*Sebald's Jews*

*Dialogue and Disjunction:*
*Studies in Jewish German Literature, Culture, and Thought*

Series Editors:

Erin McGlothlin (*Washington University in St. Louis*)
Brad Prager (*University of Missouri*)

# Sebald's Jews

## The Jew as Trope in the Narrative Fiction of W. G. Sebald

Gillian Selikowitz

CAMDEN HOUSE
Rochester, New York

Copyright © 2024 Gillian Selikowitz

*All Rights Reserved.* Except as permitted under current legislation, no part of this work may be photocopied, stored in a retrieval system, published, performed in public, adapted, broadcast, transmitted, recorded, or reproduced in any form or by any means, without the prior permission of the copyright owner.

First published 2024
by Camden House

Camden House is an imprint of Boydell & Brewer Inc.
668 Mt. Hope Avenue, Rochester, NY 14620, USA
and of Boydell & Brewer Limited
PO Box 9, Woodbridge, Suffolk IP12 3DF, UK
www.boydellandbrewer.com

ISBN-13: 978-1-64014-182-7

**Library of Congress Cataloging-in-Publication Data**

CIP data is available from the Library of Congress.

The publisher has no responsibility for the continued existence or accuracy of URLs for external or third-party internet websites referred to in this book and does not guarantee that any content on such websites is, or will remain, accurate or appropriate.

# Contents

| | |
|---|---|
| Acknowledgments | vii |
| List of Abbreviations of Sebald's Works | viii |
| Introduction: The Sebald Paradox | 1 |
| 1: The Wandering Jew in *The Emigrants* | 36 |
| 2: The Wandering Jew in *Austerlitz* | 71 |
| 3: The Jew as Other | 104 |
| 4: The Inauthentic Jew | 133 |
| 5: The Sickly Jew | 164 |
| Conclusion: Sebald and Holocaust Fiction | 194 |
| Bibliography | 199 |
| Index | 223 |

# Acknowledgments

IN PREPARING MY MANUSCRIPT for publication, I benefited from the wisdom and generosity of Jim Walker at Camden House. I am indebted to Jim for his encouragement at every stage of the writing process. I am grateful to the series editors, Brad Prager and Erin McGlothlin, for their immensely valuable advice and guidance. Thanks are also owed to the anonymous readers of my manuscript for their insightful comments and suggestions. I thank the artist, Van Hovak, for kind permission to use his compelling painting for the cover of this book.

I am grateful to my parents, the late Jack and Naomi Fletcher, who provided, against considerable odds, a culturally enriched home and an example of life-long learning.

I would not have been able to complete this project without the love and sustaining support of my husband, Mark. His clear-sighted critical perspectives have helped me to formulate my own, and I am deeply grateful for his help in proofreading and editing my manuscript. My book is dedicated with love to Mark and the special people in my life: Daniel and Michal, Anne and Alejandro, Zara and Noah.

# Abbreviations of Sebald's Works

| | |
|---|---|
| *A* | *Austerlitz* |
| *DA* | *Die Ausgewanderten* |
| *RS* | *The Rings of Saturn* |
| *TE* | *The Emigrants* |
| *V* | *Vertigo* |

# Introduction: The Sebald Paradox

GERMAN WRITER W. G. SEBALD is celebrated for his empathetic focus on Jewish victims of the Holocaust. Acclaimed as the author of "the most extraordinary novels about the erasure of Jewish life, identity and memory by a non-Jewish German writer," Sebald is widely perceived as a Holocaust author, whose final prose work *Austerlitz* is praised as "a unique example of a literary effort from within the perpetrator collective to remember the suffering of Hitler's victims."[1] Critical approbation of Sebald's treatment of Jewish life and suffering is formulated around notions of redemption, with Sebald valorized for "resurrecting the characters he communicates with by giving them back their dignity which has been taken away from them in their destruction," for "restituting individuality to the Jewish victims he portrays," and for "[saving] both the living and the dead from the oblivion of a purely physical death and [giving] them an afterlife that—one hopes—will last forever."[2] Admiration culminates in Richard Eder's claim that "Sebald stands with Primo Levi as the prime speaker of the Holocaust."[3] Although too young to have retained any lived experience of the war, Sebald perceived his own life to have been overshadowed by the war and the legacy of an unlived trauma.[4] His empathetic intention of engaging with Jewish figures as "singular individuals, who lived on the opposite side of the hallway," and his averred wish to avoid depicting Jews in generalized categories, are valued as correctives to the abstract and often stereotyped approach to Jewish characterization evident in postwar German writing, and excoriated by Sebald in critical essays.[5] Sebald's profound understanding of the complexities inherent in representing Jewish life stories from a German perspective is evident in meta- and extratextual statements that reflect his awareness of the moral constraints on his restitutive project, and set him apart from other postwar German writers. Indeed, the expatriate experience of living in England offered Sebald the opportunity of getting to know something

---

1     Bartov, "Germans as Jews," 221; Schmitz, *On Their Own Terms*, 15.

2     Jeutter, "'Am Rand der Finsternis,'" 177; Schlant, *The Language of Silence*, 234; Shulewitz, "W. G. Sebald Ransacked Jewish Lives."

3     Eder, "Excavating a Life."

4     Sebald makes this admission in "Air War and Literature," 71.

5     Boedecker, "Menschen auf der anderen Seite," 106–7. My translation. Unless otherwise noted, all translations hereafter are my own.

that no longer existed in Germany, namely, a living Jewish community, and coexistence with Jewish neighbors, a privilege that distinguished him from his contemporaries who remained in Germany.[6]

The overwhelming production of academic, literary, filmic, and artistic works, and the innumerable international conferences devoted to this unusual writer, attest to the enduring "Sebald phenomenon" that has seized the literary world since the 1990s. Sebald's "literary historiography," with its particular synthesis of the fictive-imaginative and factual, is acclaimed as an appropriate response to the challenges of writing about the Holocaust. Sebald's work has been translated into countless languages, contributing to his international standing. In his native Germany, initial resistance, based on Sebald's reputation as a polemical writer of literary criticism, has gradually given way to his inclusion within the pantheon of great German writers.[7]

In light of Sebald's extraordinary status among readers and critics alike, and the far-reaching intermedial dispersal of his work, Sebald's literary themes, and the mode of their expression, are significant. In his speech at the opening of the Stuttgart House of Literature shortly before his untimely death in December 2001, Sebald posed the question: "A quoi bon la littérature?" (What good is literature?) In answer, he stated: "There are many forms of writing; only in literature, however, can there be an attempt at restitution over and above the mere recital of facts and over and above scholarship."[8]

Sebald's plea for the privileging of the literary over and above the factual in the restitution of loss has implications for the representation of the Jewish characters in his narrative prose. His quest for a meaning "over and above the mere recital of facts" raises the question of literature's relation to reality, and the role of fiction in representing the Holocaust. This issue is rendered increasingly urgent as the Holocaust recedes into history, survivors pass away, and the question of witness authenticity becomes redundant, displaced by the fictional works of writers born too late to have any personal memory of the Holocaust. Increased distance from the event calls for new forms of representation that focus on more than just the facts, as Andreas Huyssen observes: "The old dichotomy between history and fiction no longer holds. Not in the sense that there is no difference, but on the contrary in the sense that historical fiction can give us a hold on the world, however fictional that hold may turn out to be."[9]

---

6    See Fischer, "Schreiben ex patria."

7    Sebald's photograph appears on the cover of Sørensen, *Geschichte der deutschen Literatur*, in the company of eminent German writers including Thomas Mann and Ingeborg Bachmann.

8    Sebald, "An Attempt at Restitution," 215.

9    Huyssen, *Twilight Memories*, 101.

Lawrence Langer expresses the hope that "we have finally begun to enter the second stage of Holocaust response, moving from what we know of the event . . . to how we remember it, which shifts the responsibility to our own imaginations and what we are prepared to admit there."[10] Yet while the figural element to Sebald's literary historiography succeeds in making the historical more accessible, present, and poignant, it holds the potential to allegorize his Jewish figures, and to mystify what he strove to achieve, that is, the restoration of "real" and individual human lives.[11]

Despite varied and quasi-documentary life-stories, Sebald's Jews are, in essence, tropes for conflicts that trouble his generation, allegories that vitiate Jewish singularity and conjure traditional Jewish stereotypes with a long and malign history. Sebald's figural Jews are melancholy wanderers, embodiments of a time-worn perception of the Jew as the eternal nomad, the negative pole of the dichotomy that constitutes the German as rooted and autochthonous. Alienated outsiders, who inhabit inhospitable spaces like hermits, Sebald's Jews perpetuate the perception of eternal and ontological Jewish alterity. Burdened by the past, Sebald's uncanny Jews pursue an exhausted "death-in-life" that evokes the disturbing image of the Jew as a living corpse, a dead man who has not yet died. His effete and neurasthenic Jews embody the trope of the sickly Jew. Eccentric in behavior and costume, Sebald's Jewish characters mimic the culture in which they find themselves and personify an historical view of the Jew as inauthentic and unassimilable. All Sebald's Jewish figures seek withdrawal from the social world, some to the point of self-annihilation.

Sebald's treatment of Jewish figures raises a number of questions: What are the implications of figuring Jewish characters in works that deal with the Holocaust and its afterlife? What are the risks of writing Jewish lives from the perspective of an empathetic non-Jewish German, even a writer as acutely aware of the ethical risks as Sebald undeniably showed himself to be? How did Sebald's German context influence his authorial perspective and the choices he made in depicting Jewish characters? What might a broader view of Sebald's literary oeuvre contribute to our understanding of his representation of Jewish figures?

---

10    Langer, *Admitting the Holocaust*, 13.
11    While I acknowledge the complexity of the terms "allegory" or "allegorical" and the potential for confusion with the metaphorical or symbolic modes, my understanding of "allegory" draws on Johnson, "The Vitality of Allegory," and is based on the definition of allegory as "that class of works that fulfills its rhetorical purpose . . . by means of the transformation of some phenomenon into a figural narrative, paying close attention to the author's rhetorical purpose, which is the governing principle behind allegory." As a device useful for encrypting what may otherwise be inexpressible or difficult, I acknowledge Fletcher's notion of allegory as that which "'says one thing and means another.'" Fletcher, *Allegory*, 2.

In seeking to answer these questions, I challenge certain widely held views in relation to this extraordinary literary figure by proposing that the elaborately figurative literary style Sebald employed to enhance the reality of Jewish characters paradoxically undermines his empathetic project to remember, and to rescue from oblivion, lives damaged by the indisputably real event of the Holocaust. In doing so, I address a deficit in Sebald scholarship by offering a sustained exploration of Sebald's treatment of Jews and Jewishness. While not wishing to discredit Sebald as a writer of subtlety, originality, and erudition, I suggest that his engagement with Jewishness and Jewish lives is more problematic and ambiguous than it is generally held to be.

My study is based on close textual analysis of Sebald's treatment of Jews and Jewishness in his narrative prose works, with particular emphasis on *The Emigrants* and *Austerlitz*, and with examples drawn from *Vertigo* and *The Rings of Saturn*. Fundamental to my argument is Sebald's tendency to figure the Jew as a trope for things other than himself.[12] I explore the meaning and implications of figural writing in relation to the representation of the historical or "real," and the perception of the figurative as holding the potential to deprive the historical of its claim to veracity, a point of particular concern in relation to the fictive representation of the Holocaust. I examine the aporia intrinsic to Sebald's literary historiography, the dual strategy he pursued in his representation of Jewish characters: this is evident in the tension between the empathetic closeness implicit in his restitutive project, and the distancing effect of figurative writing that dehistoricizes and abstracts Jewish figures and their fate.

I address the implications of Sebald's mystificatory figural style in relation to the subject of his prose writing: the genocide of the Jews and its enduring effect. In the context of the evolving discourse surrounding the ethics and aesthetics of representing the Holocaust, Sebald's privileging of the figurative narrative mode engages with the question of how the Holocaust can appropriately be presented, whether limits still prevail regarding its depiction, or whether, like other phenomena, it can be considered open to infinite interpretation.

I examine resistant moments in the interplay between figural and factual modes that subvert what I identify as Sebald's overwhelmingly figurative mode of representation. Such moments include instances when the figural mode is eclipsed by the concrete reality of documentary material, and rare occasions that provide a glimpse into the inner life of the subject, imbuing him or her with an unmediated "realism." I argue, however, that such subversions do not prevail over the pervasively figural nature of Sebald's writing. In his quest to endow the "real" with deeper

---

12     As all Sebald's protagonists are male, I use the masculine pronoun when referring to "the Jew."

significance, the profoundly literary nature of Sebald's narrative prose is informed by the desire to transcend the factual dimension to the Jewish lives he depicted.

Dominick LaCapra's notion of "ethical unsettlement" provides a framework for assessing the ethics of Sebald's empathy with Jewish subjects, a problematic dimension to his narrative writing.[13] While Sebald's prose fiction reveals an awareness of the ethical problems intrinsic to representing the Jewish other, the homodiegetic narrator frequently fails to observe the distance separating the empathic self from the other that LaCapra conceives as essential to the exercise of ethical empathy. I examine Sebald's self-reflective ethics of remembering, and the narrative strategies he adopted to avoid usurping the experience of the Jewish other.

Sebald's employment of essentializing Jewish tropes points to the dichotomy of German and Jew that pervades my study and is informed by the binary relationship evident in German literature and philosophy, in which the Jew represents negative and putatively "Jewish" traits of mobility, abstraction, and heteronomy, pitted against the autochthony, spirituality, and communal cohesion understood as essentially "German." While Sebald at times challenged this binary reading, it is implicit in the composites of German and Jew he created, exemplified by Austerlitz, introduced as a conflation of the German mythical hero, Siegfried, in the garb of the Wandering Jew.

My study is informed by German-Jewish philosopher Franz Rosenzweig's thoughts on the singularity of Jewishness as a perspective from which to evaluate the universalizing implications of Sebald's tropological representation of Jewish life in the aftermath of the Holocaust. Rosenzweig's reflections on the Jew and Jewishness, articulated principally in *The Star of Redemption* (1921), reveal an insistence on the Jew as a figure of historically and culturally determined particularity.[14] While imbued with a messianic dimension predicated on waiting or "living the chasm" between revelation and its fulfilment, for Rosenzweig, the individuality of the Jew renders him more than the bearer of a trait or a message: "I, the quite ordinary private subject, I, first and last name, I, dust and ashes, I am still here."[15] Rosenzweig's understanding of Jewishness provides a template against which to explore the paradox inherent in Sebald's writing of the Jew: despite his efforts to restore the individuality of the Jewish characters he portrayed, his figurative writing distanced and abstracted them to tropes that perpetuate universalizing and injurious perceptions of the Jew.

13   LaCapra, *Writing History.*
14   Rosenzweig, *The Star of Redemption.*
15   Rosenzweig, "*Urzelle,*" 126–27.

# Figuring Jewish Characters in
# Works that Deal with the Holocaust

### Figurative Writing

Sarah Hammerschlag defines figural language as that which "turns away" from the proper and fitting, and describes the literary figure, as metaphor or metonym, as a "bastard, imposing itself on what does not appropriately belong."[16] To Frank Kermode, the figural narrative mode implies "secret invitations to interpretation rather than appeals to a consensus. They inhabit a misty world in which relations . . . remain occult or of questionable shape."[17] He notes the tendency of the figural to treachery and distortion that conflict and interact with the clarity of the factual mode. Emphasizing the impossibility of separating the figural from the factual content of a text, Hayden White emphasizes that "language . . . is already freighted with figurative, tropological, and generic contents before it is actualized in any given utterance."[18]

Questions of truth and facticity, and the perceived dichotomy between literal and figural modes of writing, are central to the discourse on Holocaust representation. Initial debate focused on the unrepresentability of the Holocaust in language, exemplified by George Steiner's claim that "the world of Auschwitz lies outside speech as it lies outside reason."[19] In his analysis of the limitations of fictional representation of the Holocaust, Berel Lang notes the troubling potential of imaginative representation to aestheticize, distort, dehistoricize, and generalize events that occurred specifically and contingently.[20] With the passing away of the survivor generation, the discourse on Holocaust representation has evolved to greater acceptance of fictionalized representation of the Holocaust and of the compromise involved in negotiating between fact and fiction. As Efraim Sicher observes, "No story can be told with any degree of coherence without being reordered, emplotted, and retold from a point of view that will allow imaginative empathy. Imagination and fantasy do not necessarily impair authenticity. Fiction and history are not exclusive."[21] James Young's approach to writing the Holocaust acknowledges that "literary and historical truths of the Holocaust may not be entirely separable. That is, the truths of the Holocaust—both the factual and the interpretive—can no longer be said to lie beyond our

16    Hammerschlag, *The Figural Jew*, 14.
17    Kermode, "Secrets," 93.
18    White, *Figural Realism*, 5.
19    Steiner, *Language and Silence*, 123.
20    Lang, *Act and Idea*, 144–45.
21    Sicher, *The Holocaust Novel*, xiii.

understanding but must now be seen to inhere in the ways we understand, interpret, and write its history."[22]

Contemporary approaches to writing the Holocaust reveal an increasing tendency to globalized "ownership" of the phenomenon, and non-competitive comparison of the Holocaust with other narratives of suffering. Imre Kertész's question, "Who owns Auschwitz?" suggests that the Holocaust of European Jewry has become a universal paradigm of suffering that renders Jewish victimhood an increasingly accessible identity.[23] To Angi Büettner, "the more [the image of the Holocaust] has become integrated into the world's consciousness and memory, the wider and larger it has become . . . the story of the destruction of European Jewry gradually has become the story of the destruction of life in general."[24]

## The Figural Jew

Figuring the Jew endows the individual with metaphorical or analogous meaning and denotes a view of the Jew as an empty signifier to which meaning can be assigned. Chimerical in nature, the figural Jew implies perceptions of the Jew as something other than what he or she is, "an apparition, a phenomenon . . . whose essence must be searched for behind and beyond," the "phantom of the Jew," "the idea of the Jew," a figure of "universal viscosity."[25] The figural Jew signifies at once "is not" and "is like," as Paul Ricoeur observes.[26] The intrinsically deceptive nature of the Jew as trope is implied in the etymological origin of "trope" in the Greek *tropos* or "turn," implying a turn away from the original and proper. As Vivian Liska points out, "the distinction between the 'Jew in person' and the 'Jew as idea' assumes a radical gap between the real, concrete, the ethnic or historical Jew, on the one hand, and the virtual, theoretical, abstract Jew, the Jew as figure and metaphor, on the other."[27]

In postwar French philosophy, Jewish identity becomes freely transferrable in what Hammerschlag terms a "regime of equivalence."[28] This is manifest in the identification with Jewishness implicit in the student protest slogan, "We are all German Jews," an appropriation of Jewish victimhood that Alain Finkielkraut resentfully perceives as "pick[ing] my pocket

---

22    Young, *Writing and Rewriting History*, 1.

23    Kertész, "Who owns Auschwitz?"

24    Büettner, *Holocaust Images*, 51.

25    Di Cesare, *Heidegger and the Jews*, 168; Arendt, *The Origins of Totalitarianism*, 83; Sartre, *Anti-Semite and Jew*, 16; Baumann, *Modernity and the Holocaust*, 40.

26    Ricoeur, *The Rule of Metaphor*, 7.

27    Liska, "'Le juif, c'est moi,'" 243.

28    Hammerschlag, *The Figural Jew*, 4.

of my special status."[29] In her exploration of the figural Jew in postwar French philosophy and politics, Hammerschlag notes the view of the Jew as a trope for the disembedding of identity from notions of belonging and nationality; this is evident in Levinas's description of the Jew as "always free with regard to place."[30] Derrida describes himself as "the last of the Jews," employing the Jew as a trope for resistance to the notion of belonging.[31] The Jew as a symbol of the disappropriation of identity is reflected in Lyotard's 'jew' as an allegorical figure, a "*non-lieu*," condemned to "placelessness."[32]

Examination of approaches to Jews and Jewishness in postwar German literature leads Klaus Holz to ascribe to the Jew a third, unique, and transgressive form of "non-identity" beyond the binary distinction between self and other: "Im Dritten wird die Möglichkeit personifiziert, dass die nationale Ordnung der Welt, mithin die eigene Identität nicht gewiss ist . . . Die 'jüdische' Identität liegt darin, nicht identisch und die Negation von Identität zu sein." (The "Third" personifies the possibility that the national order of the world, indeed, of personal identity, is not secure . . . Jewish identity consists in being non-identical with, and the negation of, identity.)[33] The notion of the Jew as both non-identical and a "non-identity" implies a unique plasticity: both singular, and simultaneously, universal, a threat to identity itself.

In the context of the postwar German discourse on normalization, Holz observes that the Jew, as the embodiment of German guilt, is perceived as a threat to a rehabilitated German identity.

Contemporary critical perspectives on Sebald's narrative prose identify a universalizing approach to Jews and Jewishness that sees these terms employed as part of a broader critique of twentieth-century modernity. Mary Cosgrove suggests that Sebald's melancholy transcends the individual subject to represent issues related to global capitalism.[34] Drawing on Rosi Braidotti's notion of the "post-human" as a de-centering of 'Man' as the measure of all things, Russell Kilbourn describes "the typical Sebaldian subject [as] a post-apocalyptic 'post-human' avant la lettre."[35] Discussion of the discourse on representing the Holocaust, and diverse ways in which the Jew has been figured, prompts examination of how Sebald approached the conflicted issue of writing the Jewish other.

29    Finkielkraut, *The Imaginary Jew*, 18.
30    Levinas, "Heidegger, Gagarin, and Us," 231.
31    Derrida, *Acts of Literature*, 46.
32    Lyotard, *Heidegger and "the jews,"* 13.
33    Holz, "Die Paradoxie der Normalisierung," 46.
34    See Cosgrove, "Sebald for Our Time."
35    Kilbourn, *W. G. Sebald's Postsecular Redemption*, 14.

## Sebald's Literary Historiography: Transcending the "Real"

Sebald's literary historiography is lauded as a rewriting of history that privileges the figural discourse as a powerful means of enlivening the past. His documentary fiction insists on the figural elaboration of the historically "real," while at the same time utilizing historical facts to authenticate the enhanced reality he creates. As works that deal with the afterlife of the Holocaust, *The Emigrants* and *Austerlitz* are based in the ethnographic realism of the photographs, historical accounts, diaries, and handwritten notes through which Sebald sought to counter what he saw as the abstract fictions of postwar German writing. Nevertheless, Sebald's narrative prose works transcend the "real" through the metaphorical devices of dreams, visions, and allegorical figures, employed to compensate for the perceived inadequacy of the factual-historical approach to retrieving the past.

Sebald's emphasis on the "real" in portraying Jewish figures is rendered problematic by observations he made about the valuable, if paradoxical role of allegory in the representation of the "real": "The *effet du réel* (reality effect) essential to story writing does not depend on the probability of what is being written about, but on the mental possibilities the text reveals when it lends allegorical meaning to that which it describes."[36] In an interview with Ralph Schock, Sebald observed: "You see, realism, to which, on the one hand, I am very attracted, is not sufficient, one must always transcend it at particular moments."[37] He confessed to the temptation to "fill in the gaps and create out of this a meaning which is greater than that which you can prove."[38] In an observation that reflects Aristotle's opinion that "poetry is sometimes more philosophic, of greater importance than history, since its statements are by nature rather of universals, whereas those of history are singulars,"[39] Sebald remarked:

> Nevertheless, I believe that realism only really functions when it transcends itself, that is, if the text has mysterious facets that don't belong in a realistic text. In addition, I believe that the realistic text can support allegorical narrative, indeed, that it should engage with allegory.[40]

Responding to a suggestion that he was preoccupied with the truth of what he wrote, Sebald observed: "That's the paradox. You have this string of lies and by this detour you arrive at a form of truth which is

---

36      Sebald, "Der Mann mit dem Mantel," 163.
37      Schock, "Realismus reicht nicht aus," 98.
38      Bigsby, "W. G. Sebald in the Potting Shed," 153.
39      Aristotle, *De arte poetica*, 9.
40      Boedecker, "Menschen auf der anderen Seite," 5.

more precise, one hopes, than something which is strictly provable."[41] Sebald's remark touches on the "sanctioned or contractual fabrication or lie" inherent in the work of fiction, and the questions it raises concerning the veracity of its representations.[42] In relation to Sebald's depiction of Jewish figures, I argue that the unreliability of the documentary material he used reflects the subordination of the "real" to an aesthetically contrived reality.

As an event that refuses the notion of Jewish individuality, an abstraction in itself, the Holocaust of the Jews was designed almost as if to signify the non-being of those who were being annihilated. Shrouded initially in silence, the "Final Solution" was performed under the rubric *Nacht und Nebel*, implying not only night and fog, but disappearance without a trace.[43] But as Berel Lang reminds us, "If there ever was a 'literal' fact beyond the possibility of alternate formulations among which reversal or denial must always be one, it is here in the act of the Nazi genocide . . . the fact of the Nazi genocide is a crux that separates historical discourse from the process of imaginative representation and its figurative space, perhaps not uniquely, but as surely as any fact might be required or able to do."[44] While the discourse on the permissibility and possibility of representing the Holocaust has evolved beyond the totalizing view of the Holocaust as a paradigmatic event only able to be conveyed in a language purged of all metaphorical devices, the risk of employing language that "turns" away from literality to represent a morally extreme and unalterably real event remains.

Figuring the Jew, the black, the woman, or the indigene, risks reducing the complexity of individual histories to a single allegory of alterity, and perpetuating polarizing ethnic or gendered metaphors. For a postwar German writer, figuring Jewish characters remains ethically fraught: treating the Jew as an ethnicized trope perpetuates an historically freighted racialized discourse based on metaphors and binary terms traditionally used to stigmatize the Jew as deracinated, improper, and illegitimate, a "parasitical plant on the trunks of other nations," "a stranger to the soil and to men alike."[45] Allegorizing the Jew implies abstraction of the "real," and evokes the denigration of materiality associated with the Hegelian privileging of "spirit," and Kant's repudiation of Jewish bodiliness as that which resists the transformation of the other-worldly.[46] Figuring Jewish

---

41 Cuomo, "A Conversation with W. G. Sebald," 108.
42 Budick, *The Subject of Holocaust Fiction*, 11.
43 The letters NN ("Nacht und Nebel") signify the disappearance of victims without a trace following a directive by Hitler, December 7, 1941.
44 Lang, *Act and Idea*, 158–59.
45 Herder, *Reflections*, 144; Hegel, "The Spirit of Christianity," 186.
46 Hegel, "The Spirit of Christianity," 206; Kant, *Schriften zur Ethik*.

characters risks conjuring a German cultural substrate that perceives the Jew as occupying an "unselige Leere" (unholy void), and envisages his metaphorical erasure to Hegel's ontological "*Nichts*" (nothing).[47]

Sebald's highly figurative style has the potential to diminish the material reality of his Jewish characters through imagery of absence and dissolution that implies a spectral dimension to post-Holocaust Jewish existence. Images of void and desolation—the empty rookery, the dearth of any sign of life—constitute Henry Selwyn's home as a metaphor for his "death-in-life" existence. Sebald's tendency to mythologize Jewish characters de-historicizes their tragedies by distancing them from the specificity of time and place. Thus Aurach's survival in Manchester, with its "countless chimneys from which a yellow-grey smoke rose" (*TE*, 169), evokes a mythical sojourn in an infernal Underworld that he embraces as his predestined place, and reduces Aurach himself to a mythological figure who, like Orpheus or Odysseus, seeks redemptive recovery of the Dead in Hades.

In his figuration of catastrophe, the richly metaphorical writing Sebald employed has the potential to aestheticize the Jewish suffering he wished to remember: Austerlitz's lasting impression of the Theresienstadt concentration camp imagines it as "colour-washed in soft tones of grey-brown for Maria Theresia . . . and fitting neatly into the folds of the surrounding terrain," a painterly vision that diminishes the materiality of the fortress, while offering the consoling fantasy "that [the Jews] had never been taken away after all but were still living crammed into those buildings and basements and attics" (*A*, 280–81). Sebald's imaginative representation of post-Holocaust Jewish existence is a reminder of the problematic falsifications of fiction, that "turns away" from the real and has the potential to mitigate horror, as Adorno observed: "Our feelings resist any claim of the positivity of existence as sanctimonious, as wronging the victims; they balk at squeezing any kind of sense, however bleached, out of the victims' fate."[48] Through simile and metaphor, Sebald invites the reader to contemplate Jewish suffering as intrinsic to a natural history of catastrophe, divorced from historical context and human agency. Thus Austerlitz projects his feelings of alienation onto the natural world, perceiving, in the fading colors of the evening twilight, "a malevolent and lightless pallor" that reflects his sense of evacuation, and implicitly subsumes his suffering in a universal, mystificatory, and de-historicized chronicle of misery, impervious to questions of responsibility or justice.

Sebald was aware of the implications of his imaginative style: "In prose fiction, you have to elaborate. You have one image and you have to make something of it . . . and it only works through linguistic or imaginative

---

47    Hegel, "The Spirit of Christianity," 192, 197.
48    Adorno, *Negative Dialectics*, 361.

elaboration. Of course, you might well think, as you do this, that you are directing some form of sham reality."[49] With disarming candor, he observed that "the whole business of writing of course—you make things up, you smooth certain contradictory elements that you come across. The whole thing is fraught with vanity."[50] Sebald revealed a readiness to enhancing reality through the elaborations of fiction: admitting that the handwritten diary of Ambros Adelwarth (*TE*) was a falsification, he added, "What matters is all true."[51] He was aware too, of the problematic implications of writing Jewish lives from the perspective of a non-Jewish German: "I was certainly conscious from the beginning that even in talking to the people who you perhaps might want to portray, there are thresholds which you cannot cross . . . It's difficult and every case is different. Yet at the same time, of course, the likes of us ought to try to say how they receive these stories."[52]

Carole Angier's revelations about Sebald's tendency to falsification problematize more deeply the question of the "real" in Sebald's prose fiction. Her discovery that a number of Sebald's Jewish characters were based on non-Jewish models, that he lied to cover this up, and that he ruthlessly raided the work of others in the construction of his Jewish figures, is consistent with an ambiguous relation to reality, evident in Sebald's paradoxical wish to transcend the "real" through allegory, and to "fill in the gaps and create out of this a meaning which is greater than you can prove." What is at stake for my own exploration of Sebald's Jewish figures is not Sebald's deception—I take it for granted that writers of fiction may be parasitical and opportunistic in their methods—but his treatment of Jewish characters, and whether they are, in the final analysis, the "real" individuals he sought to restore. I argue that the highly imaginative mode Sebald privileged to enhance his creation of the "real" paradoxically contributes to the allegorical and abstract nature of his Jewish characters, who are, in essence, tropes that perpetuate stereotyped perceptions of Jewishness.

### Critical Reception of Sebald's Figuring of Jewish Characters

In the largely positive reception of Sebald's writing of Jewish lives, critics have tended to overlook, or have failed to engage with, the paradoxical dimension to Sebald's figuring of Jewish characters, and the potential erosion of Jewish individuality to which this gives rise. Ralf Jeutter praises Sebald's "manipulations of the narrative through the use of literary

---

49    Cuomo, "A Conversation with W. G. Sebald," 114.
50    Wachtel, "Ghost Hunter," 60.
51    Angier, "Who Is W. G. Sebald?" 72.
52    Cuomo, "A Conversation with W. G. Sebald," 112.

allusions, references, symbolic, allegorical and mythological amplifications
. . . By inscribing his own story into the narratives of people encountered
or assimilated he unearths his own truth which converges with the truths
of his subjects . . ."[53] To Mark McCulloh, "these lost lives—once examined with Sebald's allusory literary lens—often seem more intensely real
than anything we can know in the present."[54] Richard Gray describes
Sebald's characters as fictional composites of several historical people, to
create a "generalized and representative life story, thereby increasing the
potential for empathetic identification on the part of Sebald's readers."[55]
Russell Kilbourn explores the trope of the Wandering Jew as a metaphor
for alienation from *Heimat* in Sebald's narrative prose, without addressing the ethical implications, for a German writer, of employing this stereotype in relation to Jewish subjects.[56] In his essay on the significance of
Kafka's "Jäger Gracchus" fragment in Sebald's prose writing, Oliver Sill
explores Kafka's hunter as an allegory for contemporary rootlessness and
Sebald's own sense of *Heimatlosigkeit* (homelessness), but appears oblivious to the implications of perpetuating the Wandering Jew stereotype as a
metaphor for German loss in Sebald's writing.[57]

Negative critique of Sebald's troping of Jewish characters centers on
his instrumentalization of Jewish figures as emblems for his own conflicts,
and as signifiers for universal concerns. Peter Morgan describes the life
stories of *The Emigrants* as "metaphors of [Sebald's] existence"; Daphne
Merkin observes the instrumentalization of Jewishness as a transferrable
identity in Sebald's writing: "In the world according to Sebald . . . we are
all more or less Jews bound for the slaughter."[58] Karin Bauer expresses
concern about the German-Jewish dichotomy set up in *Austerlitz*
and Sebald's perhaps unwitting reproduction of the stereotype of the
Wandering Jew, condemned to an unproductive life of eternal nomadism.[59] Sebald's Jewish characters are criticized by Mary Cosgrove as
"compromised figures that do not in the first instance signify the Jewish
experience of victimization, but instead become ciphers of a problematic
German identity."[60] To André Aciman, the likeness of Sebald's melancholy Jewish lives suggests that these are not lives in a real sense, but
"tropes for depletion, longevity, and loneliness. Thus *The Rings of Saturn*
is about Sebald. All the rest is tangential."[61] Laura Martin defines the

53    Jeutter, "'Am Rand der Finsternis,'" 170.
54    McCulloh, *Understanding W. G. Sebald*, 26.
55    Gray, *Ghostwriting*, 21.
56    Kilbourn, "Kafka, Nabokov . . . Sebald," 33–63.
57    Sill, "'Aus dem Jäger ist ein Schmetterling geworden,'" 623.
58    Morgan, "The Sign of Saturn," 81; Merkin, "Cordoning off the Past."
59    Bauer, "The Dystopian Entwinement," 238.
60    Cosgrove, "The Anxiety of German Influence," 234.
61    Aciman, "Out of Novemberland," 46.

14 ♦ Introduction: The Sebald Paradox

implications of Sebald's figural treatment of Jewish figures when she observes:

> The life events of Bereyter and Selwyn, Adelwarth and Austerlitz, Beyle and Kafka—i.e., the protagonists from throughout his oeuvre—vary, but only in detail, and never in tone and mood. It all becomes, somehow, one vague, generalized life story, not owned by any one individual . . . By telling the tales in his own voice and with his plot embellishments, [Sebald] erases their individuality: we are in fact hearing about one individual, Sebald—or "Sebald."[62]

Ruth Franklin approaches the paradox in Sebald's writing when she suggests that, in seeking to record suffering, the patterns he traced, "by virtue of their very beauty . . . extinguish the grief that they seek to contain," implying that his intricate figural writing creates not the "real" suffering individuals he sought to remember, but aestheticized and allusive metaphors, abstractions beyond individual pain.[63]

Sebald's figuring of Jewish characters has significant implications for his literary project to remember and restore Jewish lives. Despite his attentiveness to biographical detail, Sebald's privileging of the fictive dimension to his literary historiography has the potential to mystify the reality of the individual life, to aestheticize Jewish suffering, and to undermine the empathetic intent implicit in his undertaking to restore "real" Jewish lives. The paradox between Sebald's empathic dedication to remembering "real" Jewish life and his troping of Jewish characters calls for an exploration of empathy and its ethical implications.

## Writing Jewish Lives from the Perspective of an Empathetic Non-Jewish German

### Empathy: Definition and Ethics

Sebald depicted a fallen world in which misery is endemic. His empathy is democratic, encompassing the suffering human body, the dying, the insane, and the dead. Sebald's gaze is inevitably drawn to the mortified body—of Rembrandt's Aris Kindt, Austerlitz's foster-mother, Gwendolyn, and the "gashed bodies" of Grünewald's imagination. Sebald's empathy extends to all creaturely life, including piles of lifeless herring, who, having endured "the most extreme of the sufferings undergone by a species always threatened by disaster" (*The Rings of Saturn*,

---

62  Martin, "Reading the Individual," 41–42.
63  Franklin, "Rings of Smoke," 126.

57), are metaphorical of the extermination of the Jews in Sebald's writing.[64] While Sebald's narrative fiction invites us to engage with the suffering of the Jewish other, his much-lauded empathy is problematic for its slippage into inappropriate identification. It is important to examine the meaning of empathy in order to engage with its more controversial implications in Sebald's writing of Jewish lives in the shadow of the Holocaust.

The concept of empathy covers a wide range of capacities that enable us to emotionally engage with, and share, the thoughts and feelings of others. Amy Coplan defines empathy as "a complex imaginative process involving both cognition and emotion," during which reader or empathizer imagines the experiences of the other, while never losing "the separate sense of self."[65] Coplan clarifies the concept of empathy by acknowledging the complexity of ethical judgment and the importance of avoiding the creation of binary oppositions between perpetrators and victims, pointing to the importance of a dialogic relation to the other, however limited or compromised this may be. As Coplan notes, empathy in itself is not sufficient for moral behavior, but requires consideration of the other as distinct from the self. This notion is supported by Peter Goldie, who cautions against the "perspective-shifting" implicit in imagining the mental life of others, and underlines the importance of retaining an external perspective that allows us to imagine the other in all his or her singularity, and to appreciate the perspective of others as irreducibly theirs.[66]

My study is informed by the concept of empathy theorized by Dominick LaCapra as "a kind of virtual experience through which one puts oneself in the other person's position while recognizing the difference of that position and hence not taking the other's place."[67] LaCapra's concept of "empathic unsettlement" offers a nuanced perspective on the ethical relation between the empathic self and other that allows understanding of the victim's trauma without empathic overidentification giving way to vicarious victimhood. In relation to Sebald's representation

---

64    In his oblique and figural treatment of Jewish genocide through the metaphor of the mass-elimination of herring in early twentieth-century England, Sebald draws on the stereotype of the Wandering Jew in his designation of the herring as "the restless wanderer of the seas"; the analogy between the extermination of the herring and the genocide of the Jews is implied in the reference to transporting "the restless wanderer of the seas" by railway goods wagons "to those places where its fate on this earth will at last be fulfilled" (*RS*, 54). The meaning of this cryptic observation is made clear in the double-spread photograph of partially covered corpses in a forest clearing, in the context of a report on the liberation of the extermination camp of Bergen Belsen on April 14, 1945 (*The Rings of Saturn*, 59–61).

65    Coplan and Goldie, *Philosophical and Psychological Perspectives*, 143–44.

66    See Goldie, "Dramatic Irony, Narrative, and the External Perspective."

67    LaCapra, *Writing History*, 78.

16 ◆ INTRODUCTION: THE SEBALD PARADOX

of Jewish figures in a post-Holocaust context, LaCapra's concept of "empathic unsettlement" offers a framework for considering the complexity of writing the Jewish other from the perspective of an empathic non-Jewish German, and for my argument that Sebald's empathy with suffering Jewish characters is compromised by the over-identification of his German narrator with Jewish subjects.

Sebald was acutely conscious of the ethical risks, for a non-Jewish German author, of writing empathetically about Jewish lives damaged by the Holocaust, specifically, the risk of inappropriate identification in an imagined exchange of places:

> I think certainly for a German gentile to write about Jewish lives is not unproblematic. There are examples of that, writers attempting this in Germany in the 1960s and 1970s, and many of these attempts are—one can't say it really otherwise—shameful. In the sense that they usurp the lives of these people. Perhaps not consciously so; it might be done with the best of intentions, but in the making it comes so that it isn't right, morally not right.[68]

To Christopher Bigsby, Sebald admitted that

> . . . anything one does in the form of writing, and especially prose fiction, is not an innocent enterprise . . . Writing is by definition a morally dubious occupation, I think, because one appropriates and manipulates the lives of others for certain ends. When it is a question of the lives of those who have survived persecution the process of appropriation can be very invasive.[69]

Sebald refuted any sense of personal investment in the Jewish experience, insisting that his interest in Judaism and the Jewish people was in essence, sociocultural, based on the perception that "[the Jewish people] were part of a social history that was obliterated in Germany and [he] wanted to know what happened."[70] The finely drawn biographies of Sebald's Jewish characters reflect his desire to explore German-Jewish life, because it was, in his opinion, "one of the most central and most important chapters of German cultural history."[71] Sebald acknowledged the potential for usurpation through empathetic identification—"When you get interested in someone . . . you begin to occupy this person's territory, after a fashion."[72] In Sebald's narrative prose, the narrator of "Paul Bereyter"

---

68    Cuomo, "A Conversation with W. G. Sebald," 111–12.
69    Bigsby, "W. G. Sebald in the Potting Shed," 153.
70    Lubow, "Crossing Boundaries," 167.
71    Wachtel, "Ghost Hunter," 47.
72    Wachtel, "Ghost Hunter," 42.

admits to wanting to avoid "wrongful trespass" in writing about his former teacher (*TE*, 29), while the narrator of "Max Aurach" describes himself as "tormented by scruples" in his efforts to write the life of the Jewish artist (*TE*, 230).

Through symbolic gestures of affiliation, the narrator nevertheless seeks to "inhabit" or appropriate the other's identity, violating the distance between self and other that is intrinsic to LaCapra's theory of ethical empathy. This is evident in the narrator's visit to the Jewish cemetery of Bad Kissingen and his identification with the deceased German-Jewish writer Friederike Halbleib, expressed in the sense that "now, as I write these lines, it feels as if *I* had lost her, and as if *I* could not get over the loss despite the many years that have passed since her departure" (*TE*, 224–25). The apparent conflation of narrator and author in Sebald's narrative fiction complicates ethical judgment of the narrator's numerous instances of inappropriate identification with the Jewish subject. While Sebald remained reticent about the identity of his narrator, shared biographical details, including birth date, first name, initials, an identity document, and photographs, reinforce the idea that the narrator and author are one and the same person. Sebald's comments on the relationship between author and narrator are ambiguous: "Ich glaube auch, daß man heute nicht mehr so schreiben kann, als sei der Erzähler eine wertfreie Instanz. Der Erzähler muß die Karten auf den Tisch legen, aber auf möglichst diskrete Art." (I am of the opinion that one can no longer write these days as if the narrator were transparent and of no importance. The narrator must lay his cards on the table, but in the most discreet way possible.)[73]

Questions of empathy and appropriation of the lives of others have been highlighted by the furore surrounding the publication of Jeanine Cummins's novel *American Dirt* (Flatiron, 2020).

## Sebald and "the Right to Write the Other"

In her book, Jeanine Cummins, a white American, deals with the fictional story of a Mexican mother and son's journey to the Mexico-United States border after the rest of their family has been murdered by a cartel, and aims to empathetically engage with the suffering of illegal Mexican migrants to the US. The argument around *American Dirt* centers on the question of "the right to write the other," and is instructive insofar as the reception of Cummins's book reflects on critical response to Sebald's writing of the Jewish other from a non-Jewish German perspective. *American Dirt* has been criticized as "fantasy fiction for suburban

---

73    Poltronieri, "Wie kriegen die Deutschen das auf die Reihe?" 144.

18  ♦  Introduction: The Sebald Paradox

readers with its plétora of italicized Spanish words,"[74] and the author has been charged with "opportunistically, selfishly, and parasitically" telling a fictional story of traumatic Mexican migrant experience.[75]

By contrast with the intense debate catalysed by Cummins's book, Sebald's right to narrate the Jewish other is seldom explicitly challenged. There is widespread critical appreciation, particularly among Anglophone critics, of his empathetic and sensitive treatment of suffering Jewish characters, and his oblique, respectful approach to the Holocaust. This is based on a perception of Sebald as the "longed-for *good German*, indeed Messiah-figure, who had hoped to repair the German-Jewish cultural symbiosis destroyed by the Nazis," supplemented by the view of Sebald as a melancholy anchorite in self-imposed exile, and by appreciation of his empathetic dedication to the literary memorialization of Jewish lives.[76] Among Anglophone readers, a perception of Sebald as quasi-Jewish can be traced to his preoccupation with ruin, the diasporic notion of text implicit in his writing, and his reflection on the German past that make him somehow legibly "Jewish," as Leslie Morris observes.[77] The posthumous awarding of the Koret Jewish Book Award to Sebald in 2002 would appear to confirm a perception of his metaphorical Jewishness.

Approval of Sebald's empathy with Jewish victims suggests, at times, a notion of shared German-Jewish victimhood: for Ana-Isabel Aliaga-Buchenau, "the Holocaust is the shadow that hangs over each one of [Sebald's] fictional lives as well as the author's own life."[78] Richard Gray describes the "shared marginality" between narrator and subjects as indicating empathetic consonance that links the narrator to the subject.[79] In relation to *The Emigrants* and the Jewish tradition of *Yizkor* Books, Katharina Hall commends Sebald for attempting, and in her opinion, succeeding in avoiding "improper" identification with his Jewish subjects by juggling a documentary approach with fictive writing in order to acknowledge the limits to what can be empirically known about the other, and to enhance the "real" through imagination.[80] While acknowledging that Sebald was guilty of cultural appropriation in his writing of the Jewish other, Carole Angier nevertheless refrains from condemnation on the basis of his avowedly ethical intentions, the "Skrupulantismus" (scrupulousness) he attributed to the narrator of "Max Aurach" (*Die Ausgewanderten*, 344), and which he articulated in interviews. Angier

74   Boyagoda, "The *American Dirt* Controversy."
75   Bowles, "American Dirt."
76   Schütte, "Von der Notwendigkeit," 11.
77   Morris, "How Jewish is it?" 113.
78   Aliaga-Buchenau, "'A Time He Could Not Bear to Say Any More About,'" 141.
79   Gray, *Ghostwriting*, 9.
80   Hall, "Jewish Memory in Exile" 152–64.

argues that "because he was so aware of it, he was terribly careful. In other words, he never tells a Jewish story . . . It's always the Jewish character survivor who's telling the narrator the story . . ."[81] Judith Shulewitz justifies Sebald's "usurpation" of Jewish lives on the grounds of his artistic greatness, concluding that, "if Sebald the man ransacked lives unscrupulously, Sebald the artist did so with superb literary tact."[82]

Negative critical response to Sebald's empathy centers on the ethics of his identification with Jewish victimhood. Katja Garloff asks "how . . . someone who has not suffered under the Nazis [can] legitimately speak for, or at least about, a Jewish victim of Nazi persecution."[83] Brad Prager argues that the moral basis of Sebald's authorial position is troubled by his narrative position as an empathetic German, noting that Sebald's context imposes "considerable limitations on empathy in relation to key issues surrounding Holocaust writing."[84] To Morgan, Sebald takes the stories of his subjects and represents them through his own narrative voice, obscuring the boundaries between self and other.[85] Kirstin Gwyer expresses concern about Sebald's denigration of witness accounts in favor of secondary or imaginative witnessing, and his establishment of a hierarchy of realities according to which his postmemorial experience of unlived trauma becomes the overriding reality of his childhood, validating the perception of Sebald as a more eloquent spokesperson of the Holocaust and guardian of its memory than anyone else.[86]

German critics have generally proved to be more sensitive to what they see as Sebald's appropriation of the Jewish experience. An early review of *Austerlitz* in the Zurich *Tages-Anzeiger* implicitly accuses Sebald of exploiting Jewish lives, and poses the question: "Does a German author have the right to play aesthetic games with real Jewish biographies?"[87] The question of proximity and distance in relation to Sebald's empathic stance has given rise to debate, with Thomas Wirtz deriding his empathic gestures as "schwarze Zuckerwatte" (black candyfloss.)[88] In Sebald's conflation of author, narrator, and Jewish subject, Fridolin Schley notes a strategy of identificatory empathy that validates him as a secondary witness and undermines his avowals of ethical scrupulousness.[89] For Marco Gotterbarm, Sebald's empathy is compromised by the "autofictive" nature of his narrative prose that betrays "a not-unproblematic 'Opferstolz,'"

81    Angier, *Speak, Silence*, 21.
82    Shulewitz, "W. G. Sebald Ransacked Jewish Lives."
83    Garloff, "The Task of the Narrator," 158.
84    Prager, "The Good German as Narrator," 76.
85    Morgan, "'Your Story Is Now My Story.'"
86    Gwyer, "'Schmerzensspuren der Geschichte(n),'" 112–36.
87    Doerry and Hage, "Ich fürchte das Melodramatische," 230.
88    Wirtz, "Schwarze Zuckerwatte."
89    See Schley, *Kataloge der Wahrheit*.

20 ♦ Introduction: The Sebald Paradox

manifest in numerous instances of identification with Jewish victims.[90] In Sebald's elaborately falsified report of the liberation of Bergen-Belsen (*The Rings of Saturn*, 59–62), Gotterbarm detects a subversive authorial strategy of self-insinuation into Jewish victimhood that compromises Sebald's expressions of empathy.

Examination of Sebald reception suggests that critics have for the most part been persuaded by the empathy of his restitutive project and the pathos of his authorial persona as an exiled, contrite, and ethically aware German writer, factors that appear to legitimize his right to narrate the stories of the broken Jewish figures he sought to memorialize. More controversially, it may be that Sebald's writing of the Jewish other reflects a broader issue in contemporary culture, which routinely employs Holocaust identities, language, terms, and images to confront contemporary fears and treats the Jew as a trope for a universalized narrative of destruction that subsumes the suffering of the "real" Jew.

### Postmemory and the Ethics of Empathy

The ethical dimension to Sebald's empathy is complicated by statements of affiliation that reflect Sebald's perception of his own life as overshadowed by the unlived experience of the war, suggesting his postmemorial identification with Jewish suffering:

> At the end of the war, I was just one year old, so I can hardly have any impressions of that period of destruction based on personal experience. Yet to this day, when I see photographs or documentary films dating from the war I feel as if I were its child, so to speak, as if those horrors I did not experience had cast a shadow over me, from which I shall never entirely emerge.[91]

Central to Marianne Hirsch's notion of postmemory is imaginative and emotional identification with the victim, and the adoption and validation of "the traumatic memories . . . of others as experiences one might oneself have had, and of inscribing them into one's own life story."[92] As one not genealogically related to survivor witnesses, but affiliated only through empathetic "kinship" with them, Sebald belongs to Hirsch's expanded category of postmemorial victims, to whom she attributes the experience of adopted memories so powerful as to constitute them as personal memories. Sebald's membership of the German perpetrator group

---

90     "Opferstolz" signifies pride in being a victim. Gotterbarm, *Die Gewalt des Moralisten*, 384.

91     Sebald, "Air War and Literature," 71.

92     Hirsch, "Surviving Images," 10.

nevertheless means that his relation to Jewish postmemory is "thin" according to Avishai Margalit's understanding of "thick" relations to the tribe, family, and nation with whom we share a history as a "community of memory," as opposed to our relations with others not bound to us by anything more than shared humanity.[93] In the sense of "afterwardness" that marks postmemorial writing, Kirstin Gwyer notes a rehabilitation of belatedness that confers a privileged insight on the secondary or postmemorial witness, giving him or her an advantage in understanding that eludes the primary witness. Commenting on the problem of fictional representation of the Holocaust, and the question of who has the right to bear witness, Gwyer notes the tendency to validate fictional, imaginative efforts to remember the Holocaust, and to replace first-generation Holocaust writing with the work of writers with no personal experience of the Holocaust.[94] To Cosgrove, Sebald's perception of himself as a creditable literary "heir" to the Holocaust, almost a witness in his own right, is rooted in a wishful sense of belonging and an underlying desire to reclaim past trauma as a form of compensation for his own lack of access to the traumatic event.[95] Postmemory is thematized in *Austerlitz*, in which the German narrator exhibits responses that suggest the postmemorial experience of unlived trauma and guilt: on hearing about the burning of the Lucerne station, he experiences "an uneasy, anxious feeling, which crystallized into the idea that I had been to blame" (*A*, 12). In the former Nazi prison of Breendonk, he experiences the resurgence of childhood trauma that he intuits to be the postmemorial endurance of unlived suffering: ". . . as the nausea rose in me I guessed at the kind of third-degree interrogations which were being conducted here around the time I was born" (*A*, 33).

Sebald's postmemorial claim to the experience of unlived trauma, like his tendency to over-identification with Jewish subjects, exposes a problematic dimension to a writer valorized for his empathy with the Jewish other. As a non-Jewish German author, Sebald's right to depict Jewish victims of the Holocaust is not disputed. Indeed, the discourse on representing the Holocaust has moved beyond the restrictions on non-Jewish German writers explored by Hamida Bosmajian in 1985.[96] There is no implication that only survivors are in a position to write about the Holocaust; indeed, Primo Levi, Auschwitz-survivor and writer, rejected any claim to having privileged access to the truth of the Holocaust: "We who survived are not true witnesses . . . We, the survivors . . . never touched bottom. Those who have . . . did not return, or returned

93  Margalit, *The Ethics of Memory.*
94  Gwyer, "An Absence in Context," 13–14.
95  Cosgrove, "Melancholy Competitions," 221.
96  Bosmajian, "German Literature about the Holocaust," 51–61.

22 ♦ INTRODUCTION: THE SEBALD PARADOX

wordless."[97] The educational and socially transformative potential of literature to stir empathy with the other imbues it with moral and altruistic power, and Sebald, as a non-Jewish German, was exemplary for his interest in Jewish victimhood, and for his acute awareness of the ethical risks of writing about Jewish lives.[98] What is at stake is not Sebald's right to "write the Jewish other," but the mode he employed to do so. While Sebald was undoubtedly an empathetic and sensitive writer, troubled by the genocide of the Jews, and conscious of the long-term suffering of survivors, his figurative representation of Jewish lives has the potential to transform Jewish individuals into tropes, eroding their subjectivity, and universalizing their individual significance.

Sebald's empathetic concern with the Jewish experience is problematic for its potential to appropriate the identity of the Jewish other and to displace the Jewish subject. His tendency to over-identification violates the distance between empathic self and other that is intrinsic to LaCapra's notion of ethical empathy. Questions of German and Jewish identity, and the significance of the latter to the formation of a democratic, postwar German identity, can be traced to Sebald's German milieu, troubled by the strategies of guilt-deflection, denial, and relativization that have marked German *Vergangenheitsbewältigung* (mastering of the past). This was a background Sebald sought to abandon, but with which he continued to engage, admitting ruefully: "I have inherited that backpack and I have to carry it whether I like it or not."[99]

## Sebald's German Context

Sebald's figural Jewish characters arise from a troubled postwar German milieu overshadowed by the Nazi past, and reflect the ongoing process of *Vergangenheitsbewältigung*. As studies by Lars Rensmann, Klaus-Michael Bogdal, and others suggest, 1945 did not prove to be a new beginning for German writers in terms of how Jewish characters are perceived.[100] While interest in a Jewish presence in Germany has largely been motivated by the desire to validate a newly democratic Germany, the picture of the Jew remains dominated by that of the Holocaust victim and exotic outsider. Research on Jewish stereotypes in postwar German writing indicates a perception of the Jew as an obstacle to the formation of a positive national identity, and the re-emergence of time-worn tropes of the Jew

97   Levi, *The Drowned and the Saved*, 83–84.
98   For discussion of the altruistic power of literature, see Nussbaum, *Poetic Justice*.
99   Wachtel, "Ghost Hunter," 51.
100   Rensmann, *Demokratie und Judenbild*; Bogdal et al., *Literarischer Antisemitismus*.

INTRODUCTION: THE SEBALD PARADOX    ♦    23

as an invisible economic power broker, and emblem of the social antagonisms of capitalist modernity.[101] The 1980s and 1990s witnessed a shift in West-German politics and culture from a discourse of guilt and shame towards one focused on normalization of the national narrative, acknowledgment of German victimhood, and integration of the Holocaust into the continuum of German history. The new discourse is evident in controversial attempts to relativize the suffering of Germans and their victims, such as the opening of the *Neue Wache* memorial in 1993 and the Bitburg incident.[102] The *Historikerstreit* (Historian's Debate) of the late 1980s on the hegemonic position of the Holocaust in German history advocated a more empathetic approach to the imbrication of Germans in the *Wehrmacht*. On a cultural level, the *Literaturstreit* (Literary Debate) of 1989–90 exposed the desire to move beyond constraints on what could be written about Jews, an unspoken postwar taboo challenged by Rainer Werner Fassbinder's provocative *Die Stadt, Der Müll und Der Tod* (The City, Garbage, and Death, 1975), and Martin Walser's anti-Semitic *Tod eines Kritikers* (Death of a Critic, 2002).[103]

Born in 1944, Sebald occupied a complicated position in relation to the milieu in which he was situated: a child of the perpetrator generation, who shared with his cohort the sense of being marked by a legacy of guilt relating to the involvement of their parents in the war, but at the same time, an expatriate who lived and worked for the greater part of his life in England, and considered himself privileged to have encountered living Jews at a time when this was scarcely possible in his native Germany.[104] His anomalous position has given rise to a perception of his

101    Haury, "'Ziehen die Fäden.'"

102    The *Neue Wache* memorial has the all-inclusive inscription, "To the victims of war and violent rule." In 1985, Ronald Reagan was invited to join West-German chancellor, Helmut Kohl, in commemorating the fortieth anniversary of the end of the war. At the military cemetery of Bitburg, Kohl paid homage to soldiers of the *Waffen-SS*, whom he described as "victims of Nazism also . . . just as surely as the victims of the concentration camps."

103    Walser's speech on receiving the German *Friedenspreis* (Book Industry Peace Prize) in 1998 reflected an intensified concern with German victimhood, the desire to equalize German and Jewish culpability, and the wish to end the narrative of guilt and shame in relation to the Holocaust.

104    Post-1945, a temporal paradigm of generation implicitly apportions culpability and epistemological privilege according to proximity to the catastrophic events of the war. On the basis of this generational model, postwar German history is counted in generations, starting with the calamitous collapse of 1945, designated the site of origin or *Stunde Null*. Acknowledging his expatriate privilege, Sebald stated: "In the 1960s you grew up [in Germany GS] for twenty years and you never bumped into a Jewish person, so you didn't know who they were. Just some kind of phantom image of them. And so I go to Manchester . . . And there they were all around me." Cuomo, "A Conversation with W. G. Sebald," 105–6.

writing as aloof from the context within which postwar German writing is typically evaluated, as Taberner has pointed out.[105] While Sebald's narrative prose does not directly acknowledge significant shifts in postwar German historical consciousness, it engages obliquely with the process of *Vergangenheitsbewältigung* and the ongoing debate on German guilt and the Nazi past that continues to divide the postwar German discourse. To Angier, Sebald confirmed the determining role of his German context in his life: "If you have grown up in the kind of environment I grew up in, you can't put it aside just like that. In theory I could have had a British passport years ago. But I was born into a particular historical context, and I don't really have an option."[106]

Although Sebald lived and worked in England for most of his adult life, his narrative prose is shaped by uniquely German contextual factors he shared with his postwar generation: the psychosocial experience of a childhood haunted by war and ruination, and the continuing transgenerational burden of trauma and guilt relating to the Nazi past. The conflicted and changing postwar German discourse can be detected in the specifically German conflicts with which he engaged in his narrative prose. These relate principally to *Heimat*, with its fraught connotations of homeland and belonging, the wish to reverse victim and perpetrator roles, and to oppose the hegemony of Jewish victimhood by presenting German suffering as a competing narrative.[107] In his prose fiction, Adornian alienation from *Heimat* is exemplified by the austere, even hostile living spaces of his Jewish outsiders, and reflected in their suffering at Ithaca and Jerusalem, mythical paradigms of "home."[108] As "Wandering Jews," Sebald's Jewish figures are embodiments of reproach in relation to the Nazi past, and reminders of the "negative symbiosis" in which Germans, Jews, and the Holocaust remain enmeshed.[109] Sebald's solitary Jewish protagonists are unable to sustain meaningful relationships, and manifest the rejection of genealogical continuity common to the children of the perpetrators. His inauthentic Jewish figures touch on the anxieties of his generation regarding belatedness and illegitimacy.

105   Taberner, "German Nostalgia?" 181.

106   Angier, "Who Is W. G. Sebald?" 69.

107   See Assmann, *Der lange Schatten*.

108   Following the catastrophe of the Second World War, Adorno refuted the notion of "home," stating that it is "part of morality not to be at home in one's home." Adorno, *Minima Moralia*, 39.

109   Diner, "Negative Symbiose," 9–10.

## Sebald and the Writing of His Generation

Sebald's subtle and allusive narrative prose does not immediately align his writing with the genres associated with his generation, the protest writing and *Väterliteratur* (father literature) of the 1970s and 1980s. Nevertheless, his ambivalence towards *Heimat*, and his resentment relating to the guilt of the parent generation, reflect the sense of self-pity and injury that Michael Schneider ascribes to the German second generation, "paralyzed by a stray bullet that, over a period of time, has crippled all its social organs, its energy, its will, its courage, its capacity to hope, its utopian phantasies, and along with these, its ability to creatively transform social relations."[110] While Sebald disavowed interest in the 1968 German protest movement, dismissing its ideology as "junk," studies by Mererid Puw Davies, Ben Hutchinson, Gillian Selikowitz, and others have drawn attention to the affinities between his prose writing and the literature of the 1960s protest movement.[111] Sebald's subdued tone differs from the confrontational and often crude narrative tenor of protest writers such as Rolf Dieter Brinkmann, Hubert Fichte, and Herbert Achternbusch; nevertheless, his prose writing, like theirs, reflects an oppressive consciousness of the Nazi past and ambivalence towards social institutions and genealogical continuity. The documentary element to Sebald's literary historiography, and his privileging of the detached outsider position, are evidence of his debt to the Frankfurt School of philosophy, which exerted a significant influence on the ideology of the protest movement. His opposition to psychiatric practice reflects the thinking of the anti-psychiatry movement generated by R. D. Laing and Leo Navratil, integral to protest writing such as Bernward Vesper's *Die Reise* (The Journey, 1977), and Peter Handke's *Die Angst des Tormanns beim Elfmeter* (The Goalie's Anxiety at the Penalty Kick, 1970), and thematized in the "martyrdom" of Ambros Adelwarth at the Samaria psychiatric sanatorium (*TE*).

Sebald's elaborately figural style and metaphysical worldview would seem to preclude a connection with the intensely personal and typically inquisitorial style of *Väterliteratur* (Father Literature). Through this genre, the sons and daughters of perpetrator parents expressed their protest within the private sphere of the family, and confronted their parents, principally their fathers, in attempts to expose a past concealed by the pervasive postwar "conspiracy of silence" that formed the crux of Sebald's controversial Zurich lectures of 1997.[112] While Sebald's distanced tone

110   Schneider, "Fathers and Sons, Retrospectively," 50.

111   Kunisch, "Die Melancholie des Widerstands," 20; Davies, "An Uncanny Journey"; Hutchinson, "The Shadow of Resistance"; Selikowitz, "'Connected but not Congruent.'"

112   Sebald's Zurich lectures became the essay collection, *Luftkrieg und Literatur*. In its English translation by Anthea Bell, it is known as "Air War and

differs markedly from the stridency of Vesper or the expository urgency of Meckel and Seuren, tropes of *Väterliteratur* are embedded in his writing, manifest in resentment towards the burden of inherited guilt, and ambivalence about genealogical succession.[113]

Sebald is allusive in his thematization of the resentment of the second generation toward fathers: the narrator's memory of his father's loathsome scrubbing brush, evoked by the smell inside the Nazi torture camp of Breendonk, conflates the father and the domestic space of home with Nazi terror ( *A*, 33). While the quest for exposure in *Väterliteratur* is deeply personal, manifest in Seuren's search to "discover" his father in incriminatory photographs, Sebald's compulsion to expose what had been concealed by the silence of the parent generation takes the form of uncovering Jewish lives, exemplified by the narrator's quest for understanding in *The Emigrants*. The question of Jewish affiliation, a critically debated theme in relation to Sebald's prose texts, generally takes the form of a tokenistic relationship with a stereotyped or idealized Jewish figure in *Väterliteratur*. Thus Vesper claims to identify with the feelings of a Jewish victim he discovers in a book on the Holocaust: "Ich kannte diese Angst, es war die Angst meines Traumes, der jede Nacht zurückkehrte . . . Wie durch einen unterirdischen Tunnel war ihre Angst mit der meinen verbunden." (I knew this fear, it was the fear of my dream that recurred every night . . . As if through a subterranean tunnel, her fear was linked to mine.)[114]

The tropes and conflicts of *Väterliteratur* are similar to those expressed in the writing of the survivor second generation. Erin McGlothlin explores the shared legacy of the Holocaust from the perspective of the children of survivor and perpetrator groups. For both groups,

> the Holocaust figures as an intimate companion during childhood and adult life . . . The children of the victims and perpetrators alike grew up with the simultaneous presence and absence of Holocaust memory in their everyday family lives, and thus feel profoundly stamped by its legacy.[115]

As McGlothlin observes, for the children of perpetrators, the Nazi past is inscribed into the present as "a stain upon their souls."[116] Thus the protagonist of Peter Schneider's *Vati* remarks bitterly: "Der Spruch von 'der Gnade der späten Geburt' war damals noch nicht erfunden . . . ich

---

Literature" in the essay collection, *On the Natural History of Destruction*.

113   Vesper, *Die Reise* (1977); Meckel, *Suchbild: Über meinen Vater* (1980); Seuren, *Abschied von einem Mörder* (1980).

114   Vesper, *Die Reise*, 486–87.

115   McGlothlin, *Second-Generation Holocaust Literature*, 8.

116   McGlothlin, *Second-Generation Holocaust Literature*, 9.

spürte lange, bevor ich es wußte, daß ich schuldig geboren war." (The expression, "the grace of a late birth" had not yet been invented . . . I suspected, long before I knew, that I was born guilty.)[117] In *Väterliteratur* parental guilt is perceived to irrevocably contaminate the identity of the second generation: "Ja, ich wußte genau, daß ich Hitler war, bis zum Gürtel . . . seine gottverdammte Existenz hat sich an meine geklebt wie Napalm . . ." (Yes, I knew I was Hitler, in every way . . . his goddamned existence had stuck itself to mine like napalm.)[118] The sense of being impacted by the unlived trauma of the Holocaust is expressed by Sebald, who perceived it as an ineluctable "part of my own baggage no matter where I go. One cannot easily escape it."[119] It is implicit in Aurach's perception of being "eingeprägt" ("impressed" or "marked") by the sight of the smoking chimneys that constitute Manchester as a metaphor for Auschwitz, the fate he evaded, but feels compelled to embrace (*TE*, 251). For Aurach, the sense of being metaphorically marked is significant as a simulacrum of the tattoo with which Auschwitz prisoners were branded, emphasizing his allegorical significance as a belated Holocaust victim.

Sebald's focus on the Jewish experience in his narrative prose sets him apart from the overt intergenerational conflict and antiauthoritarian writing of his generation. His allegorical style distinguishes his narrative prose from the writing of his literary cohort. Nevertheless, as examination of his affinity with the literature of his generation demonstrates, Sebald was not immune to the conflicts of the German context he shared with his cohort: these relate to guilt and shame about the Nazi past, a debilitating sense of belatedness and epistemological deficit in relation to the traumatic past, and an identity marked by a self-perception of victimhood. While Sebald dealt with many of these issues explicitly in his non-fiction, critics have drawn attention to the significant impact of Sebald's essays and literary criticism on his prose narratives in terms of imagery, philosophical perspective, and thematic material, factors that shaped the way he conceived of, and employed Jewish figures.

## Sebald's Broader Literary Oeuvre

Sebald first came to public attention as a writer of provocative critical essays, and for his 1997 Zurich lectures that became the essay "Air War and Literature." The theme of German victimhood is central to this work, reflecting Sebald's response to what he perceived as the failure or inability of postwar German writers to explore the problem of evil and

---

117   Schneider, *Vati*, 10.
118   Vesper, *Die Reise*, 107.
119   Schock, "Realismus reicht nicht aus," 101.

the suffering it caused to the German people.[120] The essay reflects the personal quest that motivated Sebald's literary project, to compensate for the epistemological deficit in relation to experiences he was born too late to have had. In "Air War and Literature," Sebald's focus on German suffering as a result of the Allied bombing of German cities is explicit and visceral, reflecting his aim to expose what he believed postwar German writers had left invisible, and to compel the reader to confront suffering and death in the form of victims "roasted brown or purple," "clumps of flesh and bone or whole heaps of bodies that had cooked in the water gushing from bursted boilers," "the roasted corpse of a child, shrunk like a mummy."[121] Traces of such imagery can be found in Sebald's narrative prose: the corrupted picture of Jerusalem, with its vision of "coagulated blood, heaps of entrails, blackish-brown tripes, dried and scorched by the sun" (*TE*, 137), is part of an extended metaphor that degrades Jerusalem as the symbol of "home" in Jewish messianism, and reflects the deeper alienation from notions of home and belonging that underlies Sebald's narrative prose works.

"Air War and Literature" reflects a Benjaminian view of history as calamity, evident in visions of destroyed German cities, and echoed in Sebald's narrative prose in the ruined and deserted landscapes the narrator traverses along the Suffolk coast (*The Rings of Saturn*).[122] It is manifest in apocalyptic fantasies of destruction, such as the narrator's nightmare of the Great Fire of London that ends in the vision of "a silent rain of ashes" (*Vertigo*, 263), metonymic of the Holocaust that is central to Sebald's narrative perspective. Sebald's obsession with corpses in the cellar in "Air War and Literature" is implicit in visions of a renovated Germany that, in his prose fiction, appears to conceal a traumatic past, and in the allegory of institutions built on, and concealing trauma, such as the *Bibliothèque Nationale* of Paris, constructed over the depot of expropriated Jewish possessions. The striking difference in representational strategy between Sebald's confrontational and explicit non-fiction, and his indirect, highly figural narrative prose, reflects the view that shapes his prose fiction, namely that "it is only in the process of metaphorization that history becomes empathetically accessible."[123] Sebald's explicit use of Holocaust imagery and Nazi language of extermination to represent German suffering in "Air War and Literature" reveals a controversial dimension to

120   Bohrer, "Die permanente Theodizee."
121   Sebald, "Air War and Literature," 28–29. Sebald's claim about the "scandalous deficit" of German attempts to deal with German suffering as a result of the Allied air war has been strenuously challenged by Bill Niven, *Germans as Victims*, and Joachim Günter, "Der Bombenkrieg findet zur Sprache," among others.
122   See Benjamin, "On the Concept of History."
123   Löffler, "'Wildes Denken,'" 137.

his non-fiction: describing the bombing of Hamburg in summer 1943, terms such as "Vernichtung" and "Einäscherung" (extermination and cremation), and descriptions of people, "überwältigt von Monoxydgas . . . andere . . . verkohlt und zu Asche geworden" (overwhelmed with carbon monoxide, others charred and reduced to ash), and the image of "grauenvolle Körperberge" (horrible mountains of corpses), create a correspondence between Jewish and German suffering, and establish a moral parallel between the Allied bombing of Dresden and the crimes of Nazism.[124]

Sebald's literary criticism of other German writers for what he perceived as deficient depictions of Jewish lives suggests that he was unaware of parallels between their writing and his own evocation of the Jewish experience. He accused postwar German writers of knowing little of the fate of the persecuted Jews, lamenting that "the real people who we were ready to sacrifice to our master race have not yet appeared before the perception of the senses."[125] In observations that reveal his failure to see the correspondences between his literary style and that of Günter Grass, he criticized the latter for creating a sentimental German-Jewish relationship premised on the wishful idea "that there were really Germans of a better kind, a thesis that stakes its claim to a high degree of probability through the combination of fiction and documentary material."[126] Sebald's censure of writers such as Alfred Andersch provides a sense of what he sought to avoid in his own portrayal of Jewish figures: he was deeply critical of Andersch's stereotyped Jewish characters in *Zanzibar* (1957), and for "putting himself into the character" of the eponymous protagonist of *Efraim* (1967), dismissing Andersch's literary process as "a means of straightening out one's own past."[127] He accused Hans Nossack, Hermann Kassack, and Peter de Mendelssohn of pursuing a "rhetoric of fatefulness," and for concealing painful reality through a lamentable tendency to myth and allegory.[128]

Sebald's non-fiction writing provides an insight into the *Heimat* ambivalence that plagued him and informed the treatment of Jewish displacement and assimilation in his narrative prose. Conflicting visions of *Heimat* are explored in the essay collection *Unheimliche Heimat*: the idealized *Verlustort* (lost space) of Luisa Lanzberg's memoirs evokes the sentimental vision of the irretrievable *Heimat* outlined in Sebald's essays on Eastern-European Jewish writers such as Joseph Roth, Karl-Emil Franzos, and Leopold Sacher-Masoch. The dystopic *Heimat*, "cold and dusty and

124   Sebald, "Luftkrieg und Literatur," 33–36.
125   Sebald, "Constructs of Mourning," 114.
126   Sebald, "Constructs of Mourning," 115.
127   Sebald, "Between the Devil and the Deep Blue Sea," 138–45.
128   Sebald, "Air War and Literature," 55–57.

full of the past," to which Paul Bereyter returns towards the end of his life (*TE*, 60), reflects antipathy to the notion of home, explored by Sebald in essays on exiled Jewish writers, such as Jean Améry.[129] The "lightless and godforsaken" German *Heimat* to which the narrator returns (*Vertigo*, 177), recalls the deterritorialized perception of *Heimat* implicit in the visions of ruin that pervade "Air War and Literature."[130]

Sebald's fascination with Jews and Jewishness is evident in his essays on conflicted Austro- and German-Jewish writers including Peter Weiss and Jean Améry. His interest in gradations of Jewishness and German-Jewish relations informs his conception of ambiguous figures such as Paul Bereyter and Ambros Adelwarth (*TE*). The negative messianism of Franz Kafka, another conflicted Jewish figure, examined in Sebald's essays, "Das Gesetz der Schande" (The Law of Ignominy) and "Das unentdeckte Land" (The Undiscovered Land), pervades Sebald's narrative prose through fragmentary allusions to Kafka's "Hunter Gracchus" story, the hunter's fate an allegory for the permanent homelessness of Sebald's Jewish characters. Sebald's essays on Améry reveal his admiration for the displaced writer whose focus on subjective experience shaped Sebald's biographical approach to representing history.[131]

Critical essays on Kafka, Hugo von Hoffmannsthal, Arthur Schnitzler, and Adalbert Stifter in *Die Beschreibung des Unglücks* reflect Sebald's "pathographic" approach to literary analysis, evident in his tendency to interpret texts as projections of the author's psychological frailties. Sebald's pathographic approach is manifest in the mental and physical enfeeblement of his Jewish characters, and their employment as tropes for the impairment of his own generation, and for a broader, problematic view that attributes the historically contingent suffering of Jewish characters to incomprehensible natural forces. His essays on the work of Ernst Herbeck and Peter Handke reflect Sebald's tendency to valorize mental illness as productively creative, a theme explored in *Austerlitz*.

Sebald's non-fiction explores the question of German-Jewish assimilation as a precursor to the Holocaust. His interest in Jewish assimilation is articulated in an early essay, in which he explored the tension between toleration and persecution inherent in Jewish assimilation.[132] While his narrative prose deals indirectly with the origins of Jewish genocide, in his critical writing Sebald drew on Gershom Scholem, Theodor Adorno, and Max Horkheimer, to identify the persecution of the European Jews as the culmination of a centuries-long process of Jewish assimilation to

---

129    Sebald, "Verlorenes Land."

130    Sebald's figuring of varied conceptions of *Heimat* is examined by Fuchs, *Die Schmerzensspuren der Geschichte*.

131    Sebald, "Against the Irreversible," and "Jean Améry und Primo Levi."

132    Sebald, "Die Zweideutigkeit der Toleranz" (The Ambiguity of Tolerance).

non-Jewish, bourgeois society.[133] Sebald's MA and PhD theses are deeply judgmental of assimilationist Jews such as Carl Sternheim and Alfred Döblin, whom he condemned for mimicking the habits and values of the bourgeoisie.[134] The problem of German-Jewish assimilation is thematized in Sebald's narrative prose; indeed, most of his Jewish figures are examples of failed assimilation, and many experience a deep sense of rejection. The fate of Paul Bereyter and his family is presented as the logical, indeed, inevitable outcome of their assimilation to bourgeois German society. By contrast, the possibility of a German-Jewish existence that preserves the unique identity of both sides is depicted in the wistful memoirs of Luisa Lanzberg and the vignette of harmonious German-Jewish life in New York's Lower East Side ("Ambros Adelwarth," *The Emigrants*).

Research into Sebald's non-fiction writing has uncovered unexplored dimensions to his writing. Contributions in Schütte's text *Über W. G. Sebald: Beiträge zu einem anderen Bild des Autors* (On W. G. Sebald: Contributions to a Different Picture of the Writer) offer novel perspectives on Sebald's non-fiction writing, including Ulrich Dronske's reevaluation of Sebald's critique of Döblin, Markus Joch's reappraisal of Sebald's polemical attacks on Andersch and Becker, and Sven Meyer's exploration of Sebald's unorthodox scientific beliefs and affinity with the discredited British scientist Rupert Sheldrake.[135] Essays in Schütte's collection contribute fresh views on Sebald's approach to German-Jewish assimilation, the relationship between his critical and imaginative writing, and his adherence to a questionable view of history as detached from causality, evident in his tendency to attribute Jewish suffering to a natural history of destruction. Schütte's "Troubling Signs" explores controversial dimensions to Sebald's prose fiction, such as his use of the discredited term "Neger" (negro), and his relativizing approach to the Holocaust, evident in his controversial employment of the mass destruction of herring as a metaphor for the industrial murder of Jews (*The Rings of Saturn*).[136] Drawing on critique of Sebald's dissident literary persona, Mario Gotterbarm accuses him of perpetrating "hermeneutic violence" against writers he considered to be unethical or inappropriate.[137]

Studies by Christian Hein, Melissa Etzler, and Andrew Sutcliffe have contributed significantly to the relatively limited body of critical work on Sebald's engagement with psychiatry. Hein's *Traumatologie des Daseins*

---

133   Scholem, *Jews and Germans*; Adorno and Horkheimer, *Dialectic of Enlightenment*.
134   Sebald, *Carl Sternheim*; *Der Mythus der Zerstörung*.
135   Schütte, *Über W. G. Sebald*.
136   Schütte, "Troubling Signs."
137   Gotterbarm, *Die Gewalt des Moralisten*. Earlier work on Sebald's polemical criticism includes Simon, "Der Literat als Provokateur," and Schütte, "Ein Porträt des Germanisten als junger Mann."

(Traumatology of Being) explores Sebald's tendency to approach mental illness within the context of the natural world.[138] Etzler and Sutcliffe examine Sebald's approach to mental illness and psychiatry against the background of the anti-psychiatry movement of the 1970s and 1980s. Etzler's study draws attention to Sebald's rejection of the psychiatric approach to mental illness in favor of a more holistic and naïve approach to mental suffering and its treatment. Sutcliffe's thesis is a comparative exploration of Sebald's engagement with psychiatry as it relates to melancholia.[139]

## Rosenzweig's Philosophy of Jewishness

In my reading of Sebald's Jewish figures, I draw on German-Jewish philosopher Franz Rosenzweig's reflections on the Jew as a material being, a figure of historically and culturally determined particularity who refuses subsumption by philosophy. Articulated principally in *The Star of Redemption*, Rosenzweig's contention that the individual "is still here," with a first and last name, provides a perspective from which to evaluate the universalizing implications of Sebald's tropological representation of Jewish life in the aftermath of the Holocaust. Rosenzweig's insistence on the singularity of the individual provides a template against which to explore the paradox inherent in Sebald's writing of the Jew: his abstraction of Jewish particularity—the "real" lives he sought to restore—to tropes that reflect the conflicts and concerns of Sebald's own context and perpetuate universalizing and damaging perceptions of the Jew. Rosenzweig conceived of the Jewish people as living the interval between revelation and redemption, not as "a contingent bearer of a trait or a message," but as a necessary link between the originary event on Mt. Sinai and a messianic end. Suspended between life and death, past and present, Sebald's Jewish figures exist in a condition of permanent waiting that is not predicated on redemptive "return," but on its opposite, the permanent exile that is allegorical of Sebald's own alienation from *Heimat*.

In his response to Jewish suffering, Sebald was conscious that "the abstract memory of the dead is of little avail against the lure of waning memory if it does not also express sympathy—sympathy going beyond mere pity—in the study and reconstruction of an actual time of torment."[140] Like Peter Weiss, whom he cited, he understood his role as that of the artistic self, engaged in the process of reconstruction to ensure the continuance of memory. Paradoxically, the substitutions and

---

138 Hein, *Traumatologie des Daseins*.
139 Etzler, "Writing from the Periphery; Sutcliffe, "Reimagining Melancholia."
140 Sebald, "The Remorse of the Heart," 177.

elaborations of his figural mode created Jewish figures who function as tropes for rootlessness, alterity, and other universalizing perceptions of Jewishness, thus diminishing the singularity of the lives he sought to remember. Franklin encapsulates the ambiguous potential of Sebald's depiction of Jewish lives: "Art is the preserver of memory, but it is also the destroyer of memory: This is the final tug-of-war in Sebald's work and the most fundamental one."[141] My engagement with Sebald's figuring of Jewish characters acknowledges the irreducibly problematic nature of his art, while retaining an awareness of the restitutive intention that underlies his literary project.

## Chapter Outline

In chapter 1, I explore the trope of the "Wandering Jew" in *The Emigrants*. Sebald's displaced Jewish figures are projections of his restitutive literary project, through which he hoped to restore "real" Jewish lives, and expressions also of a more personal alienation from *Heimat*. I examine Sebald's repudiation of home through the nexus he established between *Heimat* and death in his figuring of Henry Selwyn's inhospitable home, the suffering of Ambros Adelwarth at Ithaca and Jerusalem, mythical emblems of home, and in the allegorization of Max Aurach as the Wandering Jew whose spectral existence in Manchester, depicted as an allegory for Auschwitz, offers a disconsolate view of death as the "*Heimat*" of the Jews. I explore the pervasive imagery of desert nomadism that configures Sebald's Jewish characters as emblems of ontological Jewish rootlessness and posits the desert as the "place" of the Jews and nomadic wandering as their existential destiny. I examine the enduring emblem of Ahasverus, the Wandering Jew, and Sebald's integration of Kafka's "Wandering Jew" story, "The Hunter Gracchus," a negative messianic narrative that infuses Sebald's prose fiction with the bleak promise of eternal homelessness. Like the hunter, Sebald, and the Wandering Jews of his imagination, will remain forever exiled. Repudiation of home is explored in thwarted fantasies of homecoming: Max Aurach's fantasy of return to the Franconian *Wohnzimmer* (drawing room) of his parents (*TE*), is a negative messianic episode in which Frohmann's model of the Temple of Jerusalem is a metaphor for the heritage that Sebald's displaced Jews have lost. Sebald's construction of hybrid figures of German and Jewish identity reveals a troubling dimension to his writing: a provocative conflation of German and Wandering Jew, perpetrator and victim, Paul Bereyter's *Wehrmacht* (army) service in occupied Europe and perverse return to Germany after the war, are examined in relation to the discourse

---

141   Franklin, "Rings of Smoke," 126.

on German guilt, and the desire to reverse the roles of victim and perpetrator, reflected in Sebald's narrative fiction.

Chapter 2 explores the figure of Austerlitz as the Wandering Jew, whose restless itinerancy is motivated by the quest for origins from which he was traumatically ruptured in early childhood. In *Austerlitz*, Sebald radicalized the trope of the Wandering Jew by presenting his protagonist as a largely metaphorical figure, whose rootlessness is ontological, a Wandering Jew whose quest to confirm his origins is at the same time a quest to verify his own existence in reality. In relation to Austerlitz's unknown origins, I explore the philosophical association of the Jew with void and absence, and the desert as an onto-historical signifier of Jewish deracination. The theme of "drowning" pervades Austerlitz's story as a metaphor for his submerged origins and connects him to Levi's "Muselmann," the living dead of Auschwitz, remembered in *The Drowned and the Saved*. I examine Austerlitz's intuitive affiliation with images and sounds that connote an atavistic, nomadic existence, and suggest that his "true" origin is in the desert of Jewish exile, and not in the European cities and sites of suffering in which he seeks it. I consider the implications of Austerlitz's allegorization as the radically dispossessed Wandering Jew, an emblem for Sebald's second-generation insecurity about origins and an expression of a deeper philosophical unease about post-Holocaust Jewish existence.

The third chapter is an examination of Jewish alterity in *Vertigo*, *The Emigrants*, and *The Rings of Saturn*, drawing on historical perceptions of Jewish heteronomy in German literature and philosophy, including Luther, Kant, Hegel, and Heidegger. Sebald's Jewish figures personify the multiplicity of perceptions that, over centuries, have contributed to problematic notions of Jewish alterity that have made the Jew "the most essential outsider of society."[142] These include the Jew as Simmel's "familiar stranger," the metaphysical Jew who arises from the philosophical reflections of Hegel and Heidegger, and the Jew as the embodiment of the abstract and corrosive features of modernity—the inauthenticity, materialism, and abstract intellectuality—that Weininger identified in the figure of the *fin-de-siècle* Jew. I probe the notion of Jewish alterity as a transferable identity, thematized in "Ambros Adelwarth," and Sebald's construction of Jewish figures "in both camps," who reflect his fascination with variations of Jewishness. In relation to Paul Bereyter, I consider the aporia of the Jew in the context of catastrophe, for whom Jewishness is an alien identity imposed by decree. Sebald's displaced Jewish characters perpetuate the view of the Jew as alienated from the world, their outsiderliness reflected in homes that are typically peripheral to the social world. In the affiliation of Sebald's Jewish characters with manifestations

142   Zukier, "The Essential 'Other,'" 1151.

of an Oriental nomadic identity, I consider Sebald's attribution of an innate, Orientalized Jewishness to his acculturated Jews, an "essential" identity that migration, changing one's name, and disguise cannot eradicate. Sebald's narrative prose chronicles the conflicts and failure of assimilation and the erosion of Jewish lives, unsustained by what he saw as the "wholeness" of traditional Judaism, lived with an awareness of its own particularity, within the broader social world.

Chapter 4 is devoted to the problematic question of Jewish inauthenticity, evident in the perceived tendency of Jews to mimic the society in which they find themselves. In *The Emigrants*, *Vertigo*, and *Austerlitz*, strategies of concealment, and the configuration of Jewish characters as actors and opera singers, convey the notion of Jewish dissimulation. Sebald's figurative writing imbues his Jewish figures with an intrinsic affinity with manifestations of their putative Jewish origins in the desert of the Middle East, while the motif of the *Doppelgänger* who shadows his assimilated Jews suggests the unlived, authentic life they have discarded. In doing so, Sebald reflects a long-held perception of the Jew as an inauthentic mimic who attempts to conceal his innate Jewishness to pass unnoticed in gentile society, but as unable to do so owing to his immutable alterity, implied to have its roots in the desert of the Middle East. I explore the memoirs of Luisa Lanzberg as an example of what Sebald appeared to have considered "authentic" Jewishness, and the problematic notion that this is immutably bound to the traditions associated with exilic Jewish life, a view that tends to cultural essentialism and conflicts with contemporary approaches to Jewish authenticity that acknowledge the dynamism and multiplicity of the phenomenon.

In my final chapter, I examine Sebald's enfeebled Jewish figures in *The Emigrants*, *Vertigo*, and *Austerlitz* as personifications of the trope of the Sickly Jew. The view of the Jew as predisposed to illness is reflected in the hypochondria and hysterical paralysis of Dr K. at the Riva Spa, the suffering bodies of Ambros and Cosmo at the Samaria sanatorium, and Austerlitz's mental instability. The implications of the numerous exclusionary therapeutic spaces—the hospital, sanatorium, or spa—to which Sebald's Jewish characters are delivered or have themselves admitted, are considered in relation to the nexus between Jewish illness and alterity in Sebald's prose writing, and in the context of the antipsychiatry movement and the influence on Sebald's writing of Navratil, Reich, and others. I explore Sebald's rejection of conventional medical treatment and his attribution of Jewish illness and suffering to the vicissitudes of an indifferent natural world as obfuscating the question of German agency in the conception and execution of the Holocaust. Weininger's *Sex and Character* provides stereotyped perceptions of the Jewish body and Jewish behavior that I examine as manifestations of *fin de siècle* Jewish anxieties in relation to assimilation and masculinity.

# 1: The Wandering Jew in *The Emigrants*

> *In his dreams he had already crossed*
> *all the deserts of sand and stone*
>
> —*The Emigrants*

EXILED IN HIS GARDEN HERMITAGE, Henry Selwyn's original exodus from Lithuania to England underpins his metaphorical role as a Wandering Jew. Paul Bereyter is remembered by his students as "the very image of the German *Wandervogel*" (*TE*, 57); his "continued absence from the town" (*TE*, 28) suggests his exiled condition in postwar Germany.[1] For the "desert wanderers," Ambros Adelwarth and Cosmo Solomon, Jerusalem and Ithaca, mythical paradigms of home, offer only suffering and death. Born into an assimilated German-Jewish family that traced its Franconian roots to the late seventeenth-century, Max Aurach appears to emerge from, and belong within, the Wadi Halfa desert fresco, implying his immutable and conspicuous nomadism that three centuries of assimilation cannot disguise. Exiled from home, Sebald's displaced Jewish figures are projections of his restitutive literary project, through which he hoped to restore "real" Jewish lives. His Wandering Jews are expressions also of a deeper and more personal alienation from *Heimat*, that ineffably German concept with its emotive but fraught connotations of homeland and belonging.[2] Indeed, Sebald presented himself as an exile from Germany, "I hardly knew Germany . . . in a sense it's not my country."[3] Sebald's identification with Jewish exile has led to his description as the "fifth emigrant," who suffered from the loss of his German homeland and who, like the other wanderers in his texts, was unable to find a replacement for it in the modern world.[4] Despite his empathetic tracing of displaced Jewish lives, Sebald's troping of Jewish figures subsumes their individuality in a universalizing allegory of exile that undermines his restitutive literary intentions.

Considered unique among German writers for his concern with post-Holocaust Jewish suffering, Sebald's employment of the Wandering

---

1    The "Wandervögel" was a back-to-nature, all-male German youth group, founded in 1896 by Karl Fischer.
2    See Boa and Palfreyman, *Heimat—A German Dream*.
3    Wachtel, "Ghost Hunter," 50–51.
4    Fink, "W. G. Sebald—der fünfte Ausgewanderte," 227.

Jew stereotype is significant for what it reveals about his perception of the Jew in the post-Holocaust context. Sebald figures *Heimat* as a contaminated, if not fatal place from which his Wandering Jews have been expelled, but to which many feel compelled to return, a home experienced only *ex negativo* in the metaphorical exile of elective death, or in dreams.[5] The Wandering Jew is employed as a trope to convey a deeply pessimistic vision of Jewish existence after the Holocaust, one that reflects the fatalism and resignation that Schneider detects in Sebald's generation.[6] Sebald's narrative world forecloses the possibility of home beyond the ironic promise Sebald identifies in Kafka's writing: "Die Heimat ist der gute Ort. Und der gute Ort ist der Friedhof der Juden"[7] (The homeland is the good place, and the good place is the cemetery of the Jews) manifest in Sebald's peaceful Jewish cemeteries, in which graves "crumble and gradually sink into the ground" (*TE*, 223), and "lime trees and lilacs grow" (*A*, 408). For Sebald's Wandering Jews, only death provides a "home": for Henry Selwyn, this is the imagined icy tomb uniting him in *Liebestod* (love-in-death) with his beloved Naegeli; for Max Aurach, it is the "necropolis" of Manchester. Paul Bereyter's violent death is implicit in the photograph of railway tracks against a brooding background of firs with which his story begins, and he inhabits the text as "a dead man . . . who only by chance was not yet where he properly belonged."[8] To the doomed nomads, Ambros and Cosmo, Jerusalem and Ithaca are depicted as contaminated spaces that refute the idea of home they symbolize. Kafka's negative messianic narrative, "The Hunter Gracchus," pervades Sebald's narrative prose as an allegory for estrangement from "home," imbuing it with the bleak assurance of eternal homelessness. Kafka's hunter falls to his death in pursuit of a chamois, but a wrong turning by the helmsman of the funeral barge precludes Gracchus from metaphorically reaching home, condemning him to drift forever in a state of "living death." Like the hunter, Sebald and the Wandering Jews of his imagination will remain forever exiled.

Sebald's rootless Jewish figures revive the myth of the Wandering Jew, a late medieval legend in which Jewish guilt, initially embodied by the figure of Judas, was projected onto the Jewish people as a whole, personified by the figure of Ahasverus. While the myth of the Wandering Jew persists, and changes according to context, "what endures . . . is the use of the Jew

---

5    In a dream, Max Aurach returns to his family home in Kissingen (*TE*); Michael Hamburger's dream of return to his family home in Berlin is described in *The Rings of Saturn*.

6    Schneider, "Fathers and Sons, Retrospectively."

7    Sebald, "Westwärts–Ostwärts," 54.

8    Améry, "On the Necessity and Impossibility of being a Jew," 86.

as a screen on which individuals and societies project their anxieties."[9] A symbol of collective and inexpiable Jewish guilt, the figure of Ahasverus the Wandering Jew is arguably the principal emblem referring to Jews in European culture.[10] According to legend, Ahasverus refused Jesus rest on his *via dolorosa* to Calvary, and was condemned by him to eternal wandering: "I will stay but you shall go." Indeed, despite centuries-old Jewish settlement in urban and rural communities, the Oriental traces left on the map of Europe by the Wandering Jews are perceived as destabilizing to the orderly division between West and East.[11] Examining the evolution of the Wandering Jew myth sheds light on the philosophical and historical substratum on which Sebald, perhaps unconsciously, drew, in his construction of displaced Jewish figures as allegorical of post-Holocaust Jewish existence, and of the conflicts that burdened his generation.

## Historical Background to the Wandering Jew Trope

The earliest German reference to the Wandering Jew is found in a pamphlet from 1602, *Kurtze Beschreibung und Erzehlung von einem Jude mit Namen Ahasuerus* (Short Description and Story of a Jew by the Name of Ahasverus), in which reference is made to Jesus's cursing of Ahasverus for refusing him rest on the wall of his house on his way to Golgotha.[12] Beyond cursing him with eternal wandering, Jesus condemns Ahasverus to a life of alienation, to "walk until the end of time . . . to be a father without children, a husband without a wife, a traveler who knows not the destination of his voyage, an eternal pilgrim among men."[13] As the personification of the guilt of the Jewish nation, Ahasverus's punitive wandering is posited to continue until he is at last redeemed by extinction and subsumption into the wholeness of humanity.[14]

In the writing of Hegel, the notion of Jewish rootlessness is implicit in the historical dispossession of the Jewish people, precluded from land ownership by Jewish Law: "For the land is mine, and ye are strangers and

---

9    Marcus, *The Definition of Anti-Semitism*, 140.

10    See Hasan-Rokem, "Joban Transformation of the Wandering Jew," 151.

11    The phenomenon of Jewish wandering is explored in Hasan-Rokem, "Jews as Postcards," 507–10.

12    The oldest source of the legend is found in *Ignoti Monachi Cisterciensis S. Mariae de Ferraria Chronica et Ryccardi de Sancto Germano Chronica priora*, Bologna, beginning of the thirteenth century. Pöhlmann, "Ahasver, der wandernde Jude," 345.

13    Edelman, "Ahasuerus, the Wandering Jew."

14    For discussion of the evolution of the wandering Jew trope, see Rose, *German Question/Jewish Question*, 23.

sojourners with me" (Leviticus 25:23). As "a stranger on earth, a stranger to the soil and to men alike," rootlessness is implicit in Abraham's disseverance from nature and other peoples.[15] Unable to own land, the rootless Jew is expelled from Hegel's vision of the state, "since they held their possessions only on loan and not as property, since as citizens they were all *ein Nichts*" [nothing].[16] Hegel's relegation of the Jew to the status of *Nichts* is echoed in the evacuation of Jewish selfhood implicit in Sebald's picture of annihilated and rootless Jewish existence after the Holocaust.

The myth of Ahasverus becomes increasingly secularized in the Enlightenment of the eighteenth century, during which time the suffering of Christ, attributed to Ahasverus's pitiless indifference, is replaced by the suffering of Germans and humanity, and Jewish heteronomy replaces deicide as a sin redeemable only through death. This is implicit in the annihilatory fantasies of German Idealists, exemplified by Kant's "euthanasia" of the Jews, and Fichte's "decapitation" of all Jews.[17] The notion of "wandering" is intrinsic to nineteenth-century German Romantic writing, with its myriad portrayals of the wandering artist, whose itinerancy is metaphorical of existential unhousedness, exemplified by Friedrich Hölderlin's Hyperion, who feels "dazu geboren, heimathlos und ohne Ruhestätte zu seyn." (Born to be homeless and without a refuge.)[18] For the Romantics, "wandering" is allegorical of the artistic process itself, conceived as infinite: "Die romantische Dichtart ist noch im Werden; ja, das ist ihr eigentliches Wesen, daß sie ewig nur werden, nie vollendet sein kann." (Romantic poetry is still in the process of becoming; indeed, that is its essence, that it is always in the process of becoming, and can never be concluded.)[19] As Paul Lawrence Rose notes: "An allusive, plastic myth, comprehending themes of death, eternal Jewish character, and final redemption, Ahasverus supplied the most potent vehicle for the secular mythology of the 'destruction of Judaism' that came to dominate German revolutionary anti-Semitism in the nineteenth century."[20] The extinction of Jewishness becomes overt in notions of destruction that increasingly characterize nineteenth-century German philosophical writing, exemplified by Schopenhauer's vision of Jewish erasure through assimilation: "Ahasverus will be buried, and the chosen people will not know where their abode was."[21] For Richard Wagner, redemption of the Wandering Jew is predicated on self-destruction: "Only one

---

15    Hegel, "The Spirit of Christianity," 185.

16    Hegel, "The Spirit of Christianity," 197.

17    Kant, *The Conflict of the Faculties*; Fichte, *Beitrag zur Berichtigung*, 149.

18    Beissner, *Hölderlin: Sämtliche Werke*, 7.

19    Schlegel, "Athenäum Fragment 116."

20    Rose, *German Question/Jewish Question*, 24.

21    Schopenhauer, *Parerga and Paralipomena*, 164.

40 ◆ THE WANDERING JEW IN *THE EMIGRANTS*

thing can redeem you from the burden of your curse—the redemption of Ahasverus—*Untergang*! (downfall)"[22] The tenacity of Jewish particularism, evident in the refusal of the Jew to relinquish Judaism, gives rise to the sinister trope of the Jew as the living, wandering dead:

> Ahasverus' tragic fate is not his violent and unsuccessful search for death, but rather his exhausted dusk-watch, his outliving of himself, his obsolescence. Time itself always remains young: new peoples arise, new heroes, new empires. Only Ahasverus stays on, a living corpse, a dead man who has not yet died.[23]

In her study of the Jew as the living dead, Shapiro notes the perception of the Jew as "always already dead, but somehow, and problematically, still apparently present":[24]

> Since its formative development with the advent of the Jewish Question in the emancipation, to its so-called "Final Solution" in the terrible literalizing of this image in the manufacture in the Shoah of the "living-dead" [the *Muselmänner*], the image of the Uncanny Jew has, as it were, had a kind of "afterlife."[25]

In post-1945 German writing, the Wandering Jew is depicted as the embodiment of the past that will not "die," a cause of German suffering, and a threat to the formation of a normalized German self-identity. Perceived as a *Schuldvorwurf* (accusation of guilt,) the Wandering Jew as a revenant is a reminder of German guilt. This view is complicated by the question of Jewish guilt attached to the trope of the Wandering Jew through Ahasverus's inhumane treatment of Jesus: the persistence of the Wandering Jew myth in postwar German literature suggests a self-exculpatory equalization of Jewish and German culpability, while perpetuating the polarizing view of Jews as embodiments of rootlessness in relation to Germans, perceived as grounded in *Heimat* and *Nation*. The question of Jewish guilt is significant in the context of the shift in West-German politics and culture in the 1980s and 1990s, from a discourse of guilt and shame to one focused on normalization of the national narrative, acknowledgment of German victimhood, and integration of the Holocaust into the continuum of German history. The new discourse is evident in attempts to relativize the suffering of Germans and their

---

22   Wagner, *Judaism in Music*, 81–82.
23   Gutzkow, "Plan for an Ahasverus," 199.
24   Shapiro, "The Uncanny Jew," 161.
25   Shapiro, "The Uncanny Jew," 170.

victims, and to approach more empathetically the imbrication of Germans in the *Wehrmacht* (German army).[26]

Sebald's employment of the Wandering Jew trope in his narrative prose is explored as an intricate manifestation of a persisting perception of Jewish rootlessness in the German cultural imagination, and as a reflection of a shifting cultural and political discourse in relation to the Holocaust and its position in German consciousness.

## Henry Selwyn, the Wandering Jew

Henry Selwyn's once "real" itinerancy supports his metaphorical role as a Wandering Jew. Born Hersch Seweryn, his childhood in a Lithuanian *shtetl* (village) is ruptured by emigration, but remembered with increasing clarity as he ages. Journeys are a pervasive motif in his life: by cart from his *shtetl* to Grodno in the wake of unstated anti-Semitic violence, by train to Riga, followed by a sea voyage with negative messianic implications, which delivers the emigrants to London instead of the "Promised City" of New York. In an effort to assimilate to English society, Henry Selwyn changes his original name and conceals his Jewish origins, even from his wife. As an English country doctor, his life "in the grand style" (*TE*, 21) is one of travel and material acquisition, represented by the cars that stand idle in his garages, symbols of his former itinerancy. Retired from the social world and alienated from his wife, Henry Selwyn has exiled himself to his garden hermitage, situated in a remote corner of the garden. The narrator and his wife encounter him in his garden, and are struck by Henry Selwyn's chimerical appearance—"tall and broad-shouldered, he seemed quite stocky, even short," his movements "at once awkward and yet perfectly poised" (*TE*, 5). His wispy hair, strikingly high forehead, and stooped, "almost supplicatory posture" (*TE*, 5) evoke Gustave Doré's iconic woodcuts illustrating the Wandering Jew. In Doré's depictions, he is surrounded by images that conjure injurious perceptions of the mythical figure: the image of Christ's crucifixion is a reminder of Ahasverus's original guilt, the far-off church spires signify the Jew's metaphorical distance from Christianity, while the ominous landscape of mountains, forests, thicket and river suggest hostility to the ragged Jew on his eternal wandering.[27] Sebald's literary evocation of an artistic vision of the Wandering Jew distances Henry Selwyn from reality, and allegorizes him as a trope for stigmatized rootlessness.

---

26    The new discourse flowed from the "Historikerstreit" or Historian's Debate, and is evident in the Bitburg memorialization and *Neue Wache* dedication, which included both perpetrators and victims.

27    Doré, *The Wandering Jew*, 12 woodcuts, 1856.

Mountaineering in Switzerland with his beloved Alpine guide, Naegeli, is the apotheosis of Henry Selwyn's existence, and after Naegeli's disappearance in the Alps, Henry succumbs to a paralyzing depression from which he never recovers. When the narrator and his wife first encounter him on the grounds of his uncanny residence, Henry Selwyn has ceased his travels and withdrawn from the social world into nature, a retreat from life that signals, in Sebald's writing, the nearness of death. To the narrator, Henry Selwyn confesses to feeling *Heimweh* (homesickness) for Lithuania and his irretrievable past. Burdened by all he has lost, and haunted by guilt at repressing his Jewish origins and evading the fate of his fellow-Jews, Henry Selwyn takes his own life. His failure to ultimately find a "home" is metaphorical of Sebald's pessimistic vision of post-Holocaust Jewish existence, and of his own alienation from home, depicted in "Henry Selwyn" as hostile to human habitation.

Consistent with his averred interest in empathetically representing "singular individuals who lived on the other side of the hallway," Sebald provides a meticulous biography of the Lithuanian Jew, much of it through the voice of Henry Selwyn himself, lending his story a first-person narrative authenticity that recalls the oral testimony of the survivor generation.[28] Nevertheless, Henry Selwyn is more than an individual whose life has been damaged by displacement and persecution: beyond the personal, often poignant details Sebald supplies, Henry Selwyn's individuality as "man in the utter singularity of his being" is undermined by Sebald's elaborately figural writing that universalizes him as eternally exiled, a trope for Sebald's conflicts surrounding *Heimat* and guilt about the past, and a cipher for vitiated Jewish existence in the shadow of the Holocaust.[29] Henry Selwyn's relationship with the Swiss-German Alpinist Naegeli, and his metaphorical union with Naegeli in a form of Romantic *Liebestod*, suggest a reimagined German-Jewish symbiosis, implied, through Naegeli's death, to be a futile aspiration. A destitute figure, whose spectrality is conjured by imagery of absence and emptiness, Henry Selwyn represents the trope of the dead but still eerily existent Wandering Jew, whose appearance is an unspoken reproach in relation to the traumatic past.

### Alienation from *Heimat*: The Nexus of Home and Death

"Henry Selwyn" opens with the ominous conjunction of home and death created by the juxtaposition of the narrator's *Wohnungssuche* (quest for a home) and the brooding image of a graveyard overshadowed by a tree, the first of a number of interlinking images of overshadowing trees, metaphorical of the shadow the Holocaust casts on the lives of those affected

28  McGlothlin et al., *The Construction of Testimony.*
29  Rosenzweig, *Star of Redemption*, 10.

by it.[30] Imagery of absence and lifelessness—the empty market place, the proximity of the cemetery, the deserted crows' nests that form "dark patches" in the beeches or *Buchenstand* with its sinister connotations of Buchenwald (*TE*, 4 / *DA*, 8), the funereally black front door—suggests Henry Selwyn's spectral existence, and the Holocaust that is central to his deepening self-alienation. Henry Selwyn's house is figured as the antithesis of "home" as a term that connotes belonging and *Hineingelebtheit* (familiarity): in close proximity to the dead, hostile to human habitation behind an impenetrable thicket and high wall, inhabited by "ghostly creatures" (*TE*, 10), and concealing the "buried" secret of his origins, it is an allegory for the notion of death as the "home" of the Jew. The opening image of the graveyard is structurally significant, linking the introduction to the epilogue by foreshadowing the morbid iconography with which "Henry Selwyn" concludes: the return of Naegeli's remains. A pile of bones and a pair of boots, this is synecdochic of the Holocaust, and of the mythical Wandering Jew, Ahasverus, known also as the "shoemaker of Jerusalem," a reminder of Henry Selwyn's tropological role as a Wandering Jew.[31] Overshadowed by death, his story posits post-Holocaust Jewish existence as fundamentally rootless, metaphorical of Sebald's own estrangement from home.

## The Trope of Endless Wandering: Kafka's "Hunter Gracchus"

The frontage of Henry Selwyn's house reminds the narrator of an impressive but pointless project pursued by two French brothers who devote decades to constructing a façade resembling the Palace of Versailles for their country house. The ateleological project is a recurring motif in Sebald's narrative prose, and is allegorical of an eschatology premised not

---

30    The shadow of the Holocaust is a pervasive metaphor in postwar German writing, exemplified by the title of Aleida Assman's exploration of memory and history in *Der lange Schatten der Vergangenheit* (2006), and Sebald's own acknowledgment of a life overshadowed by trauma in "Air War and Literature." The metaphor recurs in Max Aurach's recollection of his parents' suffering and its effect on his life: "That tragedy in my youth struck such deep roots within me that it later shot up again, put forth evil flowers, and spread the poisonous canopy over me which has kept me so much in the shade and dark in recent years" (*TE*, 191). It returns in the nostalgic memoirs of Aurach's mother, Luisa Lanzberg, who recalls her youth in Franconia, and her memory of a "square shaded by a gigantic chestnut tree" (*TE*, 194), an image that links mother and son in a community of suffering.

31    Ahasverus is known in Finnish as "Jerusalemin suutari" ("shoemaker of Jerusalem"), implying that he may have been a cobbler by trade.

on the "end," but on its deferral or failure.[32] This notion is central to Kafka's "Hunter Gracchus" story (1917), a Wandering Jew myth and a negative messianic narrative that refuses the possibility of "homecoming." Kafka's story pervades *The Emigrants* as a reminder of the negative messianism that underlies the lives of the emigrants: like the hunter, Sebald's Jews will never reach "home," but are condemned to metaphorically drift forever. This is the fate of Henry Selwyn, and, as Sill observes, of the homeless writer himself.[33]

In "Henry Selwyn," Kafka's hunter is evoked by a convoluted network of imagery relating to the hunt: Henry Selwyn's former name, "Hersch" conjures *Hirsch* or stag, the traditional prey of the European hunter; Henry's hunting rifle, acquired in India as the obligatory equipment for an English gentleman, is synecdochic of the big game hunting in which the young Henry Selwyn fails to participate during his time in India, and evidence of his inability to successfully recreate himself as an English gentleman, and to metaphorically find a "home" or new identity. Gracchus alludes to the hunting rifle before embarking on his eternal journey: "I lived a happy life, and would happily have died, joyfully I flung away my knapsack, my bag, and my hunting rifle before I stepped on board."[34] Connected through the motif of the hunt, Gracchus and Henry Selwyn are condemned to endless "wandering," with *Heimkehr* (homecoming) an ever-deferred aspiration.

The motif of the butterfly hunter, encountered in the context of Henry Selwyn's Cretan journey, relates Henry's story to that of Kafka's hunter. In Kafka's fragment, the hunter compares his trapped situation with that of a butterfly in a state of pointless, perpetual motion: "I roam around on this infinitely wide flight of steps, sometimes up, sometimes down, sometimes to the right, sometimes to the left, always in motion. From being a hunter, I've become a butterfly. Don't laugh."[35] In the slide show of his journey to Crete, Henry Selwyn is depicted in the guise of a butterfly hunter, "in knee-length shorts, with a shoulder bag and butterfly net" (*TE*, 16). This evokes a similar photograph of Vladimir Nabokov, Russian expatriate writer, whose autobiography is a meditation on the ambiguity of memory, posited as potentially both redemptive and fatal to the remembering subject.[36]

---

32  The ateleological project is exemplified in Sebald's narrative prose by Alec Garrard's never-to-be-completed model of the Jerusalem Temple (*RS*), the unfinished embroidery of the Ashbury sisters (*RS*), Henry Selwyn's counting of blades of grass (*TE*), and the turbaned cleaner's Sisyphean sweeping of the Liverpool Station (*Austerlitz*).

33  Sill, "Aus dem Jäger," 605.

34  Kafka, "The Hunter Gracchus."

35  Kafka, "The Hunter Gracchus."

36  Nabokov, *Speak, Memory*.

The stories of Gracchus and Henry Selwyn are interlinked as allegories that explore the possibility of messianic recuperation of the prelapsarian past: for Gracchus, "return" is posited as impossible through Kafka's adumbration of an open-ended messianic narrative: "The Messiah will come only when he is no longer needed, he will come only on the day after his arrival, he will not come on the last day, but on the very last day."[37] As Kilbourn observes, the "quasi-allegorical butterfly man represents in *The Emigrants* the always-imminent promise, if not the *immanent* reality of redemption; a metaphor for an ever-deferred (secular) salvific principle that is nevertheless present in Sebald's *seemingly* heavy-handed intertextual homage."[38] Overwhelmed by the memory of all he has lost in the process of assimilation, Henry Selwyn can never "return" to the Jewish Lithuanian home and identity he relinquished.

## Mythologizing Jewish Fate

In Sebald's prose writing, the ineluctability of Jewish fate is reinforced by mythological allusions that transform his Jewish figures into paradigms of human existence, invest Jewish suffering with universal significance, and promote a fatalistic view of Jewish suffering as eternal and predestined, an ironic proposition, in view of Sebald's critique of other German writers for engaging in a "rhetoric of fatefulness" that undermines the reality of German suffering during the Allied bombing of German cities.[39] Doomed to remain homeless, "an eternal stranger and pilgrim on earth," Henry Selwyn's exile is figured as inescapable through Sebald's conflation of his story with that of the mythical figure of Hippolytus.

At their first encounter, Henry Selwyn shows the narrator around his estate, and introduces him to three aged and decrepit horses rescued from the knackery, who function as metaphors for his own abjection. Henry Selwyn has named one of the pitiful horses "Hippolytus," conjuring the eponymous protagonist of Euripides' play.[40] The theme of hunting relates Henry Selwyn to the mythical figure of Hippolytus, adherent of Artemis, goddess of the hunt. On the level of structural significance, Aphrodite's opening prophecy augurs the death of Hippolytus, giving the action a sense of inescapability.[41] In "Henry Selwyn," such fatalism is implied in the proleptic image of the cemetery that opens the story, and aestheticizes it with a morbid beauty. Literary-dramatic figures, Hippolytus and Henry Selwyn linger on the threshold of death: Euripides' play ends with the

---

37   Kafka, *Hochzeitsvorbereitungen.*
38   Kilbourn, "Kafka, Nabokov . . . Sebald," 62.
39   Sebald, "Air War and Literature," 50–51.
40   Euripides, *Hippolytus.*
41   See Dunn, *Tragedy's End.*

46 ◆ THE WANDERING JEW IN *THE EMIGRANTS*

death of Hippolytus as an event yet to be played out, while Henry Selwyn lives on as a revenant, haunting the memory of the narrator. Linked to the doomed mythical figure of Hippolytus through an act of redemption, the pathos of Henry Selwyn's exile is universalized, encapsulating the paradox inherent in Sebald's figuring of the Jew: Sebald's efforts to deepen the reality of Henry's life through myth and allegory render him more abstract, distant, and inaccessible.

### The Wandering Undead

The Jewish characters the narrator encounters in *The Emigrants* are, figuratively, dead: Henry Selwyn, pursuing a "death-in-life" existence after the disappearance of his beloved Naegeli, Paul Bereyter, dead before his story begins, and the uncanny couple, Ambros and Cosmo, who wander Europe and the Middle East like phantoms and who, as the narrator observes, "dissolved before [his very eyes], leaving behind them nothing but the vacant space they had occupied" (*TE*, 123). Max Aurach pursues a ghostly existence in the "necropolis" of Manchester, enacting in this emigrant city of Germans and Jews, the fate for which he feels destined as a Jew, postulating the bleak view of death as the destination he instinctively identifies as "home" (*TE*, 192). The spectral existence of Sebald's figural Jews symbolizes the enduring effect of the Holocaust on their lives. As the Wandering Undead in Sebald's narrative prose, they imply a perception of the post-Holocaust Jew as a *Schuldvorwurf*, a reproachful revenant who haunts the German present as a reminder of the unresolved past, and threatens the formation of a democratic postwar German identity. The trope of the Wandering Jew as the Undead reflects Sebald's incorporation of trauma theory, which postulates the transmission of trauma across generations by means of "phantoms," incorporeal embodiments of that which has been left unsaid.[42]

Henry Selwyn is a revenant who haunts the German present as a reminder of the unresolved past. This is implied in his leave-taking from the narrator not long before his suicide: "Rising, he made a gesture that was most unusual for him. He offered me his hand in farewell" (*TE*, 21). In the original German, this reads, "Dr Selwyn erhob sich und gab mir, was äußerst ungewöhnlich war, zum Abschied die Hand" (*DA*, 35; Dr Selwyn rose, and with a gesture that was most unusual for him, offered me his hand in farewell). This is a faint allusion to the second stanza of "Allerseelen," Richard Strauss's elegiac song, "All Souls," with its invocation to the Dead, "Gib' mir die Hand, daß ich sie heimlich drücke . . ." (Give me your hand to press in secret).[43] In the light of Henry Selwyn's

---

42    Abraham and Torok, *The Shell and the Kernel.*
43    Richard Strauss, "Allerseelen."

life, the nostalgic refrain of Strauss's song, "As once in May," is a reminder of the happier past, the unbearable memory of which is the source of Henry Selwyn's sorrow, and ultimately, his death.

Henry Selwyn's wandering does not end with his suicide: "Unverhofft und unvermutet" (*DA*, 36), an allusion to Hebel's story of loss and resurrection, he unexpectedly returns to the narrator's memory as the Wandering Undead, a metaphor for the unburied past, and the enactment of the narrator's homiletic reflection, "And so they are ever returning to us, the dead" (*TE*, 23). Translated as "unanticipated and unsuspected," Sebald alludes to Johann Peter Hebel's story, "Unverhofftes Wiedersehen" (Unexpected Reunion), an exploration of death and redemption, in which the "resurrection" of a young miner occurs sadly too late:

> The hearts of all those there were moved to sadness and tears when they saw the former bride-to-be as an old woman whose beauty and strength had left her, and the groom still in the flower of his youth; and how the flame of young love was rekindled in her breast after fifty years, yet he did not open his mouth to smile, nor his eyes to recognize her.[44]

For Henry Selwyn too, the return of his lover's remains comes too late. In the form of "a few polished bones and a pair of hobnailed boots" (*TE*, 23), they educe a Holocaust iconograph, and are a reminder of the fatal role of memory in Henry's life. The evocation of Hebel's poignant story of belated return reflects the paradox in Sebald's writing: while he empathically sought to restitute the reality of Henry Selwyn as an individual, displaced by anti-Jewish violence, and conflicted by guilt at abandoning his Jewish identity in order to assimilate to an English one, Sebald's allegorization of Henry Selwyn shaped him as an uncanny Wandering Jew.

Sebald's figuring of Henry Selwyn as a revenant is ambiguous: it manifests the refusal of the Jew's living reality, and the obliterating impulse that underlies the persistence of this negative trope; at the same time, the haunting return of Henry Selwyn in the context of Hebel's story, conjures Rosenzweig's "infinitesimal remnant" or "Übriggebliebener," who remains standing on the bank, and whose significance lies in the interim and perpetual condition of waiting for redemptive return:

> There is a feeling in him as if both things, the Having and the Waiting, are most intimately connected with one another . . . And

---

44 Hebel, "Unexpected Reunion." In Hebel's story, a young miner goes down a mine, and is tragically killed. His perfectly preserved body is exhumed decades later, and welcomed back by his aged bride. For Sebald's engagement with Hebel's story, see Veraguth, "W. G. Sebald und die alte Schule."

that is precisely the feeling of the "remnant" which has the revelation and awaits the salvation.[45]

Henry Selwyn's return as the Wandering Undead raises the question of whether Sebald's writing offers a vision of ethical pessimism that encompasses consolation or hope, as elucidated by Mara van der Lugt, and whether Henry's "reappearance" in the memory of the narrator advances the possibility, if not necessarily the actuality, of "resurrecting" the dead.[46] In acknowledging that the past cannot be laid to rest, Sebald engaged with Benjamin's view of "illuminating moments," while refuting their transformative potential in the post-Auschwitz period. In Sebald's narrative world, as Judith Ryan observes, "illumination . . . stands under the sinister signs of the darkness in the human psyche that enlightenment only superficially represses: imperialism, genocide, and war."[47]

## Paul Bereyter as the Wandering Jew

"Mostly abroad, no-one quite knew where" (*TE*, 28), Paul Bereyter embodies the allegorical Wandering Jew, forever displaced, never "at home." At the same time, in his windcheater, and with his characteristically "long and springy steps" (*TE*, 41), Paul appears innately German to his students, indeed, "the very image of a German *Wandervogel*" (*TE*, 40). "Paul Bereyter" is a problematic story that confirms Sebald's interest in exploring "people who belonged in both camps": a troubling conflation of Jew and German, victim and perpetrator, he is a figure of deep ambiguity, whose sense of autochthony makes him unique among Sebald's Jews.[48] For Paul, "German to the marrow, profoundly attached to his native land in the foothills of the Alps" (*TE*, 57), *Heimat* is a "lived" experience, embodied in hiking, music, and the German history and folksongs he teaches his pupils on educational excursions into nature. These folksongs—"Auf den Bergen die Burgen," "Zu Straßburg auf der Schanz," and "Wir gleiten hinunter das Ufer entlang"— are imbued with the themes of exile, wandering, and the longing for homecoming; "Im Krug zum grünen Kranze" articulates the *Wandervogel* hiking spirit that symbolizes Paul Bereyter's love for his German *Heimat*.[49] These are themes Sebald explored not only in his narrative prose, but in

45    Rosenzweig, *Star of Redemption*, 405.
46    Van der Lugt, *Dark Matters*.
47    Ryan, "Fulgurations."
48    Poltronieri, "Wie kriegen die Deutschen das auf die Reihe?" 93.
49    The titles of the songs translate as follows: "The Castles on the Mountains"; "At Strassbourg on the Ramparts"; "We glide along the Bank"; "At the Inn with the green Wreath."

THE WANDERING JEW IN *THE EMIGRANTS* ♦ 49

his non-fiction, such as his essays on Keller, Hebel, and Améry.[50] Indeed, Améry's conflicted relation to his Austrian *Heimat* is a model for Paul Bereyter's fatal ambivalence towards Germany.

Excursions with his students to historical sites—the ceremonial canon of the Veteran's Association, and a derelict tunnel abandoned after the First World War—recall Germany's traumatic past, and reveal the darker side to Paul's unswerving loyalty to *Heimat*: Paul's ineradicable devotion to Germany sees him traverse Europe in the service of the *Wehrmacht* and participate in the *Bitzkrieg* that lays waste to the continent, becoming complicit in the persecution of his own people. Categorized as a "three-quarter Aryan," a "Mischling ersten Grades" according to Nazi racial laws, with little awareness of his Jewish origins, Paul remains, nonetheless, a victim of anti-Semitic persecution that precludes him from teaching, and displaces him from his beloved homeland. After the war, his futile attempts to abandon his *Heimat* result in restless wandering and deeper estrangement from a homeland in which he recognizes himself to be an exile. Paul Bereyter is figured as a trope for Jewish homelessness in postwar Germany, and for the conflict of the second generation in relation to a *Heimat* that is a reminder of an inherited legacy of guilt.

In keeping with his aim of depicting "real" Jewish lives, Sebald reconstructed the life and tragedy of Paul Bereyter within a specific historical context, namely, the persecution of individuals of Jewish origin during the Nazi era. The narrator's task is motivated by receiving news of Paul's suicide on the railway track outside his hometown. In a factual episode that briefly suspends the figural narrative style, reference is made to particular historical events, such as the Gunzenhausen pogrom of 1934, the destruction of Jewish property on the infamous *Kristallnacht*, and the deportation of Jewish individuals to Theresienstadt. The circumstances of Paul Bereyter's life are researched by the narrator, who pieces together remembered and received fragments of his former teacher's life in a process that resembles the ethnographic *Exil-Forschung* (reseach into exile) of Benz and others.[51]

Beyond the gathering of historical facts, Paul's life and the life of the Bereyters is a metaphor for the demise of the German-Jewish "symbiosis." The Bereyters' social ascendancy and assimilation to the German world is symbolized by the establishment of the elegant Bereyter emporium, and the acquisition of a luxurious Dürkopp motor car, a photograph of which emphasizes their bourgeois status, while simultaneously gesturing to their putatively innate Jewish itinerancy. The rise of the Nazis and the aryanisation of the emporium sees the end of the German-Jewish

50    Sebald, "Her kommt der Tod"; "Es steht ein Komet"; "Against the Irreversible."
51    Benz, *Das Exil der kleinen Leute*.

"symbiosis" represented by the Bereyter department store. Paul flees to France in the hope of continuing his teaching career, abandoning his Jewish fiancée who, together with her mother, is deported, and presumably murdered at Auschwitz. Returning to teach in his hometown after the war and *Wehrmacht* service, Paul is consumed by resentment towards his students and the country that persecuted him. His experience of rejection leads to the recognition, "that he belonged to the exiles, and not to the people of S." (*TE*, 59), and to his suicide on the railway line outside his village.

An emblem of infinite homelessness, Paul's individual tragedy is diminished by figural writing that allegorizes his life and universalizes his fate. Projected onto the narrator-figure, Sebald's empathetic intention, to "get closer to him, to imagine what his life was like" (*TE*, 29), is undermined by figuring Paul's rootlessness as mythically predestined, thus dehistoricizing and distancing Paul's fate, and evading questions of historical and personal responsibility.

## Paul Bereyter's Fate as Mythically Predestined

A symbol of travel and displacement, the motif of the train underlines Paul's tropological role as an ever-wandering Jew, whose life unfolds as the enactment of an "Orakelspruch" (oracular premonition), the implacable logic of the German rail system functioning as the central metaphor for his doomed existence as a Jew in Germany. In the story of Paul Bereyter, the German railway system offers a template for a life presented as mythically predetermined. Indeed, the structure of Paul's story, beginning and ending with a reference to the railways, implies a life that follows a relentless sequence, according to which Paul's suicide confirms to his fellow-villagers "that things had happened as they were bound to happen" (*TE*, 28). Paul's suicide on the railway tracks is the fulfilment of his uncle's ominous prediction, "he will end up on the railways" (*TE*, 62). Paul's companion, Lucie Landau, misses the vernacular meaning of this German expression, and interprets it as having the dark implication of an oracular prophecy, evoking the oracle of Delphi, whose prophecies, feared as inescapable, endow the trajectory of Paul's life with a sense of mythical inevitability.[52] To his students, Paul's slight speech impediment suggests a "mechanical human made of tin and other metal parts," a being "powered by clockwork that could be put out of operation forever by the smallest functional hitch" (*TE*, 35). This metaphor conjures the image of Paul as a clockwork train clinging to the tracks, reinforcing the notion

---

52    The oracle, originally named Gaia in Aeschylus's *Eumenides*, was consulted by kings such as Aegeus and Croesus. Her prophecies were often cryptic and incoherent.

THE WANDERING JEW IN *THE EMIGRANTS* ♦ 51

of an existence driven by unthinking forces, on an implacable trajectory that will lead to self-destruction. The metaphor implies Paul Bereyter's unshakeable belief in *Heimat* as an embodied ideal to which he adheres resolutely, the "logic" that determines the perverse actions that reveal his divided identity as both victim and perpetrator.

In Paul's story, the pervasive motif of the train on its unalterable course on the tracks reflects a fatalistic view of his destiny: synecdochic of the Holocaust and the transportation of Jews to their death, the train is proleptic of Paul's suicide, through which he enacts the fate for which, as a Jew, he believed himself to have been destined. This notion is implicit in the blurred photograph of train-tracks leading into obscurity at the opening of Paul's story, a scene that functions as a *mise-en-abîme* for Paul's life, that ends with his self-willed death as an act of identification with the anonymous dead of Auschwitz. The motif of the train as emblematic of mythical predetermination pervades Paul's life: a childhood memory of trains that "trundled from the mainland to the island and from the island to the mainland" (*TE*, 62) fascinates him with its relentless logic. Recalling the *Märklin* model train the adult Paul had laid out on a table, Lucie Landau interprets the railway as "the very image and symbol of Paul's German tragedy" (*TE*, 61).

As a teacher, Paul uses the railway system to convey the notion of systematic organization, and his pupils engage in drawings and diagrams of all aspects of the German rail system. The rail system becomes a metaphor for the euphemistically termed "logic of the whole wretched sequence of events" (*TE*, 50), that sees the exclusion and dispossession of the Bereyters, despite a long history of German-Jewish assimilation, and confirms Paul's own exiled status. To Lucie Landau, "Paul had found his fate already systematically laid out for him in the railways, as it were" (*TE*, 62), and with the wisdom of hindsight, she observes that "perhaps he felt they were headed for death" (*TE*, 61).

Sebald's discursive network of creativity constructs Paul as an inextricable part of modern German and European culture. Paul's obsession with the German railway system, and the ineluctable trajectory of a life that ends in suicide under a train characterizes him as intrinsic to what Todd Presner describes as the "meta-epistemology of the railway system, a configuration characterized by the dissolution of the very possibility of solid ground, the utter destruction of a knowing subject with a transcendental perspective on the world."[53] Paul's suicide occurs in the *heimatliche* (homely) context of forests and mountains; "the snow-white silhouettes of three mountains, the Kratzer, the Trettach and the Himmelsschrofen" (*TE*, 29) are the last image he sees before being crushed under the train. The photograph that prefaces his story depicts rail tracks against a

53    Presner, *Mobile Modernity*, 95.

somber background of fir trees, and implies the ambiguous conjunction of *Heimat* and the deadly train on its inexorable course, metaphorical of Paul's own ambiguous identity: a German, bound to his "heimatliche Alpenland" (Alpine homeland), and a Jewish victim of his beloved *Heimat*. Motivated by empathy, the narrator's intention to approach Paul by visualizing the details and events that constituted his life, and imagining his last moments, is undermined by an imaginative literary mode that depicts Paul's rootlessness as mythically ordained.

Figured as inevitable, the fate of the Jews is disconnected from the brutal actuality of the Holocaust authored by the Germans, and from the long and pernicious history of persecution that preceded it. Empathy in this context asks for acknowledgment of the distinct categories of victims and perpetrators. In the figure of Paul Bereyter, Sebald conflated and confused these roles, obscuring the distinction between self and other, perpetrator and victim, fundamental to LaCapra's theory of ethical empathy on which the present study is based. While this offers a consoling response to the guilt that plagues the second generation, it enacts a further abstraction of Jewish reality: the empathetic intention to re-animate the lives of "real" individuals is paradoxically weakened by a dehistoricizing and mitigative narrative mode.

### The Wandering Jew in the *Wehrmacht*

Paul's service in the *Wehrmacht* is an ethically complex episode in the story of this curious perpetrator-victim.[54] From Lucie Landau's embedded narrative of Paul's life, the reader learns that Paul, in an ironic subversion of his tropological role as a Wandering Jew, serves for six years in the *Wehrmacht* motorized artillery that traverses Europe as part of the annihilative German *Blitzkrieg*, an accessory to the persecution of his own people, or, at the very least, as witness to acts of atrocity. A passing reference to spending an "unending white winter near Berdichev" (*TE*, 56) in the service of the *Wehrmacht* is telling: a Ukrainian city occupied by the Germans from August 1941 to June 1942, the Jewish population of Berdichev was annihilated in a number of murderous operations.[55] Sebald's allusion to Berdichev implicates Paul, without comment, in the eradication of the city's Jewish population.[56] Viewed within the context of Sebald's *Trauerarbeit* or project of empathetic restitution, this problematic point has been largely overlooked in critical approbation for *The Emigrants*.

---

54    See Rigg, *Hitler's Jewish Soldiers.*
55    Berdichev was liberated by the Red Army on January 5, 1944.
56    The role of the *Wehrmacht* has been exposed by Daniel Goldhagen, *Hitler's Willing Executioners.*

The brief episode outlining Paul Bereyter's service in the *Wehrmacht* is curiously distanced, the narratorial voice describing Paul's story of complicity even and neutral, and the murderous German conquest of Europe framed within the natural world of seasonal change, imbuing it with a sense of inevitability and emphasizing the inscrutable nature of the event: "The seasons and the years came and went. A Walloon autumn was followed by an unending white winter in Berdichev, spring in the department of Haute-Saône, summer on the coast of Dalmatia or in Romania . . ." (*TE*, 56). The objective listing of place names—"He was in Poland, Belgium, France, the Balkans, Russia and the Mediterranean"—diminishes the singularity of the horror perpetrated in each place, while conveying the extent of the campaign, and the numbing effect of military service. The metaphor of "an unending white winter in Berdichev" implies timelessness, obfuscation of detail, and the sanitizing or "bleaching" of horror that abstracts this very real episode and the suffering it entailed, from history, while at the same time indicating the emotional coldness of the perpetrators. Paul's response to the trauma implicit in his military role is a growing sense of losing, "with every beat of the pulse . . . more and more of one's qualities," and becoming "less comprehensible to oneself, increasingly abstract" (*TE*, 56), the impersonal pronoun implying his psychic dissociation from his military role. The repetitive rhythm of "day by day, hour by hour" conveys a sense of hypnotic compulsion, evoking the train-metaphor that represents Paul's machine-like adherence to a predetermined course, and implies Paul's gradual evacuation to the status of a machine. Sebald's obfuscation of violence and destruction through a mystificatory figural mode draws attention to his distance from the actual horror as a non-Jewish German writer, born too late to have experienced the event. His neutral representation of the German *Blitzkrieg* (lightning war) manifests a refusal to engage with the brutality of the historical event: attributed to a natural history of destruction, the *Blitzkrieg* of the Germans is rendered incomprehensible and blameless.[57] Justifying his figurative approach, Sebald observed:

> Das ist wohl die einzige Form, in der der Erzähler es sich erlaubt, diese [katastrophischen Ereignisse] zu erklären, nämlich im Sinne einer Naturgeschichte. Es ist meines Erachtens tatsächlich so, in dem Gesellschaftsgeschichte und Zivilisationsgeschichte sich auflösen und der weitere Zusammenhang, nämlich die naturgeschichtlichen Abläufe, absehbar wird.[58]

---

57  Mosbach, *Figurationen der Katastrophe*, 10.
58  Köhler, "Katastrophe mit Zuschauer."

[This is the only form the writer permits himself to narrate these catastrophic events, namely, as a natural history. In my opinion, this is so because social history and the history of civilization disintegrate, and the results are observable in natural history.]

Sebald's picture of Paul Bereyter as a Jew in the *Wehrmacht*, both victim and perpetrator, underlines the fact that the "Third Reich" created a complex environment that compelled moral compromise in order to survive, made accomplices of victims, and continues to complicate binary moral judgment.[59] Such an environment calls for the "complex position" LaCapra describes in relation to the judging of perpetrators and collaborators, one that avoids simple identification with either victim or perpetrator perspective.[60] In what he described as the "gray zone" or ambiguous network of human relations inside the concentration camps, Primo Levi cautioned against reducing these relations to "the two blocs of victims and persecutors." Crucially, he nevertheless emphasized awareness of the distinction between these two categories: "To confuse the [murderers] with their victims is a moral disease or an aesthetic affectation or a sinister sign of complicity; above all, it is a precious service rendered (intentionally or not) to the negators of truth."[61]

Depicted as a Wandering Jew in the *Wehrmacht*, Paul is a radical construct, a reversal of victim-perpetrator roles, and a provocative *Wunschfigur* (wishful figure) for a writer burdened by guilt relating to the war and the Holocaust. Paul's postwar return to Germany, colloquially described by Jews as "the land of the hangman," is described as an "aberration" (*TE*, 56), motivated by the self-serving desire to "consider those twelve wretched years over and done with and simply turn the page and begin afresh" (*TE*, 56–57), and by his unswerving loyalty to his *Heimat*. Paul's return to the country that had extruded him reflects the urge to "move on" that characterized the "economic miracle" of postwar German reconstruction. Sebald's employment of the terms, "Schlußstrich" and "Neuanfang" (*DA*, 84), characterizes Paul's response as typical of the postwar German approach to the past.[62] Implicit in this is Paul's unwavering belief in his identity as a German, a belief that is only abandoned after a lengthy process of deepening disillusionment that culminates in his acknowledgment of his exiled status in postwar Germany.

---

59    According to the Nuremberg Laws of 1935, Germans of partial Jewish ancestry were designated "Mischlinge." Those with two Jewish grandparents were identified as "Mischlinge ersten Grades." In *Hitler's Jewish Soldiers*, Rigg describes the precarious position of partial Jews in the *Wehrmacht*.

60    LaCapra, *History and Memory*, 41.

61    Levi, "The Gray Zone," 23, 33.

62    *Schlußstrich* translates as "drawing a line" under something, *Neuanfang* as "a new beginning."

Sebald represented Paul as a Jewish victim, motivated at all times by a morally numbed, and unswerving loyalty to Germany—like a train, riveted to the tracks—and acknowledged, without judgment, the aberrant nature of Paul's actions. His construction of Paul Bereyter as a fractional Jew, imbricated in German guilt, is a problematic reversal of moral roles that betrays the longing for a shared community of victims and perpetrators, and reflects the controversial discourse of Sebald's postwar German context in relation to a *Heimat* contaminated by guilt and shame.[63] Reflecting on the irreducible gulf between victim and perpetrator, the impotence and passivity of the former in the face of the overwhelming power of the latter, Assmann observes: "Der entscheidende Unterschied zwischen dem Verhältnis von Siegern und Besiegten einerseits und zwischen Tätern und Opfern andererseits ist der, dass zwischen letzteren keinerlei Formen der Wechselseitigkeit bestehen." (The defining difference between the relationship of the victors and the defeated on the one hand, and the perpetrators and victims on the other is that no form of reversal is possible between the latter.)[64] The desire to reverse roles and to equalize German and Jewish guilt are strategies of deflection overtly thematized in the story of "Ambros Adelwarth."

## Ambros Adelwarth:
## The Wandering Jew and
## the Reversal of Roles

Among the stories of Sebald's emigrants, "Ambros Adelwarth" is an anomaly: the only narrative in which the central protagonist is not a Jew, but a German, the focus is on German suffering, and the story unfolds before the Holocaust. In the character of Ambros Adelwarth, Sebald created a figure who embodies essentialized traits of both Jews and Germans: an allegorical Wandering Jew, indeed, the most rootless and cosmopolitan of all Sebald's protagonists, Ambros Adelwarth is, at the same time, depicted as impeccably German through extensive exploration of his genealogical connections, and through the stereotyped traits of orderliness and decorum Sebald ascribed to him. Ambros's house is "always very neat and tidy" (*TE*, 102), and on his deathbed he is described as "wearing full uniform, so to speak" (*TE*, 116). Ambros Adelwarth is the German narrator's great-uncle, who migrated to America from Germany in the 1920s, and whose life is marked by early loss, deprivation, and constant

---

63    Implicit in this discourse is the desire for a shared community of victimhood, manifest in the controversial Bitburg and *Neue Wache* incidents that memorialized both victims and perpetrators.

64    Assmann, *Der lange Schatten*, 74.

wandering, exemplified by the steamers, trains, and hotels that feature in his story. A German and a rootless "Wandering Jew," Ambros Adelwarth's life and death are allegorical of German suffering in the form of prewar privation, emigration, and exile.

Ambros's life is characterized by extensive travel. Having left his homeland at an early age, his travels take him to France, Switzerland, Japan, the Middle East, and New York, where he becomes a valet and later, butler for a wealthy Jewish family, and forms a love relationship with the unstable son, Cosmo, whose name implies his cosmopolitan rootlessness. Ambros accompanies the wayward and vulnerable Cosmo to Deauville as his "friend and guide . . . watch[ing] over him as one would a sleeping child" (*TE*, 91). As the "frères Solomon," Ambros and Cosmo undertake a journey to Jerusalem; repelled by the degradation of the city, they return to New York, where Cosmo suffers a mental breakdown, and, in a state of catalepsis, is admitted to the Samaria sanatorium at Ithaca, where he dies. Overwhelmed by loneliness and anguish after the death of his partner, Ambros re-enacts Cosmo's suffering by submitting himself to a radical form of Electro-Convulsive Therapy that destroys him mentally and physically. For Ambros, self-exiled from his German *Heimat*, Jerusalem and Ithaca, mythical emblems of "home," are contaminated and annihilative spaces, allegorical of the disillusionment of the second generation with the idea of home and belonging. While the close relationships between Jews and Germans in Sebald's narrative prose suggests a wishful desire for a renewed German-Jewish symbiosis, it suggests that Sebald was unable to conceive of a German-Jewish relationship uncontaminated by genocide.

German suffering is central to the story of Ambros Adelwarth, whose torment at the Samaria sanatorium reflects the discourse on German victimhood that shaped Sebald's writing, and formed the focus of his controversial 1997 Zurich lectures, in which he argued that German writers had avoided the subject of German wartime suffering. Through the "martyrdom" of Ambros, Sebald created a troubling equivalence of German and Jewish victimhood: Ambros's torture, carried out by Jewish psychiatrists in a reversal of victim-perpetrator roles, reflects the shifting discourse on German guilt that posits a more inclusive, but ethically problematic notion of victimhood, that encompasses both victim and perpetrator groups. Despite his empathetically rendered account of Ambros's biography, Sebald's figuring of Ambros as a displaced "Wandering Jew," whose passive suffering evokes that of the Holocaust victim, deprives him of the Rosenzweigian quality of *Eigenheit* or "particularity," and undermines the individual pathos of his life. A trope for Sebald's ambivalence towards *Heimat*, and for his commitment to the remembrance of German victimhood, the suffering figure of Ambros Adelwarth suggests Sebald's perhaps unconscious susceptibility to the changing discourse on German victimhood, that demanded an end to the "Dauerrepräsentation" or continued avowal of German guilt.[65]

## The Journey to Jerusalem

Through a plot structure based on the progression from hope to disappointment, the journey to Jerusalem is constructed as a negative messianic narrative that suggests the impossibility of redemptive return to *Heimat*. On their journey to Jerusalem, the site "where, at the end of time, it is said, the entire human race will gather in the flesh" (*TE*, 141), Ambros and Cosmo are depicted as "Wandering Jews": from the hills of Delphi, Ambros reflects on his travels and marvels at seeing the same stars he saw "above the Alps as a child . . . above the Japanese house, above the Pacific, and out over Long Island Sound" (*TE*, 129). In Constantinople, the wanderers have themselves photographed in the costume of Turkish nomads, assuming a nomadic Middle Eastern identity. In Ambros's diary, the sea journey to Greece is characterized by a sense of being "outside of time"; ellipses underline the temporal vagueness that suggests the mythical nature of this metaphorical journey of return. Intertextual fragments of the "Hunter Gracchus" story link the fate of Gracchus to that of the travelers, the hunter's inability to reach home allegorical of the wanderers' failure to experience messianic redemption in the debased city of Jerusalem. Ambros's reference to "two men . . . squatting on the quay playing dice" (*TE*, 133), alludes directly to the opening of Kafka's story, the dice, as a symbol of chance, evoking Cosmo's passion for gambling and linking the travelers to the hunter, whose interminable living-death results from the helmsman's chance error: "My death ship lost its way—a wrong turn of the helm, a moment when the helmsman was not paying attention . . . I only know that I remain on the earth and that since that time my ship has journeyed over earthly waters."[66] In Constantinople, "a grey pigeon about the size of a full-grown cockerel" (*TE*, 134) leads the desert travelers on their way, recalling "a dove . . . as large as a rooster" that, in Kafka's story, heralds the hunter's arrival in Riva, a stop on his interminable journey, and a reminder of the impossibility of homecoming.

Ambros's travel diary thematizes deception: Ambros momentarily mistakes Mount Olympus for the Swiss Alps, or, more disturbingly, his rejected homeland. As Sebald confessed, the diary itself is "a falsification. I wrote it. What matters is all true . . . the invention comes in at the level

---

65    Martin Walser used his acceptance speech for the 1998 Peace Prize of the German Book Trade to argue against the continuous representation of what he termed "our disgrace."

66    Kafka, "The Hunter Gracchus."

of minor detail most of the time, to provide *l'effet du réel*."[67] Although in Sebald's hand, it was taken from a nineteenth-century travelogue by François-René de Chateaubriand, *Itinéraire de Paris à Jérusalem et de Jérusalem à Paris* (Itinerary from Paris to Jerusalem and from Jerusalem to Paris, 1811). Taken together with images suggestive of illusion—Constantinople appears "like a mirage at first" (*TE*, 130), and the bogus identity of "the frères Solomon" under which the wanderers sign into their hotel—the falsified diary complicates the meaning of the "real," illustrating Sebald's poetics of ambiguity, and foreshadowing the disillusionment that awaits the travelers in Jerusalem.

### The Wandering Jew and Rejection of Home

Of the four stories in *The Emigrants*, "Ambros Adelwarth" manifests most explicitly the resentment of the second generation towards a *Heimat* perceived as contaminated by the Nazi past. The "return" of the wanderers to Jerusalem is a deeply figurative episode that mystifies the notion of home, and, through metaphors of disease and destruction, relates it to the Holocaust.

Jerusalem, the biblical symbol of redemptive homecoming, is portrayed as a debased city, an ironic refutation of the Isaiahan prophecy that predicts the role of Jerusalem as "a light unto the nations."[68] Ambros's description of Jerusalem is highly emotive, evident in imagery of disease borrowed from Flaubert's *Voyage en Orient* (Voyage to the Orient): "The erstwhile pools of Siloam are no more than foul puddles and cesspits, a morass from which the miasma rises . . ." (*TE*, 140).[69] Multiple exclamation marks and scatological imagery express horror and revulsion—"*On marche sur des merdes!!!*" (*TE*, 203). Such images are intensified by visions of physical despoilment and creaturely life reduced to "coagulated blood, heaps of entrails, blackish-brown tripes, dried and scorched by the sun . . ." (*TE*, 137). The seemingly endless list of the city's curative institutions underscores the contamination of the city, in which trauma and tragedy mark it as forever tainted. The hypotactic cataloguing of institutions devoted to healing and social care provides a sense of materiality that yields to the imaginative mode with the description of the "misshapen little man" (*TE*, 140) who evokes the "bucklicht Männlein" (little hunchback) of Benjamin's *Berlin Childhood around 1900*, a reminder of that which has been forgotten and deformed in the process of remembering.[70]

---

67    Angier, "Who Is W. G. Sebald?" 72. For further exploration of falsification in Sebald's writing, see Schowengerdt-Kuzmany, "To the Funhouse."
68    Isaiah 42:6.
69    Flaubert, *Voyage en Orient* (*1849–1851*).
70    Benjamin, *Berlin Childhood*.

Sebald's acute figuring of the dwarf-like guide to Jerusalem emphasizes his imperfection, obsolescence, and inauthenticity: the detailed description of his "cucumber of a nose . . . crooked legs . . . clad in what had once been a dragoon's breeches with sky-blue piping" (*TE*, 140), and incomprehensible language that mimicked German and English, evokes negative traits traditionally imputed to the Jew. With his malevolent gaze, the spurious guide to Jerusalem is a metaphor for the moral and material degradation of Jerusalem as the spiritual home of the Jews, forever foreclosed to them, and for the impossibility of "return," for Sebald and his generation, to a *Heimat* contaminated by the past.

Sebald's figural narrative of decline and degeneration is mixed with material details that contribute to the visceral reality of the wanderers' experience: in this befouled city, even "the few plants which have survived the drought that has lasted since May are covered in this powdery meal as if by a blight" (*TE*, 137). Annihilatory visions that foreshadow the Holocaust reflect bitter repudiation of "home": Jerusalem is described as "burnt and blasted . . . until at last the desolation was complete and nothing remained" (*TE*, 142), and the passing reference to the "tallow and soap factory and a bone-and-hide works" (*TE*, 137) is a reminder of the reduction of human lives to utilitarian byproducts in the attempted genocide of the Jews.[71]

The travelers' approach to Jerusalem is marked by imagery of stone, the city in the distance "a ruined and broken mass of rocks" (*TE*, 136), a metaphor for the petrification of the messianic promise, reduced to "dry stone and a remote idea in the heads of its people, now dispersed throughout the world" (*TE*, 142). Petrification is implicit in the haunting vision of "the silent city ris[ing] from the white limestone with its domes, towers and ruins" (*TE*, 141). The stone and dust of Jerusalem suggest a Hegelian view of Jewishness as ontologically petrified in its adherence to Jewish Law, that precluded Jews from owning land, and condemned them to permanent rootlessness.[72] In Ambros's account of the journey to Jerusalem, Sebald's figural writing subsumes the materiality of stone into a natural history of atrophy and disintegration. Thus, in the white moonlight, the "domed stone rooftops" of the city resemble "a frozen sea" (*TE*, 136–37), and the disintegration of the ancient city is implied in the voids of ellipses and dashes that fracture the narrative. Extinction of messianic hope is conveyed through the picture of "great clouds of dust rolling through the air," and "pulverized limestone ankle-deep in places" (*TE*, 136–37). Insistence on the negative—"over the rooftops not

---

71    Such human by-products include soap manufactured from human fat and lampshades fashioned from human skin.

72    "For the land is mine and ye are travellers and sojourners with me" (Leviticus, 25:23).

60 ◆ The Wandering Jew in *The Emigrants*

a sound, not a trace of smoke, nothing. Nowhere, as far as the eye can see, is there any sign of life, not an animal scurrying by, or even the smallest bird in flight. *On dirait que c'est la terre maudite* (It looks like the cursed land) . . ." (*TE*, 141)—conveys the metaphysical void at the heart of the messianic dream of return, and presages the fate of the travelers, Ambros and Cosmo, to be reduced, ultimately, to "nothing."

Crossing the "glaring emptiness of the Jordan valley" (*TE*, 142) on the way to Jericho, Ambros dreams of finding himself in his home village of Gopprechts. In language that evokes *Altneuland* (1902), the novel written by Theodor Herzl, the founder of political Zionism, Ambros's recollection of the nightmare describes a tainted *Heimat*, dirty, arid, and inhospitable, with "sand and dust swirling about it," inhabited by malevolent "beggars and footpads . . . gouty, hunchbacked or disfigured . . . others are lepers or have immense goiters" (*TE*, 142), imagery that suggests the failure of the dream of redemptive return, and its dissolution in filth and disease.[73]

## Ain Jidy and German Victimhood

In the epilogue to "Ambros Adelwarth," the spring of Ain Jidy offers the "Wandering Jews" an ambiguous moment of respite after the traumatic experience of Jerusalem, a last, transient pause in their nomadic existence before returning "home" to Ithaca, a metaphor in this story for death. Biblical in its imagery and archaic syntax, the Ain Jidy episode is in part a utopian fantasy of purity, plenitude, and infinity, "a blessèd spot with pure spring water and rich vegetation" (*TE*, 144), and a meditation on loss. The butterfly with gold-speckled wings offers a fleeting moment of transcendence, but is a reminder of Graccchus's eternally trapped predicament, and for Ambros and Cosmo, an aestheticized harbinger of death. Darker pictures, of the travelers descending into the underworld of "the lowest region on earth" (*TE*, 143), of "shores destroyed by fire and brimstone, a thing of salt and ashes" (*TE*, 143), of the Dead Sea, with its "aura of the grave, the colour of absinthe, rising from its depths" (*TE*, 143), signal the failure of the travelers' messianic "homecoming." Ambros's recollections of Ain Jidy are followed by a nostalgic reflection on memory, annotated in his diary after the return of the travelers to Jerusalem: "Looking out of the hotel window at the city, white in the falling dusk, it made him think of times long ago" (*TE*, 145). The blurring of the city in the snow suggests the elusiveness of memory, the difficulty of capturing the exactitude of a distanced life or event, and the dissolution of reality

---

73    Herzl, *Altneuland*, 1902. Translated as "*The Old-New-Land*," the novel reflects Herzl's initial, negative impressions of what would become his utopian vision of a Jewish state.

that gives the story the sense of a fable. Almost imperceptibly, the notion of martyrdom intrudes on Ambros's melancholy reflection on memory: his final diary entry is notated on the Feast of Stephen, a reference to the earliest Christian martyr, stoned to death by the Jews for affirming his faith. With this picture of suffering inflicted by Jewish perpetrators, Sebald suggests the equivalence of Jewish and German guilt.

Sebald's insistence on the figurative as a means of enhancing the "real" is aestheticizing in its effect. Imagery of evanescence—the falling snow that veils the degraded city of Jerusalem, and the towers that disappear from view in the clouds, obscures the boundaries of past and present, the real and the illusory, victims and perpetrators, and frames the city, and the messianic return of the protagonists, within an indifferent world of dissolution and loss, countermanding Sebald's restitutive undertaking.

## The Wandering of Max Aurach

Max Aurach is the Wandering Jew who has, metaphorically, "come home."[74] Indeed, he avers that Manchester, his adopted home, "has taken possession of me for good. I cannot leave, I do not want to leave, I must not leave" (*TE*, 169). With its interminably smoking chimneys, the city is a metaphor for Auschwitz, the destination Aurach believes himself to have evaded, but to which he is drawn, embracing it as the "Ort meiner Bestimmung" (*DA*, 251; The place for which I was destined), offering a bleak view of death as the *Heimat* of the Jews.[75] The desolation of this view is compounded by Aurach's name, with its echoes of Auschwitz, by his alienated existence in Manchester, described as a "necropolis or mausoleum" (*TE*, 151), and the annihilative artistic process through which he seeks to restore his lost lineage.

Max Aurach is born into a middle-class German-Jewish family who settled in rural Franconia in the seventeenth century. The family's

74    In *The Emigrants*, the protagonist of the final story was renamed "Max Ferber" in response to objections by British artist Frank Auerbach, on whose life Sebald based the story. For reasons of greater resonance, I shall be referring to him by the name Sebald originally gave him.

75    This is a reference to "Meine Ortschaft," an essay by Austro-Jewish writer Peter Weiss, chronicling his visit to Auschwitz in 1964. Aurach's conviction that, in Manchester, he had "come home" (*TE*, 192), draws on Weiss's account of visiting Auschwitz. Like Aurach, Weiss was never interned there, but nevertheless regarded it as the place for which he was destined. Weiss's use of the possessive pronoun—"meine Ortschaft"—indicates a sense of belonging to the "community" of Auschwitz, and expresses, as it does for Aurach, a belated gesture of identification with Jewish victims who were murdered there. Through allusion to Weiss, Sebald links Aurach's fate to that of an historical survivor, validating and deepening its significance.

idyllic prewar life, illustrative of the putative German-Jewish symbiosis, is recorded in the memoirs of Aurach's mother, Luisa Lanzberg (*TE*, 193–218). Nazi persecution of the Jews sees the Aurach family dispossessed, and Aurach's father, an art dealer, interned at Dachau. The fifteen-year-old Aurach is sent by his parents to England for safety; they, and the extended family, perish in the Holocaust. In England, an uncle enables him to attend an inferior boarding school, after which Aurach studies art in Manchester, and makes this emigrant city of expatriate Jews and Germans his home. In Manchester, Aurach is an isolated figure, deeply averse to travel, and obsessed with his art, through which he attempts to recreate his destroyed lineage. Aurach lives and works in his studio in the Manchester Docklands, where by chance, the young German narrator encounters him and learns something of Aurach's life during their weekly meetings at the *Wadi Halfa* café. Constrained by guilt and fear of trespass, the narrator refrains from enquiring more deeply into the circumstances of Aurach's migration to England. After a hiatus of twenty years, they resume their meetings, during which the narrator discovers the details of Aurach's life, and the persecution of his family. When Aurach is dying, the narrator returns to Germany on his behalf, to visit the graves of Aurach's family in the Jewish cemetery of Bad Kissingen.

Aurach has, paradoxically, not travelled widely. Having fled Nazi Germany for the safety of England, he desires only stasis, and declares that "he never felt more at home than in places where things remained undisturbed, muted under the grey, velvety sinter left when matter dissolved, little by little, into nothingness" (*TE*, 161). Aurach's wandering is ontological, "a hovering on the verge."[76] He resembles Rosenzweig's endlessly vigilant remnant: "Something in him waits. And he has something within himself. What he waits for and what he has, to that he may give different names, and often even scarcely be able to name."[77] While this suggests a messianic dimension to Aurach's survival, it is inflected with Kafka's negative messianism, which perceives messianic redemption in its inverted form, as Gershom Scholem captured in a poem: "So allein strahlt Offenbarung / in die Zeit, die dich verwarf. / Nur dein Nichts ist die Erfahrung, / die sie von dir haben darf." (Only so does revelation shine, / in times that have rejected you. / The only experience they may have of you, / is of your nothingness.)[78] To Löwy, messianic redemption appears in Kafka's work "only in the 'lining' of reality, or as if drawn in contrast against the dark contours of the present world."[79]

76    McCulloh, "Stylistics of Stasis," 38.
77    Rosenzweig, *Star of Redemption*, 405.
78    Scholem, "Mit einem Exemplar von Kafkas 'Prozeß,'" 73.
79    Löwy, "Theologia negativa," 79.

## Wadi Halfa and Aurach's Atavistic Rootlessness

Born into a German-Jewish family with a long history of accultura-tion, Aurach's rootlessness is implied to be atavistic and innate to his Jewishness. Every day, before and after work, Aurach patronizes the Wadi Halfa transport café, situated on the verge of Trafford Park, and frequented by "lorry drivers, refuse collectors and others who happened to be out and about" (*TE*, 164).[80] Unlicensed and illegitimate, its name deriving from a city on the border between Sudan and Egypt, the Wadi Halfa transport café is a metaphor for Aurach's liminality as an émigré, occupying a tenuous position between the German *Heimat* from which he was extruded, and his adopted home of Manchester. Allusion to the "Wanderschaft" (wandering) of the Kenyan proprietor and his family (*DA*, 241) evokes the wandering of Eastern-European Jews to the West, thematized in Joseph Roth's *Juden auf Wanderschaft* (1927), and is a reminder of Aurach's own history of displacement that connects him to the Maasai proprietor and his family's experience of wandering and dislo-cation in their migration from Kenya to Britain. Recounting his meetings at the Wadi Halfa with Aurach, the narrator recalls:

> At every hour of the day and night, the Wadi Halfa was lit by a flick-ering, glaringly bright neon light that permitted not the slightest shadow. When I think back to our meetings in Trafford Park, it is invariably in that unremitting light that I see Aurach, always sitting in the same place in front of a fresco painted by an unknown hand that showed a caravan moving forward from the remotest depths of the picture, across a wavy ridge of dunes, straight towards the beholder. The painter lacked the necessary skill, and the perspec-tive he had chosen was a difficult one, as a result of which both the human figures and the beasts of burden were slightly distorted, so that, if you half shut your eyes, the scene looked like a mirage quiv-ering in the heat and light. And especially on days when Aurach had been working in charcoal, and the fine powdery dust had given his skin a metallic sheen, he seemed to have just emerged from the des-ert scene, or to belong in it. He himself once remarked, studying the gleam of graphite on the back of his hands, that in his dreams, both waking and by night, he had already crossed all the earth's deserts of sand and stone (*TE*, 164).

In this strongly visual scene, the reader's attention is drawn to Aurach, positioned in front of the desert fresco in such a way as to imply that he is part of the desert scene. The allegory of the fresco implies the

---

80   Sebald, *The Emigrants*.

essentially nomadic identity of Aurach, who was born into an assimilated German-Jewish family that traced its Franconian roots to the late seventeenth century. Indeed, to the German narrator, Aurach seems to have "just emerged from the desert scene, or to belong in it," emphasizing his nomadism as a conspicuous and immutable trait that three centuries of assimilation cannot disguise, while implying that he belongs in an "elsewhere" conceived as radically remote. Figured as his "home" or natural habitat, the desert, abstract and hostile to life, is a metaphor for Aurach's ontological rootlessness and alienation from a world in which he is not fully existent, but lives on as a remnant in his stygian studio, in which dust and charcoal, residues of burning, connote the Holocaust, and transform his appearance into that of a Semitic desert nomad. Impervious to the world, the stony deserts of his dreams are metonymic of an historical perception of petrified and unassimilable Jewishness, the Jewish heteronomy central to Aurach's tragedy.

Through the substitutive devices of metaphor, allegory, and metonymy, Aurach is transformed from a displaced and wounded individual into a "Wandering Jew," an emblem of historical Jewish displacement. Sebald's empathetic intention to restore the singularity of a Jewish life lost to anonymity is undermined by the artistry of his figural writing, which mystifies the reality of Aurach's individual tragedy—of loss, dislocation, and guilt at having evaded his destiny—and subsumes it in his universalization as a trope for Sebald's own debilitating sense of alienation from *Heimat* and notions of belonging.

The flickering light and unsteady lines of the desert fresco evoke Kaspar Hauser's dream of the Caucasus in Werner Herzog's film *Jeder für sich und Gott gegen alle* (Everyone for Themselves and God against Everyone), and imbue Aurach's story with Hauser's emblematic homelessness.[81] Herzog's film is based on the historical figure of Kaspar Hauser, a mute and socially deprived individual, abandoned on a Nuremberg square, and gradually socialized, only to be stabbed to death by a stranger years later. On his deathbed, Hauser recounts a dream in which a tribe wanders in the Sahara, led by a blind Berber. In Hauser's dream, the desert is allegorical of his homelessness. Implied, through Sebald's ekphrastic depiction of the Wadi Halfa fresco, to be Aurach's "home" or natural habitat, the desert is a symbol of his ontological rootlessness and estrangement from the world in which, like Kaspar Hauser, he is not fully existent. Aurach lives on as a remnant in his stygian studio, in which dust and charcoal, and his restless artistic process, imply his putatively nomadic origins. Aurach's artistic struggle to recreate his lost heritage is mirrored by the German narrator's thwarted efforts to reconstruct Aurach's life, suggesting that, in the parallel he establishes between the two figures,

81    Herzog, dir., *Jeder für sich.*

the Wandering Jew may be a trope for German suffering as well. Stuart Taberner draws attention to the aporetic nature of Sebald's relationship to the subjects of his prose narratives when he notes that "Sebald is the 'fifth exile,' the German exile whose story is adumbrated throughout—and even by means of—the Jewish narratives," observing that "even as he excavates Jewish lives, the author also—perhaps unintentionally—opens up a form of melancholia that frames Jews and Germans as traumatized victims of the catastrophe of modernity."[82]

## Death as the *Heimat* of the Jew

Aurach is more than an individual whose life has been damaged by history: the elaborate figural writing that makes Manchester metaphorical of Auschwitz, "the place I saw as my destiny, but which I evaded," implies his allegorical role as the Wandering Jew who lives on as the "Undead," a paradoxical embodiment of nomadism and "suspenseful stasis," a trope for the exile of post-Holocaust Jewish existence, and the impossibility of "homecoming" for Sebald's generation.[83]

In the story of Max Aurach, Manchester is allegorized as a mythical Underworld, and Aurach's descent from the moorlands into the realm of the dead is a *katabasis*, motivated by the desire for apomnesis or "unremembering":[84]

> Naturally I took steps, consciously or unconsciously, to keep at bay thoughts of my parents' suffering . . . I did not want to be reminded of my origins by anything or anyone, so instead of going to New York, into the care of my uncle, I decided to move to Manchester on my own. Inexperienced as I was, I imagined I could begin a new life in Manchester from scratch (*TE*, 191).

Blinded by optimism, Aurach's first impression of the city is expressed in imagery that posits deception: he perceives the city laid out "as if in the heart of a natural amphitheatre" (168), illuminated "as if by firelight or Bengal flares" (168), and fails to notice the material reality of "crammed and interlinked rows of houses . . . textile mills . . . chemical plants and factories of every kind . . ." (*TE*, 168). The interweaving of figural and factual observation yields to the imaginative mode in Sebald's allegorization of Manchester as a simulacrum of Auschwitz: as the illusory light dies away, Aurach discerns, in the "solid mass of utter blackness, bereft

82    Taberner, "German Nostalgia?" 184, 182.
83    McCulloh, "The Stylistics of Stasis," 41.
84    This is one of many instances in which Sebald draws on the mythical *katabasis*, Greek for "descent into the Underworld," to suggest the subject's penetration of repressed memory.

of any further distinguishing features," the "chimneys . . . belching out smoke by day and night" that evoke the ceaselessly working crematoria of Auschwitz, and the anonymity of industrial genocide perpetrated there (*TE*, 168–69). Metaphorical of Auschwitz, Manchester provides a space of postmemorial experience that allows Aurach to enact the fate for which, as a Jew, he believes himself to be destined. Aurach's sense of being "eingeprägt" (*DA*, 251) or "impressed" by the sight of the smokestacks that dominate Manchester, implies his identification with Jews on whom victimhood was physically branded in the form of a tattooed number that metaphorically annihilated them as individuals. The coercion implicit in Aurach's claim, "Manchester has taken possession of me for good. I cannot leave, I do not want to leave, I must not" (*TE*, 169), suggests the inescapability of his fate, reinforcing the desolate view of death as the *Heimat* of the Jews.

Aurach's memory of his first encounter with Manchester concludes with a fleeting vision of a herd of deer, "like the shadow of a cloud, flit[ting] across the fields" (*TE*, 169). The image conjures the hunt, and Kafka's Hunter Gracchus, who dies in pursuit of his prey, imbuing Aurach's first perception of Manchester with a bleak fatalism. The simile that likens the fugitive deer to "the shadow of a cloud" frames Aurach's vision of Manchester, and the memory of the Holocaust it holds, within a perspective of natural history that evades questions of agency.

With its "single row of empty houses, the wind blowing through the smashed windows and doors," reduced to the "grid-like layout of the streets" (*TE*, 157), the once-thriving Jewish quarter of Manchester evokes, through confluence of fact and imagination, both the violence and systematization of genocide, and the evacuation of the Jewish presence that makes the area an allegory of Jewish loss. Metaphorical of Jewish identity and persecution, the "star-shaped complex of Strangeways prison" at its center recalls other stellate fortresses, Breendonk and Theresienstadt, dedicated to the torture and imprisonment of Jews. Sebald mythologizes the abandoned Jewish quarter as an ironic "Elysian Fields," in Greek mythology, the final, paradisal resting place given to heroes on whom the gods conferred immortality. With its flickering fires and shadowy figures, it is a vision of Hades, borrowed from Heinrich Böll's novel, *Der Engel schwieg* (The Silent Angel, 1951), peopled only by the ghosts of its former Jewish inhabitants, and the spectral figures of homeless children:[85]

> When night fell upon those vast spaces . . . fires would begin to flicker here and there and children would stand around them . . .

85    Böll, *Der Engel Schwieg.*

shadowy figures . . . they strayed in small groups, in gangs or quite alone, as if they had nowhere to call home (*TE*, 157–58).

The *Trümmer* or rubble that signifies German displacement in Böll's novel is missing in Sebald's evocation of Jewish absence; the "bare terrain . . . like a glacis" is a haunting visual trope for Jewish erasure (*TE*, 158). Sebald's depiction of the "Elysian Fields" evokes postwar *Trümmerfilme* that depicted ruined postwar German cities, in which an annihilated population was reduced to a foraging, prehistoric existence.[86] In the allegory of homelessness among the vacant spaces from which even the rubble has been removed, Sebald mythologizes Jewish exile as a mythical and inevitable phenomenon, detached from historical determinants. Aurach's belief that, in Manchester, he has "found his place," is ironically realized: metaphorical of Auschwitz, the necropolis of Manchester represents the ultimate resting place of the Wandering Jew, the fulfilment of the curse of Ahasverus, to wander until he is at last redeemed by death.

### The Wandering Jew and the Dream of Return

The Wandering Jew who feels compelled to remain, Aurach eschews travel, claiming "it is torture to me" (*TE*, 169). He cannot bring himself to return to Germany, describing it as "a country frozen in the past, destroyed, a curiously extraterritorial place . . ." (*TE*, 181). It is primarily in dreams or by proxy that Aurach returns to his *Heimat*.

In one such dream, Aurach imagines returning to his family home, a fantasy characterized by imagery of illusion, exemplified by the "glittering Crystal Palace" in which his father's gold-framed art collection is exhibited, the ornately painted *trompe-l'oeil* doors through which Aurach passes into his parents' home, and the "gallery covered in layers of dust" (*TE*, 176) that he recognizes as their drawing room. Through such imagery of deception, Sebald calls into question the truth value of his own artistic project, to "resurrect" the dead through literary commemoration, admitting to the endless exile of post-Holocaust Jewish existence, and the impossibility of "homecoming" for his own generation. Aurach's parents are absent, but in the drawing room, a stranger, Frohmann of Drohobysz, holds a miniature replica of the Temple of Solomon, perfect in every detail. The figure of Frohmann derives from Joseph Roth's collection of stories, *Juden auf Wanderschaft* (The Wandering Jews), in which the character of Frohmann wanders from ghetto to ghetto exhibiting his

---

86    *Trümmerfilme* include *Die Mörder sind unter uns* (The murderers are among us), dir. Wolfgang Staudte, 1946; *Germania anno zero* (Germany Year Zero), dir. Roberto Rosselini, 1948; *Irgendwo in Berlin* (Somewhere in Berlin), dir. Gerhard Lamprecht, 1946.

meticulously constructed model.[87] As the "guardian of tradition" in Roth's text, Frohmann is a reminder to the dispersed diaspora Jews of their Jewish heritage and communitarian values: "Herr Frohmann, der mit seinem Kunstwerk von einem Ghetto zum andern fährt und gelegentlich nach Berlin kommt, versteht sich als Hüter der Tradition." (Herr Frohmann, who travels with his work of art from one ghetto to another, and from time to time comes to Berlin, sees himself as the guardian of tradition.)[88] Aurach's recognition of the fragile structure as "a true work of art" (*TE*, 176), is a validation of its auratic power to represent, in perfect form, the ruined temple and the longing it embodies, and an implicit acknowledgment of his own destructive, post-Holocaust art as a corruption of the heritage the miniature temple represents. But the fragility of the structure, constructed of *papier-mâché*, pinewood, and gold paint, suggests the precariousness of the messianic dream of redemptive return.

Aurach "returns" vicariously to his German *Heimat* through the narrator, who visits the Jewish cemetery of Bad Kissingen after reading the affecting memoirs of Aurach's mother. Described by Aurach as "one of those evil German fairy tales" (*TE*, 193), Luisa Lanzberg's memoirs are given to the narrator by Aurach, in an act of cultural transmission that confers on the German narrator guardianship of Jewish memory and legacy in a revived notion of German-Jewish "symbiosis." The narrator is directed to the "Israelite cemetery" of Bad Kissingen, the archaic term evoking the nomadic Biblical tribe, and implying Jewish presence as anachronistic in contemporary Germany. Designating Jews as "Israelites" is a reminder of the Nazi *Law on the Alteration of Family and Personal Names* (August 17, 1936), according to which first names of non-Jewish origin required the addition of the generic name "Israel" for Jewish men, "Sara" for women, in a generalizing gesture that conflated the complexity of Jewish identity into a single notion of stereotyped otherness. The brief account of the history of the Kissingen synagogue reflects a perception of Jewishness as implicitly Middle Eastern, "the earlier temple had been replaced by what is known as the new synagogue, a ponderous turn-of-the-century building in a curiously Orientalized, neo-Romanesque style" (*TE*, 221). In a heavy-handed metaphor that signals Jewish heteronomy, the keys to the cemetery do not fit the gate, and the narrator climbs over the cemetery wall to gain entry, an allusion to Kafka's *Schloß*: "Again and again, memories of *Heimat* returned and filled his consciousness . . . where he had previously failed to scale the wall, he succeeded in clambering over it, a small flag between his teeth."[89]

---

87 Roth, *Juden auf Wanderschaft*.
88 Sebald, "Ein Kaddisch für Österreich," 117.
89 Kafka, *Das Schloß*, 49.

While Sebald interprets K.'s successful scaling of the wall as signifying metaphorical "return" to *Heimat*, it is a home that signifies death: "Weil der Tod stets als die andere Heimat des Menschen galt, durchziehen auf dem Weg ins Schloß deren Bilder die Imagination K.s." (Since death is our other homeland, visions of home passed through K.'s imagination on his way into the Castle.)[90] The cemetery in which K. triumphantly plants his small flag is "the undiscover'd country, from which no wanderer returns," a reminder that for the narrator, and for Aurach himself, return to *Heimat* is, at best, illusory.[91] With its "tall grass and wild flowers under the shade of trees that trembled in the slight movement of the air" (*TE*, 223), the Jewish cemetery of Kissingen is a peaceful place. The faded, almost undecipherable German-Jewish names on the ancient gravestones—Blumenthal, Grunwald, Hamburger, Kissinger—reflect their owners' affinity with the land, and the imagined German-Jewish symbiosis to which they were in thrall. Overgrown and neglected, the "gradually sinking" cemetery (*TE*, 223) symbolizes the fading from view and memory of Germany's lost Jews, and the idea of death as the only "*Heimat*" to which the Wandering Jews can return, be remembered as individuals, and be peacefully absorbed into the *Heimat* earth.

Sebald's empathetic intention of restoring the lives of real Jewish individuals is compromised by his privileging of the figural literary mode that subsumes their individuality in a universalizing allegory of exile. His rootless Jews revive the myth of the Wandering Jew, and the problematic historical and philosophical substrate that sees the Jew as innately rootless and alien, implying the troubling view that there is no place for the Jew in the post-Auschwitz world.

In Sebald's narrative prose, the Wandering Jew trope reflects the bitterness of the second generation in relation to a *Heimat* perceived as contaminated and irrecuperable. Repudiation of *Heimat* is taken to an extreme in Aurach's embrace of Manchester as a surrogate for Auschwitz, the "home" in which, like Kafka's K., he seeks to pursue his remnant existence: "Die Sehnsucht nach unabänderlicher Ruhe, der in der Welt K.s allein der Tod eine mögliche Erfüllung verspricht . . . diese Sehnsucht und diese Angst dürfen als die Motive gelten für diese Reise K.s in 'das unentdeckte Land, von des Bezirk kein Wandrer wiederkehrt.'" (The longing for everlasting peace, the possibility of which is promised only by death in K.'s world . . . that longing and anxiety may be what motivate K. to journey to "the undiscovered land, from which no wanderer returns.")[92] Despite the European context into which they are born, all Sebald's Jewish protagonists are depicted as intuitively drawn to

90   Sebald, "Das unentdeckte Land," 86.
91   Shakespeare, *Hamlet*, III, 1.
92   Sebald, "Das Gesetz der Schande," 92.

imagery that posits the desert nomadism of the Middle East, implying Jewish rootlessness as innate and eternal, and perpetuating one of the most insidious and pervasive Jewish stereotypes. In his characterization of Jewish figures as "Wandering Jews," Sebald revealed the provocative side to his literary persona by creating ambiguous conflations of Jew and German: thus Paul Bereyter occupies the morally problematic position of being both a "Wandering Jew," thrust into exile, and a member of the notorious German *Wehrmacht*, participating in the invasion of Europe that casts him in the compromised role of perpetrating atrocities against his own people, a reversal of victim-perpetrator positions that serves to equalize Jewish and German guilt. Sebald's construction of hybrid figures of German and Jewish identity suggests a wishful desire for a renewed German-Jewish symbiosis, and an inability to envisage a German-Jewish relationship uncontaminated by the Holocaust.

# 2: The Wandering Jew in *Austerlitz*

*I have never known who I really was*

*—Austerlitz*

THE WANDERING JEWS in *The Emigrants* are exiles who preserve memories of the *Heimat* from which they have been banished: Henry Selwyn's *shetl* in Lithuania, Paul Bereyter's Allgäu of fir forests and mountains, Aurach's fragmented recollections of assimilated German-Jewish life in Munich. Depicted as unassimilable, the emigrants are never "at home." Austerlitz, by contrast, has no "home": neither archival research, nor the intuitive visions that resurface in his unconscious enable him to validate his origins. In *Austerlitz*, Sebald radicalized the trope of the Wandering Jew by presenting his protagonist as a metaphorical figure, whose rootlessness is ontological, and whose quest to confirm his origins is at the same time a quest to verify his own existence in reality. His search is haunted by the resurrective hope "that time will not pass away, has not passed away, that I can turn back and go behind it, and there I shall find everything as it once was" (*A*, 144), a yearning for a coexistent temporality that would erase the boundaries between the living and the dead and restore to him the origins he has lost. Austerlitz's existence is defined by deficit and by corrosive doubt in his own reality; indeed, he describes himself as having "no place in reality, as if I were not there at all" (*A*, 261). His origin in a metaphorical void evokes Jewish cosmogony, and provides a clue to his identity: "In the beginning God created the heaven and the earth. Now the earth was unformed and void, and darkness was upon the face of the deep . . ." (Genesis: 1–2).[1]

The narrative of *Austerlitz* traces the protagonist's forlorn search for *arche* or "origin," to fill the "internal mnemic void" created by a traumatic rupture from his parents in early childhood.[2] Raised in Wales by a childless Welsh couple who change his name and erase all evidence of his origins, his early, painful history of loss is deeply buried in his mind and inaccessible to him. While fragmentary memories of Austerlitz's early childhood emerge as flashes of Benjaminian *Jetztzeit*, they are ultimately insufficient and unsatisfying.[3] Such moments of anamnesis are

1    *The Holy Scriptures*, 3.
2    Long, *Image, Archive, Modernity*, 152.
3    Translated literally as "now-time," Benjamin's "Jetztzeit" refers to a notion of time that is imbued with revolutionary potential, in which the present

72 ♦ THE WANDERING JEW IN *AUSTERLITZ*

supplemented by the prosthetic memories of others whose testimony is doubtful. Documentary material, photos, the Theresienstadt film, and archival research do not, in *Austerlitz*, confirm the protagonist's understanding of his origins, but distance him further from what he seeks. A radio interview overheard by chance instils in Austerlitz the belief that he had been a Czech *Kindertransport* child, sent to England at the age of four for safety. From Vera, the woman he believes to have been his nanny, Austerlitz learns the putative details of his separation from his mother when she sent him from Prague to England as a *Kindertransport* child. But Vera's memories—of the station scene, Agáta's anguish, his little rucksack "avec quelques viatiques" (with some provisions), and the terrifying German presence—are presented as "an indistinct, rather blurred picture" (*A*, 245) that, rather than confirming his search for self, underlines the precarious nature of his quest.

Austerlitz has no name that can give him individuality as Rosenzweig understands it: "That which has a name of its own can no longer be a thing, no longer everyman's affair. It is incapable of utter absorption into the category, for there can be no category for it to belong to. It is its own category."[4] The significance of the name is implicit in Rosenzweig's assertion of singularity: "I first and second name, I dust and ashes, I am still here."[5] For Rosenzweig, naming is significant as a means of inscribing the individual into history:

> Through his surname, man belongs to the past; all that coerces him is contained in that name. Fate has a hold on him and his surname is the gate by which fate enters . . . A man's proper name serves as a declaration that this is to be a new human being; it lays claim to the present by confronting man with a future. It always bears with it dreams and desires.[6]

The allusiveness of Austerlitz's richly multivalent name—a Napoleonic battle, a Parisian railway station, a storage depot for expropriated Jewish property, the original name of the entertainer, Fred Astaire, and the hunched *mohel* who circumcised Kafka's nephew—vitiates his individuality. The similarity of Austerlitz's name to Auschwitz, the extermination

---

and past are drawn into a messianic relation: "History is the subject of a structure whose site is not homogenous, empty time, but time filled by the presence of the now or 'Jetztzeit.'" "Jetztzeit" is predicated on "saving" the past from the threat of irretrievable disappearance: "The true picture of the past flits by. The past can be seized only as an image which flashes up at the instant when it can be recognized and is never seen again." Benjamin, "On the Concept of History," XIV, V.

4    Rosenzweig, *Star of Redemption*, 186–87.
5    Rosenzweig, "'Urzelle,'" 126–27.
6    Rosenzweig, *Understanding the Sick and the Healthy*, 82.

camp that determines his alienation from origins, universalizes him as a trope for post-Holocaust existence. Austerlitz's ignorance of his origins estranges him from his own history, and from the obligation to the past that envisages the Jew as "riveted or bound, if not to his body, at least to the generations that precede and bind him, like Isaac in the *Akedah*, to the Covenant as ligature that constrains the individual."[7] Austerlitz's rupture from his beginnings is a break with that which gives substance and meaning to the present, leaving him feeling that "[he] had never really been alive . . ." (*A*, 194).[8]

In his last work of prose fiction, Sebald complicates the Wandering Jew trope by depicting Austerlitz as dispossessed of origins, and consumed by the longing to discover who he really is, and from where he is exiled. Austerlitz's search for origins is made mythical by the mysterious and disordered worlds through which he passes on his quest, and by his resemblance to mythological figures. While the biographies of the emigrants are supplemented with documentary material to enhance their reality, in *Austerlitz*, Sebald's resurrective mission to restore the lives of "real" Jewish characters is difficult to detect. Austerlitz's biography is meagre in its details, and he has been interpreted not as a "real" character, but an allegorical one, "less as an autonomous 'I' than as a locus of connections," a metaphysical figure who has "no essence and resides in no place," and who disappears from the text as enigmatic a figure as when he entered it.[9] In his construction of Austerlitz as the Wandering Jew who does not know from where he is exiled, Sebald's writing resonates with philosophical perceptions that sought to abstract the Jew to an ontological void, evident in Kant's "euthanasia" of the Jew, Hegel's relegation of the dispossessed Jew to a *Nichts*, occupying an "unhappy void," and Heidegger's coded allusions to the desert, conceived as a boundless void with no beginning or end, an onto-historical signifier of Jewish deracination and estrangement from the notion of beginning. On his search for identity, Austerlitz responds intuitively to atavistic visions of nomadic Jewishness: the motif of the desert, replete with caravan, palm trees, tents, and nomads, recurs in his story, suggesting that his "true" origin or "place" is in the *midbàr* or desert of Biblical Jewish wandering, and not in Central Europe, as Austerlitz comes to believe, and where he engages in a vain search for traces of his parents. Sebald's depiction of Austerlitz, a putatively European Jew, as responding instinctively to visions of desert nomadism betrays a problematic view of Jewishness, that sees the Jew as "from elsewhere," unassimilable, and immutably other, and perpetuates

---

7    Chaouat, "Being and Jewishness," 101.

8    The "Akedah" refers to the Pentateuchal narrative of the "binding" of Isaac." Genesis 22: 1–19.

9    Pelikan-Straus, "Sebald, Wittgenstein," 48.

the trope that insists that Jews do not belong, and are destined to remain peripheral to society.

## The Wandering Jew without Origins in German Philosophy

Sebald's depiction of Austerlitz as originating in the void resonates with images encountered in the philosophical writing of Kant, Hegel, Heidegger, and others, in whose writing the Jew is associated with the boundless void of the desert, and conceived as an Orientalized nomad, "a stranger to the soil and to men alike."[10] For Kant, the Jews are perceived as "the Palestinians among us," for Friedrich Nietzsche, the "mixed character" of the Jews retains an Oriental and nomadic dimension that offers the potential for a new European identity of the future.[11] Implicit in such philosophical reflections is the notion of the void or desert, the "nothingness" intrinsic to Judaism, epitomized by the "empty space" within the *Kodesh Kodeshim* (Holy of Holies) of the Jerusalem Temple, discovered by the Roman leader Pompey in his quest to expose the mysterious Jewish God: "When Pompey had approached the heart of the temple, the center of adoration, and had hoped to discover in it the root of the national spirit, to find indeed in one central point the life-giving soul of this remarkable people, there was nothing."[12]

Hegel relegates the Jew, dispossessed by Judaism of the right to own land or property, to a void, "*ein Nichts*."[13] Implicit in Hegel's pronouncement is a metaphorical death sentence that extrudes the Jews from existence on the grounds of implacable heteronomy, and refusal to be subsumed into the absolute unity of Christianity. For Hegel, the Jews were a people without a soul, whose existence was founded on emptiness. Excluded from his dialectic of universal history, fossilized as historical remnants, and petrified before their Law, the Jewish people occupied "an unhappy void [*unselige Leere*]."[14] Hegel's view of the Jews as alienated from origins is manifest in his vision of Abraham, who

> had in youth already left a fatherland in his father's company. Now, in the plains of Mesopotamia, he tore himself free altogether from his family as well . . . The groves which often gave him coolness and shade he soon left again; in them he had theophanies, appearances of

10   Hegel, "The Spirit of Christianity," 186.
11   Kant, *Anthropology*, 100; Large, "Nietzsche's Orientalism."
12   Hegel, "The Spirit of Christianity," 192.
13   Hegel, "The Spirit of Christianity," 197.
14   Hegel, *Phenomenology of Spirit*, 206.

his perfect Object on High, but he did not tarry in them . . . He was a stranger on earth, a stranger to the soil and to men alike.[15]

In the rootless wandering of Abraham, Hegel identifies a relentless heteronomy that disqualifies the Jews from history:

> The same spirit which had carried Abraham away from his kin led him through his encounters with foreign peoples during the rest of his life; this was the spirit of self-maintenance in strict opposition to everything . . . With his herds Abraham wandered hither and thither over a boundless territory without bringing parts of it any nearer to him by cultivating and improving them.[16]

Heidegger's *Black Notebooks*, first published in 2014, contain coded allusions to the Jew as rootless and alienated from origins. The metaphor of the desert, an empty, limitless space with no beginning or end, pervades his notebooks as the onto-historical signifier of Jewish deracination and estrangement from the notion of beginning. In *Ponderings XII–XV*, references to *Ver-wüstung* or "desertification" signify "not the laying waste of something present at hand," but an ontological expansion of the desert in a process of "desertification" that Heidegger imputed to the Jew.[17] As Donatella Di Cesare notes: "It is not difficult to perceive in desertification the ultimate symbol of Judaism. And not only because the desert is a symbol of the Hebrew people, but also because desertification is the impossibility of having a relationship with the beginning."[18] Heidegger takes the notion of Jewish abstraction further in his description of the Jew as "weltlos" (without the world), an idea he initially applied to stone, conceived as having no access to the world, and as thus failing to "be" or exist: "The stone is never dead because its being is never in the sense of what is instinctual or subservient."[19] The "worldlessness" of the Jew is implicit in Heidegger's vision of the "metaphysical Jew," an abstraction, an insidious agent of desertification, invisible, and other. Heidegger's view of the "metaphysical Jew" followed in a tradition of philosophers who similarly sought to abstract the Jew to nothingness: Kant accepted Jews as citizens only on the condition of abjuring or "annihilating" their Judaism; Hegel relegated the Jew, unable to own possessions or land, to *Nichts* or nothingness. The void implicit in Heidegger's notion of the metaphysical Jew had political implications in light of the genocide of the Jews: in his essay on "nothingness" in Heidegger, Taubes traces Heidegger's perception of

15  Hegel, "The Spirit of Christianity," 192.
16  Hegel, "The Spirit of Christianity," *192.*
17  Heidegger, *The History of Beyng,* 42.
18  Di Cesare, *Heidegger and the Jews,* 100.
19  Heidegger, *The Fundamental Concepts of Metaphysics,* 236.

the Jew to its inevitable conclusion, observing in it "the secret appointment between philosophy and politics."[20] Heidegger's extrusion of the Jew from the history of being is implicit in his obscure reference, in 1940, to the "first purification of being in the face of its profound disfigurement by the domination over being."[21]

Sebald died before the publication of the Black Notebooks, and could not therefore have been directly influenced by them. I do not wish to impute to Sebald an affinity with Heidegger's manifest anti-Semitism. Nevertheless, Sebald's Jewish tropes, and the metaphors that animate them, resonate with figural elements and philosophical notions in Heidegger's coded reference to Jews and Jewishness in the *Black Notebooks*, and in works published earlier.

# Austerlitz's Quest

Austerlitz's identity is resolutely withheld from him. His quest for origins in the internment camps, archives, museums, and railway stations of Central Europe yields no lasting resolution to his sense of incompleteness. His wanderings across Europe, to Prague, Bohemia, and Paris, confirm the failure of his archival quest to validate his Czech Jewish origins; his intuitive response to iterations of nomadic Oriental images implies that he originates not in Europe, but in the desert of Biblical Jewish exile. Austerlitz identifies the children of Israel's camp in the wilderness as his "proper place," suggesting instinctive consciousness of his nomadic, Semitic origins. As a metaphor for Auschwitz, the camp of the Israelites signals the impossibility of "home," foreshadowing the futility of his quest. Austerlitz's origins are obscured by the testimony of unreliable witnesses, and the epistemological ambiguity of the sites where he seeks to restore memory of his lost parents. An eternally Wandering Jew, he disappears from the text into the void from which he emerges.

### Antwerp Centraal Station: Nomadic Identity and Myth

Austerlitz is physically absent from the opening pages of the text, suggesting the ontological void from which he arises. His quest for origins is implied in street names, "Jerusalemstraat" and "Paradijsstraat" (*A*, 1), that conjure the Jewish narrative of foundation, the former a reference to the messianic "home" of the Jews to which, at the end of time, they will return (Isaiah: 40), the latter to the creation of man and woman and their prelapsarian existence in Paradise (Genesis 2:10). With its dark station concourse and confusion of streets and alleys, Antwerp is figured as

20     Taubes, "Vom Adverb 'Nichts.'"
21     Heidegger, *Ponderings XII–XV*, 187.

ominous and labyrinthine, prefiguring the impossibility of Austerlitz's quest to confirm who he is and where he originates. Austerlitz's exile from origin is intimated by the depiction of the Antwerp *Nocturama*, with its "bats and jerboas from Egypt and the Gobi desert," the first of a series of images conjuring an Orientalized and nomadic identity that hints at Austerlitz's putative origins or "place" in the desert of the Middle East.[22] Sebald's tendency to figure Jewish characters as intuitively susceptible to visions of an atavistic "desert" Jewishness, confounds the problem of their homelessness by suggesting that the Jew has no place in Europe, and that the desert of the Middle East is the true "home" of the Jew.

In the monumental hall of the Antwerp Centraal station, waiting passengers resemble "the last members of a diminutive race which had perished or had been expelled from its homeland" (*A*, 6); personifications of Austerlitz's exiled condition, they are metaphorical of the Jewish remnancy Rosenzweig describes:

> [The remnant] is always somehow someone left over, an interior whose exterior has been seized and swept away by the current of the world while he himself, what is left over of him, remains standing on the bank.[23]

As if in response to the implicit void of Austerlitz's origins, the vision of the "verdigris-covered negro boy" on his dromedary hints at Austerlitz's putatively nomadic, Orientalized identity (*A*, 4). It is against a background of exile and immanence that Austerlitz appears for the first time. With his heavy walking boots and rucksack, he is a striking embodiment of the mythical Wandering Jew; but his curiously waved blond hair resembles that of the actor who plays the role of Siegfried in Fritz Lang's *Nibelungen* film series (1924), based on the ancient Germanic myth of origin, *Das Nibelungenlied*.[24] A profoundly allegorical figure, indeed, a conflation of two myths, Austerlitz's origins are implied as mysterious, distanced in time, and ahistorical. Austerlitz and Siegfried are linked by a shared anxiety about origins: Austerlitz's search for traces of his mother in the Theresienstadt propaganda film affiliates his quest with Siegfried's forlorn longing to "find" his mother by interrogating Mime: "Nun melde,

---

22    Other references include Adela's identification of Austerlitz's Jewish identity in her vision of "palm trees . . . the caravan coming through the dunes . . ." (*A*, 158–59), the postcard Austerlitz sends the narrator with its picture of tents in the desert (*A*, 166), the Rembrandt painting, "The Flight into Egypt" (*A*, 169) that resonates with Austerlitz's own history of displacement, and the Biblical illustration of "the camp of the children of Israel in the wilderness" (*A*, 78–79).

23    Rosenzweig, *Star of Redemption*, 404–5.

24    Lang, dir., *Die Nibelungen*.

78 ♦ The Wandering Jew in *Austerlitz*

wie hieß meine Mutter?" (Tell me, what was my mother's name?)[25] Austerlitz's origins, like those of the mythical Siegfried, are obscure: both are raised by people not their parents, and the lives of both figures are determined by destruction. For Siegfried, this lies in the future, in the *Götterdämmerung* (twilight of the gods) that completes the *Nibelungen* saga; for Austerlitz, in the past, the Holocaust that destroyed all evidence of his origins.

Filled with "subterranean twilight," its mirrors half-obscured, as the place of the first encounter with the protagonist, the Antwerp Centraal station waiting-room is a mythical space in which time seems to stand still. In this otherworldly domain, the "goddess of time past" files her nails, an image of stasis that contributes to the mythical timelessness of the episode (*A*, 8). The dial of the "mighty clock" that dominates this space is blackened by soot and tobacco smoke, making it difficult to discern the passing of time. The violence of the simile that compares the movement of the clock's hand to a "sword of justice, slicing off the next one-sixtieth of an hour from the future and coming to a halt with a menacing quiver" (*A*, 9), and the implicit personification of Justice as the ancient Greek goddess, *Dike*, imbue the episode with a fatalistic determinism, according to which Austerlitz's past is "sliced off" forever from his present and future, and dehistoricized as myth. Sebald's mythologizing of Austerlitz's quest for origins implies a vision of the Holocaust, the trauma at the heart of his tragedy, as an event outside of history, paradigmatic, and detached from the question of German agency. This reflects the "rhetoric of fatefulness" Sebald criticized in the work of other postwar German writers, such as Hermann Kassack, Hans Nossack, and Peter de Mendelssohn, and suggests Sebald's perhaps unconscious affinity with the themes that dominated the writing of his generation.[26]

Questions of origins, guilt, and punishment are explored in Austerlitz's disorientated wandering in the Brussels Palace of Justice, "the singular architectural monstrosity on which [he] was planning to write a study" (*A*, 38).

### The Brussels Palace of Justice and Austerlitz's Irretrievable Origins

Situated on the ominously-named Gallow's Hill, the Brussels Palace of Justice is a spatial allegory for the devastating role of sanctioned power in depriving Austerlitz of his origins and identity. "The largest accumulation of stone blocks anywhere in Europe," the grandiose "Palace" is symbolic of the oppressive authority and pitilessness of the Justice system. With its "corridors and stairways leading nowhere," and "doorless

25   Wagner, "Siegfried," Act 1, scene 1.
26   Sebald, "Air War and Literature," 51.

rooms and halls where no one would ever set foot" (*A*, 39), it is emblematic of Austerlitz's impenetrable memories, and of the imperviousness of the Justice system to human comprehension and need. The reference to Gallow's Hill is a reminder of the crude notion of guilt and punishment the Palace represents. Like other fortifications encountered on his wandering across Europe—Theresienstadt, the Salpêtrière hospital, the "hideous outsize building" of the *Bibliothèque Nationale* (*A*, 386), the Palace of Justice is a metaphor for Austerlitz's defenses against the incursion of traumatic memory.

Allusion to "empty spaces surrounded by walls and representing the innermost secret of all sanctioned authority" (*A*, 39) evokes Hegel's vision of the void at the center of Jewishness, the "nothingness" Pompey found in the most sacred Jewish space, and suggests the metaphorical void of Austerlitz's Jewish origins, erased by history. Austerlitz's disoriented wandering—"once or twice he had climbed flights of creaking wooden stairs . . . branching off from the main corridors here and there and leading half a story up or down" (*A*, 40)—recalls Kafka's Gracchus in his incarnation as a trapped butterfly, whose predicament provides a desolate undertone to Austerlitz's forlorn quest.

Imagery relating to the world of nature subsumes Austerlitz's tragic quest in an indifferent natural history of suffering: Austerlitz wanders through the labyrinthine structure, "a mountain range of stone . . . through forests of columns," and looks out at "the leaden grey roofs of the palace, crammed together like pack ice, and down into ravines and shaft-like interior courtyards never penetrated by any ray of light" (*A*, 39). The metaphor of impenetrable darkness returns at the end of *Austerlitz*, in the narrator's description of the diamond mines of Kimberley and the author Dan Jacobson's futile search for traces of his family's Lithuanian roots, described in his novel, *Heshel's Kingdom*, which the narrator reads on his return to the fortress of Breendonk: "The chasm into which no ray of light could penetrate was Jacobson's image of the vanished past of his family and his people which, as he knows, can never be brought up from those depths again" (*A*, 414).[27] In the context of Austerlitz's search for origins, the impenetrable depths of the Palace of Justice are metaphorical of the futility of his quest in a world devoid of justice or redemption.

### The Great Eastern Hotel: Flood, Origins, and Guilt

As part of the railway system that is synecdochic of genocide in Sebald's narrative prose, the Great Eastern Hotel hints at the Holocaust that is the source of Austerlitz's alienation from origins. With its connotations of colonialism and capitalist expansion, the once-luxurious railway

27   Jacobson, *Heshel's Kingdom*.

80 ♦ THE WANDERING JEW IN *AUSTERLITZ*

hotel reflects Sebald's view of the Holocaust as the end-result of bourgeois capitalism and the concomitant pressure on Jews to assimilate, a theory that derived from the Frankfurt School, and touches on Sebald's awareness of his own petit bourgeois background. Austerlitz's instinctive desire to explore this site—"obeying a sudden impulse, he had gone into the foyer" with its faint evocations of an Orientalized, nomadic identity—(*A*, 57), suggests that it arises from an unconscious awareness of his "true" origins.

Housed within the hotel, the freemasons' temple is a secret space, metaphorical of Austerlitz's hidden origins. The theatrical "unlocking of the portal" by the hotel manager suggests that the hotel may contain clues to Austerlitz's identity. This is implied in the portal, "paneled in sand-colored marble and red Moroccan onyx" (*A*, 57), conjuring the originary narrative of the Israelite exodus from Egypt, and their forty-year wandering in the desert. The allusion to the desert sand suggests that this may be the "home" from which Austerlitz is exiled, and that his origins are to be found in atavistic Jewish nomadism. With no beginning or end, the desert carries with it the connotations of ontological nothingness that Heidegger imputes to the Jew, that marks him as immutably other, and excludes him from Being.

On the vaulted ceiling of the Freemasons' temple, the "single golden star emitting its rays into the dark clouds all around it" (*A*, 57–58) is allegorical of Austerlitz's quest for enlightenment. Recalling the Star of David and the yellow star Jews were forced to wear in Nazi Germany, the star provides a clue to Austerlitz's presumed Jewish identity. While the gold-painted picture of Noah's ark beneath a rainbow, and the dove returning with the olive branch in her beak, offer the promise of redemption, the flood implies the "submersion" of Austerlitz's past, manifest in his confession, "I have never known who I really was" (*A*, 60). In the vision of Noah's ark, Austerlitz's estrangement from origins is tied to the question of guilt that sees the flood as punishment for man's wickedness on earth, and Austerlitz's incarceration in the oppressive Elias house as retribution for abandoning his parents, "whom I had left, I feared, through my own fault" (*A*, 62).[28] The picture of Noah's ark on the flood catalyzes in Austerlitz the desire to recount to the narrator what he remembers about his Welsh childhood, dominated by an eschatology of guilt and punishment absorbed from Elias's apocalyptic sermons, and through exposure to the phenomenon of flood, exemplified by the haunting image of the drowned Welsh village of Llanwddyn. A photograph album depicting the drowned inhabitants of a flooded village functions as a metaphor for

---

28 "And God said unto Noah: The end of all flesh is come before me; for the earth is filled with violence through them; and behold, I will destroy them with the earth." Genesis 6: 6.

Austerlitz's own "buried" origins, and his sense of not being truly alive: "I leafed again and again through these few photographs . . . until the people looking out of them . . . became as familiar to me as if I were living with them down at the bottom of the lake" (*A*, 73–74).

## The Ladies' Waiting-Room: The Maternal Space, Memory, and Redemption

Austerlitz's experience in the Liverpool Street station marks a critical moment in his search for origins: an allegory of the quest to discover his repressed identity, his entry into "one of the darkest and most sinister places in London, a kind of entrance to the underworld," is motivated by an instinctive, and inexplicable impulse he ascribes to the "slight inner adjustments of which we are barely conscious" (*A*, 189). Having avoided all clues to his real identity, Austerlitz's experience in the Liverpool station leads him to confront for the first time, a vision of his young self at the place of arrival as a *Kindertransport* child.[29] In this atemporal, highly figurative episode, mythological and intertextual allusions, surreal visions, and the extended metaphors of inundation and stone allegorically transform Austerlitz into an emblem of radical homelessness. Austerlitz's encounter with his child-self is framed in myth: his compulsion to descend into the Underworld of the station places him in the company of mythical figures such as Odysseus and Orpheus; the repetitive and pointless labor of the white-turbaned station cleaner evokes the eternal punishment of Sisyphus; like Charon, the mythical ferryman who takes the souls of the dead across the river Styx to the Underworld, the cleaner leads Austerlitz, a "dead soul" who doubts his own existence in reality, into the mysterious realm of the Ladies' Waiting-Room, to confront the past (*A*, 194). The waiting-room is a fantastical universe in which time is suspended, "minutes or even hours may have passed" (*A*, 189), "the laws of physics are violated," and perspective is "improbably foreshortened" (*A*, 191). In the "icy grey light, like moonshine" (*A*, 189), Escher-like architectural conundrums of "huge halls . . . rows of pillars . . . viaducts and footbridges" (*A*, 190–91) become visible. Hallucinatory visions of guilt and punishment, of "prisoners, in search of some way of escape from their dungeon," conflict with images of liberation, the "ferns, young willows, heron nests . . . and the birds [who] spread their great wings and fly away" (*A*, 191), to render the waiting-room metaphorical of the confusion of Austerlitz's unconscious mind, in which fragments of memory

---

29  The *Kindertransport* was an organized rescue effort of children from Nazi-controlled territory during the nine months prior to the outbreak of the Second World War.

emerge, "all interlocking like the labyrinthine vaults . . . which seemed to go on for ever and ever" (*A*, 192).

In this "Underworld" of stifled memory, Austerlitz's search for origins sees him allegorically return to the hidden, maternal space of the Ladies' Waiting-Room. Stepping past a heavy curtain, and entering into "the large room . . . disused for years," Austerlitz likens himself to "an actor, who, upon making his entrance, has completely and irrevocably forgotten not only the lines he knew by heart, but the very part he has so often played" (*A*, 189), a theatrical metaphor that emphasizes the illusionary nature of his experience, and the revelation it engenders. In an epiphanous vision that evokes a "nativity scene" of mother, father and child, Austerlitz sees himself as a *Kindertransport* child in the station waiting-room, and the adults who would become his foster parents. The redemptive connotations of this tableau are undermined by the physical separation of the boy from the parent-figures, and the rucksack by which Austerlitz recognizes himself, and which functions as a reminder of his alienation from his beginnings. Austerlitz's response to the vision of himself as a *Kindertransport* child—"I felt something rending within me" (*A*, 193)—recalls the rending of the temple veil at the moment of Jesus's death. Symbolizing the opening of the Covenant to the world, it suggests the redemptive potential of Austerlitz's epiphany.[30] "Rending" implies also the Jewish mourning ritual of Kriah, the act of tearing one's clothes as an expression of grief at the loss of a loved one, and expresses the overwhelming sense of loss the vision engenders in Austerlitz, who confesses to feeling that "I had never really been alive, or was only now being born, almost on the eve of my death" (*A*, 194).[31]

The Liverpool station episode thematizes the possibility of redemption through numerous Christological symbols that posit the possibility of hope or salvation. Austerlitz enters the station on a Sunday morning, the cleaner or mythical "guide" wears a "snow-white turban," signifying purification, and the name of Austerlitz's lover, Marie de Verneuil, conjures salvation, as does the church in which he visualizes her in a flood of returning memories. Kilbourn (*W. G. Sebald's Postsecular Redemption*), identifies an ambiguous form of redemption, understood as signifying return to a place, time or condition. Sebald's secular redemption persists negatively as a thematic or structural absence that, while ironic, remains open to the idea of hope. Sebald borrows from Kafka the view of redemption as "asserting itself only by its total absence . . . the messianic promise of the future [as] . . . only implicit in the religious form of conceiving

---

30    "And behold, the veil of the temple was torn in two from top to bottom; and the earth shook and the rocks were split" (Matthew 27:51).

31    David rent his garments when he heard that Absalom had slain his brothers (Samuel 13:31).

(and rejecting) the contemporary world as infernal."[32] The idea of hope postulated in Sebald's writing is premised on acceptance of the unlikelihood or impossibility of hope, which, even if forlorn, remains valuable in the desire for its realization. Sebald noted: "What is important in messianic thought is solely the possibility of what Ernst Bloch called 'das Prinzip Hoffnung,' a principle which to Franz Rosenzweig appeared to be 'the Star of Salvation.'"[33]

Beyond the suggestion that he may have been a *Kindertransport* child, Austerlitz does not discover, in this symbolic space, who he is, or from where he is exiled. Recalling his experience, he likens the black and white diamond pattern of the stone slabs beneath his feet to "the board on which the endgame would be played" (*A*, 193), an allusion to Samuel Beckett's drama, *Endgame* (1958), and an acknowledgment of the futility of his search. This is implicit in the opening line of Beckett's nihilistic play: "Finished, it's finished, nearly finished, it must be nearly finished."[34] Austerlitz's cryptic allusion to Beckett's absurdist play refutes the redemptive connotations of the Ladies' Waiting-Room episode, and suggests his nascent awareness of death as the place from which he is exiled.

### Prague: Austerlitz's Quest for Origins

The experience of overhearing a radio conversation between two former *Kindertransport* children, brought to England on a ferry named "Prague," stirs in Austerlitz the conviction that he too, had been a *Kindertransport* child, and precipitates his impulsive return to the putative city of his birth to engage in an archival quest for traces of his origins. The radio interview reawakens in him vague memories of "waiting on a quay in a long crocodile of children . . . most of them carrying rucksacks or small leather cases," and of seeing "the great slabs of paving at my feet, the mica in the stone" (*A*, 200). The rucksacks are emblematic of Austerlitz's tropological role as the endlessly wandering Jew, for whom the stone slabs, prefigured in the Liverpool Station Ladies' Waiting-Room, evoke Beckett's drama, *Endgame*, and signify the futility of his search for self. While Prague represents, in the writing of Bachmann, Celan, and others, a lost, uncontaminated *Heimat* and a source of utopian hope, the destruction of its Jewish population makes it a site of persisting memory and unresolved mourning.[35] Austerlitz's return to his putative birthplace of Prague does not offer the consolation of certainty, or redemption from the anguish of his originless existence. For Austerlitz, Prague remains emblematic of

32    Löwy, "'*Theologia negativa*,'" 81.
33    Sebald, "Das Gesetz der Schande," 99.
34    Beckett, *Endgame*.
35    See Thomas, *Prague Palimpsest*.

origins, a maternal space he recalls when prompted by the memories of others, but a space that cannot validate his genesis.

Austerlitz arrives in Prague on a day "too bright, almost overexposed" (*A*, 203), a photographic metaphor that touches on the epistemological uncertainty that motivates his quest for identity. With its "labyrinth of alleyways, thoroughfares and courtyards" (*A*, 212), Prague is figured as a mystifying city in which the blurring of boundaries between past and present, nature and art, obscures the certainty of what he seeks, and compels him to visit the state archives in search of factual traces of his mother, and his presumed European Jewish identity. "Standing outside of time altogether" (*A*, 203), an "illusionist," fantastical structure that resembles a prison, a monastery, an opera house, and an English "folly," the archive building is a repository of the past, an ahistorical space that confounds Austerlitz's quest for archival validation of his origins and existence in reality.

An enigmatic porter leads Austerlitz down into the "Underworld" in which, like Odysseus, he seeks his beloved mother. Unlike Odysseus, who embraces the shade of his mother Anticlea, Austerlitz does not encounter his mother, but is guided to traces of her by the archivist, Tereza Ambrosova, whose sudden appearance, "as if she had, as they say, sprung from nowhere" (*A*, 206), touches on Austerlitz's own mysterious origins, and contributes to the fantastical nature of this episode. To Tereza Ambrosova, Austerlitz confesses the dispossession that motivates his quest—"my origins had been unknown to me" (*A*, 208)—and his hope that archival information might fill the void in his consciousness. Evoking St Teresa of Avila and the ambrosia of the Greek gods, thought to confer immortality, the name of the archivist connotes redemption, and indeed, her archival research directs Austerlitz to the probable home of his mother Agáta.[36] But in the nightmare that follows his visit to the archives, Austerlitz imagines "climbing up and down flights of steps" (*A*, 210), recalling Kafka's Gracchus, trapped in a condition of thwarted mobility that underlines his eternal alienation from home. In the "dungeon-like basement" of his repressed memories, Austerlitz imagines himself as the last survivor of the "tribe of the Aztecs [which] had died out years ago" (*A*, 210), a metaphor for Jewish exile and remnancy, and an admission of the futility of his archival search for traces of his parents.

Austerlitz is directed by Tereza Ambrosova to 12 Sporkova, the likely last known address of his mother and the presumed space of his childhood, where "the uneven paving of the Sporkova underfoot," and "the artificial stone of the hall" (*A*, 214) stir memories, "long numbed and now coming

---

36    St Teresa of Avila, a sixteenth-century Carmelite nun, was associated with the Prague statuette of the Infant Jesus, whose mysterious origins make it a metaphor for Austerlitz's lost origins.

back to life," a hope qualified by the observation "it was true that I could recognize nothing for certain . . ." (*A*, 212–13). The "star-like mosaic flower" in the hall suggests Austerlitz's Jewish origins, evoking the yellow star emblematic of Jewish persecution in Nazi Germany, the source of his trauma. At 12 Sporkova, Austerlitz encounters Vera, whom he believes to have been his childhood nursemaid, with whom Austerlitz and his mother lived after his father left for Paris. Although the apartment reveals "everything was just as it had been almost sixty years ago" (*A*, 216), there are proleptic hints of the catastrophe to come in the "blue-tinged aquatint of the Bohemian mountains" that foreshadows an aquatint Austerlitz sees in the Terezin museum, depicting the "star-shaped fortification, colour-washed in soft tones of grey-brown for Maria Theresia" (*A*, 287). This would later become the Bohemian concentration camp of Theresienstadt to which his mother Agáta was deported, before being "sent East" (*A*, 287), a sinister euphemism for the extermination camps of Poland. Vera shares with Austerlitz her memories of his lost parents and what she knows of his origins: of his mother, whose Orientalized Jewish origins are hinted at by the "fez and slipper factory" of her grandfather, and of his paternal grandfather, whose Jewishness is implicit in his occupation as an itinerant trader in spices from St Petersburg. From Vera, Austerlitz learns about the erosion of their lives with the advent of Nazism, that reduced his father's family to Wandering Jews, "peddlers . . . just as their ancestors had once walked the countryside of Galicia" (*A*, 240–41). A clear strategy of identifying voices—"said Vera," "said Austerlitz"—indicates the mediated nature of the narrator's account, and guards against violating the principle of ethical distance between self and other in his retelling of Austerlitz's story, confirming Sebald's awareness of the risk of inappropriate identification of narrator-author with Jewish subject.

By her own admission, Vera's memories are occluded and unreliable, "as if you were looking at the past through a glass mountain . . ." (*A*, 224). Prompted by Vera, the memories that return to Austerlitz's mind are not his own, but prosthetic memories belonging to others, confirming Thomas's description of Prague as a site of secondary memory: "Prague exemplifies this palimpsestic process by which every attempt to reach an authentic state of being through unmediated memory is exposed as secondary and citational."[37] Unable to recognize or remember himself in a photograph of a small page at a masked ball, Austerlitz's desolate confession that "all memory was extinguished in me" (*A*, 259) acknowledges the impossibility of his quest. Looking out of the window into the garden of 12 Sporkova, surrogate memories supplied by Vera conjure for Austerlitz the hunchbacked tailor Moravec in his workshop, depicted as a nostalgic *Heilsraum* (sacralized space), with its lilac trees, "sweet fragrance wafting

37    Thomas, *Prague Palimpsest*, 8–9.

up from the walled garden, the waxing moon . . . the sound of church bells ringing in the city" (*A*, 221). The hunched figure of Moravec evokes Benjamin's "bucklicht Männlein," an allegorical figure of childhood terror, who appears in Benjamin's *Berlin Childhood around 1900*, in which he pleads to be remembered: "Liebes Kindlein, ach ich bitt,' / Bet fürs bucklicht Männlein mit." (Dear little child, I entreat you / pray for the little hunchback.)[38] A reminder of the literary project, to remember, and to restore the past, the figure is a reminder too, of the paradox inherent in Sebald's figural representation of Jewish loss, that subsumes the suffering individual in a universalizing allegory of homelessness and imperfection.

Austerlitz's traumatic severance from the utopia of childhood is implied by the metaphor of Moravec's "big scissors," and the knife he sharpens to cut a slice of sausage (*A*, 220). Severance is a recurring motif in Sebald's prose fiction—the weavers' scissors at the conclusion to "Max Aurach," and the razor and scythe in *Vertigo*, the latter signifying the severance of Germany from a more positive past. "Cutting" signifies Austerlitz's putative Jewish singularity, and the act of circumcision that inscribes a Jewish male into Jewish particularism, while simultaneously "cutting" him off from broader society. In the historical context of Austerlitz's life, the pervasive metaphor of severance implies his own expulsion, and the extrusion of his parents from the *Reich*, indicating Sebald's privileging of the figurative over the objectively factual in the representation of the "real" and historical. The depiction of Moravec, "mending the worn hem of a jacket, or sewing a quilted lining into an overcoat," evokes Benjamin's description of Kafka's negative messianism: "It was on the *Kehrseite* (reverse side) of this 'Nothingness,' in its *Futter* (lining), if I may say so, that Kafka sought to brush redemption with his finger." For Benjamin, Kafka envisaged the possibility of redemption in a different world, "which Kafka did not find but glimpsed in flight, or in a dream."[39] In an essay on Benjamin, Scholem observed: "In Kafka's world, Benjamin perceived the negative inversion to which the Jewish categories are subjected . . . there the teaching no longer conveys a positive message, but offers only an absolutely Utopian promise . . . as yet undefinable . . . Benjamin knew that in Kafka we possess the *theologia negativa* of a Judaism not a whit less intense for having lost the Revelation as a positive message."[40]

In the vision of the tailor Moravec at work, Sebald presents the iconography of rupture and repair McGlothlin identifies in the metaphor of sewing in survivor and perpetrator writing of the German second generation:

38    Benjamin, *Berlin Childhood*, 652.
39    Benjamin, *Briefe II*, 614.
40    Scholem, *On Jews and Judaism*, 196.

Second-generation literature thus mourns the dead with its own metaphorical rendering of *keri'ah*, the marking of memory in the evocation of rupture. At the same time, by using their writing to express the fracture caused by the Holocaust, second-generation writers forge a link to Jewish mourning ritual, reinscribing their murdered family into both personal and Jewish memory and effecting a sort of repair of their torn legacy.[41]

Imagery of rupture and repair is part of a network of emblems in Sebald's writing—needle, scissors, spindle, thread—that imply the hope, if not the reality, of repairing the past. The image of Moravec mending the lining of a coat suggests the possibility of redemption for Austerlitz from the pain of alienation; but the scissors, with its implication of severance, undermines this hope by implying that Austerlitz will remain cut off from the world in which he believes himself to have "no place."

Jewish homelessness is thematized in a brief episode recounting Austerlitz's dream of returning to his parents' home in Prague. His dream of homecoming is one of several fantasies of return to the parental home in Sebald's prose fiction that reflect the nostalgic longing of the German second generation for wholeness, for a repaired relationship with their homeland, and for restitution of the past.[42] Echoing his return to 12 Sporkova, Austerlitz finds all the furniture in its "proper place," but his parents are absent and when they return, are unconscious of his presence, and speak in "the mysterious language of deaf mutes" (*A*, 261), a metaphor for the incomprehensibility and inaccessibility of the past. Language of uncertainty—"I am not aware . . . I simply think . . . It does not seem to me . . . I feel more and more as if time did not exist at all" (*A*, 260), imbues Austerlitz's fantasy of homecoming with a sense of imminence that imagines "home" as precariously suspended between life and death. While Aurach's return to the home of his parents ends in an epiphany on the nature of true art that underscores the heritage he has lost and cannot recover, "homecoming" for Austerlitz is foreclosed by the nihilistic acknowledgment that "I have always felt as if I had no place in reality, as if I were not there at all . . ." (*A*, 261). His confession reflects a recognition of allegorical erasure that echoes Hegel's relegation of the Jew to a void, and Heidegger's abstraction of the Jew to metaphysical "nothingness."

41   McGlothlin, *Second-Generation Holocaust Literature*, 24.
42   Such fantasies include Max Aurach's dream of returning to the drawing room of his parents (*TE*), and Michael Hamburger's fantasy of returning to his parental home in Berlin (*RS*).

## The Search for Agáta: Absence and Remnancy

On his way to Terezin, site of the concentration camp of Theresienstadt to which, as he discovers from Vera, his mother was transported before being sent east to her death, Austerlitz is overcome by the sense of "going further and further east and further back in time" towards the Holocaust. The vision of "a petrochemicals plant half eaten away by rust with clouds of smoke rising from its cooling towers and chimneys as they must have done without cease for many long years," evokes the Holocaust that dominates Austerlitz's imagination as the source of his alienation from his beginnings (*A*, 263). To Austerlitz "walking down the straight road, always looking ahead to see if the silhouette of the fortifications . . . was in sight yet (*A*, 264), Terezin is "not so much a fortified town as one half-hidden and sunk into the marshy ground of the flood plain" (*A*, 264), a reminder of the flooded Welsh villages of his childhood, metaphorical of his irretrievably "drowned" origins. Austerlitz's confrontation with Terezin, the historic site where he hoped to "encounter" his mother, is presented in a deeply figurative episode in which Sebald employed the distancing devices of allegorical writing to suggest the catastrophe of human destruction, reflecting Sebald's observation: "Ein Massengrab läßt sich nicht beschreiben. Das heißt, man muß andere Wege finden, die tangentieller sind . . ." (A mass grave cannot be described directly. That means, one must find other, more tangential ways of describing it.)[43] As a belated "witness" to destruction, Austerlitz is distanced by the topography of the village, its "star-shaped ground plan" barely emerging above the fields, hidden by the "shrubs and bushes [that] covered the former glacis and the grass-grown ramparts" (*A*, 264). To Bettina Mosbach, Sebald's detachment in relation to depicting Jewish tragedy sees him adopt a "geometry of representation" based on simultaneous contemplation of violence, and avoidance of its depiction.[44]

To Austerlitz, "the most striking aspect of the place was its emptiness," suggesting the absence of what was once a captive, vitiated Jewish presence. The village of Terezin is devoid of human presence except for "a bent figure" (*A*, 266), and a mentally disturbed man of incomprehensible speech, who disappears, "swallowed up by the earth, as they say" (*A*, 266), imbuing the episode with the surrealism of a fairy tale. The Terezin episode is characterized by stasis: in the blank windows and ruined doorways "there was no more movement at all apart from the spiders spinning their threads" (*A*, 272), an ambiguous image that suggests both abandonment and neglect, and the ironic possibility of repair, implicit in the threads they weave. To Austerlitz, "the gates and doorways of Terezin,

---

43 Hage, *Zeugen der Zerstörung*, 264.
44 Mosbach, *Figurationen der Katastrophe*, 59.

all of them ... [obstruct] access to a darkness never yet penetrated" (*A*, 267–68), a mystification of destruction that suggests the futility of Austerlitz's attempt to penetrate the meaning of this enigmatic space, and Sebald's refusal to confront the horror perpetrated at this site of destruction. The obscurity of Austerlitz's past is allegorized in his dream of gazing into a Terezin barrack, and finding it "filled floor to ceiling with layer upon layer of cobwebs." Trying to retain the "powdery grey dream image ... to discover what it concealed," the vision only dissolved all the more (*A*, 272–73). Austerlitz's inability to discern with clarity the village of Terezin, associated with his mother and his origins, points to a deeper ontological uncertainty about the reality of his own existence. It reveals Sebald's oblique figuration of catastrophe as a strategy of avoidance, a pretense to historical ignorance that detaches the violence of the trauma inflicted on Austerlitz from its origin in human agency, and undermines his statements of empathy.

Austerlitz is mesmerized by the immanence of the objects on display in the window of Terezin's only shop, Antikos Bazar, remnants of past lives that seem to hold the promise of resolution to his question of origins, "as if one of them or their relationship with each other must provide an unequivocal answer to the many questions I found it impossible to ask in my mind: what was the meaning of the festive white lace tablecloth ... What secret lay behind the three brass mortars of different sizes ... or the tin advertising sign bearing the words *Theresienstädter Wasser*" (*A*, 275). Sebald's "museal" representation of these objects manifests a strategy of remembrance that resembles that of the twentieth-century Holocaust museum, with its consciousness of the ethics and limitations of representation, and reflects his avowed intention to create, in *Austerlitz*, an alternative Holocaust museum.[45] Like Austerlitz himself, the objects are ciphers for their absent owners, detached from their origin and function in the lives of the individuals for whom they represented belief in the continuity of life, permanency, and tradition. While the articles do not provide Austerlitz with an answer to his question, Sebald's detailed listing of the objects imbues them with an auratic quality that constitutes them as ghostly markers of past lives extinguished in Auschwitz, reminders of the bourgeois life of which they were once a part. Sebald's delicate figuring of these remainders offers clues to Austerlitz's Jewish identity: "the festive white lace tablecloth hanging over the back of the ottoman" is a poignant reminder of traditional Jewish life to which the gathering of family and observance of ritual were integral; the tin advertising sign labeled *Theresienstädter*

---

45    See Krauthausen, "Sebald: creci en una familia postfascista alemana" (Sebald: I grew up in a post-fascist German family).

90  ♦  THE WANDERING JEW IN *AUSTERLITZ*

*Wasser* hints at Agáta's fate. The trapped "marine flowers swaying inside their glassy spheres . . . the model ship, the squirrel perched forever in the same position," and the ivory-colored porcelain group of a hero in the act of rescuing an innocent girl from a cruel fate, are allegorical of Austerlitz's fate, to have survived those to whom his existence was once meaningful, and to be trapped in a mnemic void. An inventory of an ultimately destroyed world, the meaning of the objects remains closed to Austerlitz, as Martin Modlinger observes:

> As a place of suffering and death, it cannot—and should not—be fully accessible to the living . . . For Sebald, literary historiography can never claim to present the factual or emotional truth of suffering; it can only describe the path of necessary failure towards such an understanding. Theresienstadt as the place of the dead remains forever closed to the living.[46]

Sebald's poignant evocation of loss is at the same time, an aestheticization of remnancy: this is implicit in adjectives connoting delight—the "wonderful marine flowers," and the minutely detailed description of a "leaf-embroidered jacket of pale, summery linen . . . and the olive-green uniform tunic with gilt epaulettes that went with it" (*A*, 275). His elaborately figural mode suggests the aestheticizing gaze of the collector, as Iris Radisch points out.[47] The sonorous invocation of "three brass mortars of different sizes, which had about them the suggestion of oracular utterance" (*A*, 275), imbues the objects on display with philosophical gravity, while implying that the calamity of Jewish destruction was predestined by a mythical conception of fate. Implicit in the portrayal of a lampshade depicting "a river never rising from any source, never flowing into the sea but always back into itself" (*A*, 276), is the notion of Jewish catastrophe as inevitable and endemic to a natural history of catastrophe. To Austerlitz's hungry gaze, the vestigial objects have grown "quite naturally into the black branches of the lime trees" reflected in the windows of the shop; emblematic of Germany, the lime trees are a faint reminder of German agency in the causation of such remnancy (*A*, 274). The indistinct reflection of Sebald's own face in the window of Antikos Bazar (*A*, 276) suggests that he partakes of Austerlitz's dispossession, hinting at a "negative symbiosis" of Jews and Germans, unified in a community of victimhood.

Sebald's figural representation of the Terezin ghetto holds the potential to mystify and obscure the trauma and atrocity associated with this site. Presented as a "fairy tale" in which time is suspended, the bizarre and fantastical make illusory appearances, and remnant objects in a shop

---

46    Modlinger, "The Kafkaesque in Adler and Sebald," 219.
47    Radisch, "Der Waschbär der falschen Welt."

window are sacralized and imbued with the power to answer the question of Austerlitz's origins, Sebald's privileging of the figural mode underlines the troubling discrepancy between his choice of narrative mode and his subject, the genocide of the Jews and its enduring effect. Through pervasive imagery of concealment, blankness, obscurity, and darkness, Sebald forecloses understanding of the trauma that underlies Austerlitz's alienation, and perpetuates a rhetoric of incomprehensibility in relation to the Holocaust that evades the question of responsibility. Indeed, in the representation of the ghetto, references to Germany and the German language are exemplified only by the lime trees in the park, and the mentally deranged man who tells a tale "in a kind of broken German" (*A*, 266), and are subtle to the point of being almost imperceptible.

At a later time, in the reading room of the *Bibliothèque Nationale* in Paris, Austerlitz discovers a photograph of the records room in the Theresienstadt ghetto. The sight of the room, "filled with open shelves up to the ceiling" (*A*, 395), catalyzes in him the epiphany that "my true place of work should have been there, in the little fortress of Terezin, where so many had perished in the cold, damp casemates, and it was my own fault that I had not taken it up" (*A*, 395). Austerlitz's identification with the Jewish dead of Theresienstadt reflects the guilt of the survivor, in whose memory the dead survive only as a faint recollection. It is a recognition, shortly before he disappears from the text, that his own "true place" is among the dead.

In the nightmare that follows Austerlitz's visit to Terezin, the postapocalyptic fantasy of an extinguished landscape is a projection of his sense of annihilation, and an allegory of an irredeemably fallen world: "Where roads had once passed over firm ground, where human beings had lived, foxes had run across country and birds of many kinds had flown from bush to bush, now there was nothing but empty space, and at the bottom of it stones and gravel and stagnant water" (*A*, 285). With its vision of tall chimneys and plumes of smoke, "stars [that] showed only on the pallid side of the firmament, sooty, smoking lights extinguished one by one," and the "cones of extinct Bohemian volcanoes," Austerlitz's nightmare is a deeply pessimistic vision of an annihilated "post-human" world that the Holocaust has allowed us to imagine.

### The Quest for Origins: The Film and the Archive

From Vera, Austerlitz learns that his mother, Agáta, was transported to Theresienstadt, before her likely deportation to "the east," a euphemism for the extermination camps of Poland. In his anxious search for traces of his origins, Austerlitz seeks Agáta's image in the Nazi propaganda film, "Der Führer schenkt den Juden eine Stadt" (The Führer grants the Jews a city).[48] The name by which the film is known is false: originally named "Theresienstadt: A Documentary Film from the Jewish Settlement Area," the discrepancy points to the intention to deceive that underlies the later name, with its implications of the Führer's largesse.[49] Designed to falsely depict life in the Theresienstadt ghetto, camp inmates were forced to "act" the role of a contented populace, and to "mask" their suffering. Unable to recognize his mother with certainty in the film, Austerlitz watches a slowed-motion copy that "revealed previously hidden objects and people, creating, by default as it were, a different sort of film altogether" (*A*, 345). In this "different film," Sebald aestheticizes and obfuscates historical reality to create a picture of camp life that adds yet another layer of deception to a film already burdened by falsity.

In the slowed-down version, the image of Jewish workers who "looked as if they were toiling in their sleep," evokes a fantastical world: the bodies of the workers are de-materialized and spectral, "hovering rather than walking" (*A*, 348), "dissolved at the edges, resembling . . . the frayed outlines of the human hand shown in the fluidal pictures and electrographs taken by Louis Draget" (*A*, 348). Sebald's dissolution of reality distances his portrayal of camp life from historical reality; what remains is the shadow of the real, evident in "those fleeting faces . . . which seemed to dissolve even as they appeared" (*A*, 345), and in Austerlitz's recollection of "the face of a young woman . . . barely emerging from the black shadows around it" (*A*, 345). While Austerlitz attempts to "see" Agáta by examining a slow-motion fragment of the film, imagery of deliquescence underscores the impossibility of his quest, obstructed by damaged sections of the tape [that] "now melted the image from its center . . . blotting it out . . ." (*A*, 348). Death is a lurking presence in camp life, melodramatically portrayed in Sebald's slowed-down version of the film, in which "the merry polka" on the soundtrack becomes "a funeral march dragging along at a grotesquely sluggish pace, and the rest of the musical pieces accompanying the film . . . also moved in a kind of subterranean world, through the most nightmarish depths . . . to which no human voice has ever descended" (*A*, 348–49).

Austerlitz's quest to see his mother is complicated by the false reality portrayed in the film: drawing on H. G. Adler's description of Theresienstadt, Sebald's depiction of the "Maskendasein" (masked existence) of the inmates conceals the horror of the concentration camp behind a grotesque farce, in which Agáta's professional identity as an opera singer imbues her with an innately deceptive quality, and the inauthenticity of the setting, with its carefully staged concert and tavern, unsettles

---

48    Gerron, dir., *Der Führer schenkt den Juden eine Stadt.*
49    Margry, "Theresienstadt," 150.

Austerlitz's perception of the "real."[50] To Austerlitz, scrutinizing the fragment, the vague image of Agáta emerging from the shadows around it is a wishful fantasy, as he admits, "she looks . . . just as I imagined the singer Agáta from my faint memories and the other few clues to her appearance that I now have, and I gaze and gaze again at that face which seems to me both strange and familiar . . ." (*A*, 351). Austerlitz's encounter with the illusory picture of his mother confirms only the uncertainty of her identity, and the futility of his quest. As Prager observes, "Sebald's Austerlitz does not encounter his mother, but rather encounters a voiceless image of a victim who resembles his memory of his mother."[51]

Recovering from a breakdown after visiting Terezin and Germany, Austerlitz undertakes archival research into Theresienstadt by reading Adler's epic work on the concentration camp. The episode opens with a map of the camp, somewhat damaged by a dark smudge, suggesting the inadequacy of Adler's monumental attempt to render Theresienstadt comprehensible, and the unreliability of his documentary account. In the most conspicuously factual episode in *Austerlitz*, the figural is displaced temporarily by the "pseudo-technical jargon governing everything in Theresienstadt" (*A*, 330), recording inmate numbers, occupations, disease and death rates, forced labor, and the sham clean-up campaign for the Red Cross inspection. Nevertheless, the figural mode prevails through the extended metaphor of incomprehensibility: Austerlitz's attempt to read Adler is compared with the process of "deciphering an Egyptian or Babylonian text" (*A*, 330), while reference to the self-administration housed in barrack block BV as "The Castle," evokes Kafka's obscure text, and serves to obfuscate comprehension of Theresienstadt and the destruction perpetrated there. Sebald's privileging of the figurative mode is manifest in the detailed description of the sinister ghetto hearses, relics of ancient funeral coaches, "covered by ulcerations of peeling black varnish," with "rows of letters and numbers coarsely painted in lime-wash" (*A*, 334), a vision that implies Jewish suffering and the Holocaust through images of ulceration and lime, and suggests, through the depiction of the silver-bronzed funeral coaches, the notion that Jewish genocide originated in the assimilation of Jews to the seductions of eighteenth-century bourgeois Enlightenment.[52]

### Marienbad: "The Drowned and the Saved"

Austerlitz's experience at Marienbad is the culmination of an extended metaphor of flood and submersion that implies the irretrievable nature

---

50 Adler, *Theresienstadt, 1941–1945.*
51 Prager, "Interpreting the Visible Traces," 182.
52 Lime was used to capture the smell of decaying bodies in mass graves.

of his origins, and the sense of annihilation that affiliates him with the "drowned" of Primo Levi's memoir of Auschwitz.[53] The metaphor of submersion links his quest for origins to his childhood memories of flooded Welsh villages, in which drowned inhabitants pursued their lives "at the bottom of the lake," and he too, felt as if he "had been submerged in that dark water" (*A*, 74). It is through imagery of water and submersion that the deforming effect of his alienation from origins is acknowledged: Austerlitz's lover Marie compares him to "a pool of frozen water" (*A*, 303), while his inaudible, almost subaquatic attempts to speak betray him as "drowned."

Austerlitz's return to Marienbad is a reprise of a former visit, the memory of which inexplicably "wrenches [his] heart" as a reminder of an idyllic time with his parents and Vera in 1938 (*A*, 300). The connotations of Marienbad are ambiguous: the spa town, famous for the curative properties of its spring water, and a favorite retreat for European Jews, offers the possibility of rehabilitation; indeed, the salvific implication of the name, "Marienbad," points to the healing function of this spa town.[54] Formerly known as Auschowitz Springs, its assonance with Auschwitz is a baleful reminder of the trauma that constituted Austerlitz as a Wandering Jew, alienated from his beginnings. Austerlitz's visit to Marienbad begins with an ominous descent into the Underworld of the "deathly and still" Palace Hotel (*A*, 291). The village of Marienbad is untouched by time, evinced by the dust on the writing desk. Imagery of submersion evokes Austerlitz's "buried" memories, and links Marienbad to the drowned Welsh villages of his childhood: the reception clerk is preternaturally wrinkled as if through prolonged immersion in water, hotel workers move sluggishly, as if under water, and, listening to the rain falling, Austerlitz feels his mind "becoming gradually submerged" (*A*, 297). The restorative associations of Marienbad are undermined by reference to the "dark sea" (*A*, 298), and to the "insidious illness" that Austerlitz imagines to be infecting all guests. A tin of broken glass outside his hotel room evokes the *Kristallnacht* pogrom of November 9, 1938, and binds Austerlitz's quest for origins to the Holocaust as the paradigmatic "negative myth of origin."[55] The "drowned" village of Marienbad is the externalization of Austerlitz's submerged, inaccessible memories, and the trauma that has made him unable to breach the defensive barriers of memory.

Austerlitz's experience at Marienbad is haunted by awareness of the composer, Schumann, whose failed attempt to drown himself in "the icy waters of the Rhine" (*A*, 301) gestures to Austerlitz's own submerged origins. Indeed, his companion Marie recounts to him the story of

53  Levi, *The Drowned and the Saved.*
54  See Zadoff, *Next Year in Marienbad.*
55  Margalit and Motzkin, "The Uniqueness of the Holocaust," 65–83.

Schumann's madness and incarceration as a cautionary tale that compares Austerlitz's repressed mental state to the deranged condition that led to Schumann's attempted drowning. While the simile through which Marie likens Austerlitz's psychic repression to "a pool of frozen water," links his mental torment to Schumann's suicide attempt (*A*, 303), it is a reminder also of the Nazi hypothermia experiments on Jewish and other concentration camp inmates, connecting the suffering of Schumann and Austerlitz with theirs in a universalizing perspective of pain.[56] Imagining the incarceration of "poor Schumann in his Bad Godesberg cell" (*A*, 301), Austerlitz recalls a decaying dovecote at the nearby country estate of Königswart, the two images related by the wretchedness they represent:

> The floor inside was covered with pigeon droppings compressed under their own weight . . . a hard, desiccated mass on which lay the bodies of some of the birds who had fallen from their niches, mortally sick, while their companions, surviving in a kind of senile dementia, cooed at one another in the darkness under the roof, and a few downy feathers, spinning round in a little whirlwind, slowly sank through the air (*A*, 302).

Pigeons, in *Austerlitz*, are an ambiguous symbol of the possibility of homecoming, but also its failure: in Austerlitz's badminton games with Gerald at Andromeda Lodge, the feathered shuttlecocks follow an infallible trajectory of return, "a streak of white drawn through the evening hour" (*A*, 158), that Gerald mimics in his Cessna flights. Gerald's failure to return from one of his flights, and the dead pigeons in the decayed dovecote of Königswart, signify Austerlitz's own intractable failure to return to his origins.

An uncanny troupe of figures appears at the spa resort, shortly after Austerlitz, unable to accept the redemptive love offered by Marie de Verneuil, breaks off his relationship with her. Following his rejection of Marie, Austerlitz remembers

> . . . a little company of ten or a dozen small people [who] emerged from the dark as if out of nowhere, at a place where white mist was already rising from the ground, and crossed our path. They were the sort of visitors sent to the spa because of their failing health by some Czech enterprise or other, or perhaps they came from one of the neighboring Socialist countries. They were strikingly short, almost dwarfish figures, slightly bent, moving along in single file, and each of them held one of those pitiful plastic mugs from which the water of the springs was drunk in Marianske Lazne at the time. I

56 Berger, "Nazi Science."

also remember, added Austerlitz, that without exception they wore raincoats of thin blue-grey Perlon . . . To this day I can sometimes hear the dry rustling with which, as suddenly as they had appeared on one side of the path, they vanished again on the other (*A*, 305).

The ghostly troupe of dwarfish figures recalls Austerlitz's haunting childhood memories of the wandering Welsh dead and drowned villages, and of his own nascent awareness of a "submerged" reality: "All the years I spent at the Manse in Bala I never shook off the feeling that something obvious, very manifest in itself was hidden from me" (*A*, 76). The dwarflike creatures are ambiguous emblems of misfortune, distortion, and foreboding, metaphorical of Austerlitz's psychic deformation that issues from the repression of memory. Emerging "as if out of nowhere," their poverty implied by the "pitiful plastic mugs" they hold, the phantasmal figures are allegorical of Austerlitz's ontological destitution, and manifestations of his sense that "all my life had been a constant process of obliteration" (*A*, 174). Their individuality effaced by the "white mist rising from the ground," and by the uniformity of their identical raincoats, the hunched figures recall Primo Levi's description of the "drowned" of Auschwitz, who "form the backbone of the camp, an anonymous mass, continually renewed and always identical, of non-men who march in silence."[57] Dispossessed of his origins, Austerlitz is a "non-man," who imagines himself to be "submerged in that dark water," and whose psychic paralysis reflects the imperviousness of the dead.

The "dry, rustling sound" created by the Perlon raincoats worn by the dwarfish figures conjures Odradek, Kafka's mysterious creature, whose laugh is described as "the kind of laughter that has no lungs behind it. It sounds rather like the rustling of fallen leaves."[58] A combination of wood, metal, and thread, its star-shape relates it to the stellate objects that function as emblems of Jewishness in Sebald's narrative prose.[59] To Benjamin, Odradek is "the form things assume in oblivion."[60] To Adorno, Odradek signifies "bare life," the configuration things take when they have no clear purpose, "a sign of distortion but also of the . . . reconciliation of the organic and inorganic, of overcoming death."[61] Odradek is "a creature of the intermediate, the in-between, and the threshold"; Austerlitz's

---

57 Levi, *The Drowned and the Saved*, 90.

58 Kafka, "The Cares of a Family Man."

59 These include the "white furry stars" of the hoya plant in Luisa Lanzberg's memoirs (*TE*, 196), the "star-shaped bastion" of Breendonk (*A*, 25), and the octafoil design of the mosaic floor of Austerlitz's childhood home in Prague (*A*, 213).

60 Benjamin, *Selected Writings* 2, 811.

61 Benjamin and Adorno, *The Complete Correspondence 1928–1940*, 69.

foothold is similarly provisional.[62] The image of the creature, "always rolling down the stairs, with ends of thread trailing after," offers a vision of distortion and survival, and posits a view of Austerlitz as a "broken" remnant, unable to restore the threads that might connect him to his origins and make him whole again.[63]

## Austerlitz's Nomadic Jewish Origins

After his traumatic encounter with the past at Terezin and Marienbad, and his lengthy incarceration in a mental hospital following a breakdown, Austerlitz wanders through the half-deserted area between the tracks of the *Gare d'Austerlitz* and the *Quai d'Austerlitz,* where he comes upon the tent of the Bastiani Travelling Circus in one of the "empty spaces not far from the station itself," suggesting the void of his origins that Austerlitz seeks to fill in. The circus tent, the troupe of musicians in Oriental clothing, the exotic instruments on which they performed, and their music that seemed to him to come from "somewhere very distant, from the east . . . from the Caucasus or Turkey," stir in Austerlitz an incomprehensible and profound reaction: "I still do not understand . . . what was happening within me as I listened to this extraordinarily foreign nocturnal music conjured out of the air . . . nor could I have said at the time whether my heart was contracting in pain or expanding with happiness for the first time in my life" (*A*, 383). Austerlitz's profound engagement with the music of the circus troupe suggests his instinctive identification with an Orientalized, nomadic identity. Sebald's tendency to depict Jewish characters as intuitively susceptible to visions and to exotic sounds that conjure an atavistic Jewish identity reflects a troubling view of the Jew as inherently foreign to Europe, and evokes the exclusionary perception of the Jews as "restless wandering Bedouins."[64] Implicit in this is the idea of the desert as the "place" of the Jews, a notion that is increasingly thematized on Austerlitz's forlorn path through the storage depots and train stations of Paris.

Built over the "rotting corpse" of confiscated Jewish possessions held in the Austerlitz-Tolbiac storage depot, the *Bibliothèque Nationale* embodies the failure of Cartesian rationality and Enlightenment notions of progress. Indeed, to Austerlitz, the grandiose building represents a negative dialectic that sees "the degree of complexity . . . and absolute perfection [of any project we design and develop], coincide with its chronic dysfunction and constitutional instability" (*A*, 392–93). Austerlitz reflects the idea, derived from Adorno and Horkheimer, that the Enlightenment

62   Levine, "Of Big Ears and Bondage," 211.
63   Kafka, "The Cares of a Family Man."
64   Sombart, *The Jews and Modern Capitalism.*

project was based on the dialectical relationship of progress to cruelty, and was fundamentally motivated by the desire to eliminate otherness. On his search for origins, the library signifies for Austerlitz the failure of archival research, noting that it "proved useless in my search for any traces of my father who had disappeared from Paris more than fifty years ago" (*A*, 393). A "hideous, outsize building," the library is an intimidating and disorientating space, inimical to human beings, and designed to alienate the reader. Sebald employs imagery of exile and dissolution to suggest the depletion of the present by the hidden, but contaminating past, evident in the "desolate no-man's-land" that must be crossed to reach the library, the birds that fall to their death in the "artificial pine grove," and the "pines from the Forêt de Bord transported to this place of banishment" (*A*, 391), imagery that evokes Austerlitz's own displacement from his origins.

Images conjuring a nomadic, Middle-Eastern identity—the "wandering tribe encamped here on their way through the Sahara or the Sinai desert," the "red Sinai hall" of the inner citadel of the library (*A*, 390), and the faint echoes of Jewish exile implicit in the allusions to Babylon— convey the notion that Austerlitz's true origins are to be found in Orientalized Jewish nomadism.[65] Sebald's figuring of Austerlitz as a Wandering Jew, whose rootlessness is innate and ineradicable, illustrates the paradox inherent in his empathetic writing about Jewish lives damaged by the Holocaust: in depicting the tragic futility of Austerlitz's search for origins in the archives, libraries, storage depots, and train stations of Europe, Sebald's elaborate and allusive figuration perpetuates the negative trope of the eternally wandering Jew.

### Origins, Heritage, and "Homecoming"

Austerlitz's account of his visit to the *Gare d'Austerlitz*, "the most mysterious of all the railway terminals of Paris" (*A*, 407), is haunted by thoughts of his father's fate: described as a "terminal space," the final episode in Austerlitz's quest for origins implies ends, and the foreclosing of hope. With its "labyrinthine underpasses," it hints at hidden terror in the form of the German occupation of Paris that precipitated Maximilian's flight and presumed death.[66] Iconography evoking transgression and punishment—"a scaffolding reminiscent of a gallows," rusty iron hooks, a roughly-assembled wooden platform, pigeon feathers, and disturbing

---

65    The lower storey of the library is likened to a "ziggurat," a Babylonian structure (*A*, 387). Following the fall of the First Temple in 586 BCE to Nebuchadnezzar, the Jews were exiled to Babylon.

66    According to Greek myth, the labyrinth of Crete was designed to contain the terrifying Minotaur, part-bull, part-man.

dark patches of an unidentified leakage—points to "an unexpiated crime" (*A*, 407), the persecution of the Jews that underlies Austerlitz's vain quest. Here, as elsewhere, the pigeon feathers signify Austerlitz's failure to return to origins. In these last moments of Austerlitz's textual presence, "two tiny figures . . . moving about on ropes, carrying out repair work, like black spiders in their web" (*A*, 407–8), suggest the hope of repairing the past, underscored by Austerlitz's intention of continuing his search for traces of his father and Marie de Verneuil. In a thoughtful exploration of the open-ended conclusion to *Austerlitz*, Zilcosky questions whether it holds the promise of "homecoming," understood as the possibility, for Austerlitz, the narrator, and the author, of achieving a recuperated self, or whether such a conclusion would indicate a turn to the melodramatic that Sebald strove to avoid. In the "lost-and-found" narrative structure of *Austerlitz*, Zilkosky detects the seeds of melodramatic "homecoming": "*Austerlitz* . . . exhibits melodramatic tendencies not present in Sebald's earlier works," but leaves the ethical question of representing the Holocaust as melodrama unanswered.[67] Analysis of Sebald's figuration suggests that the possibility of a potentially melodramatic, redemptive conclusion is thwarted by the sense of doom that attends Austerlitz's departure from the text: the workers carrying out the repair work at the *Gare d'Austerlitz* are precariously balanced; Austerlitz's wandering around the deserted station, "up flights of steps on one side and down on the other" evokes the eternal homelessness of Kafka's Hunter Gracchus (*A*, 406), and implies Austerlitz's own failure to "return to his origins." Austerlitz's hope of finding traces of his father in the Pyrenees is shadowed by the unstated parallel between Maximilian and Walter Benjamin, who, fleeing from the Germans, committed suicide at Portbou on the French-Spanish border in 1940. In a symbolic gesture that appears to foreshadow his own imminent death, Austerlitz gives the German narrator the keys to his home, enjoining him to study his legacy of photographs, "all that was left of his life" (*A*, 408).

In a gesture of identification that is at the same time an appropriation of Jewish heritage, the narrator receives the keys to Austerlitz's house and access to the adjoining Ashkenazi cemetery, investing him with guardianship of Jewish legacy. While Sebald sought to avoid the many overt instances of inappropriate identification to which he succumbed in *The Emigrants*, in establishing the German narrator of *Austerlitz* as the interlocutor of the Jewish victim, he established a relationship that validated his own, belated writing of Jewish lives, and positioned himself as a secondary witness, whose detached and skillful mediation of Jewish memory could be considered more truthful than the testimony of the witness generation, disfigured by trauma, amnesia, dissociation, and falsification.

67    Zilcosky, "Lost and Found," 697.

Sebald's desire for an alternative legacy is evident in the narrator's recounting of author Dan Jacobson's quest for his own Jewish heritage in the form of traces of his Lithuanian ancestors, and of discovering, at the German prison at Kaunas, that Jewish prisoners had carved their initials and birthdates, one of which matched Sebald's own, suggesting his metaphorical adoption of Jewish victimhood as an alternative "heritage."[68]

The dubious notion of handing over Jewish legacy for German safekeeping is expanded in Austerlitz's account of finding the Ashkenazy Jewish cemetery adjacent to his London home. Hidden "behind that wall, although he had never been able to see it from any of his windows" (*A*, 408), the scene allegorizes the question of origins and heritage, previously hidden from Austerlitz. The gate in the cemetery wall "stood open for the first time in all the years he had lived in Alderney Street (*A*, 409), suggesting his receptivity to the possibility of discovering himself. A plot where "the bright spring sun [shone] through the newly opened leaves" (*A*, 408–9), the Ashkenazy cemetery is an enchanted and peaceful space. But like the cemetery of Bad Kissingen in *The Emigrants*, it suggests the dispiriting notion that it is only in death that Jews find an enduring "*Heimat*." The "dwarf-like" caretaker and her oversized dog are magical figures in an experience likened to "entering a fairy tale which, like life itself, had grown older with the passing of time" (*A*, 409). With this homiletic phrase, Sebald appears to consign Austerlitz's story, and indeed, the story of European Jewry in the twentieth century, to the mystificatory realm of a "fairy tale." *Austerlitz* ends as it begins, with the absence of the protagonist, who, after acknowledging "I don't know what all this means" (*A*, 408), disappears from the text into obscurity.

### The Children of Israel's Camp in the Wilderness: Austerlitz's "Proper Place"

As a small child exiled in Wales, Austerlitz recalls feeling an instinctive affiliation with the stories in his Welsh children's bible, sensing that "some meaning relating to [himself] lay behind the Bible stories [he] was given to read in Sunday school from [his] sixth year onwards" (*A*, 76). His anxious identification with the fate of the baby Moses, given away to save his life, suggests a dim apprehension of his own fate as a *Kindertransport* child, while a Biblical illustration of the children of Israel's camp in the wilderness stirs feelings of recognition in him that "the desert of Sinai look[ed] just like the part of Wales where [he] grew up, with bare mountains crowding close together" (*A*, 77). As a displaced child, Austerlitz intuitively affiliates with the Israelites on their wandering in the Sinai

---

68    See Taberner, "German Nostalgia?" for an insightful exploration of the relative trajectories of narrator and Jewish subject in *Austerlitz*.

desert, and senses that his "proper place was among the figures populating the camp," and that "the children of Israel's camp in the wilderness was closer to [him] than life in Bala" (*A*, 77, 80). In this Biblical illustration, Austerlitz unconsciously confronts what he believes an anonymous power has preserved him from discovering, namely, the secret of his own origins.

At first glance, the illustration of the camp of the children of Israel in the wilderness conveys a vision of Jewish nomadism in a desert camp enclosed by stony mountains. Evoking the mountainous Sinai desert where Moses received the Ten Commandments, the bedrock of Judaism, the scene is endowed with messianic expectancy, recalling Rosenzweig's vision of the Jew as remnant, suspended between the originary site of exile at Sinai, and redemption at the end of history. It is a picture of nomadic Jewish existence in the desert, isolated by stony mountains, and severed "from men and soil alike," that Austerlitz identifies as his own.

Closer examination reveals a more sinister interpretation that links this scene to the eschatology of sin and guilt that underlies Austerlitz's story. With its ordered rows of identical huts signifying coercion and control, its stylized human forms, stony mountains incised by railway tracks, and at its centre, a parade ground on which a structure emits white smoke, the camp of the children of Israel that Austerlitz identifies as his "proper place" is allegorical of Auschwitz, the paradigm of suffering to which his own name fatalistically gestures. Austerlitz's confession that his "proper place" was among the tiny figures or "winzige Figuren" populating the camp (*A*, 85), points to his function as a trope for the nameless dead, and for annihilated Jewish existence after Auschwitz. The term "Figuren" was used by the SS to refer euphemistically to the corpses of *Muselmänner*, inmates dehumanized beyond the point of being considered worthy of dying, as Levi concurs, "One hesitates to call their death death."[69] For Giorgio Agamben,

> This—that the death of a human being can no longer be called death—is the particular horror that the Muselmann brings to the camp and that the camp brings to the world. But this means . . . and that is why Levi's phrase is terrible—that the SS were right to call the corpses *Figuren*. Where death cannot be called death, corpses cannot be called corpses.[70]

The woodcut illustrating the Israelite desert camp is a vision of Jewish exile as total and annihilating, reflecting Sebald's extreme pessimism in relation to the deformation of both Jewish and German consciousness by

---

69    Levi, *The Drowned and the Saved*, 90.
70    Agamben, *Remnants of Auschwitz*, 70.

102 ◆ The Wandering Jew in *Austerlitz*

the Holocaust. Peter Morgan observes: "Auschwitz becomes the literary symbol of the over-determination of Sebald's generation by the national past . . . [Sebald's] awareness of Auschwitz has become so overwhelming that there can be no moving beyond it."[71] While Austerlitz experiences an intuitive insight into his identity as a Jew, the resemblance of the camp to Auschwitz, and the connotations of the desert as a metaphor for absence, suggest that it is to death that he metaphorically belongs, confirming his radical homelessness in the postwar world.

Eric Santner offers an illuminating interpretation of Sebald's employment of the trope of Jewish wandering, evident in imagery of desert nomadism that illuminates various points in Austerlitz's life.[72] It is implicit in the depiction of the desert camp of the Israelites in a Welsh children's Bible perused by the young Austerlitz, and in Adela's instinctive acknowledgment of Austerlitz's Semitic identity when, on his visit to Andromeda Lodge, she points out to him an imaginary desert scene: "Do you see the fronds of the palm trees, do you see the caravan coming through the dunes over there?" (*A*, 158–59). Atavistic Jewish nomadism is implied in a postcard depicting "a camp of white tents in the Egyptian desert" (*A*, 166), sent by Austerlitz to the narrator.[73] Jewish nomadism is unstated in the scene from Leni Riefenstahl's Nazi propaganda film, *Triumph des Willens* (Triumph of the Will, 1935), described by Austerlitz's father Maximilian, who remembers "a city of white tents extending to the horizon . . . from which as day broke the Germans emerged singly, in couples, or in small groups, forming a silent procession and pressing ever closer together as they all went in the same direction, following, so it seemed, a higher bidding, on their way to the Promised Land at last after long years in the wilderness" (*A*, 239–40).[74] Drawing on Alain Badiou, Santner interprets Sebald's seemingly perverse appropriation of the symbols of Jewish wandering as a means of representing the "deception, swindle, simulation," intrinsic to Nazism: "When a radical break in a situation, under names borrowed from real truth-processes, convokes not the void, but the 'full' particularity or presumed substance of that situation, we are dealing with a *simulacrum of truth*."[75] Badiou sees in such forms of deception the evil of simulacrum and terror that appropriates the language of "truth-events" to consolidate a closed particularity that condemns those excluded from it to the status of animality.

71    Morgan, "The Sign of Saturn, 75, 92.
72    Santner, *On Creaturely Life*, 123–24.
73    In the context of Austerlitz's wandering in search of origins, the postcard of the tents in the desert functions as a *mise-en-abîme* of the narrative structure that traces his mobility.
74    Riefenstahl, dir., *Triumph des Willens*.
75    Badiou, Alain, *Ethics*, 73–74.

Santner's invocation of Badiou suggests that, beyond the evocation of a putatively innate Jewish identity, originating in the desert of Jewish exile, Sebald's iteration of the imagery of Jewish wandering illustrates the profoundly fraudulent nature of the Nazi regime that perversely used the symbols of Jewish exile, messianism, and redemption, to assert the veracity of the communitarian ideals from which Austerlitz is excluded.

In his last work of prose fiction, Sebald radicalized the Wandering Jew trope by depicting Austerlitz as dispossessed of origins, and consumed by the longing to discover who he really is, and from where he is exiled. Sebald's depiction of Austerlitz, a putatively European Jew, as responding instinctively to visions of desert nomadism, betrays a problematic view of Jewishness, that sees the Jew as "from elsewhere," unassimilable, and immutably other. Austerlitz personifies Sebald's inability to conceive of a future, or to imagine redemption. This can be traced to his context as a second-generation German, responsive to a postwar German imaginary described by Julia Hell: "While there is continuity in German culture between the apocalyptic thinking after World War II and the catastrophic visions so prominent after World War I, there is also a significant difference: after World War II the belief in redemption, or in the redemptive potential of violence and revolution, no longer exists."[76]

76    Hell, "The Angel's Enigmatic Eyes," 363.

# 3:  The Jew as Other

> *In the middle of this crowd, which had merged*
> *into a single living organism . . . he had felt like a*
> *foreign body about to be crushed and then excreted*
>
> *—Austerlitz*

ALIEN AND ISOLATED, Sebald's Jews manifest traits that derive from diverse perceptions of Jewish alterity. In *Vertigo*, the spectral presence of Malachio, and the philosophical-theological perspective he embodies, evoke the metaphysical Jew, and the Jew as an emblem of abstract rationality. For Henry Selwyn, Jewishness is a communitarian experience bound up with his early life in a Lithuanian *shtetl*, and concealed as a shameful secret in his assimilation to English culture. He is Georg Simmel's *Fremder*, the "familiar outsider," who comes and stays, positioned between near and far, the foreign and the known, conceived "not as an individual, but as a stranger of a specific type."[1] Henry Selwyn's affiliation with symbolic manifestations of Eastern landscape implies his Oriental origins that conflict with his appropriated English identity, and constitute him as a trope for unreconciled Jewish alterity. Paul Bereyter is the Jew in the context of catastrophe, for whom Jewishness is an identity imposed on him according to a notorious system of identification, a death-sentence that compels him to acknowledge his alien status in the land of his birth. The only figure whose name concedes his putatively cosmopolitan Jewishness, Cosmo Solomon embodies Holz's "Third" category of identity, a "non-identity" that, as a symbol of internationalism, threatens the concept of identity itself.[2] Cosmo is the Jew in the modern world, who violates notions of homogeneity, and does not fit the category of either native or foreigner, but, as his name implies, falls between the borders that separate different nations. Conflicted between fragile memories of a Benjaminian Berlin childhood, and the obliterating emptiness of a ruined postwar Germany, Michael Hamburger (*RS*) represents Hegel's dispossessed Jew, whose alienation renders him irreducibly other.

The homes of Sebald's Jewish figures reflect their outsiderliness: Henry Selwyn occupies a *faux* hermitage in his garden, Paul Bereyter's "continued absence from the town" implies the provisional nature of his

---

1    Dilger and Wössner, "Georg Simmels Exkurs," 14.
2    Holz, "Die Paradoxie der Normalisierung."

home in the village of S. Aurach's studio near the Manchester docklands is figured as a crepuscular space, in which dust, a gas cooker, and "the grey velvety sinter left when matter dissolved, little by little, into nothingness," gesture towards the Holocaust (*TE*, 161), the trauma at the heart of his self-exclusion.

## The Jew as the "Essential 'Other'"

In his exploration of the Jew as the "essential 'Other'" in history, Henri Zukier observes that "the Jew has become the most universal and most intimate outsider in the Western mind, the consummate carrier of difference."[3] Owing to the medieval association of the Jew with the idea of exclusion, "the Jew remains forever in the mind of the West the most readily available target for exclusion, the most essential outsider of society."[4] As history's paradigmatic other, the Jew occupied the position of "familiar Outsider," a known, yet threatening figure, a figment of society's imagination, the other against whom the dominant group could measure its foundational values, and the stranger who enabled the establishment of a binary worldview that distinguished between "us" and "them." The doctrinal universalism of the Christian Church contained within it a new category of exclusion: defined as not belonging to the universal human category promoted by the Medieval Church, the Jews were excluded from the category of humanity itself. This is evident in Kant's "elimination" of the Jews from the perfect body politic, Hegel's extrusion of the Jews from history, Fichte's annihilatory fantasy of decapitating all Jews, and Heidegger's expulsion of the Jew from Being. Reflecting on the afterlife of the Jew as the excluded outsider, Zukier observes with irony: "The Jew became the familiar Outsider of Western society, ever ready to be effortlessly picked off the historical-cultural shelves in times of need."[5]

In the history of the Jewish outsider, it is the heteronomy of the Jew, and the refusal of the Jew to be subsumed in Christianity, that gives the trope its enduring power. Sebald valorized Jewish heteronomy as a challenge to the homogenizing impulse he saw as intrinsic to the bourgeois mentality. His narrative prose chronicles the conflicts and failure of Jewish assimilation, and the erosion of Jewish lives, unsustained by what he saw as the "wholeness" of traditional Judaism, lived with an awareness of its own particularity within the broader social world. Sebald's privileging of the figural narrative mode has given rise to Jewish figures who embody a multiplicity of traits that perpetuate negative perceptions of the Jew.

3    Zukier, "The Essential 'Other,'" 1120.
4    Zukier, "The Essential 'Other,'" 1151.
5    Zukier, "The Essential 'Other,'" 1148.

## Historical Background to the Jew as Other

In "Generation and the Ground of Jewish Identity," Daniel and Jonathan Boyarin examine the question of Jewish otherness articulated in the letters of St Paul.[6] Paul's writing reveals a shift towards a homogenizing approach to the Jews, who replace pagans as prime exemplars of intolerable difference. This is evident in efforts to universalize the Torah, and to break the particularism of the Jewish religion: "There is neither Jew nor Greek . . . For you are all one in Christ Jesus . . . If you belong to Christ . . . then you are Abraham's offspring, heirs according to the promise" (Galatians 3: 26–29). According to Pauline doctrine, baptism replaces a literal genealogy with an allegorical one that effaces all differences, "for in the Spirit such marks do not exist" (Romans 2: 27). Indeed, the Pauline doctrine of Christianity is marked by a compulsion towards sameness, and a view of Jewish identity as "the very sign of discord and disorder in the Christian polity."[7] In the contemporary philosophical writing of Alain Badiou and Slavoj Žižek, Jayne Svenungsson finds the re-emergence of Pauline universality that excludes all particularity, personified in the rhetorical use of "Jews" and "Judaism" to illustrate a negative construction of particularity. For both philosophers, only Jews who have abjured their Judaism, such as Spinoza, Marx, and Trotsky, are identified with the more universalist element in Judaism, the "rootless and universal cosmopolitanism indifferent to all particular ethnic forms."[8]

The drive to sameness is intensified in Luther's approach to the Jews. For Luther, Jewish alterity was tainted by the perception of Jews as alien, deceitful killers of Christ. Luther Germanized traditional hostility to the Jews, replacing the suffering of Jesus at the hands of the Jews with that of the German people: "What shall we do with this rejected and condemned people? Since they live among us we dare not tolerate their conduct . . . we must practise sharp mercy to see whether we might save at least a few from the glowing flames."[9] Eradication of Jewish heteronomy becomes fundamental to Luther's hate-filled proposals: "First, to set fire to their synagogues or schools and to bury with dirt whatever will not burn" . . . advising that "their homes also be razed and destroyed . . . and all their prayer books and Talmudic writings . . . be taken away from them."[10] For Luther, the "openness" of Jewish scriptural interpretation threatened the single and unquestionable truth of his reformed Christianity, and contributed to his metaphorical expulsion of the Jews from the German world.

6    St. Paul the Apostle, known as Saul of Tarsus, c. 4 BCE–c. 62–64 CE, one of the first Christian leaders.
7    Boyarin, "Generation," 694.
8    Svenungsson, "Enlightened Prejudices," 8.
9    Luther, *On the Jews and Their Lies*, 48.
10    Luther, *On the Jews and Their Lies*, 63, 64.

In his exploration of the philosophy of German Idealism, and its relation to social and philosophical manifestations of anti-Semitism, Michael Mack raises an issue that has implications for reading Sebald's troping of the Jew. Sebald's perpetuation of negative perceptions of Jewish alterity resonates with a philosophical substrate that includes German Idealism, and its later manifestation in the writing of Heidegger, among others. In the philosophy of German Idealism, Mack observes the interrelation between Kant and Hegel's anti-Semitic fantasies, and the attribution to the Jew of injurious characteristics and conduct that contradict the rationalism they are held to represent. In the writing of Kant, Mack sees the characterization of the Jew as the opposite of reason's purity: "They [the Jews] embodied the impurity of empirical reality, of 'matter.'" Mack identifies in the philosophical reflections of Kant and Hegel a vision of the Jews as representing "this earthly remainder of incompleteness, of imperfection . . . they embody all that which hinders the construction of a perfect body politic in the here and now . . . They come to embody the worldly, which resists an immanent and imminent transformation into the other-worldly."[11] Mack's hermeneutic reading of Kant, Hegel, and Wagner exposes the relation of the "hidden" metaphysical anti-Semitism of German Idealism and its injurious function as part of the broader public entity: drawing on Berel Lang, he identifies in Nazi assertions of Jewish alterity a totalization of the universalism promoted in the writing of Kant and Hegel, that envisaged the exclusion of the Jew on the grounds of irreconcilable difference.

To Kant, the Jews were "the Palestinians living among us," a statement that implied that the Jews had no place in Europe, and should be expelled from the German body politic.[12] Perceiving Jews as "a nation of cheaters," orientated towards the goods of the world, and corrupting of the German body politic, Kant recommended the *Absterben* (dying away) or "euthanasia" of Jewishness, conceived as "the leaving behind of all ancient regulatory teachings [to follow] the religion of Jesus . . . there being only one shepherd and one flock."[13] Intrinsic to Kant's view of Jewish heteronomy is the immutability of "Jewish essence," based on the unalterable tie between the Jews and their God. Articulated in *Religion within the Boundaries of Mere Reason*, Kant's notion of Jewish immutability was an attempt to erase Christianity's Jewish origins, and to make renunciation of heteronomy the moral basis of his body politic.[14]

For Hegel, the figure of Abraham embodied Jewish heteronomy in the form of relentless opposition to the world:

11    Mack, *German Idealism and the Jew*, 3–5.
12    Kant, *Anthropology*, 100.
13    Kant, *The Conflict of the Faculties*, 248.
14    Kant, *Religion within the Boundaries*.

108 ♦ THE JEW AS OTHER

> Abraham left a fatherland in his father's company. Now, in the plains of Mesopotamia, he tore himself free altogether from his family as well, in order to be wholly self-subsistent . . . The first act which made Abraham the progenitor of a nation is a disseverance which snaps the bonds of communal life and love . . . Among men he always was and remained a foreigner . . . The whole world Abraham regarded as simply his opposite . . .[15]

Hegel saw Judaism, immutable and heteronomous, as that which deviates from an idealist account of the world. The antithesis of transcendental autonomy, to Hegel, the Jews were trapped in the immediacy of being and excluded from history: "They stand before the portal of salvation . . . but refuse to go through it . . . Therefore, they will be locked out of the gates of salvation forever. In other words, they will no longer have a history."[16] Prohibited, by God's injunction, from the autonomy implicit in ownership, the dispossessed Jew is excluded from Hegel's ideal of homogenous society. Kant and Hegel underpinned their universal principles with negative stereotypes about Jews and Jewishness, among which is the enduring perception of the Jew as foreign and alienated, "a stranger on earth, a stranger to the soil, and to man alike."[17]

The nineteenth century witnessed a change from theologically determined Jewish alterity, to a biological vision of Jewish otherness that reinforced the notion of Jewishness as ineradicable, and Jewish assimilation as impossible: "Jews will never become true Germans . . . The more they try to change, the more they reveal themselves as fundamentally defective . . . Jews see and represent the world differently from Germans . . . No healthy assimilation is possible . . ."[18] For Ernst Reventlow, the Jews "remain an alien and hostile element amid such a nation as the Germans."[19] Richard Wagner identified the otherness of the Jews as manifest in immutable adherence to Jewish law: "But the Jew has stood quite apart from this community [of European nations], alone with his Jehovah in a dispersed and barren stock, incapable of real evolution."[20] In his opera cycle, *The Ring of the Nibelungen*, Jewish heteronomy is allegorized in the opposition between the autonomy of Siegfried and the objectionable otherness of Alberich and the Nibelungen: for Siegfried, the ring is a symbol of transcendental freedom, which he values more than his own life; for Alberich, the value of the ring is purely material, and he will not sacrifice his life for it.

15  Hegel, "*The Spirit of Christianity*," 185.
16  Hegel, *Phenomenology of Spirit*, 248.
17  Hegel, "The Spirit of Christianity," 186.
18  Gilman, *Kafka, the Jewish Patient*, 13.
19  Reventlow, "Was sind für uns die Juden?" 17.
20  Wagner, *Stories and Essays*, 27–28.

In *Sex and Character* (1903), a grandiose attempt to explain the modern world on the basis of the putative opposition between male and female principles, and the struggle between the Aryan and Jewish mind, Otto Weininger identified Jews with the abstract and corrosive features of modernity—the inauthenticity, materialism, and liminality that threatened social and economic stability.[21] Perceived as mobile and as adhering to a mechanistic and calculative worldview, to Weininger, the Jew posed the threat of *Weltherrschaft* or world-domination. This notion has its precursor in the writing of von Treitschke, in whose opinion the Jews are guilty of creating the materialism of the modern age, "that reduces all work to money and threatens to choke the pleasure our people have traditionally taken in their work."[22] Implicit in this is the view of the German economy as traditional and frugal, and Germans as rooted in *Heimat* and *Nation*. To Werner Sombart, the urban nature of the Jews could be traced to their exile, "a selective process whereby the best elements of Jewry . . . were forced to revive their nomad instincts and to gain their livelihood as townsmen."[23] For Sombart, "the modern city is nothing else but a great desert as far from the warmth of the earth as the desert is, and like it, forcing its inhabitants to become nomads."[24]

Heidegger's view of Jews as agents of modernity shares some of Weininger's attitudes. To Heidegger, the *Machenschaft* or manipulative power of the Jews, and their "subjection to the indiscriminately uniform, morally oblivious demands of *Technik*," constituted them as symbols of an impersonal urban modernity from which they were seen as profiting.[25] The picture of the Jew as the embodiment of cold rationality reemerges in Heidegger's criticism of the Jewish intellectual, evident in his observation that "the Jewification (*Verjudung*) of our culture and universities is certainly horrifying."[26] In his *Black Notebooks*, Heidegger goes further:

> The occasional increase in the power of Judaism is grounded in the fact that Western metaphysics . . . offered the point of attachment for the expansion of an otherwise empty rationality and calculative capacity, and thereby created for themselves an abode of the "spirit."[27]

Fundamental to Heidegger's antipathy to Jews was the belief that they embodied the abstract thought intrinsic to the corrosive spirit of

---

21 Weininger, *Sex and Character*, 281.
22 Von Treitschke, *Unsere Aussichten*.
23 Sombart, *The Jews and Modern Capitalism*, 230–31.
24 Sombart, *The Jews and Modern Capitalism*, 233.
25 Weston, "Thinking the Oblivion," 282.
26 Heidegger, "The Jewish Contamination," 1.
27 Heidegger, *Ponderings XII–XV*, 37.

modernity, and were responsible for modernity's degenerative tendencies. Richard Wolin notes: "Heidegger's defense of ontological rootedness betrayed a long-standing German Romantic prejudice concerning the unique spiritual confluence between the *Volk* (the people) on the one hand, and *Heimat, Boden, Landschaft* (homeland, earth, landscape) and 'Mother Earth' on the other."[28] To Wolin, this represented a distinctly German response to the dislocations of modernity, particularly, the risks of destabilization and loss of identity associated with the transition from *Gemeinschaft* (organic communities) to *Gesellschaft* (modern mass society).

In the *Black Notebooks* of 1941, Heidegger observed: "The question of the role of World Jewry is not a racial question, but a metaphysical question concerning the kind of humanity which, free from all attachments, can assume the world-historical 'task' of uprooting all beings from being."[29] For Heidegger, the Jew, ineffably threatening and irreducibly foreign, becomes a metaphysical entity, to be excluded from history and from Being. The metaphysical basis of Heidegger's rejection of the Jew is congruent with a philosophical tradition exemplified by Kant, who accepted Jews as citizens on condition of their "euthanasia," understood as abjuration of all traces of "the Jewish," and Hegel, for whom the dispossession of the Jews, prohibited from land-ownership, reduced them as citizens to the status of "nothing." A "worldless," duplicitous machinator, for whom uprootedness constitutes an ontological condition, Heidegger's metaphysical Jew is defined on the basis of traditional oppositions that reduce him to an abstraction. Extruded from history and existence, the fate of the Jew, relegated by Heidegger to a metaphysical essence, is realized in Auschwitz.

In the context of collective identity-building in the newly-democratic Germany, there is an awareness that perception of the Jew constitutes an indicator of the nation's moral standing. While attitudes to the Jew in postwar Germany remain ambivalent, Ulrike Dünkelsbühler notes the continuing desire among Germans, to define themselves in relation to the Jewish other:

> Der Signifikant 'jüdisch' tritt als Einbruch auf, als Bedrohung des Eigenen, als radikale Differenz, zu der er allererst gemacht werden muß und wird, denn nur durch die Setzung dieser Differenz — und in Absetzung zu ihr— kann sich die Identität des Eigenen kulturell, textuell und eben nicht nur theoretisch konstituieren, sondern damit ineins politisch *legitimieren*.[30]

28    Wolin, *Heidegger in Ruins*, 250.
29    Heidegger, *Überlegungen XII–XV.*
30    Dünkelsbühler, "Zur Irr-Rede gestellt," 146.

[As a signifier, "Jewishness" appears as an intrusion, as a threat to one's own, as a signifier of radical difference, and it is only through positing of this difference—and in erasing it, that self-identity can not only be culturally and textually constituted, but politically *legitimized.*]

In postwar German literature, the trope of the Jew as other undergoes further deformation as the externalization of repressed German guilt. Lars Rensmann reveals the negative troping of the Jew as the reminder of unwanted memory in relation to the Holocaust. His research reveals the re-emergence of negative stereotypes relating to Jews as covert manipulators of world power, emblems of modernity, and the abstract power of money, the antithesis of the autochthonous German, perceived as embedded in homeland and nationhood.[31] Eva Reichmann notes the perpetuation of Jewish stereotypes in postwar German and Austrian literature, including that of the Jew as the personification of abstract rationality, or "homo judaicus mentalis." In her analysis of the character of Professor Singer in Inge Merkel's *Das andere Gesicht* (*The Other Face*, 1982), she observes the depiction of the Jew as a "trockene Verstandesmensch," or dry intellectual.[32] Analysis of Sebald's narrative prose reveals that his Jewish figures resonate with the multiplicity of perceptions that, over centuries, have contributed to problematic notions of Jewish alterity.

## The Jew as Other in *Vertigo*, *The Emigrants*, and *The Rings of Saturn*

### Malachio, the Metaphysical Jew

"All'estero," the second story in *Vertigo*, sees the narrator aimlessly wandering the streets of Vienna. His thoughts are preoccupied with death, allegorized in a dream of "cross[ing] a wide stretch of water during the hours of my nocturnal absence. Before I opened my eyes, I could see myself descending the gangway of a large ferry . . ." (*V*, 37), a vision that suggests the mythical journey across the river Styx to the world of the Dead, and foreshadows the allegorization of death and resurrection that pervades this episode. From the windows of a Jewish Community center, the narrator hears children singing Christmas songs, a curiously ecumenical experience in the context of the nearby synagogue and kosher restaurant that signal Jewish heteronomy. Outside the Jewish center, the narrator becomes aware of his "tattered, and, as it seemed, ownerless shoes. Heaps of shoes and snow piled high" (*V*, 37), a Holocaust image

31  See Rensmann, *Demokratie und Judenbild.*
32  Reichmann, "Jüdische Figuren," 239.

112 ◆ THE JEW AS OTHER

that signifies his momentary identification with Jewish victimhood, and, like the coalescence of Jewishness, Christmas, and community, implies an inchoate longing to resurrect the lost German-Jewish relationship.

On the narrator's journey to Venice, images of destruction—"mounds of rubble and piles of stones" (*V*, 51)—recall Sebald's childhood memories of ruined postwar German cities, graphically described in "Air War and Literature." The narrator's conflation of the despoiled landscape with a Tiepolo painting of a plague-ravaged town, and St Thecla, interceding for its inhabitants, suggests his own yearning for release from the shame and guilt of belonging to a contaminated country. It is in the context of death and the longing for redemption that, on the eve of All Souls' Day, the German narrator of "All'estero" falls into a conversation with a Venetian named Malachio in a bar "on the Riva" of Venice, the liminality of the location suggesting the marginality of Malachio's identity as a metaphysical Jew, neither fully human, nor divine, bearer of the messianic message of redemption from exile.

Malachio's Jewishness is implied in his name, *mal'ach*, Hebrew for angel, and confirmed by his words of farewell, "*ci vediamo a Gerusalemme*" (see you in Jerusalem), the traditional Jewish Passover greeting that expresses hope of redemption from exile (*V*, 62). A manifestation of abstract intellectualism, he is the Jew as "Verstandesmensch" (intellectual), an astrophysicist, who sees the world *sub specie aeternitatis*, meditates on the aporetic notion of resurrection implicit in the Book of Ezekiel, and represents both the hope of redemption and a reminder of its impossibility, implied in the eternal futurity of the Jewish messianic dream of return. Malachio's reflections on Ezekiel's notion of resurrection do not find answers, but he "believed the questions were quite sufficient for him" (*V*, 62), a statement that implies the principle of hope Sebald derived from Bloch: "Wichtig ist am Messianismus allein, wie Ernst Bloch gezeigt hat, die Lebendigkeit des Prinzips Hoffnung." (The importance of Messianism, as Bloch demonstrated, lies solely in the hope implicit in it.)[33] An abstraction, an apparition, he is the metaphysical Jew, whose appearance is never described, and after their encounter, the narrator is unable to recall his facial features.[34] Metaphors of the mystical and other-worldly contribute to his auratic quality: Thomas Mann's profoundly symbolic novella, "Der Tod in Venedig" ("Death in Venice," 1912) haunts Sebald's story, and allusion to the "celestial city" evokes Jerusalem and the dream of return that underlies the Jewish messianic message implicit in Malachio's farewell.

In a symbolic gesture, Malachio ferries the German narrator out of the "real" world of the city to the allegorical "Underworld" of the Canale

33 Sebald, "Das Gesetz der Schande," 99.
34 Di Cesare, *Heidegger and the Jews*, 169.

della Giudecca (Canal of the Jews), where, on a "nameless island," he confronts him with a vision of Jewish death.[35] The *Inceneritore Communale* (communal incinerator), a "silent shell" with its "white pall of smoke" and "fires that never go out," calls to mind the ceaseless working of the crematoria of Auschwitz (*V*, 61); despite its inclusive name, it represents the unique otherness of Jewish genocide, through which "the miracle of life born of carbon, [goes] up in flames" (*V*, 61). Sebald's figural writing distances and mystifies Jewish suffering: the calamity of Jewish erasure is implied as inexpressible—"without a word, my guide pointed out the Inceneritore Communale," a strategy of silence that reflects Sebald's oblique approach to representing the Holocaust. The narrator's confrontation with Jewish death occurs in a timeless void—"it seemed to me that a long time passed"—that dehistoricizes Jewish suffering as an eternal phenomenon. On the Canal of the Jews, the vast Stucky flour mill, "built from millions of bricks," recalls the faceless dead of Auschwitz, its "blind windows" allegorical of absence, and its likeness to a bone mill a crude reminder of human extermination.[36] Implied to be a charnel house through the narrator's arch question as to whether "it was really only grain that was milled in there" (*V*, 61), the flour mill is aestheticized in a captivating vision of "the moon [that] came out from behind the clouds and struck a gleam from the golden mosaic" (*V*, 62), an image of transcendence that mitigates the unease the mill evokes.

With its floating cemetery islands and ancient, decaying buildings, Venice is a city characterized by the nearness of death, where even a flour mill is tainted by intimations of genocide, and the golden mosaic emblem of the Stucky flour mill conceals violence and death. Depicting a monumental reaper woman and sickle, the mosaic recalls a painting by Nazi propaganda artist Josef Hengge, reference to whom recurs in the narrator's childhood memory of a Hengge mural, depicting a "fearful battle scene, [that GS] frightened me so that whenever I passed, I had to avert my eyes" (*V*, "Il ritornio in patria," 207). The Nazi provenance of the emblem suggests the continuity of the contaminating past in the present, the sickle, with its implications of "cutting," metaphorical of the violent "severance" of Jewish others from Germany.

The sickle symbolizes also the abrupt ending of the episode, denoting rupture from the allegorical, and return to the quotidian: "The boat docked. We shook hands. I stepped ashore" (*V*, 62). After his encounter with Malachio, the narrator remains troubled by thoughts of redemption, recollecting, on All Saints' Morning, "the two days of

35    "Giudecca" is a probable corruption of the Latin "Judaica" (Jewish).
36    The image of the "blinde Fenster" (blind windows) occurs in Peter Handke's novel *Langsame Heimkehr* (1979), in which it functions as a metaphor for that which was once there.

114 ♦ THE JEW AS OTHER

remembrance devoted to the suffering of the sainted martyrs and poor unredeemed souls" with whom he identifies, imagining himself to have died, and to be "already interred or laid out for burial" (*V*, 64–65). In a mythologizing fantasy, he imagines "crossing the grey lagoon to the island of the departed" (*V*, 65), an allusion to the legendary "Islands of the Blessed" where Greek heroes were laid to rest. Malachio returns to the consciousness of the narrator, who ponders the meaning of Malachio's messianic words, but is unable to comprehend their redemptive message. In this allegory of the post-Holocaust German-Jewish relationship, the German narrator's encounter with Malachio, the metaphysical Jewish other, is an obscure reminder of the impossibility of redemption from shame and guilt.

**The Jew as the Orientalized Other**

Sebald posits Jewish alterity as innate and ineradicable, inhibiting Jewish characters from maintaining an assimilated life. His Jewish figures intuitively identify with allegorical reminders of a nomadic, "Eastern" Jewish identity, an echo of Kant's designation of the Jews as "the Palestinians among us": for Henry Selwyn, the slide show of his journey to Crete is a reminder of his putatively Oriental origins; Cosmo Solomon, an assimilated American Jew, is overcome by a filmic reminder of his supposed nomadic Jewish origins, and imagines returning to them by following the mirage of a desert caravan; on his daily visit to the Wadi Halfa café, Max Aurach takes up a position in front of a frieze depicting a desert scene from which he appears to emerge, and in which he seems to belong.

Henry Selwyn's affiliation with the symbolic landscape of the East, manifest in the slideshow of his journey with Edwin Elliott to Crete, implies his hidden Oriental origins, and evokes the stereotypical perception of the Jew as "Eastern" and other. The concealed secret of Henry's putatively Oriental identity is implicit in the "veiled" Cretan landscape, and the "dust in the room . . . [that GS] glittered and danced in the beam of light by way of a prelude to the pictures themselves" (*TE*, 15). Henry Selwyn and his friend Edwin's intense engagement with the slideshow— "for both of them this return of their past selves was an occasion for some emotion" (*TE*, 17)—suggests an affinity with the "East"; ekphrastic description of the slides depicting Henry's journey to Crete, reflects an Orientalizing gaze that sees the Cretan landscape as feminized and "supine" from a distanced Western perspective (*TE*, 17), "veiled in bright green as it lay before us" (*TE*, 15).[37] The conflation of the Cretan landscape with Kaspar Hauser's dream of the Caucasus, depicted in Herzog's

---

37    The Orientalizing gaze can be seen in Novalis's depiction of the seductive Zulima, encountered by the protagonist in Novalis, *Heinrich von Ofterdingen*, 57–60.

film as having a "distinctly Indian look to it, with pagoda-like towers and temples with strange triangular facades . . . follies, in a pulsing dazzle of light . . ." (*TE*, 17–18), links this mysterious landscape to Henry Selwyn's life in his garden folly, hinting at the Oriental exoticism implicit in his Jewish otherness.[38] Indeed, Richard Gray observes that "it is tempting to read this insistence on the 'Oriental' as an allusion to Selwyn's own Jewish, in the metaphorical sense 'Oriental,' origins."[39]

Neither Oriental, nor able to sustain an appropriated English identity, Henry Selwyn is an emblem of unreconciled Jewish alterity. A recluse and a "dweller in the garden," Henry's exiled existence in his hermitage increasingly resembles an "afterlife," in which the boundaries of the quotidian fall away, evident in the entropy of his untended garden with its neglected tennis court, "tumble-down Victorian greenhouses, and overgrown espaliers . . ." (*TE*, 7). His withdrawal into nature resembles a living death, evoking Karl Gutzkow's image of the Jew as a living corpse, "a dead man who has not yet died."[40]

Indeed, Henry Selwyn undergoes several "deaths": by changing his name and thus erasing his Jewish identity in an act of renunciation he describes as a "second confirmation" (*TE*, 20), and through his disengagement from life after the death of his lover, Naegeli. Through such acts, he is transformed into the Jew as Uncanny Other, occupying an uncertain border between life and death, returning as a phantom to haunt the German narrator's consciousness. Henry's "second confirmation" is an ironic reference to the *Bar-Mitzvah* ceremony through which a thirteen-year-old Jewish boy is accepted as a man in the Jewish community. Henry Selwyn abandons his original Lithuanian name as evidence of his Jewish origins in order to assimilate, or to pass as "invisible" in English society.[41] In a metaphorical sense, Henry Selwyn kills his Jewish identity, which becomes a guilty secret that haunts him increasingly with age. Henry Selwyn's original family name, "Seweryn," evokes the first name of nineteenth-century Polish Romantic poet, Seweryn Goszczynski (1801–1876), who participated in the "Great Polish Emigration" that followed the failure of the November uprising of 1830–31. His name, and his nationalistic poetry, foreshadow the themes of emigration, displacement, and exile in Henry Selwyn's life. Viewed from a Rosenzweigian perspective, Henry Selwyn's relinquishment of his name cuts him off from his

38    Herzog, "Jeder für sich und Gott gegen alle."

39    Gray, *Ghostwriting*, 185.

40    Gutzkow, "Plan for an Ahasverus," 157.

41    Fermaglich, "Names, Name-changing," 34–57. Fermaglich explores name-changing among Jewish emigrants to the US between 1917 and 1942, noting the desire for invisibility as a significant motivation for such a step. Fermaglich's research indicates the potentially negative effects of Jewish name-changing, including self-hatred and guilt.

116 ♦ THE JEW AS OTHER

own singularity—"that which has a name of its own can no longer be a thing, no longer everyman's affair"—and from the history he shares with his fellow Jews: "Through his surname, man belongs to the past; all that coerces him is contained in that name. Fate has a hold on him and his surname is the gate by which fate enters."[42]

Henry Selwyn's second "death" occurs after Naegeli's disappearance in the Alps. As recounted by Henry to the narrator, his relationship with Naegeli has the quality of an Alpine idyll, charged with the transcendence associated with the mountains of German Romanticism.[43] Henry Selwyn's otherness is emphasized through the polarity Sebald established between Henry and his Swiss-German lover and guide, Naegeli: Henry is the Jewish other, the cerebral *Verstandesmensch*, who places great emphasis on his academic achievements; by comparison, Naegeli represents the hard physicality implied in his name (*Nägel*, or nails), an echo of Klaus Theweleit's "Stahlgestalt," the figure of steel intrinsic to the fascist fantasy of the hard male body.[44] Naegeli embodies the "Alpine sublime," associated with the cosmic, the gigantic, and the extreme. Undaunted by the terrors of nature, in death he becomes one with the snow and ice. After Naegeli's disappearance, Henry Selwyn relinquishes the trappings of his assimilated life and chooses the eternal exile of death. His vision of "being buried under the snow and ice" (*TE*, 15) is a fantasy of reunion with Naegeli in a form of *Liebestod* (love-in-death) that evokes Wagner's opera *Tristan* (1859), and with that, the substrate of negative perceptions of Jews and Jewishness that characterizes Wagner's literary and musical works, and the philosophical reflections of nineteenth-century German philosophers. United in a consummation of love-in-death, the relationship between Henry Selwyn and Naegeli reflects Sebald's wishful desire to "make good" the once productive German-Jewish relationship. But, like Castorp's dream of love and death in Mann's novel of 1924, *Der Zauberberg* (The Magic Mountain), Henry Selwyn's fantasy of *Liebestod* leads to no lasting insight and offers no enduring solace or enlightenment. Overwhelmed with sorrow at the magnitude of his losses, unable to "bury" his past or conceive of a future, Henry Selwyn takes his own life.

### The Assimilated Jew in the Context of Catastrophe

Born into an assimilated German-Jewish family, Paul Bereyter is a fractional Jew who believes himself to be "German to the marrow" (*TE*, 57).

---

42    Rosenzweig, *Star of Redemption*, 186–87; *Understanding the Sick and the Healthy*, 82.
43    Denham, "W. G. Sebald's Magic Mountains," 321.
44    See Theweleit, *Männerphantasien*.

Paul is a "Catastrophe Jew," on whom the Nuremberg Laws impose the sentence of Jewishness, according to which he is "firmly promised to death, already in the midst of life."[45] Explaining the ambiguity of Paul's position as a three-quarter Aryan, rejected as a Jew, and utilized in the *Wehrmacht* by the German *Heimat* to which he returns after the war, Sebald observed:

> So perhaps he did return to Germany because simply this was the place he knew best . . . And I also think . . . he was very much in the German mold . . . an idealist, coming out of the *Wandervogel* movement, as it were, a little bit like the young Wittgenstein when he went to upper Austria to teach the peasant children there, full of idealism, educational zeal, and so on. And this return to Germany in that sense is not altogether surprising.[46]

The Bereyter emporium symbolizes the apex of the Bereyter family's assimilation to middle-class German society; its fate is a metaphor for the immutability of Jewish alterity, and the failure of the putative German-Jewish symbiosis. The perception of the Jew as other and unassimilable is manifest in Paul's story by the "perfidious" way in which his mother was excluded from entering a coffee shop in their village, by the "meanness and treachery that a family like the Bereyters were exposed to in a miserable hole such as S." (*TE*, 50), by Paul's exclusion from teaching in Germany, and, with increasing violence, by the pogrom against the centuries-old Jewish population of Gunzenhausen, and the deportation of his fiancée to her death. Germany's expulsion of its Jewish others is attributed to the "logic of the whole wretched sequence of events" (*TE*, 50), a resignatory observation that reflects the overarching metaphor of the train in Paul's story: clinging relentlessly to the tracks, it is an emblem for the inevitable destruction of the Jewish other, represented by Paul, and by the Bereyter emporium established by his father.

The emporium episode is prefaced by the history of Paul's family in Germany. Narrated by his companion Lucie Landau, it is a story of German-Jewish intermarriage and assimilation that sees the Bereyter family's rise from humble beginnings to bourgeois respectability. Stereotyped perceptions of Jewish alterity are implicit in the story of the Bereyters' assimilation, manifest in the strong commercial drive imputed to them, marking their ascendancy from junk shop to emporium, and the detailed account of Theo Bereyter's mercantile ambitions, displayed by "working his way up to the higher echelons," before opening an emporium "with capital saved partly from his earnings and partly borrowed" (*TE*,

---

45    Améry, *At the Mind's Limits*, 85.
46    Wachtel, "Ghost Hunter," 46.

## 118 ♦ THE JEW AS OTHER

51). The chronicle of the Bereyter family history is narrated in a factual mode, emphasizing precise details of age, years, and stages of professional advancement, implying the pragmatism of Paul's antecedents, the material reality of their ascent, the scale of their achievement, and the tragedy of its destruction. The reference to Nuremberg, where Paul's father had worked as an apprentice, and his mother as an actress, momentarily disturbs the detached narrative tone by foreshadowing the laws that would put an end to the Bereyter's assimilatory aspirations, and see them dispossessed and persecuted.

Paul's description of the Bereyter family emporium, mediated by Lucie Landau, is a sentimentally evoked *Gedächtnisort* or "sacralized island of memory" that resembles Pierre Nora's "lieu de mémoire" (place of memory), and symbolizes the vanished *Heimat* and lost "German-Jewish symbiosis" of Paul's imagination.[47] The social ascendance of Paul's family is symbolized by the establishment of the Bereyter emporium, in which the comprehensive store contents suggest a commitment to a Germanness that is both *völkisch* (folkish) and bourgeois. The episode posits the unspoken polarity of German and Jew: against the paradigm of German stability and tradition, the dimly outlined figure of Paul on his tricycle represents the itinerant, chimerical Jewish other. Cuckoo clocks, bales of loden cloth, and Gütermann's sewing thread suggest the German cultural tradition to which assimilating Jewish families like the Bereyters aspired. Carved in the Black Forest since the early eighteenth century, the cuckoo clocks are redolent of the *völkisch* artisanship perceived as harmonizing with the environment. With its traditional earthy green color, loden cloth is used for traditional *Tracht* worn in the Tyrol, and by Paul and his fiancée during their brief idyll together, depicted in black-framed photographs of the happy couple that constitute a *memento mori* (a reminder of the inevitability of death) for the lost German-Jewish symbiosis. Originating in the Middle Ages, the colorful Gütermann sewing threads, displayed behind glass windows like jewels, imply the inestimable value of German tradition. Paul's recollection of the "case that seemed especially magical to him, in which rolls of Gütermann's sewing thread were neatly arrayed . . . in every color of the rainbow" (*TE*, 52), conjures the fantasy of German-Jewish assimilation. The emporium attendants, in "waistcoats and sleeve bands," and Theo Bereyter himself, resplendent in frock coat, or pin-stripe suit and spats, represent the bourgeois status the Bereyters sought to attain. Reminders of the German countryside— the *Maiglöckchen* (lily of the valley) soap, the gleaming leather boots, and the whip stand—hint at a deeper yearning to belong, evinced in Paul's immersion in the land through hiking as a *Wandervogel*, and through

47   Nora, "Les lieux de mémoire."

excursions into nature that characterize his "Anschauungsunterricht" (object lessons).

Imagery connoting illusoriness and hesitation suggests the precariousness of the putative German-Jewish symbiosis: "The light in the emporium . . . was dim even on the brightest of days, and it must have seemed all the murkier to him as a child, Paul had said, as he moved on his tricycle, mostly on the lowest level, through the ravines between tables, boxes and counters" (*TE*, 51). The figuratively rich but ironic picture of the "seemingly endless dark rows of bolts of material" (*TE*, 51) suggests the hope intrinsic to the belief in the German-Jewish relationship as an infinite boon, darkened by a premonition of its tragic failure. Objects devoted to preservation and to halting inevitable decay, such as the mothballs, preserve jars, and galvanized watering cans, are rendered ironic by the catastrophic trajectory of Paul's life, and that of his family and their emporium, sold to an Aryan for a pitiful sum following the death of Paul's father after the Gunzenhausen pogrom. The juxtaposition of a photograph depicting the Bereyter family in their luxurious Dürkopp motorcar (*TE*, 53), with the account of the Gunzenhausen pogrom of 1934, indicates the tragic disjuncture between their assimilatory aspirations and the German response. Noting the one-sided nature of the German-Jewish "dialogue," Scholem observed ironically, "Where Germans ventured on a discussion with Jews . . . such a discussion was always based on the expressed or unexpressed self-denial of the Jews, on the progressive atomization of the Jews as a community in a state of dissolution . . ."[48] The death of Paul's father, attributed to anguish over the attacks on long-standing Jewish inhabitants of his hometown, and his burial in a remote part of the cemetery reserved for "suicides and people of no denomination" (*TE*, 53), symbolize the perception of immutable Jewish outsiderliness, and the vanity of the Jewish dream of assimilation.

### "People who Belonged in Both Camps"

The story of Paul Bereyter reveals Sebald's fascination with nuances of Jewishness. Discussing the complex identity of Paul Bereyter, designated a "three-quarter Aryan," Sebald observed: "Es gibt viele solche Schicksale, Leute, die weder in die eine noch in die andere Schuhschachtel gepaßt haben . . . Was bislang kaum gemacht worden ist in der Literatur, das sind diese Übergänge. Daß es Leute gibt, die in beide Lager gehört haben." (There are many such fates, of people destined not to fit into either shoebox . . . What has not yet been explored in literature are the transitions, people who belonged in both camps.)[49] Paul is figured as part of the

---

48    Scholem, "Against the Myth," 63.
49    Poltronieri, "Wie kriegen die Deutschen das auf die Reihe?" 142.

## 120 ♦ THE JEW AS OTHER

fabric of German life, yet extruded, "a German to the marrow," but fractionally Jewish, a victim, but also, as a soldier in the *Wehrmacht*, a perpetrator. On researching the prototype for Paul Bereyter, Sebald admitted: "Once you get hold of a thread you want to pull it out and you want to see, you know, what the colors of the pattern are."[50] Sebald's non-fiction reflects his interest in divided Austro- and German-Jewish figures, such as Peter Weiss, Ludwig Wittgenstein, and Jean Améry, from whom Sebald derived elements of Paul Bereyter's life and character. Peter Weiss, writer and artist, was half-Jewish, survived the war by fleeing to Sweden, and acknowledged his passive imbrication, as a German, in what he identified as the social and economic preconditions for genocide. Weiss's depiction of Jewish figures as conflations of perpetrator and victim prefigured Sebald's own hybrid characters, Ambros Adelwart and Paul Bereyter (*TE*).[51] Sebald valorized Weiss's identification of himself as both victim and perpetrator, noting that, to Weiss,

> . . . rulers and ruled, exploiters and exploited are in fact the same species, so that he, the potential victim, must also range himself with the perpetrators of the crime or at least their accomplices, and not just in a purely theoretical sense either. Weiss' willingness to take this heaviest of all moral obligations on himself raises his work far beyond all other literary attempts to "come to terms with the past," as the usual phrase runs.[52]

Material details of Paul's life are informed by the character and biography of Ludwig Wittgenstein: like Paul, Wittgenstein spent a period as an elementary school teacher in a remote village. Paul's love of the outdoors is modelled on Wittgenstein's love of nature, as is his hiking apparel, and the windcheater he habitually wore. The motif of Wittgenstein's windcheater aligns Paul's life and death with that of the philosopher: worn in his incarnation as a German *Wandervogel*, the jacket is emblematic of Paul's love of *Heimat*; its absence from the hall in which it had hung for forty years is metonymic of Paul's death, and it is implied that he wore it as a "shroud" when he committed suicide, aligning him with Wittgenstein's philosophical profundity, and imbuing his death with a deeper significance.

Sebald constructed the character of Paul to closely resemble the Austro-Jewish writer Jean Améry: both are fractional Jews for whom

---

50    Wachtel, "Ghost Hunter," 43.

51    In his play *Die Ermittlung* (The Investigation, 1965), Weiss depicted Jews as pitiless torturers, implicated in medical execution. In *Nacht mit Gästen* (Night with Guests, 1963), he gave stereotypically Jewish names, such as Rosenrot, Liebseel, and Gotthilf, to agents of cruelty.

52    Sebald, "The Remorse of the Heart," 190.

Jewishness was largely irrelevant, and for both men, Jewishness is an identity imposed on them by decree: "I am a Jew . . . I mean by that those realities and possibilities that are summoned up in the Auschwitz number."[53] In his essay, "On the Necessity and Impossibility of Being a Jew," Améry reflects on the condition of being "condemned" to Jewishness: "To be a Jew meant for me, from this moment on, to be a dead man on leave, someone to be murdered, who only by chance was not yet where he properly belonged."[54] As vestigial Jews, Améry and Paul Bereyter remain consumed by conflicted feelings of longing for, and repudiation of home. Améry's belief in *Heimat* as inalienable—"What do we have, if not our homeland?"—becomes, over time, acceptance that loss of *Heimat* implies loss of self: "I was a person, who could no longer say 'we' and who could therefore only out of habit, but not with any feeling, say 'I.'"[55] Paul's deep attachment to *Heimat*, like that of Améry, undergoes a transformation from perceiving *Heimat* as an idyll, to recognizing it as a *Trugbild* or illusion. This is reflected in the image of "the pine forests . . . black on the mountainsides . . . and the sky . . . so low and dark, one expected ink to run out of it any moment" (*TE*, 61), an ominous vision of German landscape that bars itself to affiliation, and gives this scene, from Paul's final visit to Germany, its proleptic power. Both men commit suicide when the burden of irreconcilable conflict in relation to *Heimat* becomes too great to bear, and for Améry and Paul, the place of suicide is symbolic: both choose to kill themselves "at home," Améry in Salzburg, and Paul Bereyter outside his hometown, allegorically enacting the notion that it is only in death that the Jew can be assimilated to *Heimat*.

Sebald's conflation of Paul with the characters and lives of Weiss, Wittgenstein, and Améry is misleading, and overlooks the fact that these conflicted, partially Jewish figures were passive victims of anti-Semitism; by contrast, Paul's stubborn refusal to acknowledge his extrusion as a Jew in Germany, to "correct his patchy knowledge of the past" (*TE*, 54), or to intervene when bad news reached him, amounts to a negation of his Jewishness, and of any affiliation with the plight of his fellow-Jews. While Weiss's consciousness of his own moral ambiguity is based on his belief that he had passively "absorbed" fascist ideas, Paul's actions—his service in the motorized artillery of the *Wehrmacht*, and his perverse return to Germany after the war—reflect indifference to the moral implications of war, and participation in the perpetration of evil. Paul's response to persecution reflects the unswerving loyalty to his German *Heimat* that engenders his students' perception of him as a "mechanical human made of tin and other metal parts" (*TE*, 35), emblematic of the trains that

53 Améry, "On the Necessity," 94.
54 Améry, "On the Necessity," 86.
55 Sebald, "Verlorenes Land," 139.

fascinate him with their relentless adherence to the tracks. Paul does not share Wittgenstein's self-scrutiny in relation to his Jewishness: as Monk points out, Wittgenstein "felt he was hiding something. He felt that he was allowing people to think of him as an aristocrat when in fact he was a Jew," suggesting deep ambivalence about his Jewishness.[56] Unlike Améry, whose conflicted feelings towards his former homeland precluded his return to Austria until shortly before the end of his life—"In a Wirtshaus, aus dem ma aussigschmissn worn ist, geht ma nimmer eini" (One never returns to an inn from which one has been thrown out)—Paul's return to Germany after the war is a self-serving manifestation of the wish for "Schlußstrich" and "Neuanfang" that characterized the postwar response of Germans, wishing to draw a line and begin afresh.[57] Améry's suicide followed years of introspection, analysis, and philosophical reflection on the meaning of *Heimat*, loss, identity, and human cruelty.

By associating Paul with historically conflicted Jewish figures of profound sensibility and self-awareness, Sebald's story of Paul Bereyter represents a distorted moral perspective. While Paul is undeniably sensitive to his own predicament, and indeed, seeks consolation in the thoughts of suicidal German-Jewish writers, he is portrayed as indifferent to the plight of others, and to the moral contradictions inherent in his ambiguous identity as a Jew, and as a willing participant in the *Wehrmacht*, a reordering of roles that deflects the idea that Germans bear sole responsibility for the genocide of the Jews.

## Ambros Adelwarth: The Suffering Jew as Other

Examination of the language employed to describe Ambros's torture at the Samaria sanatorium suggests that, in a troubling reevaluation of moral order, Sebald depicted Jews as Nazi perpetrators and Germans as Jewish victims. Holz ironically notes the ethically problematic nature of such a reversal:

> Die beste Lösung ist eine Täter-Opfer Umkehr, durch die der neue Deutschland seine Schuld vorwerfende Täter im vormaligen Opfer gefunden wird ... Die Täter-Opfer-Umkehr ermöglicht die Normalisierung der deutschen Nation, indem der Schuldvorwurf als "jüdische Tat" demaskiert wird.[58]

---

56   Monk, *Ludwig Wittgenstein*, 279.
57   Améry, *Örtlichkeiten*, 89.
58   Holz, "Die Paradoxie der Normalisierung," 53.

THE JEW AS OTHER ♦ 123

[The best solution is a reversal of perpetrator-victim roles, through which the new Germany can exchange its perpetrators, reminders of guilt, for former victims . . . The perpetrator-victim reversal enables the normalization of the German nation by exposing the accusation of guilt as a "Jewish act."]

Through the torment of Ambros Adelwarth, Sebald created a troubling equivalence of German and Jewish victimhood and guilt. In a provocative reversal of the roles of German and Jew, perpetrator and victim, the treatment that destroys Ambros is carried out by Jewish psychiatrists, Fahnstock and his assistant, Abramsky.[59] Fahnstock is presented as the successor to German psychiatrist and ECT pioneer, Anton Edler von Braunmühl (1901–57), whose "Blockmethode" was devised to anaesthetize animals to be slaughtered, and associated with Nazi euthanasia methods. Fahnstock adopted this method, which not infrequently involved more than a hundred electric shocks at intervals of only a very few days.

Sebald borrowed from Nazi language to implicate Jewish figures in the annihilative torture of a German, and employed the Nazi "voice" of detached rationalism to describe and quantify the infliction of extreme suffering.[60] Fahnstock's description of earlier forms of electro-convulsive therapy notes that "patients would be convulsed for minutes, seemingly on the point of death, their faces contorted and blue" (TE, 111), an image that conflates Ambros's suffering with the agony of Jewish victims, asphyxiated in the gas chambers of Auschwitz and Treblinka. While appropriating the language of Holocaust victimhood to describe German suffering has been explored, Sebald's employment of the Nazi language of annihilation in relation to Jewish characters as perpetrators suggests a troubling indifference to the resonance of such language.[61] Indeed, Abramsky, without recourse to euphemism, describes the treatment of Ambros by means of the "Annihilierungsmethode" (annihilation method). In exploring the language of Nazi propaganda against the Jews, Jeffrey Herf draws attention to key verbs and nouns that formed the core of the language of mass murder:

59    The Jewish identity of psychiatrists Fahnstock and Abramsky is implied by hints the reader is given about their Eastern European origins, and the impact on their career paths of Austrian anti-Semitism, euphemistically referred to as "circumstances" (TE, 114) or "den damals herrschenden Verhältnissen" (DA, 167).

60    The language of Nazi medical reporting is evident in "The Dachau Human Hyperthermia Study" (August 1942–May 1943), carried out at Dachau by Doctors Holzloehner, Rascher, and Finke, and submitted to Himmler on October 21, 1942. Berger, "Nazi Science."

61    See Moeller, "The Politics of the Past."

124 ♦ THE JEW AS OTHER

> They were the verbs vernichten and ausrotten, which are synonyms
> for "annihilate," "exterminate," "totally destroy," and "kill," and
> the nouns Vernichtung and Ausrottung, meaning "annihilation,"
> "extermination," "total destruction," and "killing." Whether taken
> on their own from the dictionary meaning or placed in the con-
> text of the speeches, paragraphs, and sentences in which they were
> uttered, the meaning of these terms was unambiguous . . . When
> [the Nazis] imputed such intentions to the Jews and when they
> spoke of their own intentions, the evidence does not support the
> view that the Nazi leaders were speaking euphemistically. The mean-
> ing of their words, for those who took them seriously, was plain. The
> Nazis said what they meant and meant what they said.[62]

Through the figure of the German Ambros, Sebald instrumentalized
the trope of the Jewish other to convey the theme of German victimhood that dominated his controversial essay, "Air War and Literature,"
in which Sebald castigated German writers for "individual and collective
amnesia" regarding what he described as "the darkest aspects of the final
act of destruction," and which he believed "remained under a kind of
taboo like a shameful family secret, a secret that perhaps could not even
be privately acknowledged."[63] In his depiction of Ambros Adelwarth's
suffering, Sebald inverted the roles of victim and perpetrator by presenting Jewishness as a transferrable identity. Ambros is depicted in the passive habitus of the suffering Jewish other, "sitting on the stool outside
the door at the appointed hour, leaning his head against the wall, eyes
closed, waiting for what was in store for him" (*TE*, 111). Sebald's reversal of victim-perpetrator roles in his construction of Ambros as a "docile
Jewish victim," reflects his wish to redress the deficit in postwar German
literature in relation to the controversial question of German suffering.
Ambros's "martyrdom" reflects the shifting discourse on German guilt
that posits a more inclusive, ethically problematic notion of victimhood,
encompassing both victim and perpetrator groups.

Sebald's description of Ambros's suffering as "Martyrium" (martyrdom), imbues his torment with profound, heroic, even religious, significance. In her discussion of the ambiguous concept of "sacrifice," Aleida
Assmann distinguishes between self-willed victimhood, in which the victim
engages in the "Akt des freiwilligen Erleidens des Opfertodes" (the act of
voluntary sacrificial death), and purely passive victimhood that entails no
active engagement on the part of the victim, but is nevertheless imbued
with religious significance.[64] While Jewish Holocaust victims belong to
the second category, Ambros voluntarily submits himself to a repeated

62    Herf, "The Jewish War," 55–56.
63    Sebald, "Air War and Literature," 9–10.
64    Assmann, *Der lange Schatten*, 73.

and painful procedure that ultimately kills him. Describing Ambros's passivity to the narrator, Abramsky observes that Ambros's docility "was in fact due simply to your great-uncle's longing for an extinction as total and irreversible as possible of his capacity to think and remember" (*TE*, 113–14). Sebald's conflation of Ambros's voluntary suffering with the passive "martyrdom" of the Jewish victim is a misrepresentation, and a willful reversal of the moral hierarchy that distinguishes victims from perpetrators. His representation of Jewish characters as perpetrators confirms what Ruth Angress describes as a disturbing pattern in postwar German fiction, evident in "the impetus to resurrect not the memory of German Jewry, but the myth of Shylock, as victim and victimizer."[65]

Retired from his work as a psychiatrist at the Samaria sanatorium, and withdrawn into nature as a bee-keeper, Dr Abramsky's fantasy of the destruction of the sanatorium and everything it contains is a comment on the impossibility of representing the Holocaust: "I do not expect anyone can really imagine the pain and wretchedness once stored in this extravagant timber palace and I hope all this misfortune will gradually melt away now as it falls apart" (*TE*, 110). It is at the same time, a wishful fantasy of undoing history, echoing the SS taunt that "however this war may end, we have won the war against you; none of you will be left to bear witness, but even if someone were to survive, the world will not believe him. There will be no certainties, because we will destroy the evidence together with you. And even if some proof should remain and some of you survive, people will say that the events you describe are too monstrous to be believed."[66] The desire to expunge a shameful past is implicit in Abramsky's hope that

> . . . all the material on file—the case histories and medical records . . . have probably long since been eaten by the mice . . . Nowadays, I place all my hope in the mice, and in the woodworm and deathwatch beetles. The sanatorium is creaking and in places already caving in, and sooner or later they will bring about its collapse (*TE*, 112–13).

Abramsky's role is ambiguous, a contrite Jewish perpetrator, but one who wishes to cover the traces of guilt, and is thus complicit in the "conspiracy of silence" that Sebald imputed to postwar Germans, engaged in the process of rebuilding a contaminated country. Abramsky's fantasy of disintegration evokes Kafka's story, "Josephine the Singer and the Mouse people" (1924), an allegory of Jewish otherness that focuses on the precariousness of Jewish existence, and negative stereotypes relating

---

65    Angress, "A 'Jewish Problem?'"
66    Levi, *The Drowned and the Saved*.

126 ♦ THE JEW AS OTHER

to Jewish imperfection. Josephine's singing is derided as "piping," her physiognomy as "frail . . . crippled."[67] The mice, like the Jews, are bound by a shared history of persecution and suffering: "our life is very uneasy, every day brings surprises, apprehensions, hopes, and terrors," and the threat of pogroms is implicit in the fear of being "unexpectedly flushed by the enemy and many of our people left lying for dead."[68] Sebald's allusion to Kafka's story is at once a reflection on Jewish otherness that emphasizes its imperfection, and a comment on the indestructible nature of Jewishness that survives as memory. Abramsky's vision of the sanatorium, ultimately disintegrating into "a great yellowish cloud that billows out and disperses," leaving only "a heap of powder-fine wood dust, like pollen" (*TE*, 112–13), posits, through the generative connotations of "pollen," the potential for redemption of Jewish life through the literary project that seeks its survival.

## The Jew as Embodiment of the Ills of Modernity

The figure of Cosmo Solomon personifies the stereotype of the Jew as the embodiment of the ills of modernity: its cold materialism, obsession with technology, and dissolution of national, social, and sexual boundaries. This view is evident in the writing of Sombart, for whom the Jews represent the negative pole of the opposition between "ink and blood, understanding and instinct, abstraction and reality."[69] With his agile mind that engages with aeronautical design and gambling strategies, Cosmo exemplifies the putatively Jewish qualities of calculative rationalism. Scion of an American-Jewish family, described as "amongst the wealthiest of the Jewish banking families in New York" (*TE*, 88), Cosmo conjures the enduring notion of Jewish world domination. His heteronomy is implicit in his name: his first name connotes internationalism, while his second name inscribes him into Jewish history and marks him as indelibly Jewish, manifest in his intuitive and disastrous identification with a cinematic representation of a nomadic, "Oriental," and allegedly Jewish identity. An assimilated American Jew, "other" in attire and behavior, and relentlessly cosmopolitan, Cosmo represents Holz's Third category of identity, a threat to notions of belonging and national identity:

> Der Dritte ist etwas, das es eigentlich, gemäß der binären Unterscheidung, gar nicht geben dürfte . . . Das Judenbild wird paradox, also etwas das seine eigene Unmöglichkeit einschließ . . . Sie sind eine partikulare Gruppe wie alle anderen, sind aber zugleich

67    Geller, "Of Mice and Mensa," 375.
68    Geller, "Of Mice and Mensa," 368.
69    Sombart, *The Jews and Modern Capitalism*, 185.

von einem "unerbittlichen Universalismus." Der Universalismus ist wie der Internationalismus eine Konkretion der Figur des Dritten, nämlich Negation der Unterscheidung zwischen partikularen Völkern, Negation der nationalen Ordnung der Welt.[70]

[The "Third" is an entity that, in terms of the binary distinction should not, in fact, exist. The image of the Jew is paradoxical, indeed, it announces its own impossibility . . . [Jews] are a particular group, like all others, but are at the same time, "relentlessly universal." Like their internationalism, their universality is a concretion of the figure of the Third, namely, the negation of the distinction between particular peoples, the negation of the national order of the world.]

The dissolution of boundaries is a feature of Deauville, the French casino where Cosmo embarks on a gambling spree calculated to ensure a never-ending source of income. With its atmosphere of unbridled greed, Deauville forms the background to Cosmo as the personification of the ills of modernity, reflecting Weininger's assertion, "Judaism is the spirit of modern life."[71] Cosmo's gambling mania evokes the negative stereotype of the rapacious Jew, whose materialism Weininger attributes to his sense of ontological nothingness: "Because he believes in nothing, he takes refuge in material things, and that alone is the origin of his avarice: it is here that he seeks a reality."[72] Cosmo's spectacular gambling success leads to rumors of fraud and mysterious powers that raise the suspicion of Jewish *Machenschaft*, the invisible "pulling of strings" historically imputed to the Jew.[73] The exoticism of Deauville represents the dissolution of identity associated with modernity, and evident in its architectural *mélange* of pseudo-Balinese and Tyrolean hotels, Gothic castles, Swiss chalets, and mock-Oriental residences, and its visitors, described as "a veritable wave of the exotic" ( *TE*, 123). With "flashing kaleidoscopic lights and tootling garlands of sound," the casinos represent the artifice of modern life, in which individuals, reduced to "contingents . . . troop over to the new casinos," and the croupier in circus costume dissolves into "pink puffy clouds . . . a whiter shade of pale" ( *TE*, 121). Depicted against the shallowness of modern life epitomized by Deauville, Cosmo exemplifies the putatively Jewish qualities Weininger disparaged: the adaptability of the Jews, the mobility of their minds, and their lack of deeply rooted and original ideas.

The overwrought atmosphere of Deauville is conveyed by the breathless listing of its fabulously wealthy clientele; the Rolls-Royce,

---

70 Holz, "Die Paradoxie der Normalisierung," 46.
71 Weininger, *Sex and Character*, 329–30.
72 Weininger, *Sex and Character*, 294.
73 Achinger, "Allegories of Destruction," 146.

"gold-plated within" (*TE*, 124), and "the yearlings of the season . . . wearing lace dresses through which their silken undergarments gleamed in Nile green crevette, or absinthe blue" (*TE*, 124), convey the superficiality of modern life. In the narrator's dream of Deauville, Cosmo and Ambros "dissolve . . . leaving behind them nothing but the vacant space they had occupied" (*TE*, 123), a vision that suggests the ontological emptiness of the Jew. The lack of reality Weininger imputes to the Jew approaches Heidegger's notion of the metaphysical Jew:

> I think that the idea of Judaism consists in this want of reality, this absence of any fundamental relation to the thing-in-and-for-itself. He stands, so to speak, outside reality, without ever entering it. He can never make himself one with anything—never enter into real relationships . . . He is without simplicity of faith, and so is always turning to each new interpretation, so seeming more alert than the Aryan. Internal multiplicity is the essence of Judaism, internal simplicity that of the Aryan.[74]

Cosmo's extraordinary success at gambling culminates in the vision of Ambros, "busy until dawn counting the money and packing it into a steamer trunk" (*TE*, 94). Cosmo's compulsion to make money reflects the enduring perception of the Jewish other as rapacious, dissembling, and exploitative. The "non-identity" implied in his name perpetuates a view of the Jewish other as fundamentally unaffiliated, an agent of dissolution, and a threat to notions of belonging and social responsibility. Cosmo's relationship with Ambros is a wishful fantasy of a resurrected "German-Jewish symbiosis," in which Ambros is a guardian-figure to the unstable, self-absorbed Cosmo, in a reversal of the post-Holocaust moral hierarchy of German and Jew, confirming Cosgrove's observation that "even the portrayal of an idealized symbiosis of relations between Germans and Jews is tainted by the negative symbiosis of their relations after the Holocaust."[75]

### Michael Hamburger: The Dispossessed Jew as Other

Conflicted between fragile memories of a vanished Benjaminian Berlin childhood to which he returns in dreams, and the obliterating emptiness of a ruined postwar Germany in which he vainly seeks traces of the life he has lost, Michael Hamburger (*The Rings of Saturn*) represents Hegel's vision of the dispossessed Jew. The German-Jewish poet's story of displacement and dispossession is framed within a narrative that thematizes

---

74    Weininger, *Sex and Character*, 324.
75    Cosgrove, "The Anxiety of German Influence," 246.

notions of alterity and loss. Such ideas are traced in the narrator's disorientating experience on Dunwich heath, and a dream in which conflicting visions of alterity—a Chinese pavilion, a Belgian villa, and a sinister lookout tower that hints at Auschwitz —jar with an allusion to Shakespeare, emblem of Englishness, confusing notions of identity, and imbuing the episode with a disconcerting nihilism: "No, nothing. Nothing but dead silence" (RS, 175), an echo of King Lear's mourning over Cordelia, "Thou'll come no more, Never, never, never, never, never."[76] The narrator's gaze takes in the "shattered ruins of a house . . . the strangely contorted bodies of those people who had lived there . . . a scene of devastation" (RS, 174), images that recall Sebald's description, in "Air War and Literature," of bombed-out German houses, outside which "horribly disfigured corpses lay everywhere."[77] Scenes of destruction culminate in the image of the Sizewell power plant, its magnus block a "glowering mausoleum . . . on an island in the pallid waters where one believes the Dogger bank to be, where, a long, long time ago, the delta of the Rhine flowed out into the sea" (RS, 175). In this allusive and complex vision, the implicit juxtaposition of Shakespeare with the quintessentially German image of the Rhine creates a universal vision of destruction that locates the origin of German guilt in the broader context of European history, reflecting Sebald's view on the Holocaust: "I do not at all perceive the disaster wrought by the Germans, horrendous though it was, as a unique event. It developed, with a certain consequentiality, from within European history."[78] Through this relativizing perspective, Sebald mitigates and evades the question of German agency in the causation of the Holocaust.

Loss is integral to Michael Hamburger's story: he notes the "disappearance of [his] Berlin childhood behind the new identity [he] assumed" (RS, 177); it is implicit in his fragmentary recollection of sights, scents, and sounds that conjure up Benjamin's *Berlin Childhood around 1900*. Like Benjamin's memories of the everyday life of his childhood, Hamburger's recollections revolve around fragments, "a Prussian lion . . . a Prussian nanny, caryatids bearing the globe on their shoulders . . . the noise made by the central-heating pipe behind the wallpaper in the dark corner . . . the nauseating smell of soapsuds in the laundry, a game of marbles in a Charlottenburg park . . ." (RS, 177). As Benjamin wrote to Gershom Scholem, "these childhood memories . . . are not narratives in the form of a chronicle but . . . individual expeditions into the depths of memory."[79] While the remembered objects are reminders of everyday

76    Shakespeare, *The Tragedy of King Lear*, 280–81.
77    Sebald, "Air War and Literature," 28.
78    Pralle. "Mit einem kleinen Strandspaten."
79    Benjamin, *Berlin Childhood around 1900*, xi–xii.

130 ♦ THE JEW AS OTHER

bourgeois life, the world in which these objects were made no longer exists for Michael Hamburger: like the enchanted Bereyter emporium and the childhood world of Luisa Lanzberg, his memories of a Berlin childhood reveal a lost world of plenitude, in which humans lived in harmony with the world of things.

Hamburger's enchanted memories of his Berlin childhood, "an obituary of a lost boyhood" (*RS*, 177), are displaced by fragmented recollections of a return visit after the war: "If I now look back to Berlin, all I see is a darkened background with a grey smudge . . . unclear numbers and letters in a gothic script, blurred and half-wiped away with a damp rag . . . houses of which only the façades were left standing, smoke-blackened brick walls and fields of rubble . . ." (*RS*, 177–78). His return to Berlin on his quest for traces of a lost life, is marked by absence: "If I now think of that desolate place, I do not see a single human being, only bricks, millions of bricks, a rigorously perfected system of bricks reaching in serried ranks as far as the horizon, and above them the Berlin November sky from which the snow would come swirling down—a deathly silent image of the onset of winter" (*RS*, 179). The poet's vision of the brick stelae, like nameless gravestones "stacked in long precise rows . . . the thousandth brick in every pile . . . stood upright on top," is symbolic of the alterity of Jewish death, meticulously planned and anonymous. The "rigorously perfected system of bricks reaching in serried ranks as far as the horizon," recalls the tightly-organized Nazi displays of force, such as the infamous Nuremberg rallies held between 1933 and 1938. Hamburger's aural hallucination of "the closing bars of the *Freischütz* overture" (*RS*, 179), conjures the substrate of *völkisch* German Romantic elements that constitutes Carl Maria von Weber's opera, *Der Freischütz* (The Marksman, 1821) as quintessentially German; in the context of Hamburger's life, Sebald's allusion to von Weber's opera is an oblique reminder of German authorship of the Holocaust.[80]

In a dream, Hamburger returns to his family home in Berlin. His imagined return is mythologized as a descent down an "imperceptibly sloping corridor" (*RS*, 180) into an Underworld where he encounters his ghostly family. Invisible to them, the poet "hesitantly crosses the threshold, and in doing so, realizes [he] no longer knows where [he] is" (*RS*, 180), reflecting his loss of identity as a German Jew, attempting to assimilate to English culture. Michael Hamburger's allegorical return is motivated by the hope of "cancelling the monstrous events that had happened since we emigrated . . . of reversing, the entire course of history" (*RS*,

---

80    Carl Maria von Weber's *Der Freischütz* (1821), represents a milestone in the development of the Romantic opera, and is considered self-consciously German in its evocation of the archetypal forest of the German Romantic imagination, and of *völkisch* elements relating to nature, hunting, superstition, and magic.

178), echoing Améry's *Ressentiment*, his counter-rational demand that "the irreversible be turned around, that the event be undone."[81] This hope is subverted in Hamburger's dream by images portending catastrophe—the black taxis speeding towards the sinister site of Wannsee, the ambulance outside his home—and through allegorization of loss, exemplified by the bare walls, and the absence of furniture in his childhood home.[82] The lifelessness of his abandoned home is conveyed by the vision of the "museum-like rooms," his grandmother laid out on a high table, and his father in the "Cold Glory" of the unheated drawing room, his words lingering like "white vapour . . . in the ice-cold air" (*RS*, 181). Glimpsed from a window, a distant view of a "golden cupola . . . a valley enclosed by blue-forested hills," evokes a lost utopia, identified by his father, in a prosopopoeic utterance, as "a place somewhere in Poland" (*RS*, 181), a tenuous reminder of the Holocaust that underlies Michael Hamburger's story of loss.

On his visit to Hamburger's home in Suffolk, the German narrator's profound affiliation with the poet is expressed through his identificatory perception that "I lived or had once lived there," and through his sense of being overwhelmed by a feeling that "the spectacles cases, letters and writing materials . . . had once been my spectacles cases, my letters and my writing materials" (*RS*, 183), the reiteration of the possessive pronoun underscoring his metaphorical usurpation of Hamburger's identity and possessions. Indeed, Hamburger is displaced from his home even as he is described as showing the narrator around the house in which domestic objects resemble "still lifes" that the narrator imagines himself to have created (*RS*, 184). As if to support his claim to appropriation, the narrator posits "elective affinities" that connect him to the poet; he suggests the possibility of a deeper, genealogical connection, even a form of legacy: "How is it that one perceives oneself in another human being, or, if not oneself, then one's own precursor?" (*RS*, 182).

The intense identification of the German narrator with Michael Hamburger is a dispossession of the Jewish other, and a misunderstanding of Jean Améry's call for *Ressentiment*, the counter-rational demand for a "moral turning back of the clock" that would allow the perpetrator to join his victim as a fellow human being.[83] Intrinsic to Améry's demand is the desire that persecutors should experience the suffering of their victims, and wish to share with them the longing to "turn back time, to undo what has been done," a desire that stems from the victim's experience of extreme loneliness and abandonment in relation to deportation,

---

81    Améry, "Resentments," 68.

82    Wannsee was the site where, on the January 20, 1942, the "Final Solution" was decided upon, authorizing the genocide of the Jews.

83    Améry, "Resentments," 77.

132 ♦ The Jew as Other

internment, torture, and continuing existential isolation.[84] Sebald saw himself as descended from the literary process of writers like Améry, who sought justice for the victims of the Holocaust. Nevertheless, the narrator's claim to Hamburger's experience, and his appropriation of the markers of that experience, constitute a violation of LaCapra's concept of ethical empathy, intrinsic to which is acknowledgment of the irreducible difference of the other, and a misinterpretation of Améry's notion of *Ressentiment*: a response to what he perceived as the German tendency to neutralize and repress their tainted national history, Améry's *Ressentiment* is a reminder of the need to acknowledge it, in the hope that "two groups of people, the overpowered and those who overpowered them, would be joined in the desire that time be turned back, and with it, that history become moral."[85]

Sebald's figural construction of Jewish alterity blurs distinctions of identity and moral category, leaving the question of agency in relation to the war open to infinite interpretation. In his analysis of the risks of a figurative approach to representing the Holocaust, Lang notes, "the implication is unavoidable, that a subject . . . could be represented in many different ways and as having no *necessary* and perhaps not even an actual basis. The assertion of alternate possibilities [of figuration] . . . suggests a denial of limitation: *no* possibilities are excluded."[86] Thus the risk remains of figuring a real person as a fictional invention, and a real event as a non-event. Notwithstanding the empathy that motivates his identification with his subject, Sebald's figural writing abstracts the person of Michael Hamburger, and dehistoricizes the specificity of his tragedy.

Sebald's Jewish figures personify the perception of the Jew as the consummate figure of difference in the Western imagination, and the embodiment of the coldness and alienation associated with modernity. Sebald's Jewish others reflect his interest in nuances of Jewishness, and the implications of such fractional identity in the complex moral environment of the "Third Reich." Jewish alterity in Sebald's work is a transferrable identity, evident in awkward conflations of German and Jew, perpetrator and victim, and problematic reversals of moral order. Sebald's repudiation of attempts to abandon Jewishness through assimilation suggests a perception of Jewish heteronomy as innate and immutable, implicit in which is the problematic historical association of the Jew with the idea of difference that has made the Jew the essential outsider of Western society.

84    Améry, "Resentments," 70.
85    Améry, "Resentments, 78.
86    Lang, *Act and Idea*, 146.

# 4: The Inauthentic Jew

> *In him he would have recognized a kind of*
> *doppelgänger . . . his other self in the dark-coated*
> *brother whom he could never and nowhere escape*
>
> —Vertigo

MANY JEWS HAVE historically been compelled to hide their identity, a contingent truth that arises from their history as victims of persecution. In the imaginary world of Sebald's prose narratives however, he figured the mimicking assimilation of his Jewish characters as a necessary truth, a rejection and concealment of their innate Jewish alterity, implied in manifestations of atavistic desert nomadism to which his assimilated Jews instinctively respond. Thus Cosmo Solomon, an assimilated American Jew, intuitively identifies with a filmic representation of an oasis, and imagines himself to have followed the mirage of a desert caravan that emerged onto the stage from a grove of palms (*TE*, 97). Through imagery that implies the theatrical world of illusion and falsity, Sebald's figural writing points to the fundamental inauthenticity of his Jewish characters: Aurach's first view of his adopted city, Manchester, perceives it as "as if in the heart of a natural amphitheater" (*TE*, 168), foreshadowing the surrogate reality of his exiled existence there. Sebald's inauthentic Jewish figures are shadowed by a double who embodies the "authentic" identity they have sought to abandon: Austerlitz's inchoate sense of an unlived identity is conveyed through his haunting awareness of a spectral, discarded twin brother; in *The Emigrants*, the notion of an unlived, "real" life is implied in Cosmo Solomon's quest to find an imaginary brother in a room that had been locked for years (*TE*, 97). For Dr K., the divisions of assimilated Jewish identity are allegorized through the motif of the *Doppelgänger* who, in the film *The Student of Prague*, makes a terrifying appearance as the inescapable "other self" (*V*, 151).

Sebald's Jewish figures mask their Jewish identity through costume: thus Austerlitz's transformation from his putatively Czech Jewish identity to an English one is manifest in a change of clothing that he perceives as a change of species: "I remember how dreadful it was, once my own clothes had disappeared, to have to go around dressed in the English fashion in shorts, knee-length socks that were always slipping down, a string vest like a fish-net and a mouse-grey shirt, much too thin" (*A*, 61–62), the "mouse-grey shirt" implying his adoption of a trans-species identity, the simile of the string vest "like a fish net" capturing his sense of being trapped inside a false identity. In *The Emigrants*, Paul Bereyter hides his Jewishness behind the uniform of a *Wehrmacht* soldier, and in costumes that are described as often flamboyantly eccentric, Cosmo hides his putatively "real" Jewish self, conceived by Sebald as Oriental and exotic, and implied in the imagery of desert nomadism with which Cosmo instinctively identifies. An indistinct photograph purporting to be of Cosmo receiving a trophy after a polo match at Deauville reveals him in an overlarge coat that conceals his physiognomy, while his facial features are shadowed by a hat. Assimilation to an alternative identity is implied to be a fraudulent process, doomed to failure, as Aurach's uncle Leo observes bitterly, "so war alles eine Fälschung von Anfang an" (*DA*, 274; So too everything else had been a fake, from the very beginning).[1] In figuring his assimilated Jewish characters as masking their essential Jewishness, Sebald perpetuated a long-held perception of the Jew as an inauthentic mimic who attempts to conceal his Jewish identity, but is unable to do so owing to his alien and ineradicable alterity, implied to have its roots in the desert of the Middle East.

The sole picture of unambiguous and vital Jewish life in Sebald's prose fiction, the representation of the Lanzberg family in the memoirs of Luisa Lanzberg, reflects an idyll of Jewishness lived with an awareness of its heteronomy within the broader gentile German world, and bound to traditional cultural practice that evokes a primal Oriental Jewishness. The dual proposition—that all Jews, even assimilated ones, manifest an affiliation with an archaic essence of Jewishness—and that sustainable Jewish existence is predicated on observance of cultural tradition and consciousness of its radical alterity, suggests that Sebald's perception of viable Jewishness was shaped by cultural essentialism. Defined as the belief that racial categories are associated with distinct, fixed, and stable cultural patterns, and that such fixed cultural patterns "definitively and permanently shape the psychological characteristics of individuals," Sebald's essentializing view implies that, in their assimilation to a foreign culture, Jews inevitably assume a role that is contrary to their essential nature, marking them as inauthentic.[2] As Luther observed in 1523: "A Jew is not a *Deutscher* (German) but a *Teutscher* (deceiver)."[3] Four centuries later, the notion of Jewish inauthenticity is echoed in Hans Blüher's description of the Jews as "the only people that practise mimicry. Mimicry of the blood, of the name, of the body."[4]

---

1     Uncle Leo's words echo Scholem's dismissal of the German-Jewish "dialogue" as "never anything but a fiction." Scholem, "Against the Myth," 61.

2     Morning, *The Nature of Race*.

3     Luther, "That Jesus Christ was born a Jew."

4     Blüher, *Secessio Judaica*, 54.

Sebald's dual perspective risks perpetuating malign historical viewpoints that see the Jew as fundamentally unassimilable; it holds the troubling suggestion that, by succumbing to the pressures and seductions of assimilation, the Jews were complicit in their own misfortune.[5] His depiction of Jewish figures as bound to an archaic and fundamental notion of Jewishness implies the impossibility of Jewish assimilation, and confirms the destruction of the German-Jewish "symbiosis" as inevitable. As Scholem remarked bitterly, "the attempt by the Jews to explain themselves to the Germans and to put their own creativity at their disposal, even to the point of self-abnegation, is a significant phenomenon . . . to the infinite intoxication of Jewish enthusiasm there never corresponded a tone that bore any kind of relation to a creative answer to the Jews."[6] Sebald's view of Jews as susceptible to the lure of assimilation at the cost of self-abnegation suggests that they hold some responsibility for their fate.[7] This notion evokes Heidegger's claim that the Holocaust was an act of Jewish self-annihilation, and his obscure assertion that, "when the essentially 'Jewish' in the metaphysical sense struggles against what is Jewish, the *zenith of self-annihilation has been achieved.*"[8]

Sebald's anti-assimilatory stance was influenced by Scholem's argument that relations between Jew and German deteriorated from the Enlightenment of the eighteenth century, and that the pressure on Jews to abandon their unique identity and customs led logically to the destruction of European Jews in the Holocaust.[9] Sebald's view of the nexus of toleration and persecution in relation to Jewish assimilation reflects Adorno and Horkheimer's negative perspective in *Dialectic of Enlightenment*:

> The dialectical link between enlightenment and domination, and the dual relationship of progress to cruelty and liberation . . . are reflected in the very essence of those assimilated. The enlightened self-control . . . led them straight from their own, long-suffering community into the modern bourgeoisie, which was moving inexorably toward reversion to cold repression and reorganization of pure "race."[10]

---

5 This view is manifest in Heidegger's notion of Jewish "self-annihilation." For Heidegger, as Di Cesare notes, the Holocaust was "'the culmination of self-annihilation in history' because 'only the chosen people' . . . were complicit with metaphysics, which brought with it the desert void, the nothingness of technical nihilism." Di Cesare, *Heidegger's Jews*, 202.

6 Scholem, "Against the Myth," 63.

7 Sebald, "Die Zweideutigkeit der Toleranz," 29.

8 Heidegger, *Anmerkungen*, 20.

9 Scholem, *Jews and Germans*.

10 Adorno and Horkheimer, *Dialectic of Enlightenment*, 169.

136 ♦ The Inauthentic Jew

To Eleanor Wachtel, Sebald articulated his nostalgia for the once productive, pre-Holocaust German-Jewish relationship:

> There was a very, very close identification between the Jewish population in Germany and the gentile population. And especially between the Jewish population and the country, the topography of the country, through their surnames . . . the relationship between the Jewish minority in Germany and the larger population was one of the most central and most important chapters of German cultural history from the eighteenth century to the present day in one form or another.[11]

Sebald's wistful observations betray a longing to return to the prelapsarian idyll of German-Jewish relations depicted in Luisa's memoirs, and for restitution of the tradition-bound and self-consciously heteronomous Jewishness on which such an idyll was founded. Exploration of the contested notion of Jewish authenticity reveals that such a view fails to consider the complexities of Jewish identity-formation in its adaptation to history.

## The Vexed Question of Jewish Authenticity

Kenneth Marcus observes: "There is no fixed, stable, and generally agreed upon notion of what it means to be Jewish," noting that Jewish identity has developed too variously in the diaspora to be "strait-jacketed" into any particular conception.[12] In "Reflections on the Jewish Question," Jean-Paul Sartre wrote: "The Israelite situation in society is as follows: it starts on the one hand with a false persona that is foisted on him, then it refuses him the ownership of whatever he can gain through his work since he is told that true possession is always beyond what he believes he owns." Sartre's notion of Jewish identity as "a false persona" reflects his definition of the Jew as a product of the anti-Semitic gaze, "one whom other men consider an Israelite . . . the replica of their hatred of analysis, spirit, of negation, of nuance . . ."[13] Sartre saw the Jew as having two choices: to deny his Jewishness, or to courageously assert it by accepting the negative identity imposed on him by others:

> Authenticity for [the Jew] is to live to the full his condition as a Jew; inauthenticity is to deny it or to attempt to escape from it . . . The Jews have neither community of interests nor community of beliefs.

11 Wachtel, "Ghost Hunter," 47.
12 Marcus, *The Definition of Anti-Semitism*, 123.
13 Sartre, "Reflections on the Jewish Question," 42–43.

They do not have the same fatherland; they have no history. The sole tie that binds them is the hostility and disdain of the societies which surround them. Thus, the authentic Jew is the one who asserts his claim in the face of the disdain shown towards him.[14]

Implicit in this is the perception of lived Jewish authenticity as resistant, manifesting moral courage in the face of hatred and opposition. To Sartre, the alternative to acceptance of Jewishness is its denial, and the attempt to escape it by seeking an inauthentic identity through assimilation. Fackenheim's insistence on the assertion of Jewishness to prevent a "posthumous victory" for Hitler can be seen as a logical development of Sartre's belief that authenticity requires defiance and commitment to survival.[15] Sebald shared Sartre's valorization of the "authentic" Jew, whose resistant power he valued over what he saw as the dissimulation of the assimilationist Jew.

Recent research emphasizes Jewish authenticity as a multivalent, dynamic, and unstable concept that implies multiple understandings of Jewishness, as Stuart Charmé observes,

> An authentic identity, therefore, is never an entity or substance that we possess, but rather a project situated in time and space. Being born into a particular Jewish situation determines many possibilities, but those possibilities are historically influenced, and new possibilities are influenced in turn by our own actions.[16]

In "Varieties of Authenticity in Contemporary Jewish Identity," Charmé observes that authenticity has become an important term in relation to the contemporary discourse on Jewish identity, tradition, culture, and religion, a term often invoked when referring to the "Jewish content" in a person's life, the normative superiority of one form of Jewishness over another, and to issues of personal values and sense of self. In the discourse on authenticity, claims are made on the basis of historical continuity with the essence of Jewish tradition, a notion that derives from the German Romantic idea of *Volksgeist* (spirit of a people), that sees a particular ethnic group as holding a unique cultural outlook, a view proposed by the eighteenth-century German philosopher, Johann Gottfried Herder.[17] Adherence to a primordial tradition located in an idealized past is intrinsic to such an essentialist model of authenticity; as a Romantic response to alienating modernity, Jewish authenticity based on traditional Jewish values is perceived as conserving a cultural integrity that has been lost in the

14      Sartre, *Anti-Semite and Jew*, 64–65.
15      Fackenheim, *Encounters*, 203–10.
16      Charmé, "Varieties of Authenticity," 47.
17      Herder, *Auch eine Philosophie*.

urban bourgeois world. Thus Jewish *shtetl* life has become symbolic of an authentic, prelapsarian Jewish existence, and of the dichotomy between this form of existence, and inauthentic, assimilated Jewish life in the modern city.

The Holocaust complicated the question of "real" Jewishness in a context that did not discriminate between degrees of Jewish authenticity, and in which Jews were forced to accept a Jewish identity imposed upon them by racial decree. In *The Imaginary Jew* (1980), Alain Finkielkraut challenges the validity of maintaining a notion of authentic Jewishness based on a destroyed, essentializing, pre-Holocaust Jewish identity. Finkielkraut explores the changing nature of what constitutes authentic Jewishness in the post-Holocaust era, in which the idea of Jewish authenticity founded on an essentialist, linear tradition has been challenged by the concept of authenticity as a response to a complex struggle of historical situations. Such a notion of authenticity has given rise to multiple "authentic Judaisms" that encompass a range of understandings of what it means to be Jewish.[18] On the question of giving the Jew an "unequivocal and precise content," Finkielkraut observes:

> To nationalize Judaism, or better yet, to make it a church, is to arrest it, in the sense of freezing a changing process . . . Restrict the word *Jew* to a single truth and there we are: suddenly capable of judging, categorizing, classifying and finally diminishing those who don't conform to our idea of our common bond.[19]

The changing discourse on authenticity, and the shift towards a more fluid and diverse approach to the meaning of Jewish authenticity, has implications for Sebald's perpetuation of an essentialist model of Jewishness in the memoirs of Aurach's mother, Luisa Lanzberg, explored in this chapter. It bears also on Sebald's construction of implicitly inauthentic Jewish figures as tropes for his own sense of inauthenticity, arising from the belatedness of his authorial position.

## The Belatedness of the Second Generation and the Trope of the Inauthentic Jew

As a second-generation German writer, Sebald was haunted by a sense of belatedness, of "writing from a site of missing the event," and by the desire to enact what Gary Weissman has described as "[the incomprehensible origin of trauma] . . . by mimicking its continuing disruptive

---

18    Shmueli, *Seven Jewish Cultures*, 2.
19    Finkielkraut, *The Imaginary Jew*, 166, 168.

after-effects in the present time."[20] Sebald's "masked" Jews are externalizations of his struggle with the problem of belatedness and inauthenticity as a writer, engaged in describing events he was too young to have witnessed or understood. As Susanne Vees-Gulani observes, "Sebald searches relentlessly for any possibilities of access to the experiences [of trauma], for gaining at least glimpses of the events . . . Sebald was not only looking for descriptions of the bombings but for a possibility to live through and to experience first-hand the events whose full reality eluded him, but which cast such a strong shadow over his life."[21]

With the demise of the Holocaust survivors, there has been a paradigm shift from representing the Holocaust as it happened, to representing it in terms of its impact on the present: from first-hand witnessing to the imaginative reconstructions of the past by authors with little or no authentic claim to experience beyond vicarious identification with the trauma of others.[22] Thus the suffering of Auschwitz has become freely available to "everyone who lives after Auschwitz, particularly those in Western countries who have Auschwitz in their history; even the following generations are assuredly survivors of the Holocaust."[23] In relation to Sebald, belatedness has come to be perceived as an advantage over primary experience:

> Despite his lack of experiential knowledge of what it was like to be a German Jew during the Holocaust, Sebald's writing is not just felt by many to have facilitated access to the survivor generation, but for some actually seems to have become a substitute for the more immediate, or less belated, accounts, factual or fictionalized, provided by those who did know.[24]

Sebald was highly self-referential in explaining his motivation for wanting to bear witness to Jewish suffering in relation to the Holocaust, citing his sense of originating in the trauma of the event, "as if I were its child, so to speak," implying a notion of having "inherited" a vicarious experience that validates his claim to the position of witness, and displacement of the survivor as the voice of the Holocaust. Validation of his privileged status as a secondary witness is evident in his claim to having been traumatized by "those horrors I did not experience," but that subordinated all other memories of "the entirely unreal idylls" of his early

---

20    Weissman, *Fantasies of Witnessing*, 37.

21    Vees-Gulani, "W. G. Sebald, the Airwar, and Literature," 343, 348.

22    See Felman and Laub, *Testimony*; LaCapra, *Writing History*; Abraham and Torok, *The Shell and the Kernel*.

23    Klüger, *Von hoher und niedriger Literatur*, 31.

24    Gwyer, "What Comes 'After,'" 2.

140 ◆ THE INAUTHENTIC JEW

childhood.[25] In what appears to be a defense of his inauthentic status as a secondary witness, Sebald pointed to the limitations of the eye-witness observer, for whom confrontation with the unbearable immediacy of trauma "must inevitably have led to . . . paralysis of the capacity to think and feel . . . The accounts of individual eyewitnesses, therefore, are of only qualified value, and need to be supplemented by what a synoptic and artificial view reveals."[26] Sebald used a dialectical metaphor to justify the advantage of his belated authorial position, noting that "if you turn the opera glass around . . . although it's further removed, the image seems much more precise."[27] In Sebald's affiliation with the witness generation through telling their stories and exploring their work in his critical writing, his self-reflective awareness of authorial inauthenticity mirrors that of the survivors themselves, overwhelmed by the sense of having escaped the destruction that others did not, and painfully conscious that the voice of the survivor was a surrogate for that of the true witness, the silent Dead.[28] In interviews and in his prose narratives, Sebald expressed a similar awareness of authorial inadequacy: "I think these certainties have been taken away from us by the course of history, and we have to acknowledge our own sense of ignorance and insufficiency in the matters and therefore try and write accordingly."[29]

In his narrative fiction, Sebald thematized authorial belatedness and inauthenticity. The photograph with which the story of "Paul Bereyter" opens depicts train tracks disappearing into a blur of oblivion. Implying the incomprehensibility of the Holocaust for which the train is synecdochic, the image simultaneously invites and obstructs a belated witnessing on the part of the reader. In *Austerlitz*, the narrator's visit to the fortress of Breendonk catalyses in him a vicarious somatic response to the torture he imagined to have been committed there; this is manifest in the "black striations [that] began to quiver before my eyes . . . I had to rest my forehead against the wall, which was gritty, covered with bluish spots, and seemed to me to be perspiring with cold beads of sweat" (*A*, 33). The narrator of "Max Aurach" laments his inability to penetrate his subject: "Often I could not get on for hours or days at a time, and not infrequently I unraveled what I had done, continuously tormented by scruples that were taking tighter hold and steadily paralyzing me. These scruples concerned not only the subject of my narrative, which I felt I could not do justice to, no matter what approach I tried, but also the entire questionable business of writing" (*TE*, 230). Austerlitz's first recorded mental

25  Sebald, "Air War and Literature," 71.
26  Sebald, "Air War and Literature," 26.
27  Wachtel, "Ghost Hunter," 57.
28  Kleinschmidt, "Schreiben an Grenzen," 77.
29  Wood, "An Interview with W. G. Sebald," 23–29.

breakdown is a radical acknowledgment of authorial inadequacy, manifest in [his] oppressive sense of "the falsity of [his] constructions and the inadequacy of all the words [he] had employed . . . there was not an expression in the sentence but it proved to be a miserable crutch, not a word but it sounded false and hollow" (*A*, 172–73). Personifications of inauthenticity, the spuriousness of Sebald's assimilated Jewish characters is conjured through imagery of deception and illusion that subverts reality, and reduces Jewish figures to surrogates and doubles, exposing the paradox that characterizes Sebald's treatment of Jews and Jewishness: the more he sought to empathetically restore the singularity of Jewish characters existing in the aftermath of the Holocaust, the further they were distanced from reality by the metaphorical mode of their representation. Emerging from the conflicts of Jewish existence in the diaspora, the notion of Jewish inauthenticity has a long history.

## Historical Background to the Inauthentic Jew

In Luther's 1543 pamphlet, *On the Jews and Their Lies*, reference is made to the Jews as "false bastards and outsiders," whose "impious" and "shameful" lies Luther aimed to "unmask." For Luther, Jewish deceit was inherent in the Jews' exegesis of the Talmud, through which "they interpret and distort almost every word," unlike the single, unchallenged meaning that characterized his own interpretation of the Bible.[30]

Luther's accusation of Jewish deceit persists in the Enlightenment, evident in the debate about Jewish emancipation and the question of Jewish assimilation in Germany. The surge in Jewish assimilation at this time led to the accusation of Jewish mimicry that has been interpreted as "a denial of Jewish genius [that] endeavored to counter Jewish acculturation and accomplishment as well as to perpetuate anti-Jewish stereotypes."[31] David Levin explores the issue of Jewish mimicry in Wagner's writings and in his operas, evident in his depiction of the dwarf Mime in *Siegfried*, and Beckmesser, the pedantic critic in *Die Meistersinger von Nürnberg* respectively.[32] In *Judaism in Music*, Wagner disparaged the "be-Jewing of modern art" as a threat to the German soul; through his operatic character, Mime, he caricatured what he saw as the Jew's ability to mimic his host culture.[33] In *Die Meistersinger von Nürnberg*, Beckmesser's contest song is described by Karl Zaencker as a "public unmasking" of the stereotypically scheming Jew.[34] Based on

---

30  Luther, *On the Jews and their lies*.
31  Geller, "Of Mice and Mensa," 363.
32  Levin, *Richard Wagner*.
33  Wagner, *Judaism in Music*, 81–82.
34  Zaenker, "The Bedeviled Beckmesser," 8.

142 ♦ THE INAUTHENTIC JEW

the fable, "The Jew in the Thornbush" by the Grimm brothers, the figure of Beckmesser manifests anti-Semitic traits relating to putative Jewish inauthenticity and lack of creativity, as well as the injurious influence of Jewishness on German art, evident in Beckmesser's screeching singing, conceived as a parody of Jewish cantorial style.

By the 1920s, Jewish mimicry had come to signify a threat to German identity. In *Secessio Judaica* (Leave, Judaism), Hans Blüher, prominent in initiating the German *Wandervogel* youth movement, demonized Jewish assimilation, accusing the Jews of imitating their hosts: "The Jews are the only people that practise mimicry. Mimicry of the blood, of the name, of the body."[35] Blüher dismissed Jewish assimilation to German culture as merely temporary, and liable to revert to innate Jewishness, observable in "the movement of the Jew, his walk, his gestures . . . the form of his hair on the nape of his neck, the eyes and the tongue . . ." Blüher predicted that once removed from the German body politic, Jewish mimicry of the German would cease and "one will see the Jews in Germany as clearly as one sees them in Russia and Poland. No one there confused him with the autochthonic man."[36] On the Jewish tendency to mimicry, Pierre Leroy-Beaulieu noted: "Jews have a remarkable faculty of taking on a new skin, without at bottom ceasing to be a Jew." For Leroy-Beaulieu, it is the voice that betrays the "real" Jew despite attempts to assimilate: "The metamorphosis was often too sudden to be complete . . . A glance, a word, a gesture, all of a sudden lays bare the old Jew at the bottom."[37] Sombart saw in Jewish adaptability a mimicry that was extraordinarily opportunistic: "How mobile the Jew can be is positively astounding. He is able to give himself the personal appearance he most desires . . ."[38] To Jünger, the Jew was "a master of all masks," a threat to German culture.[39] Self-awareness of Jewish inauthenticity is evident in Walther Rathenau's derogation of the imperfectly assimilated Jew, whose Jewishness remains conspicuous in his "slovenly shambling appearance . . . ill-constructed build . . . clumsy feet . . ."[40] In an observation that indicates his critique of Jewish assimilation to German culture, Kafka suggests that "only memories of the ghetto preserve the Jewish family," implying that the hidden Jewish self was still strong enough to reveal the superficial and falsifying nature of the German "mask" that concealed it.[41]

35  Blüher, *Secessio Judaica*, 54.
36  Blüher, *Secessio Judaica*, 55.
37  Leroy-Beaulieu, *Israel among the Nations*, 178, 194.
38  Sombart, *The Jews and Modern Capitalism*, 272.
39  Jünger, "Über Nationalismus und Judenfrage."
40  Rathenau, "Höre, Israel," 457–62.
41  Kafka, *Tagebücher 1910–1923*, 420.

THE INAUTHENTIC JEW ♦ 143

Nazi propaganda depicts the Jews as an insidious threat, with Joseph Goebbels describing them as "masters at adapting to surroundings without losing their essence. They practise mimicry," noting further that one had to be "an experienced Jew expert" to unmask them.[42] For Hitler, "The Jew is the great master of lying," who "takes over foreign culture, only imitating, or rather, destroying."[43]

In the writings of Günter Grass, Rainer Werner Fassbinder, Georg Tabori, and others, postwar German literature manifests the reactivation of negative portrayals of Jewish inauthenticity.[44] In *The Ballad of Wiener Schnitzel* (1996), Tabori explores the trope of the "hidden," ineradicable Jew, who makes a horrifying appearance as the eternally Wandering Jew to the character of Morgenstern, parodying his attempts to assimilate and overcome his innate and repulsive Jewishness. In the writing of Nobel Prize-laureate Günter Grass, Sander Gilman detects the myth of the hidden, damaging, and inauthentic Jewish discourse, based on the notion that the Jew is forever unable to master the language of the culture to which he seeks to assimilate. Citing Grass's novel, *Der Blechtrommel* (The Tin Drum, 1958), Gilman notes the characterization of the Jewish toyshop owner, Sigismund Markus, as speaking German with a Yiddish accent, the "Mauscheln" that marks him indelibly as a parvenue, "between cultures . . . moving across boundaries that are always understood as polluting and polluted."[45] In *Hundejahre* (Dog Years, 1963), Gilman observes a Weiningerian view of the hidden, polluting Jewish language, imputed to the Jewish protagonist of the novel, Eddi Amsel, who "developed his secret language, giving new names to the new surroundings."[46]

In the minor figure of the New York bootlegger, Seckler, Sebald perpetuated the notion of the contaminated Jewish discourse that hides the "real" Jew: Seckler's distorted German speech or "Mauscheln" betrays his immutable Jewish alterity: "Kannst du hingehen auf die neue Jeschiwa, wo sie brauchen Blechschmiede wie dich" ("Ambros Adelwarth," *DA*, 123; Can you go over to the Yeshiva where they need metalworkers like you; *TE*, 85). Explicitly identified as "a Jew from Brünn" (*TE*, 84), dishonest in his involvement in illicit distilleries, and mendacious in his dealings with Ambros's German relative, Kasimir, Seckler represents the trope of the dissimulating Jew, the negative pole of the binary opposition Sebald established in the story of "Ambros Adelwarth" between honest,

42    Goebbels, "Mimikry."
43    Hitler, *Mein Kampf*, 416.
44    These works include Fassbinder's *Der Müll, Die Stadt und Der Tod* (1976) and Tabori's *Die Ballade von Wiener Schnitzel* (1996).
45    Gilman, "Jewish Writers in Contemporary Germany," 220.
46    Gilman, "Jewish Writers in Contemporary Germany," 223.

144 ♦ THE INAUTHENTIC JEW

hard-working German emigrants, and exploitative Jews in the migrant population of 1920s New York.

"Masked" figures, who hide their true identity in order to live false lives as assimilated Jews, Sebald's Jewish figures reflect the trope of the mimicking Jew. The conflicted lives of Sebald's inauthentic Jews manifest the belief that assimilation cannot hide the innate, atavistic, and ineradicable Jewishness that such Jews sought to conceal: "The Jew, hidden within the chrysalis of his westernized male body, remains a Jew in all his limitations and beliefs. His body reveals him and betrays him. He is fated . . . to become that which he must become."[47] The perpetuation of this injurious Jewish trope in Sebald's narrative prose calls for critical scrutiny and consideration of its implications.

## The Inauthentic Jew in *The Emigrants,* *Vertigo,* and *Austerlitz*

### The "Faustian Pact" of Jewish Assimilation

*The Emigrants* is a sustained thematization of the failure of Jewish assimilation, through which Jews abandoned their Jewishness to embrace an alternative identity and culture. Indeed, the conflicts of assimilation are central to the story of Henry Selwyn. A Lithuanian Jew, whose emigration to England as a child occurred in the shadow of anti-Semitic violence, Hersch Seweryn aspires to exchange his Jewish identity for an English one. As the anglicized Henry Selwyn, he lives the comfortable life of a country doctor, with all the trappings—the substantial home, luxury cars, and anachronistic costume—of an English squire. When the narrator and his wife encounter him, he has exiled himself to his garden hermitage, situated in a remote corner of the garden, his *faux* gothic hermitage a metaphor for his inauthenticity as a Jew who has tried to assume an alternative identity.

"I have never been able to sell anything, except perhaps, at one point, my soul" (*TE*, 21). With this confession, the terrible pact through which Henry Selwyn exchanged authenticity for assimilation is laid bare. Part of an intricate network of allusions to the theater that conveys the inauthenticity of Henry's life as an assimilated Jew, Henry refers to Goethe's drama, *Faust* Part I, in which Faust's wager with Mephistopheles sees the former exchange his arid intellectual life for the seductions of sensuality. Henry Selwyn's costume is self-consciously theatrical: in his tweed jacket with leather patches, or disguised as an eighteenth-century squire in a tartan dressing gown and white neckerchief, he assumes the "mask" of an

47    Gilman, *Franz Kafka*, 168.

English country gentleman. Withdrawn from the social world and from his medical practice, Henry Selwyn is reduced to a "surrogate" figure. His longing to overcome the tradition-bound Jewishness into which he was born, and to assimilate to an English identity, mimics Faust's tragic conflict: "Zwei Seelen wohnen, ach! In meiner Brust." (Alas! Two souls live within me.)[48] The subtext of the Faustian pact imbues Henry Selwyn's conflict with a universal significance that diminishes the individual nature of his tragedy: echoing the divine premonition of Faust's folly, "es irrt der Mensch, so lang er strebt" (Man errs whenever he strives), Henry's unhappy, inauthentic life is emblematic of Sebald's belief that Jewish striving to assimilate would inevitably result in tragedy.[49]

## Henry Selwyn's Home as a Metaphor for his Inauthenticity

The mimicry of the "real" implicit in the metaphor of the theater is implied in the "façades" that line the marketplace near Henry's home. The "neoclassical" style of his house hints at a surrogate identity; so too, the reference that compares his house to "a replica of the façade of the palace of Versailles, an utterly pointless counterfeit. . . ." (*TE*, 4). The metaphor of the theater extends to the lavishly figured garden, "where a mossy path led . . . on through deep shadows, to emerge, as if upon a stage, onto a terrace . . ." (*TE*, 4), and a distanced view opens to the "the lawn to the west . . . and beyond . . . to the white mountains of cloud on the horizon" (*TE*, 5). On this theatrical "stage," the narrator, his wife, and Henry Selwyn are presented as "actors," their encounter invested with a sense of theatrical irreality. Imagery of concealment—"the canopy of branches overhead . . . the ground . . . thickly strewn with empty nutshells" (*TE*, 6–7)— implies the masking of the "real" in Henry's life. Secrecy is implicit in the windows of his house that "glinted blindly, seeming to be made of dark mirror glass" (*TE*, 4). The Meissen figurines on the mantelpiece, a shepherd, a shepherdess, and "a Moor rolling his eyes" (*TE*, 15), suggest artistic mimicry of the "real," the former hinting at the English pastoral idyll that Henry Selwyn sought to adopt as his own, the latter, with its implications of colonialism, a reminder of the exploitative dimension to the bourgeois life that Henry sought to make his own. Reference to the "startlingly ugly *altdeutsch* sideboard, and the refrigerator, "gas-powered and possibly not without its dangers" (*TE*, 8), suggests the precariousness of Henry's assimilated existence by gesturing to the malign German history that overshadows his life.[50] The illusiveness of Henry Selwyn's assimilation is suggested by the "false messianic

48    Goethe, *Faust*, 33.
49    Goethe, *Faust*, 11.
50    "Altdeutsch" translates as "in the old German style."

146 ♦ THE INAUTHENTIC JEW

arrival" of the Lithuanian migrants in London, instead of the "Promised City of New York" (*TE*, 19). In London, Henry's father makes a living as a lens-grinder, evoking Spinoza, a philosopher of profound vision, and a renowned maker of optical lenses, following his excommunication from the Jewish community of Amsterdam in 1656 on the grounds of heresy.[51] The obscure allusion to Spinoza is a reminder of the notion of "seeing" and its opposite, the false reality of obscured vision that signified, to Sebald, the assimilated condition.[52]

Neither Henry Selwyn's name-change, nor his adoption of the antiquated costume of a nineteenth-century English gentleman are proof against resurgent awareness of his Jewish origins. In old age, increasingly troubled by a sense of all he has lost, Henry Selwyn is conflicted between his assimilated English life, and homesickness for an older, traditional Jewish identity represented by his Lithuanian *shtetl*. This division is dramatized in the scissions that fracture his story: the "shattering crash" of the rifle-shot that is proleptic of his suicide (*TE*, 11), the Alpine fall of Naegeli that marks the end of their relationship as a reimagined "German-Jewish symbiosis," the "shattered" slide of the Lasithi plateau, that ruptures his past from the present (*TE*, 17), and his abdication from medical practice that "severed [his] last ties with what they call the real world" (*TE*, 21). Such ruptures point to the divisions of assimilated Jewish life, manifest in his conflicted consciousness of a lost Jewish identity, and the inauthenticity of his English existence.

## Paul Bereyter: The Inauthentic Jew and the Trope of Metamorphosis

Through the figure of Paul Bereyter, Sebald presented an empathetic picture of a life marked by loss: of Jewish identity, abandoned through assimilation, and of hard-won German identity, revoked by the Nuremberg Laws. This was the plight of many assimilated Jews, who would discover that the allegedly "indestructible community of Germans and Jews consisted . . . only of a chorus of Jewish voices and was, on the level of historical reality, a myth that exacted too high a price."[53] Paul Bereyter's resistance to the Jewish identity thrust on him in the context of catastrophe, echoes Améry's claim: "Keiner kann werden, was er vergebens in seinen Erinnerungen sucht," and in the painful conundrum he expresses: "So bin ich auch gerade, was ich nicht bin, weil ich nicht war, ehe ich es

51    Nadler, "Why Spinoza was Excommunicated."
52    This is evident in the deteriorating vision of Paul Bereyter, whose "blindness" precludes him from acknowledging his exiled position as a Jew in his German homeland.
53    Scholem, "Against the Myth," 63.

wurde, vor allem anderen: Jude." (No one can become that which he vainly seeks in his memories . . . And so I am that, what I am not, because I never was that which I was forced to become: a Jew.)[54] For Améry, as it is for Paul, identification as Jewish is to assume an aporetic non-identity that results in the self-annihilatory sense that "mich gibt es nicht." (There is no "I.")[55]

Sebald employed the trope of metamorphosis, borrowed from the natural world, to reveal the process of negative transformation through which Paul evolves from a view of Germany as his home to an acknowledgment of his exiled position as a Jew in Germany. As a teacher, Paul introduces the idea of metamorphosis to his students through the case of cockchafers that depicts the lifecycle of the insect on his classroom wall (*TE*, 31).[56] The trope of negative transformation is explored in Paul's attempt to seek recovery from his mental torment at the salt baths of Salins-les-Bains, the crystallization process metaphorical of the atrophy of Paul's feelings towards his German *Heimat*. On the prevalence of the motif of transformation in Sebald's prose fiction, Prager observes that "his implicit contention is that one's background or national identity may be a confining category out of which one would hope to metamorphose, but cannot."[57] Sebald rejected the conventional view of metamorphosis as resulting in something beautiful or positive: "The idea of transformation, metamorphosis, in terms of turning from a pupa into a beautiful winged thing, doesn't particularly appeal to me. It strikes me as rather trite."[58]

Paul's photograph album depicts his negative metamorphosis from a childhood and youth lived in harmony with nature and other creatures in the *Blumenstrasse*, to the dystopic world he encounters on his final visit to Germany, a vision of obliteration and absence, where "no snow had fallen" and "there was no sign anywhere of any winter tourism" (*TE*, 60). The lives of the suicidal Jewish writers that form the substance of Paul's research towards the end of his life are emblematic of the transformation from belonging, to acknowledgment of extrusion, that finally precipitates

54    Améry, *Jenseits*, 101.
55    Améry, *Jenseits*, 101.
56    The "Maikäfer" or "cockchafer" is the subject of "Maikäfer, flieg!" an old German children's song that thematizes war, expulsion, loss, and destruction, topoi embedded in the consciousness of Paul's young students in the years immediately following the war: "Maikäfer flieg!/ Dein Vater ist im Krieg. / Die Mutter ist im Pommerland, / Pommerland ist abgebrannt, / Maikäfer flieg!" (Fly away, cockchafer! / Your father is at war. / Your mother is in Pomerania, / Pomerania is burnt down. / Fly away, cockchafer!) Such themes are articulated in Sebald's own early recollections of the war, expressed in "Air War and Literature."
57    Prager, "Sebald's Kafka," 106.
58    Kafatou, "An Interview with W. G. Sebald," 35.

148 ♦ THE INAUTHENTIC JEW

Paul's suicide on the train tracks outside his village. As his vision deteriorates, the "mouse-grey" prospect Paul ultimately faces suggests a painful process of evolution that resembles a "transformation of species," an idea that resonates with Kafka's numerous elaborations on this theme, explored by Sebald in an essay in which he posited the failure of attempts to become something other than that for which one is intrinsically destined.[59] The notion of the "mausgrauer Prospekt" (*DA*, 88) that confronts Paul etymologically evokes the German word, *Mauscheln*, the corrupted German spoken by Jews that betrays their ineradicably alien Jewishness. Associated with mice as contaminatory vermin, the word evokes the rhetoric of sickness and parasitism that implicates the Jew in contagion, while suggesting the destructiveness of the Jew, manifest in German proverbs such as "Jews have as much value in the world as mice in corn."[60] In the context of Paul's life as a Jew upon whom Jewishness is imposed as a reminder of his innate identity, the oblique reference to *Mauscheln* suggests the impossibility of transcending ineradicable Jewishness.

The trope of metamorphosis implicitly places Paul's tragedy within the natural world of growth and decay that marks his transformation from a spurious sense of German autochthony, to acknowledgment of his exiled Jewish identity. While undoubtedly poignant, the pathetic fallacy of brooding fir forests and lowering skies that imply Paul's deepening despair imbues his decline with a sense of inevitability that evades questions of causality.

## The Inauthentic Jew and Imagery of the Theater

Alienated from a past he intuits only in fragments of Benjaminian *Jetztzeit*, Austerlitz is presented against a background that conveys inauthenticity through imagery relating to the theater, the world of fantasy and illusion.[61] Indeed, his resemblance to an actor who is himself a simulacrum of Siegfried, a mythical figure, implies Austerlitz's inauthenticity. The hall of Antwerp Centraal station provides a theatrical backdrop to Austerlitz's quest for origins: with its miniaturized waiting passengers, it is a "double" of the Antwerp Nocturama, itself a "topsy turvy" imitation of the "real" world, creating a profoundly illusory context to Austerlitz's quest. Sebald's employment of the "doubling effect" of the theater undermines the pathos of Austerlitz's alienation by abstracting him to the status of

---

59   Sebald, "Tiere, Menschen, Maschinen."
60   Hiemer, *Der Jude im Sprichwort*, 36.
61   Benjamin described his concept of *Jetztzeit* as follows: "The true picture of the past flits by. The past can be seized only as an image which flashes up at the instant when it can be recognized and is never seen again." Benjamin, "On the Concept of History," 390.

a simulacrum. His epiphanic experience in the Liverpool Station Ladies' Waiting-Room is presented as a dramatic moment, in which he steps onto a metaphorical stage (*A*, 189), the "heavy curtain" through which he passes into the Ladies' Waiting-Room symbolizing his transition from the irreality of a life alienated from its "true" origins, to intimation of his authentic self.

For Austerlitz, the illusionary nature of Prague, the putative city of his birth, is conjured by allusions to the world of the theater: his mother Agáta was an opera singer, and, as Vera reminds him, as a child, he attended her rehearsals in the Estates Theater, entering the building "through the stage door," a portal to the deceptive illusory world within. Returning to the theater on his quest for origins, Austerlitz experiences it as a world of surrogate reality, a transcendent space in which "tiers of seats with their gilded adornments shining through the dim light rose to the roof" (*A*, 227). Illuminated by a glimpse of "the bright strip of light between the wooden floorboards and the hem of the curtain" (*A*, 228), Austerlitz's fantasy of seeing Agáta's "sky-blue shoe embroidered with silver sequins" reveals a Romantic yearning for return to the past, and for dissolution of the boundaries between the living and the dead that would reunite him with his mother. Indeed, Vera confirms that Agáta had worn sequined sky-blue shoes with her costume as Olympia, the life-like automaton of E. T. A. Hoffmann's tale, "The Sandman," and an emblem of inauthenticity in Austerlitz's story. Agáta's blue shoe evokes Novalis's "blaue Blume" (blue flower) that, in *Heinrich von Ofterdingen*, represents the Romantic yearning for transcendence of the quotidian: "Fern ab liegt mir alle Habsucht: aber die blaue Blume sehn ich mich zu erblicken." (It is not greed, but only the blue flower I yearn to see.)[62] Agáta returns to Austerlitz's dreams, a spectral figure in an "ashen-grey silk bodice," a reminder of her death by burning in the Holocaust. Unable to discern her face behind an "iridescent veil of pale, cloudy milkiness" (*A*, 229), for Austerlitz, her spectral return signifies the "authentic" life he has lost and is unable, or afraid to imagine.

The Schönborn Garden of Prague offers a panorama of the city that seems to be "veined with the curving cracks and rifts of past time, like the varnish on a painting" (*A*, 230), a simile for the artifice and unreality against which Sebald situates Austerlitz's quest for authenticity. The convoluted roots of a chestnut tree offer incomprehensible patterns in which Austerlitz seeks an answer to the question of his origins; a recurring metaphor for the enduring effect of the Holocaust in Sebald's narrative prose, the chestnut tree is a symbol of the trauma that continues to alienate Austerlitz from his identity. In this brief episode, imagery of the natural world interweaves the remembrance of Austerlitz's putative

62   Novalis, *Heinrich von Ofterdingen*, 9.

150 ♦ THE INAUTHENTIC JEW

Czech childhood with memories of his friend Gerald and England. Ethereal imagery of faded windflowers, finely cut leaves, and snow-white blooms suggests the fragility of memory and the dissolution of past and present in an aestheticized vision that abstracts Austerlitz's tragic quest for authentic selfhood.

## The Lost Twin Brother and Allegories of Expulsion

Hoping to recapture his "true" identity by retracing his original journey as a *Kindertransport* child, Austerlitz travels by train through Germany, perceived as intrinsically inauthentic, "rooted in legend . . . a romantic stage set" with its timeless castles, fir forests, and fabled Rhine river (*A*, 318). The Germany to which he returns is a mythical land, in which boundaries of time have dissolved, and it is "difficult to say even of the castles standing high above the river . . . whether they are medieval or were built by the industrial barons of the nineteenth century" (*A*, 318), and "evening sunlight" coalesces with "the glow of a fiery dawn" (*A*, 318–19). To Austerlitz, modern Germany is founded on mimicry of the past, and ancient buildings "betray not a crooked line anywhere, not at the corners of the houses or on the gables, the window frames or the sills" (*A*, 314). Reference to the "murderous town" of Bacherach recalls the pogrom of 1287, and the eradication of Jews of the Middle and Lower Rhine and Moselle regions, and functions as a reminder of the long German history of anti-Semitic violence, and Austerlitz's own history of persecution as a putatively alien and inauthentic Jew.[63] Sebald's representation of Germany as a naïve and romanticized space—"I see the great river not yet regulated in any way, flooding its banks in places, salmon leaping in the water, crayfish crawling over the sand . . ." (*A*, 319), mythologizes and palliates the conflicted German past in a timeless vision of primordial nature.

On his journey through Germany, Austerlitz is haunted by the image of a silent twin brother whom he imagines to have accompanied him on his original journey through Germany as a *Kindertransport* child, and to have died of consumption and to have been "stowed in the baggage net with the rest of our belongings" (*A*, 317). Austerlitz's sense of inauthenticity is expressed earlier in his consciousness that "I must have made a mistake, and now I am living the wrong life," and his awareness of "someone else walking beside me, or as if something had brushed against

---

63    The Jews of Bacherach were accused of the ritual murder of Werner, aged 16, and of using his blood for Passover observances. The cult of Werner was removed from the Bishopric of Trier calendar in 1963.

me" (*A*, 298).[64] The trope of the lost brother suggests the authentic Jewish life that Sebald believed his assimilated Jewish figures discarded in their quest for *Eindeutschung* (assimilation to German culture); the spectral image of the absent brother is allegorical of the trauma that continues to haunt Sebald's Jewish figures as "the unforgettable forgotten that declines to enter the tribunal of history but has not vanished into the grave."[65] In *Rewizja procesu Józefiny K.* (Revision of the Trial of Josefine K.), an exploration of delayed trauma in Sebald's narrative prose, Adam Lipszyc notes that, for Austerlitz, the spectre of the lost brother represents the *Nachträglichkeit* or delayed trauma of the past, "Austerlitz as his own twin, the one who hides behind the silk veil that separates the living from the dead; it is himself transformed into a spectre, yet at the same time very real, whose place had been taken by Austerlitz-the-emigrant."[66] The absent brother is allegorical in Sebald's narrative prose of the irredeemable loss that is impossible to express as a primary event, and occurs always in its belated, secondary form.

Austerlitz's recollection of his journey through Germany ends with an allusion to "the great army of mice . . . said to have plagued the German countryside, plunging into the river and swimming desperately, their little throats raised only just above the water, to reach the safety of the island" (*A*, 319), evoking the legend of the "Pied Piper of Hamelin." The story is suggested earlier in the reference to the *Mäuseturm* or Mouse Tower, the sight of which illuminates for Austerlitz why the tower of the drowned Welsh village of Vrynwy disturbed him so deeply, evoking as it did, the repressed memory of his original journey through Germany as a *Kindertransport* child. The desperately swimming mice mimic Austerlitz's fate, to have been exiled from Europe as an unwanted, threatening, and alien creature. The vision of the mice with their "little throats upraised" alludes to Kafka's story, "Josephine the Singer, or the Mouse Folk," in which he explores the alleged Jewish capacity for mimicry. In Kafka's story, Josephine "stretch[es] her throat as high as it could reach," although her singing is described as mediocre mimicry:

> Was her actual piping notably louder and more alive than the memory of it will be? Was it even in her lifetime more than a simple memory? Was it not rather because Josephine's singing was already past losing in this way that our people in their wisdom prized it so highly? So perhaps we shall not miss it so very much after all.[67]

---

64    A trope in postwar German literature, the lost brother is central to Peter Handke's *Langsame Heimkehr* (1979), and Hans-Ulrich Treichel's *Der Verlorene* (1999).

65    Tagg, *The Disciplinary Frame*," 73.

66    Lipszyc, *Rewizja procesu Józefiny K.*, 71–86.

67    Kafka, *The Complete* Stories, 389.

Josephine's story thematizes the myth of the inauthentic Jewish discourse, the lack of creativity imputed to Jews and reflected in Wagner's opinion of the Jew as "innately incapable of presenting himself to us artistically through either his outward appearance or his speech, and least of all through his singing."[68] To Geller, the story of Josephine represents the tragedy of Jewish assimilation by demonstrating that "the problems of Jewish identity in post-Emancipation Europe could not be overcome by either acculturation or achievement."[69]

### *Der Sandmann* and False Reality in *Austerlitz*

A Romantic *Märchen* (fairy tale) about illusory reality, E. T. A. Hoffmann's novella, *Der Sandmann* (The Sandman, 1816) forms a subtext to Austerlitz's quest for traces of his mother, a search that is at the same time a quest for truth that would validate his own existence in reality. Hoffman's story explores the question of "authentic" vision of the real and historical, subverted in *Der Sandmann* by Olympia's illusory nature as a life-like automaton, and Nathaniel's choice to exist in a fantasy world. The question of truth and reality in relation to historical events was a fraught issue for Sebald, motivated by the desire to address historical injury in the post-Holocaust context, but oppressed by consciousness of his belatedness in doing so.

From Vera, Austerlitz discovers that Agáta was known for singing the part of the Olympia in Jacques Offenbach's opera, *The Tales of Hoffmann* (1881), based on E. T. A. Hoffmann's stories. The longing to "see" and "reanimate" Agáta by scanning the Theresienstadt film for her image, aligns Austerlitz with Hoffmann's protagonist, Nathaniel, who becomes obsessed with seeing Olympia through a spyglass that distorts reality and endows her with life. For both Austerlitz and Nathaniel, reality has been shaped by trauma: for Nathaniel, this is the fantasy of being dismembered as a child by Coppola, for Austerlitz, the psychic damage caused by rupture from his parents at a young age. Both rely on the "artificial eye"—the spyglass, the camera—to reveal to them the subjective reality they crave. At his first appearance, Austerlitz is depicted with his "old Ensign with telescopic bellows" (*A*, 7), through which he controls, and distances, what he sees. Indeed, Austerlitz's photography is a metaphor for his attempt to avoid confronting reality, and for his tentative process of remembering, illustrated by "the moment when the shadows of reality . . . emerge out of nothing on the exposed paper, as memories do in the middle of the night . . ." (*A*, 109).

---

68    Wagner, *Judaism in Music*, 87.
69    Geller, "Of Mice and Mensa, 379.

In his response to the problem of belatedness in bearing witness to trauma that was not his, Sebald employed the magical potential of the fairy tale, a problematic genre in relation to the depiction of the Holocaust and its aftermath, owing to its employment to support Nazi ideology. Hoffmann's story confirms the difficulty of penetrating the real or historical: Nathaniel never perceives Olympia as the lifeless object she is, and Austerlitz does not recognize his mother in the Theresienstadt film. Indeed, Sebald's reimagination of Hoffmann's fairy tale confirms Peter Arnds's observation that the postwar fairy tale "no longer seems to promise an intact order in which moral values can be re-established."[70] In figuring Austerlitz's inauthenticity, Sebald used Hoffmann's story as an allegory through which to posit the idea that the "real" or "true" "lies elsewhere, away from it all, somewhere as yet undiscovered" (*A*, 71–72). Sebald's oblique gaze, and the opacity of his allusive and complex figurations, suggest that, like Hoffmann's protagonist, he preferred to evade painful reality behind figural obscurity that potentially distorts and aestheticizes catastrophe. In Austerlitz's memory, great-uncle Alphonso's glasses, "with grey silk tissue instead of lenses in the frames, so that the landscape appeared through a fine veil that muted its colors" (*A*, 124), are a metaphor for Sebald's figural obscuration of historical reality, and the potential this holds to diminish and aestheticize catastrophe.

### The Divisions of Jewish Assimilation

In the figure of Dr K., Sebald dramatized the division in German-Jewish middleclass identity, between assimilation and tradition-bound Jewishness.[71] The longing for a different identity is metaphorical of Sebald's own, second-generation German yearning for an alternative identity to his tainted German one. This is implicit in Sebald's "doubling" of himself, in photographs, identity documents, and biographical information, in relation to his German narrator-figure, and his phantom presence as the *Doppelgänger* of Jewish figures, into whose lives he "sutures himself."[72] Sebald utilized the deception implicit in the theater as a simulacrum of the "real" world to suggest the inauthenticity of assimilated Jewish life. Indeed, the vision of Dr K., sitting "like a ghost at the table," conjures the specter of Banquo at Macbeth's table in Shakespeare's eponymous play, and implies the inauthenticity of Dr K.'s identity as an assimilated Czech Jew, eagerly embracing German language and culture.

70    Arnds, "On the Awful German Fairy Tale," 423.
71    In Sebald's narrative prose, biographical details and allusion to Kafka's writings suggest that Dr K. figurally embodies the writer, Kafka.
72    Long, "History, Narrative," 137.

154 ♦ THE INAUTHENTIC JEW

The notion of the "double" as allegorical of the conflict between the assimilated, implicitly inauthentic self, and the traditional Jewish self, is prefigured in the brief interlude in which Dr K. and his companions, Ehrenstein and Pick, entertain themselves in Vienna. Dr K. describes Ehrenstein as looking exactly like Pick, "whom he so resembles he could be his twin brother. As like as two eggs . . ." (*V*, 143). Dr K.'s aversion to his companion, Otto Pick, focuses on what is implied to be the latter's hidden Jewish identity, manifest as "a small, unpleasant hole in his nature through which he sometimes creeps forth in his entirety . . ." (*V*, 143), implying the notion of Jewishness as a hidden taint, and fear of its disclosure.[73] In Vienna, Dr K.'s thoughts are dominated by sexual conflict that mirrors the divisions of his assimilated identity: torn between marriage, and acknowledging his homosexuality by "tak[ing] the only possible step beyond a friendship with men" (*V*, 142), his homosexual inclinations are personified in the haunting presence of the writer, Grillparzer, whose lascivious advances, "laying a hand on Dr K.'s knee" (*V*, 142), conjure Kafka's "Hunter Gracchus" story, at the end of which the hunter lays his hand on the burgomaster's knee. In the story of Dr K., Gracchus's eternal exile becomes a metaphor for the conflicted condition of Dr K., tormented by irresolvable divisions between traditional Jewishness and assimilation, and between socially sanctioned marriage, and living an "intolerable" life as a homosexual.[74]

Imagery of deception and mirroring imply Dr K.'s consciousness that his assimilated identity masks a hidden, innate Jewishness, conflated in his imagination with anxiety about his sexual orientation. "On the borderline between grinding weariness and half-sleep," Dr K.'s sexual anxieties are explored in his fantasy of a plaster angel descending on him, its raised sword pointing forward as a (phallic) symbol of his sexual conflict, and of the act of circumcision that marks Dr K. as a Jewish other, cutting him off from wider society.[75] For Dr K., the advancing angel represents the hope of release from sexual and identity conflict: "A veritable angel . . . all day long it has flown towards me and I of little faith knew nothing of it. Now he will speak to me . . ." (*V*, 146), a longing for redemption that is undermined by his discovery that the angel is not a living angel but a painted ship's figurehead. In a church in Verona, Dr K.'s experience of being "on the threshold between the dark interior and the brightness outside" (*V*,

73    Otto Pick was a Czech Jewish author and friend of Kafka's with whom he attended a Zionist conference in Vienna in 1913. Pick belonged to the German-speaking Jewish community of Prague and to the literary circle that included Max Brod, Franz Kafka, and Franz Werfel.

74    Kafka, *Letters to Felice*.

75    Kafka, *Diaries*, 292. The account of the dream is borrowed from Kafka's recording of a daydream, June 25, 1914.

149), causes him to feel for a moment as if the church were replicated before him, "a mirroring effect he was familiar with from his dreams, in which everything was forever splitting and multiplying, over and again, in the most terrifying manner" (*V*, 149), prefiguring the mirror scene that, in the film, *The Student of Prague*, dramatically represents the divisions of Jewish identity between traditional Jewishness, and Jewishness as mimetic of bourgeois Germanness. Seeking solace from his "solitary, eccentric condition" in the *Cinema Pathé di San Sebastiano* in Verona (*V*, 150), Dr K. is believed to have watched *The Student of Prague*, a popular film at the time.[76] The name of the cinema evokes the suffering of St Sebastian and his adoption as a homosexual icon, a symbol here of Dr K.'s sexual divisions. Through the doubled figure of Balduin, *The Student of Prague* dramatizes the Faustian pact of the student's bargain with Scapinelli: "He [Balduin] sold his soul to a certain Scapinelli," thus "cutting himself off from love and life" (*V*, 150–51), and losing his own reflection. The dramatization of the disjuncture of self and threatening other within the conflicted German Jew is articulated in Balduin's anguished acknowledgment, "My own image is my opponent." Sebald suggested that the *Student of Prague* is the story of Kafka, "pursued by his own likeness," frightened by the "progressive de-realization of his own person and the approach of death."[77]

George Mosse describes *fin de siècle* Jews as "conforming to a negative stereotype of men who not only failed to measure up to the ideal [of masculinity], but who in body and soul were its foil," according to the regime of power that constituted Germans as the norm, and Jews as sites of difference.[78] This tension is manifest in the figure of the Eastern European Jewish bookseller's unmanly, bookish son, who "feels himself (as Dr K. knows) to be German and for that reason goes to the *Deutsches Haus* (German House) every evening after supper to nurture his delusion of grandeur as a member of the German Casino Club" (*V*, 166). The episode reflects the tensions between assimilatory Jews, and Jews who sought to maintain their distinct Jewishness. A critique of assimilation, the *Deutsches Haus* episode allegorizes Sebald's perception of the moral and physical deformation of the Jew who aspired to assimilate to German society: the son of the Jewish bookshop owner is presented as "in no way attractive, indeed repulsive, who has had nothing but misfortune in his life . . ." (*V*, 166). He reflects the conflict within Jewish identity, between "dusting off the prayer stoles," and "peeking out at the street through gaps between books . . . mostly of an obscene nature" (*V*, 166), between the old, authentic Jewishness, and a secular, assimilatory identity.

76    Allred, "Foreign Bodies."
77    Sebald, "Kafka at the Movies," 165.
78    Mosse, *The Image of Man*, 6.

156 ♦ THE INAUTHENTIC JEW

The episode parodies the image of the Jews as the "People of the Book," replacing the notion of Jewish obedience to the written Law with obscenity and fraudulence. The son of the bookshop owner is described as ambiguous in appearance, "it is hard to tell whether he is indeed straight as a ramrod, or malformed" (*V*, 166), a comment on the chimerical nature of his appearance as a Jew, conflicted between Jewish and German identities. Dr K.'s relationship to him is ambiguous, vacillating between revulsion and sexual attraction, metaphorical of his own division in relation to his Jewishness and sexuality. Dr K. follows him, "veritably lusting," and watches the man "enter the gates of the *Deutsches Haus* with a prurient feeling of "unbounded pleasure" that conflates capitulation to repressed sexual desire with the assimilatory urge and its fulfillment.

### The Memoirs of Luisa Lanzberg: A Vision of Jewish Authenticity?

As a trope in Sebald's writing, the inauthentic Jew presupposes the possibility of Jewish authenticity, and what this might mean in Sebald's writing. While the life stories of his Jewish figures are for the most part histories of failed adaptation to an alternative identity, the embedded narrative of Luisa Lanzberg's memoirs offers a rare insight into what Sebald appeared to have considered a desirable and "authentic" Jewishness. Luisa's memoirs reveal a conservative form of Jewish existence that adheres to tradition, and retains awareness of its otherness in the context of the broader German environment. In Luisa's nostalgic recollections of childhood and youth in rural Franconia, Jewish life is imbued with a sense of purpose and belonging through observance of the rituals and festivals that punctuate the seasons. It is through the celebration of ritual and commemoration of historical events that the traditional Jewishness depicted by Luisa betrays its roots in the Middle Eastern desert of Jewish exile: the Lanzberg family celebrates the festivals of Passover and Tabernacles that commemorate the Jewish exodus from Egypt and forty-year wandering in the Sinai desert; the *menorah* in their living room symbolizes the narrative of Maccabee resistance, while the observance of the Sabbath is a reminder of the commandments given to Moses at Sinai.

Luisa's memoirs resemble the Jewish "*Heimat* literature" of Eastern Europe that fascinated Sebald and influenced his depiction of traditional Jewish life in the embedded narrative of her diaries. A genre that looks back to a Jewish world, abandoned with the opening up of the ghettos, and the movement to the West and assimilation of Eastern European Jews to the cultures of Western Europe, these stories of Jewish life evince a sentimental sense of loss, and were generally aimed at readers who shared this feeling, or at non-Jewish readers in the hope of educating them in Jewish customs and idioms. Sebald explored ghetto stories in "Westwärts–Ostwärts: Aporien deutschsprachiger Ghettogeschichten"

(Westward–Eastward: Aporias of German-Language Ghetto Stories) and in his essay on Joseph Roth, "Ein Kaddisch für Österreich—Über Joseph Roth" (A Memorial Prayer for Austria—On Joseph Roth), both essays in *Unheimliche Heimat*. Ghetto stories offer nostalgic and idealized pictures of Jewish family life, wrily described by Sebald as "Biedermeierliches im Lampenschein" (cosy by lamplight).[79] The Sabbath meal is central to these stories, and symbolizes the observance of ritual that regulated Jewish life in the ghetto. The chronicles of Kompert, Franzos, and Roth reflect ambivalence between adherence to the traditional past and assimilation to bourgeois values; the writing of Franzos posits the pessimistic idea of the cemetery as the *Heimat* of the Jews, "wo der blaue Himmel freundlich auf das kleine Feld herablächelt, das ganz eingehüllt ist in frisches Grün." (. . . where the blue sky smiles down kindly on the small plot, and the whole scene is wrapped in fresh green.)[80] Lamenting the dearth of nature depictions in Eastern European ghetto stories, Franzos noted, "nur zwischen den Grabsteinen keimt frisches Grün, nur über den Toten weht Blumenduft." (Fresh greenery grows only between the gravestones, the fragrance of flowers wafts only over the dead.)[81] Indeed, the peaceful Jewish cemetery is a recurrent trope in Sebald's prose fiction, positing the idea that Jewish assimilation to the *Heimat* earth is possible only in death. In the writing of Roth, exemplified in *Juden auf Wanderschaft* (The Wandering Jews, 1927), Sebald identified a yearning for a prelapsarian past, pessimism about Jewish migration to the West, and a melancholy undertone that cohered with his own essentialist vision of Jewish authenticity.

As early as 2005, Klaus Gasseleder's comparative analysis exposed Sebald's extensive and unattributed appropriation of Thea Gebhardt's memoirs as a pre-text for Luisa's recollections of her youth.[82] Sebald's falsifications in relation to his source were revealed more recently by Angier.[83] Despite this, for both Gasseleder and Angier, Sebald's appropriation of Gebhardt's memoirs is mitigated by the manner in which he changed her original diaries to reflect his own melancholy worldview, and imbued them, through his figural elaborations, with philosophical depth. The narrator of her memoirs, Luisa will be murdered at Riga, and her recollections are shadowed from early childhood by awareness of the nearness of death. By contrast, Thea Gebhardt survived the war, and her retrospective gaze is a nuanced one that acknowledges the ambivalence or "zwei Gesichter" (two faces) of the German approach to Jews.

---

79   Sebald, "Westwärts–Ostwärts," 59.
80   Franzos, *Die Juden von Barnow*, 289.
81   Franzos, *Die Juden von Barnow*, 296.
82   Gasseleder, "Erkundungen zum Prätext."
83   Angier, *Speak, Silence*.

158 ◆ THE INAUTHENTIC JEW

In his construction of Luisa's memoirs, Sebald also drew on the tradition of the Yizkor (memorial) books that, since 1945, have documented and mourned lost German and European Jewish communities. The tradition of Yizkor books goes back to the thirteenth century, and the Eastern European Jewish practice of memorializing towns and villages, family, communities, and places of interest damaged or destroyed in pogroms. Post-Holocaust Yizkor books written by Holocaust survivors draw on local record books that document the social and economic aspects of lost, mainly Eastern European Jewish communities, and combine these with the tradition of the Yizkor or "memory book" that recorded the names of pogrom victims.[84] Unlike the Yizkor books, the memoirs of Luisa Lanzberg do not describe post-Holocaust Jewish life. This is left to the German narrator, whose return to Bad Kissingen exposes the forgetfulness of the German people, and his own feelings of rejection towards them. In a two-part structure, Luisa's memoirs chronicle her youth in idyllic Steinach, and her coming-of-age and the darkening of her world in the colder environment of Bad Kissingen. Sebald extends the scope of the original Yizkor books to suggest that the Holocaust is not relegated to the past, but ever-present, exemplified by the neglected Jewish cemetery with its archaic name, "israelitischer Friedhof" (Israelite cemetery), and the warning on the cemetery gate against vandalism. The narrator's ironic remark, "It goes without saying . . . that there are no Jews in Steinach now" (*TE*, 193) sets the scene for the unfolding of Luisa's recollections.

A sense of immediacy is achieved through the first-person narrative by Luisa as a member of the lost community; her narrative in the present continuous tense creates the sense of a past that is still occurring. The tone is naïve and nostalgic: in a passage largely taken from Thea Gebhardt's memoirs, Luisa imagines the meandering road to the village that she describes, with childlike innocence, as "her real home" (*TE*, 194). Her familiarity with the topography and people, identified by their occupation—Liebmann the slaughterer, Gessner the baker, Meier Frei the merchant—recalls the Eastern European *Ghettogeschichten* (ghetto stories) of Sholem Aleichem, whose idealized picture of ghetto life, peopled by Tevye the dairyman, Motl the cantor's son, and Yente the matchmaker, is evidence of a viable, pre-Holocaust Jewish life in Eastern Europe.[85] In the idyll of Luisa's chronicle, meadows "spread before you" and "the fields open out," suggesting the embrace of Jewish life in rural Franconia (*TE*, 194); the image of the Windheim woods that "nestle in a gentle curve" (*TE*, 194) implies the protective nature of this environment. The juxtaposition of Jewish tradition with emblems of the German

84    Hall, "Jewish Memory in Exile."
85    Aleichem, *Tevye the Dairyman*.

world reflects an apparently harmonious German-Jewish coexistence that sees "the old castle with its cobbled forecourt and the Luxburg arms" (*TE*, 194) counterposed with the "Federgasse" (feather lane) that evokes the rustic Eastern-European *shtetl*; so too, the conjunction of the assimilated German-Jewish poet Heine, the Jewish Sabbath, and the conservative newspaper, the *Münchner Neueste Nachrichten* (the Munich Latest News) in which Luisa's mother immerses herself every evening" (*TE*, 195). Luisa's memoirs offer a vision of traditional Jewishness, respected and tolerated within a German Christian environment: in the German school, Jewish students are excused from Christian morning prayers; for their part, Jewish students acknowledge allegiance to "the earth, the sea, and the *Reich* (*TE*, 204), and the teacher, Salomon Bein, regards himself as "a loyal servant of the state" (*TE*, 202–3).

The narrative perspective contracts from the countryside to the village, and finally, to the Jewish home itself, conceived as existing discretely within the broader enclave of the gentile German world. The reiteration of "stehen" (to stand)—"hier steht das Haus der Lions . . . es stehen die Häuser des Bäckers Gessner . . . des Schlächters Liebmann und des Mehlhändlers Salomon Stern" (There stands the house of the Lions. . . . there stand the houses of Gessner the baker . . . Liebmann the butcher and Solomon Stern the flour-merchant). . . . culminating in "jetzt stehe ich . . . wieder in der Wohnstube" (*DA*, 290–91; Now I stand once again in the living room), conveys Luisa's feeling of rootedness to this home and the *Heimat* around it. Fuchs describes Luisa's memoirs as a sentimental "Gedächtnisort" (place of memory) that draws on Pierre Nora's concept of sacralized islands of remembrance, and indeed, the Lanzberg home in Steinach is a nostalgically evoked "lost world," an icon of "Heimischkeit" (homeliness), in which Jewish religious festivals follow the rhythm of the seasons, and objects of Jewish ritual, such as the silver menorah, combine with the collected works of Heine and the photograph of a beautiful aunt, a "true Germania," to form a "reliquiary" of the German-Jewish symbiosis experienced by the Lanzberg family before its destruction in the Holocaust.[86] The tone is sentimental and celebratory in Luisa's recollection of "golden tendrils of vine" adorning the leather-bound volumes of Heine's poetry (*TE*, 195), and the "golden-green grapes" that hang from the ceiling during the festival of Sukkoth (*TE*, 201). Images suggesting preservation against decay—the evergreen bridal bouquet, and the naphthaline to protect winter clothes from destruction by moths—imply belief in the enduring nature of the German-Jewish relationship, ironically memorialized in her memoirs. Such hope is posited in Luisa's chronicling of the cycle

---

86    Fuchs, "'Ein auffallend geschichtsblindes und traditionsloses Volk,'" 95–96.

160 ♦ THE INAUTHENTIC JEW

of Jewish festivals celebrated with the change of seasons, a utopian vision of traditional Jewish life, lived unhindered in a German context; imagery of eternality, exemplified by Salomon Bein's collection of ageless gemstones, "rose quartz, rock crystal, amethyst, topaz and tourmaline," is metaphorical of the hope that the German-Jewish coexistence depicted in Luisa's memoirs would last forever (*TE*, 203).

As it is in the ghetto stories of Franzos, Kompert, and Roth, celebration of the Sabbath is a vital expression of traditional Jewishness in Luisa's chronicles, in which it is associated with the repetition of comforting rituals: the cutting of paper cuffs "especially every time" for the silver candelabrum required for the Sabbath (*TE*, 195), and the weekly visit to the "fish man," and the "baker to whom we took our Sabbath meals on Friday evenings," a reference to the injunction on cooking on the Sabbath in traditional Jewish households. Luisa's memories of the Sabbath are a conflation of Jewish tradition and secular visions of bourgeois life: of her father going to the synagogue in his frock coat and top hat, of smelling the spice box at the end of the Sabbath, and of family and friends, playing billiards and drinking beer at the Kissingen spa, where Jews came into contact with the outside world.

There are hints of the catastrophe that would befall the German Jews: the names of neighboring villages—Aschach, Kleinbrach—evoke the idea of ash, and with it, Auschwitz as emblematic of the Holocaust; so too, the cautionary tale of Paulinchen, "the girl who went up in flames," and the discovery of a solution that could fire-proof "even the finest of materials" (*TE*, 200). The figure of Kathinka, who walks endlessly around the chestnut tree in the square, "knitting something that she plainly never finishes" (*TE*, 196), is allegorical of unfinished Jewish lives, and of the enduring impact of the Holocaust. The disappearance of Siegfried Frei, thought to have emigrated to Argentina or Panama, and the spectral vision of Luisa's father "in his death robes, moving about the house like a ghost" on the Jewish Day of Atonement (*TE*, 201), are proleptic of Jewish displacement and destruction. Luisa's lively recollection of fetching a fish for the Sabbath meal darkens momentarily at the haunting memory of "the skewed fish-eyes [that] often went on watching me even in my sleep" (*TE*, 198). The "pieces of silver . . . the Hollegrasch coins" given to Luisa's brother by his godfather every year, are a poignant metaphor for the continuity of Jewish life that would be ruptured by the betrayal of German Jews that, for the Lanzbergs, still lies in the future (*TE*, 199).[87] While the motif of the overshadowing tree carries no hint of future disaster in Thea Gebhardt's memoirs, in Luisa's diaries, the chestnut tree that overshadows the Steinach square is thematically connected to other iterations of the motif to suggest its baleful significance, implicit

---

87    Judas betrayed Jesus for thirty pieces of silver (Matthew 26: 15).

in Aurach's admission that "tragedy in my youth struck such deep roots within me that it later shot up again, put forth evil flowers, and spread the poisonous canopy over me which has kept me so much in the shade and dark in recent years" (*TE*, 191). Luisa's wistful narrative voice acknowledges the shadow the past casts on the present and future, "[time] seems as if it had been open-ended, in every direction, indeed—as if it were still going on, right into these lines I am now writing" (*TE*, 207), reflecting Sebald's darker perspective, that sees the Holocaust as an event continuing into the present.

The second part of Luisa's memoirs records her coming-of-age in Kissingen, where her father hoped to establish a position in middle-class German society. By comparison with her childhood recollections, her memories of this time are dominated by bitter cold, alienation, and deepening shadow. Scenes of rustic life give way to distant views from her "top-floor window across the flower beds of the spa nursery gardens to the green, wooded hills all around" (*TE*, 210). With its somber Flemish furniture and carved columns, oppressive in the "pale, hissing gaslight" (*TE*, 209), the Lanzberg villa in Kissingen is "a strange place," in which she feels like a "visitor, passing through" (*TE*, 210), a foreshadowing of her displacement, and eventual destruction. Natural phenomena, in the form of Halley's comet that eclipses the sun and sees the "shadow of the moon blotting out the sun . . . and the birds flapping about in a frightened panic" (*TE*, 211), reflect a darkening of her world; the "huge shadow" of a zeppelin overhead hints at the war to come. As Gasseleder notes, for Luisa, even love is overshadowed by death: her meeting with her first, doomed fiancé, follows a visit to the salt-vapor frames, metaphorical of the transformation of the living into the dead. Fritz Waldorf's proposal to Luisa evokes in her the memory of a young butterfly hunter, seen once before, and remembered as "a messenger of joy" (*TE*, 214). Deriving from the sixth chapter of Nabokov's autobiographical memoir, *Speak, Memory*, the butterfly hunter signals, in Sebald's writing, "the zone of the unreal . . . the possibility that forever remains suggested but unrealized."[88] As an emblem of happiness in Luisa's memoirs, its appearance is rendered ironic by Fritz Waldorf's premature death.

Luisa's memoirs of young adulthood are dominated by the First World War, suffering, and death. Her marriage to Fritz Aurach, who hoped to set himself up in middle-class life as a dealer in fine art, is arranged by a Jewish marriage broker, suggesting the continuity of traditional Jewishness within the context of the bourgeois German world. As a measure of his identification with the lives of Luisa and her family, Sebald inscribes himself into Luisa's narrative through reference to the injury of a young German *Freikorps* (free corps) soldier by the name of Egelhofer,

---

88    Curtin and Shrayer, "Netting the Butterfly Man," 277.

162 ♦ THE INAUTHENTIC JEW

the name of Sebald's beloved grandfather, and through allusion to Luisa and Fritz's visit to the Allgäu, where Sebald himself grew up. In Luisa's memoirs, recollection of carefree activities is overshadowed by a sense of impending doom: a view from the Bavarian Alps offers a scene "so peaceful, it was as if nothing evil had ever happened anywhere on earth" (*TE*, 217), a utopian vision undermined by a storm far below, and by the faint evocation of the persecutory associations of the Jewish star-emblem in the name of Luisa's street, *Sternwartstrasse*. Her memoirs are open-ended: ice-skating on the Theresienwiese is recalled in "shades of blue everywhere—a single empty space, stretching out into the twilight of the late afternoon . . ." (*TE*, 218), an image of absence, proleptic of Luisa's tragic fate, and that of her family, murdered at Auschwitz.

The precarious idyll of German-Jewish life depicted in Luisa's memoirs contrasts with the alienation and social withdrawal that characterizes the lives of Sebald's other Jewish figures, suggesting that, in Sebald's textual world, the life of the Lanzberg family represents a desirable, "authentic" mode of Jewish existence: conscious of their non-identity with gentile German society, the Lanzbergs live a middle-class German life, dress in the style of the bourgeoisie, and aspire to middle-class measures of success, while maintaining a lived connection with an ancient Jewish identity through observance of religious and cultural traditions. The memoirs of Luisa Lanzberg present a nostalgic, traditional, and prescriptive view of "authentic" Jewish life, the stability of which functions as a reproach to the alienated Jewish figures Sebald depicted as abandoning their Jewishness in order to assimilate.

In handing Luisa's memoirs to the German narrator for safe-keeping, Max Aurach describes them as "an evil German fairytale, in which, once you are under the spell, you have to carry on to the finish, till your heart breaks, with whatever work you have begun—in this case, the remembering, writing, and reading" (*TE*, 193). The notion of the German-Jewish tragedy as an "evil German fairy tale" evokes the magical world of the *Kunstmärchen* (literary fairy tale) of Novalis and the Grimm brothers, and suggests the illusory nature of the German-Jewish relationship; more problematically, it places the genocide of the Jews in the realm of myth and fairy tale, mitigating the brutal actuality of the catastrophe.

Sebald employed the trope of the inauthentic, mimicking Jew to pursue the argument that "authentic" Jewish identity is based in awareness of an originary Jewish "essence," posited as Eastern and nomadic, and evoked in the rituals and traditions of Jewish life celebrated with self-conscious awareness of its heteronomy within the broader gentile world. Torn between the desire for an alternative identity, and the tug of what Sebald saw as the spiritual sustenance of traditional Jewishness, the lives of Sebald's assimilated Jewish figures chronicle the moral and physical deformation resulting from abjuration of Jewish tradition, and the "masking" of the Rosenzweigian quality of Jewish particularity. In portraying his assimilated Jews as mimics of the society in which they find themselves, Sebald perpetuated troubling historical perspectives that impute falseness to the Jew, potentially implicate the Jew as agent of his own destruction, and homogenize the notion of what constitutes Jewish authenticity.

# 5:  The Sickly Jew

*He feels ill, sick, as he puts it, at every point of the compass*
—"Dr K. takes the Waters at Riva," *Vertigo*

SEBALD'S NARRATIVE PROSE asks us to consider the question of suffering intrinsic to a disintegrating world, in which nature itself "groan[s] and collaps[es] beneath the burden we placed upon it" (*TE*, 7), and mortified bodies are "doubled up by grief like snapped reeds" (*TE*, 170), or implied in sheet-covered forms in a forest clearing. His prose fiction dwells on the body in pain, exemplified in Grünewald's paintings, in which "the extreme vision of that strange man . . . distorted every limb, and infected the colors like an illness" (*TE*, 170). In Sebald's writing, the decaying human body reflects a fascination with illness and disintegration, manifest in the vision of Emperor Hsien-feng's death: "The waters had already risen from his abdomen to his heart, and the cells of his gradually dissolving flesh floated like fish in the salt fluid that leaked from his bloodstream into every available space in the body tissue" (*RS*, 146). To Sebald, the human body is never a refuge, but always a source of anguish; his Jewish subjects suffer symptoms of paralysis, disabling anxiety, melancholy, and blindness, in response to a world in a relentless process of dissolution. In his narrative prose, Sebald explored the experiential dimension to mental suffering, and its creative, and indeed, resistant potential, reflecting his dictum, "Die Beschreibung des Unglücks schließt in sich die Möglichkeit zu seiner Überwindung ein." (The description of our dismal plight carries with it the possibility of overcoming that unhappiness.)[1] To Eleanor Wachtel, Sebald expressed his concern about suffering in the world:

> There is a great deal of mental anguish in the world, and some of it we see and some of it we try to deal with . . . I think the physical and mental pain in a sense is increasing. If you imagine the amount of painkillers that are consumed, say in the city of New York every year, you might be able to make a mountain out of it on which you could go skiing . . . And certainly, when it's a question of mental anguish . . . only very little of it is ever revealed . . . those of us who are spared this live unaware of the fact that there are these huge mental asylums everywhere and that there is a fluctuating part of the

---

1    Sebald, *Die Beschreibung des Unglücks*, 12.

population which is forever wandering through them. It is a characteristic of our species, in evolutionary terms, that we are a species in despair . . . We're living exactly on the borderline between the natural world . . . and that other world which is generated by our brain cells.[2]

Implicit in Sebald's observation is an ambiguity in relation to suffering and its causality: situated on the faultline that runs through our physical and emotional makeup, and the destructive power of the natural world, illness and suffering in Sebald's prose writing are posited as both intrinsic to a naïve, natural world of dissolution and pain, and contingent upon a man-made world in which genocide, dispossession, and displacement are the results of human formulation. To Santner, Sebald's "lifeless landscapes" and "humans marked by death" (*TE*, 170) are allegorical of "an absence of balance in nature . . . a nature already thrown off its tracks, a nature already 'written asunder' by human history."[3] While his literary historiography allows him to explore the human condition as shaped by such conflicting forces, Sebald is inclined to explore suffering within the context of a natural world, driven by enigmatic forces. In Sebald's prose fiction, illness is presented in veiled and mystifying terms that obscure comprehension, and treatment is sought in natural remedies, or immersion in nature. The pain of Sebald's Jewish characters is not ameliorated by discovering the origin of their trauma, which remains incomprehensible to them. Even as he recounts the story of his oppressive Welsh childhood, Austerlitz admits to a sense of being directed by an incomprehensible power, "far greater than or superior to my own capacity for thought . . ." (*A*, 60). While he discovers from Vera what he believes to be the human agency from which his trauma originates, Austerlitz nevertheless projects onto the natural world of earthquakes, desert, and impenetrable mist the pain he experiences (*A*, 322–23).

By imputing Jewish illness and suffering to the vicissitudes of an indifferent natural world, Sebald obfuscates the question of German agency in the conception and execution of the Holocaust. As Mark Ilsemann notes, *Austerlitz* "bars itself against any intrusion of psychology, choice, and comprehensible causality."[4] In Sebald's natural history of destruction, Ward sees a metaphysical explanation for suffering that refuses to name an agent in the process of ruination.[5] Sebald's tendency to view illness and human misery in the context of a universalized history of natural

---

2    Wachtel, "Ghost Hunter," 56.
3    Santner, *On Creaturely Life*, 99.
4    Ilsemann, "Going Astray," 302.
5    Ward, "Ruins and Poetics," 61.

166 ♦ THE SICKLY JEW

destruction circumvents the question of German responsibility for Jewish suffering, as Franklin observes:

> Sebald's work has always presented suffering without its cause, as merely a part of the great pattern of pain that defines the human condition. We see this in the unique brand of melancholy that afflicts his characters, a melancholy that always seems to exist outside their comprehension.[6]

Sebald's disinclination to confront the trauma central to the Jewish lives he memorializes has profound implications: his reluctance to invade what he may have perceived to be an inalienably Jewish space of mourning gives rise to a vestigial form of *Bilderverbot* (prohibition on visual representation), manifest in an allegorical and opaque narrative mode that risks mythologizing the Holocaust and the suffering of those in its aftermath, and subsuming the sickly Jew in a natural world of pain and dissolution. At the heart of this is Sebald's broader view of history that refuses causal logic:

> Wir wissen ja inzwischen, dass Geschichte nicht so abläuft, wie die Historiker des 19. Jahrhunderts uns das erzählt haben, also nach irgendeiner von großen Personen diktierten Logik, nach irgendeiner Logik überhaupt. Es handelt sich um ganz andere Phänomene, um so etwas wie ein Driften, um Verwehungen, um naturhistorische Muster, um chaotische Dinge, die irgendwann koinzidieren und wieder auseinander laufen.[7]
>
> [We know now that history does not function in the way that the historians of the nineteenth century have told us . . . that is, according to a logic dictated by great individuals, not according to any logic at all. History has more to do with completely different phenomena, with something like drifting, with natural historical patterns, with chaotic things that for a certain time coincide and then later go their separate ways.]

Sebald's resistance to causal logic affiliates his writing with the work of parascientific English biologist, Rupert Sheldrake, whose holistic "morphic field" theory has been widely condemned, if not derided, by conventional scientists, with John Maddox, editor of *Nature*, describing it as "a book for burning."[8] Sheldrake was a figure in whom Sebald found a kindred spirit, describing him as "very close to me," one of the people

6    Franklin, "Rings of Smoke," 140.
7    Hage, "Im Gespräch mit W. G. Sebald."
8    Maddox, "A book for burning?"

"without whom I couldn't pursue my work."[9] While Sebald maintained that "I don't particularly hold with parapsychological explanations of one kind or another . . . I find it all rather tedious," he insisted that "we somehow need to make sense of our nonsensical existence."[10] Sebald's morally neutral view of history underlies his universalization of Jewish genocide in a myth of natural destruction that blurs questions of agency, and potentially mitigates German guilt in relation to the Holocaust. But, as Margalit reminds us, historical specificity remains important in remembering the Holocaust, noting that "the standing of Germans as a community of memory connected to the perpetrators does not leave them the option of acting on behalf of humanity at large. They are a side to this memory."[11]

## The Sickly Jew and Sebald's Generational Predicament

Embodiments of impairment and inadequacy, Sebald's sickly Jewish figures are metaphorical of a deficit perceived by the second generation in relation to their own bodies and minds that derives from a problematic legacy of unacknowledged shame and guilt inherited from the parent generation. In her case studies of second-generation patients, Anita Eckstaedt describes the pathological absorption by the second generation of the repressed guilt of their parents: "The totality of what the parent generation had experienced, but also accepted during the 'Third Reich,' becomes evident in the second generation as a sickness," manifest in psychic deformation resulting from the repression of self in order to accommodate the parental legacy of shame and guilt.[12] In the adoption, by the second generation, of "illusory, unexpiated, and unnamed fragments of the past," Eckstaedt identifies a dispossession of self, a loss of hope, an unidentifiable but pervasive melancholy, and a sense of impending doom, evident in a tendency to apocalyptic fantasies. This is acknowledged by Morgan, for whom Sebald's "oscillation from narcissism and hypochondria, to apocalyptic destructivity [is] a late and extreme expression of the melancholy of his generation."[13] Sebald's generational predicament can be discerned in his tendency to valorize the literary mode of marginalized writers, and in his fiercely critical stance towards the theory and practice of psychiatry.

The revolutionary environment of the 1960s and 1970s encouraged reevaluation of the question of normativity, and the treatment of socially

9    Silverblatt, "A Poem of an Invisible Subject," 81.
10   Cuomo, "A Conversation with W. G. Sebald," 97.
11   Margalit, *The Ethics of Memory*, 81.
12   Eckstaedt, *Nationalsozialismus*, 17.
13   Morgan, "The Sign of Saturn," 89.

and mentally atypical individuals. This is reflected in Sebald's numerous essays on marginalized writers, including Ernst Herbeck, Robert Walser, and Herbert Achternbusch. In the work of the schizophrenic poet Herbeck, Sebald identified "a reservoir of regenerative energies," the "*pensée sauvage*" of the mentally ill that philosophers like Claude Levi-Strauss posited as having the potential to expand the limits of normal cognition.[14] To Sebald, Herbeck's writing reflected the improvisatory impulse described by Levi-Strauss as "bricolage": art produced from random or remnant objects, associated with the creative methods of socalled primitive people.[15] Sebald regarded Herbeck's "bricolage" as evidence of the return of ancient forms of creativity through the mental perspective of schizophrenia, offering an alternative to the increasing technologization of contemporary forms of expression. For Sebald, the writing of the alienated and mentally disordered poet Robert Walser, represented the naïve proposition that mental illness generated poetic ability, and that Walser's childlike "Bleistift und Zettelsystem" (pencil and note system) offered an ennobling perspective on the negligible things in life.[16] Sebald's somewhat simplistic approach to psychiatric practice is demonstrated in the treatment of Austerlitz's mental illness by remedial garden work, drug therapy having been shown to be a failure. The book of medieval remedies for mood and body disorders that Marie de Verneuil gives Austerlitz to promote his recovery from a mental breakdown is further evidence of Sebald's superficial understanding of disabling mental illness.

Sebald employed the trope of the Sickly Jew to expose what he believed were social injustices in the treatment of mental illness. While he disavowed any affiliation with the protest movement of the 1960s, work by Davies and Hutchinson demonstrates that Sebald's writing reveals themes and tropes that preoccupied the generation of 1968. To Davies, Sebald's focus on generational experience, on power structures and their impact on the individual, and on the creative potential of socially marginalized individuals, indicates his affiliation with the 1960s culture of protest.[17] This is evident in his critique of psychiatry in the Samaria sanatorium episode ("Ambros Adelwarth"), and in Austerlitz's incarceration in various mental institutions. In Sebald's reading of Sternheim and Döblin in relation to their society, Hutchinson detects a sociological approach to literature consistent with the philosophy of the Frankfurt School, central to Sebald's oppositional perspective.[18] Sebald's views were influenced by the anti-psychiatry movement of the 1960s and

14    Sebald, "Eine kleine Traverse," 133.
15    Levi-Strauss, *Das wilde Denken.*
16    Sebald, "Le promeneur solitaire," 154.
17    Davies, "An Uncanny Journey."
18    Hutchinson, "The Shadow of Resistance."

1970s, led by Navratil, Reich, and others, who questioned the foundations upon which the psychiatric institution was based: its diagnostic processes, treatment methods, and involuntary confinement of the mentally ill. Crucially, the movement challenged the notion of normality that underlies psychiatric treatment of the mentally ill, and fostered the belief that it was not the individual, but rather, the system itself that was disordered, and that the relationship between therapist and patient was inherently unjust. Both Reich and Navratil explored the notion that mental illness offered the potential for a deeper understanding of the antinomies of the socalled normal world, a conviction Sebald expressed strongly in his non-fiction, and one that underlies the Romantic approach to suffering in his prose fiction.

Beyond the social protest that informed and motivated his critique of psychiatry, Sebald's writing reflects his response to a crucial shift in psychiatric approach, from a focus on the lived experience of mental illness, to the treatment of mental illness as a neurochemical imbalance. The limited representation of psychiatric treatment in his narrative prose reveals drug therapy to be the only mode of treatment, one that is shown to be both destructive and ineffective.

### The Sickly Jew and the Creative Potential of Suffering

There is a transcendent dimension to the sickness and suffering of Sebald's Jewish figures that reflects a Romantic view of pain as positive, even transcendent: "Ich trauerte; aber ich glaube, daß man unter den Seeligen auch so trauert. Sie war die Bote der Freude, diese Trauer, sie war die grauende Dämmerung, woran die unzähligen Rosen des Morgenroths sprossen" (My suffering was the harbinger of joy, the darkening sunset from which the countless roses of dawn spring forth).[19] In Sebald's prose fiction, suffering artist figures, such as Max Aurach, and historical writers, such as Stendhal, Herbeck, Walser, and Kafka, conform to a Romantic model of the artist that valorizes illness and pain: "Fängt nicht überall das Beste mit Kranckheit an? Halbe Kranckheit ist Übel—Ganze Kranckheit ist Lust—und zwar Höhe." (Does not the best everywhere begin in illness? Half an illness is baneful. A whole illness is pleasure, indeed, a higher form of pleasure.)[20] In Joseph Görres' *Korruskationen*, melancholy is a path to transcendence, and a precondition for creativity: "Kennt ihr nicht das wahre Medium der Poesie, die Schwermuth, die wie ein Frühlingsmorgennebel die Phantasie umhüllt, und ihre Zaubergeschichte reflektirt?" (Melancholy is the true medium for poetry, enrobing fantasy

19   Hölderin, *Hyperion.*
20   Novalis, "Poetik des Übels," 245.

like the morning mist and reflecting its enchantment.)[21] The tendency to valorize suffering, even severe mental illness, reflects the idea that such conditions release creative and imaginative energies, as Vincenzo Chiarugi suggests: "Ich muß hierbei noch bemerken, daß man das Genie im Wahnsinn einen sehr hohen und bewundernswürdigen Grad von Vollkommenheit erreichen sieht" (I must note that, in madness, genius reaches a very high degree of perfection).[22]

In its most extreme form, German Romantic fascination with disease finds expression in the idea of death as the apotheosis of art, and the price of artistic fulfilment, implied in Hegel's statement, "Das Ziel der Natur ist, sich selbst zu töten und ihre Rinde des Unmittelbaren, Sinnlichen zu durchbrechen, sich als Phönix zu verbrennen, um aus dieser Äußerlichkeit verjüngt als Geist hervorzutreten." (The goal of nature is to kill itself and to break through the husk of its immediacy and sensuousness; as Phoenix, to burn itself, in order to emerge rejuvenated as spirit from this exteriority.)[23] The idea of death as the apotheosis of creativity is implicit in Max Aurach's annihilative artistic process, out of which artworks evolve "from a long lineage of grey, ancestral faces, rendered unto ash but still there, as ghostly presences, on the harried paper" (*TE*, 162). All Sebald's Jewish protagonists suffer incapacitating depression; a number of them commit suicide. For Paul Bereyter and Henry Selwyn, the most effective way of regaining any sense of agency eventually becomes the destruction of its possibility, and thus themselves. Austerlitz disappears from the narrative, having given away his legacy to the German narrator in a valedictory gesture that seems to prefigure his suicide.[24]

The suicide of Sebald's Jewish figures is *Freitod* (freely willed death,) not tied to religion or secular law, but depicted as flowing from the longing for death that increasingly consumes them, and represents the attempt to regain agency over a disintegrating self. For Sebald's Jewish characters, suicide represents the ultimate, *poetic* expression that imbues their life stories with significance. Their death confirms Nicholas Saul's understanding of Romantic suicide as "not immoral or morally indifferent," but possessing a "dignity [that] flows from the sublime aura of the act, the paradoxical recuperation of the lost self in the act of self-destruction."[25] While Sebald's sickly Jewish characters experience moments of potential

---

21   Görres, *Korruskationen*, 74.

22   Chiarugi, *Abhandlung*, 316.

23   Hegel, "Philosophy of Nature."

24   Alfred Thomas explores the coincidences posited by Sebald that point to Austerlitz's suicide in imitation of Paul Celan and Walter Benjamin. Thomas, "Prague Palimpsest," 6.

25   Saul, "Morbid?" 590–91.

transcendence, these do not open to the future, but point back to a past they do not fully comprehend, but that overshadows their lives.

Sebald resisted medicalizing illness in his narrative prose; by contrast, his non-fiction reveals a "pathographic" approach to interpreting literary works on the basis of the writer's psychological disposition, and contributing sociocultural conditions.[26] To Sebald, German-Jewish writer Carl Sternheim's pathology was central to an understanding of his work, indeed, Sebald's writing on Sternheim has been described as a "Krankengeschichte" (chronicle of illness), that attributed Sternheim's literary flaws to a "confusion of spirit" that could be traced to his failed attempts to assimilate to Wilhelminian German society.[27] Navratil's *Schizophrenie und Sprache* (1966) exerted a significant influence on Sebald's interpretation of Sternheim's writings, evident in Sebald's argument that Sternheim's conflicted attempts to be both revolutionary in his writing, and at the same time, to satisfy bourgeois expectations, reflected "an already schizoid character, with a noticeable structural similarity to exemplars of late-bourgeois ideology."[28] References to "Über-Ich," the "Es," the "orale Fixierung" and the "Ödipus-Komplex" (super-ego, id, oral fixation, and Oedipus complex) indicate that Sebald drew on Freud too, in his diagnosis of Sternheim's pathology.[29] Sebald's PhD thesis on German-Jewish writer and psychiatrist Alfred Döblin followed the pathographic mode of his work on Sternheim.[30] Sebald located Döblin's manic-depressive tendencies in his conflicted background as a Jew, eager to overcome his Jewishness in order to assimilate to bourgeois society, and to achieve political importance. To Sebald, Döblin's conflicted Jewishness, manifest in an "Assimilationskomplex" (assimilation complex), contributed to a depiction of violence that appeared to promote Nazi ideology, and was in essence, violent in itself, noting in condemnation that "'physical injury hurts the body,' as it says in *Dialectic of the Enlightenment*, 'terror hurts the spirit.'"[31]

In relation to Sebald's non-fiction, Martin Klebes observes that Sebald's "pathographic" approach to interpreting the text on the basis of the psychological disposition of the writer is contradicted by his narrative prose, which emphasizes the inaccessibility of the subject's psychic interior: Austerlitz's origins remain unreachable to him, and the narrator of Max Aurach laments his inability to penetrate the interior of his subject: "Such endeavors to imagine his life and death did not, as I had

26　See Klebes, "Sebald's Pathographies."
27　See Schley, *Kataloge der Wahrheit*, 227.
28　Sebald, *Carl Sternheim*, 61.
29　Sebald, *Carl Sternheim*, 62.
30　Sebald, *Der Mythus der Zerstörung*.
31　Sebald, *Der Mythus der Zerstörung*, 159.

to admit, bring me any closer to Paul, except at best for brief moments of the kind that seemed presumptuous to me" (*TE*, 29). Sebald's interest in the pathographic interpretation of literary text declined with time, evident in a dismissive comment on Walser's *Bleistiftgebiet* (In the Pencil Zone) that recorded his last years in Bern, and his time in the psychiatric clinic of Waldau: "Was für eine Krankheit das in einem diagnostisch genauen Sinn war, tut wenig zur Sache." (What kind of illness it was, in a diagnostic sense, doesn't matter much.)[32]

Underlying Sebald's fascination with manifestations of Jewish illness is a long tradition of designating the Jew as sickly: neurotic, physically weak, hysterical, and predisposed to blindness, and particularly, to mental instability. Through figural language suggesting contagion, and thematization of exclusionary spaces, such as the sanatorium and the hospital, Sebald perpetuated the notion of Jewishness as metaphorically contaminating and requiring seclusion, evoking Jünger's pernicious view of Jews as infective bacteria or schizomycetes, a threat to German culture and society.[33]

## The Sickly Jew: Historical Background

The idea of the Jew as metaphorically contagious is implicit in Luther's disparaging description of the Jews as "a heavy burden to [Germans] in [their] country, like plague, pestilence, and nothing but misfortune."[34] It is understood in Hegel's commendatory description of Jesus as "free of the contagious sickness of his age and his people."[35] The Jew in Medieval literature is depicted as marginalized in relation to the ideal Christian society; lacking spiritual significance, the defectiveness of the Jewish body pointed only towards destruction and mortality.[36] Often believed to provide more resistance to certain illnesses, such as smallpox or leprosy, and to supposedly lengthen one's life, such abnormalities implied the threatening power imputed to the Jew.[37] The sickly medieval Jew was characterized by a blindness allegorical of the spiritual and moral darkness of the Jewish character:

> The Jewish body and its afflictions mirrored the spiritual world, where the opposition between sight and blindness indicated the eternal life that every Christian anticipated, compared with the mortal condition of the Jews . . . the status assigned to the Jews was both

---

32    Sebald, "Le promeneur solitaire," 161.
33    See Jünger, "Über Nationalismus und Judenfrage."
34    Luther, *On the Jews and their Lies*, 35.
35    Hegel, "The Positivity of Christian Religion," 68–69.
36    Matteoni, "The Jew, the Blood and the Body," 197.
37    Trachtenburg, *The Devil and the Jews*.

a sign of inferiority and of danger: weak and deprived of both physical and spiritual sight, he was also thought of as murderous, being distinguished by an alleged blood-lust ... The apparently defective Jew's body could thus symbolize both exclusion and inversion, redirecting the powers of death towards society.[38]

The operas of Wagner manifest the allegorization of the defective Jewish body in imagery that evokes culturally pervasive bodily images indicative of racial and national identity in his world. The characters of the *Ring* embody Wagner's fear of the infiltration of European society by "Jehova's principle of power," a veiled allusion to Judaism.[39] The physical defectiveness of the Jew's body is expressed in idiosyncratic corporeal signs—of stature, voice, gait, and physiognomy—incorporated in Wagner's operas.[40] By contrast, German characters, such as the Volsungs, Siegfried, and Walter von Stolzing, are youthful and robust. In *Richard Wagner, Fritz Lang, and the Nibelungen*, Marc Weiner demonstrates that Wagner's operas repeatedly denigrate Jewish characters: "In [Wagner's] tetralogy, heroes are associated with beautiful, lithe, and powerful animals, while those figures evincing traits associated with Jews, such as avarice, egotism and lovelessness, are likened to lowly, disgusting, and clumsy creatures."[41] A superior being, Siegfried is close to nature, to the creatures of the forest, such as birds, wolves, bears, and deer, and even to the fish of the streams to which he compares himself.[42] By contrast, the entry of the toadlike dwarf Alberich into the clear waters of the Rhine brings about the end of the natural state, depicted through Wagner's utilization of opposing animal motifs that convey the fundamental irreconcilability between races.[43] In Siegfried's description of the Nibelungen, Wagner articulates the German perception of Jewish physiognomy as "ugly, disgusting and gray, small and crooked, hunchbacked and limping, with hanging ears, dripping eyes."[44]

The proliferation of institutions of isolation and healing in the nineteenth-century—the spa, the hospital, and the sanatorium in which Sebald's Jewish figures find themselves—perpetuates the rhetoric of Jewish contagion that saw the Jew as a threat to the body of the German nation. Deriving from an ancient Greek tradition that established the body as a metaphor for the nation state, the notion of Jewish contagion

38    Matteoni, "The Jew, the Blood and the Body," 193.
39    *The Ring of the Nibelungen* (1853), Wagner's four-part opera series based on Germanic myth.
40    See Levin, *Richard Wagner.*
41    Weiner, *Richard Wagner*, 92.
42    Weiner, *Richard Wagner*, 90–91.
43    Weiner, *Richard Wagner*, 92.
44    Weiner, *Richard Wagner*, 96.

174 ♦ THE SICKLY JEW

was expanded by the German Idealists to an ontotheological level that excluded the Jew from the spiritual and the other-worldly on the grounds of perceived imperfection and materiality. In the idealized body politic, the Jew is conceived as a "parasitic plant upon the host nation."[45] Responding to a discourse of parasitism and social Darwinism prevalent in Wilhelmine Germany, Nietzsche writes about the Jew in language that implies fear of contamination: "German blood has difficulty . . . in absorbing even this quantum of 'Jew' . . . let in no more Jews! And close especially the doors to the East!"[46] Eugen Dühring, proponent of the Wilhelmine discourse that saw the Jew as "most comfortable in the flesh of the peoples," advocates for the "Jews' diseased genealogy . . . to be exterminated."[47] Gerhard Kittel describes the Jew as a contaminant, infiltrating the body of the nation:

> But the poison that really eats into the nation's body like an uncanny sickness is rootless, decadent Jewry. It is this Jewry that must corrode all genuine religious, cultural, and national ideas that have grown from the people, because its rootlessness makes it essentially separate . . . it debilitates and infects others . . . devours the marrow of a people . . . It is always spiritual homelessness and hence poison and dissolution.[48]

Sebald's mentally ill Jewish figures sustain the idea of the Jew as being at greater risk of mental illness. For Eastern-European Jews, herded into barracks in Germany, loss of community and pressure to acculturate contributed to psychic pain. According to neurologist Jean Martin Charcot, Jews were "the best source of material for nervous illness"; in the Jew, "the emotions seem to be more vivid, the sensibility more intense, the nervous reactions more rapid and profound."[49] The German anthropologist-physician Georg Buschan notes the "extraordinary incidence" of hysteria in Eastern- European Jews as a sign of racial degeneration.[50] F. Köhler observes in Jewish patients a tendency to "egoism . . . manifest in extreme cases as mental illness, which is especially common among Jews . . . [predisposed] to neurasthenic and hysterical symptoms."[51] In Arthur de Gobineau's "Essai sur l'inégalité des races humaines" (essay on the inequality of the human races), concepts of biological pure-breeding and rational scientific evidence are employed to support a vision of

45    Herder, *Ideen zur Philosophie*, 270, 272.
46    Nietzsche, *Beyond Good and Evil*, 181–82.
47    Dühring, *Die Judenfrage*.
48    Kittel, *Forschungen zur Judenfrage*.
49    Charcot, *Leçons du Mardi*, 11–12.
50    Buschan, "Einfluß der Rasse," 104–5.
51    Köhler, "Tuberkulose und Psyche."

Jewish illness as an eternal and heteronomous phenomenon.[52] In "The Wandering Jew in the Salpêtrière" (1893), psychiatrist Henri Meige describes what he sees as the racial psychopathology of a Jewish patient suffering from an obsessive need to wander: "The great frequency of nervous disorders in the Jewish race" reveals a hereditary predisposition to suffer from neuropathological conditions such as ambulatory neurosis, since "it is characteristic of their race to move with extreme ease. At home nowhere, and everywhere." Meige presents the Wandering Jew as "a sort of prototype of the psychopathic Israelite peregrinating around the world."[53]

Sebald's sickly Jewish figures embody diverse perceptions of physical and mental impairment that stigmatize the Jew as imperfect and a threat to social health. While Sebald's empathetic concern with Jewish suffering is not in contention, his figuring of the sickly Jew as a trope for philosophical and social concerns tends to efface the "real" Jew, offering a problematic vision of debilitated post-Holocaust Jewish existence.

## The Sickly Jew:
## "Dr K. Takes the Waters at Riva"

The opening to the story carries implications of finitude, implicit in the image of the "ominous, deserted" station that provides a backdrop to Dr K. as the sickly Jew, who "feels he has reached the end of the line" (*V*, 141). The notion of suicide is deepened by the reference to Heiligenstadt, the emblematic site of Beethoven's suicidal despair.[54] Dr K.'s thoughts are dominated by suffering, implied in the image of "a man wounded on the battlefield," and the reference to "rescue services and hygiene" that place his story in the context of the *fin de siècle* discourse on sickness. Reference to being "on his way to Vienna," to the border post of Gmünd, and to the metaphorically significant destination of Riva (shore), implies Dr K.'s suicidal condition, an existence between life and death, expressive of Sebald's vision of mental illness as a form of "living death." Described as "extremely unwell . . . He is suffering from dejectedness, and his sight is troubling him . . . He has a sense of being continually among an alarming number of people," (*V*, 142), Dr K. is an embodiment of the neurasthenia, melancholia, and impaired vision historically attributed to the Jew. Dr K.'s feeling of social alienation and self-rejection—"at such times

52    De Gobineau, "Essai sur l'inégalité."
53    Meige, "The Wandering Jew in the Clinic." The wandering Jew as a signifier of Jewish mental illness is explored by Goldstein, in "The Wandering Jew and the Problem of Psychiatric Anti-Semitism." See also Hacking, *Mad Travelers*.
54    Heiligenstadt is the Austrian village in which Beethoven recorded his suicidal despair in his "Heiligenstadt Testament" of 1802.

176 ♦ THE SICKLY JEW

he sits like a ghost at table, suffers bouts of claustrophobia, and imagines that every fleeting glance sees right through him"—stigmatize him as the Sickly Jew, a trope for vitiated post-Holocaust Jewish existence, and an emblem of imperfection, whose visual impairment evokes the moral and spiritual blindness imputed to the Jew. Tormented by sexual conflict between conventional marriage and homosexual love, he contemplates suicide, and "wishes he lay buried there, a few stories deeper, in the ground" (*V*, 142).

Attempting to evade social duties in Desenzano, Dr K. seeks tranquillity in nature, "reclining on grass down by the lake" (*V*, 153). Tormented by his own failure to appear at a public welcome, "he feels ill, sick . . . at every point of the compass" (*V*, 154), and imagines his appearance in terms that evoke Kafka's enigmatic statements on the failure of the Messiah to return: ". . . those in whom we invest our hopes only ever make their appearance when they are no longer needed" (*V*, 154). The negative messianism implicit in these words gestures to the eternal futurity of the messianic dream, and of Jewish suffering from which it derives.[55] Dr K.'s symptoms are accompanied by self-annihilatory fantasies of being "struck . . . dead with an oar" (*V*, 143), and of lying buried in the street, the image of the oar faintly conveying a mythical allusion to the ferryman transporting the dead to the Underworld, and implying a view of Jewish suffering as timeless and ahistorical. Imagining himself "on the brink of disintegration . . . beneath this watery sky under which the very stones dissolved" (*V*, 147), Dr K.'s mental illness is experienced as self-dissolution, and projected onto the natural world: his seasickness is experienced as "the waves . . . still breaking within him," while his yearning for exculpation from sexual conflict is expressed as a longing for the "pouring rain, which veiled every outline and shape in an even grey-green" (*V*, 146), to wash away his memory of conflicted sexual desire. His anxieties about marriage and sexuality "continually come over him, like a living thing . . ." (*V*, 155–56). "The misery within him almost overflowing" (*V*, 148), Dr K.'s mental suffering is expressed through a metaphor that conjures natural catastrophe, implying the innate and inevitable nature of Jewish misery, "a condition in keeping with his nature and ordained for him by a justice not of this world, a condition that he could not transcend and which he would have to endure till the very last of his days" (*V*, 148). Dr K.'s "fretful state of mind" (*V*, 143), manifest in headaches and insomnia, and the hysterical incapacitation to which he is prone—"he often feels quite paralysed and unable to pick up his knife and fork" (*V*,

---

55   Kafka wrote: "The Messiah will come only when he is no longer needed; he will come only on the day after his arrival, he will not come on the last day, but on the very last day." *Hochzeitsvorbereitungen*, 88, 90.

156)—reflects the notion of innate Jewish neurosis described by Buschan and Köhler.[56]

At the Riva sanatorium of Dr Hartungen, the lake is "serenely peaceful in the gathering darkness" (*V*, 155), and "all is now blue on blue" (*V*, 155). Reached by steamer just before nightfall, Dr von Hartungen's hydropathic establishment at Riva is presented as an island of precautionary isolation. Water imagery underlines the relative impurity of Dr K. who seeks to "immerse himself" in the therapeutic tranquillity of the sanatorium. A Romantic sense of *Zeitaufhebung* (stasis) prevails, "nothing appears to move . . . not even the steamer, already some way out upon the water," conveying a sense of timelessness that lends a mythical quality to Dr K.'s illness. With the Genoese girl, a fellow-patient, he rows out onto the lake, an act of self-exile to a different world, aestheticized as art, "as if the entire location were an album and the mountains had been drawn on an empty page by some sensitive dilettante, as a remembrance for the lady to whom the album belongs" (*V*, 157–58). Dr K. conflates the girl from Genoa with a mermaid, her "water-green eyes" (*V*, 160) evoking for him the mythical figure of the water nymph Undine, subsuming her in the other-worldly, watery scene. The girl personifies his longing for incorporeal love, "for out there on the lake they were indeed almost disembodied, and possessed of a natural understanding of their own scant significance" (*V*, 159). Their encounter ends in a form of dissolution, with their agreement that "neither would divulge the other's name, that they would exchange no pictures, nor a shred of paper, nor even a single written word, and that once the few days that remained to them were over, they must simply let each other go" (*V*, 159). And indeed, the Genoese girl disappears from sight, a mythical figure whose dissolving outline can barely be distinguished as the steamer carrying her "slipped out into the lake . . . and the white wake which it trailed . . . was also smoothed over" (*V*, 160).

The theme of suicide returns with the death of Dr K.'s table companion, who had taken his life with his old army pistol, leaving Dr K. "quite alone at dinner, like a man with a contagious disease" (*V*, 162), evoking the trope of the Jew as a contaminant. An extended extract from Kafka's "Hunter Gracchus" story returns Dr K.'s suffering to the world of nature—of the Black Forest, wolves, chamois, "dark green country," and the sea, conjuring the hunter's unredeemed wandering, allegorical of Jewish exile, imperfection, and estrangement from bodily self.

---

56    Buschan, "Einfluß der Rasse"; Köhler, "Tuberkulose und Psyche."

## The Sickly Jew and Sebald's Critique of Psychiatry

Dr K.'s experience at the Riva Sanatorium implies notions of infective-ness and banishment integral to the *fin de siècle* discourse on illness, and exemplified in Thomas Mann's *Der Zauberberg* (The Magic Mountain), 1924. Sebald employed the trope of the sickly Jew to critique psychiatric theory and practice, reflecting the view, prevalent in the protest move-ment of the 1960s and 1970s, that mental institutions fostered oppres-sive power relations between physicians and their patients. The idea of the "fresh air cure" offered by the sanatorium was associated with a coercive medical regime, and the isolation of patients from the world.[57] Implicit in the banishment of the sick to institutions of healing is the view of sickness as a marker of degeneracy, requiring exile from society.[58] As Gilman notes, "from a Jewish perspective, the therapeutic space . . . takes on a very different meaning . . . As a commentary on the Jewish body, and the tradition of associating Jews with infectious disease, time spent in the sanatorium induced the fear of being racially predestined to nervousness and hypochondria, a reflex of the displacement of Jewish anxiety in a world no longer fixed in its Enlightenment promise of Jewish equality."[59] Dr K.'s body is the site of his anxieties, its weakness manifest in the paralysis that makes him "unable to pick up his knife and fork" (*V*, 156). Within the sanatorium, the porter's green apron is a meta-phor for hygiene, and for defense against infection; "fastened at the back with a brass chain," it is suggestive of the enforced containment of the sick. The daily routine of the sanatorium, with its "various cold douches and the electrical treatment prescribed for him" (*V*, 155) is a controlling one, manifest in drawings that illustrate methods of daily treatment (*V*, 155–56), and Dr K.'s presence at the clinic is a reminder of the rhetoric of Jewish contagion.

The weak and defective body of the sickly Jew in Sebald's writing reflects Jewish anxiety about physical and mental difference. This is evi-dent in Kafka's awareness of his own physical inadequacy: "I am a menda-cious creature; for me it is the only way to maintain an even keel; my boat is fragile."[60] Acknowledging his "solitary, eccentric condition" (*V*, 150), a reference to his conflicted sexuality, Dr K. seeks refuge in the *Cinema Pathè di San Sebastiano*, the allusion to St Sebastian evoking depictions of the body of the saint, pierced with arrows, a projection of Dr K.'s own desire to suffer. Here the unspoken fantasy of the Jewish body pierced by hidden arrows exposes Dr K.'s self-scourging anxiety about his own

57  Gilman, *Franz Kafka*, 231.
58  See Müller-Seidel, *Rechtsdenken*.
59  Gilman, *Franz Kafka*, 65.
60  Kafka, *Letters to Felice*.

masculinity, and constitutes an expression of self-hatred, disillusionment, and despair. As Gilman observes, "these arrows . . . represent Kafka's anxiety about his own masculinity, an anxiety as closely tied to his sense of self as his anxiety about his illness, each category transforms into the other; each is linked to the other in Kafka's expressions of his sense of who he is in his time and his place. For they all contribute to the complex notion of 'difference' at the heart of Kafka's self-conception."[61]

Questions of suffering, guilt, and critique of psychiatric practice, are central to the experience of Ambros Adelwarth at the Samaria sanatorium at Ithaca. On his journey to Ithaca to uncover the fate of his great-uncle, Ambros Adelwarth, the narrator perceives the region to be "in the middle of nowhere," the place names, "Monroe, Monticello . . . Delhi, Neversink and Nineveh" conjuring "another world long since abandoned" (*TE*, 105). Reference to René Magritte's *Empire des Lumières*, a series of paintings that confuse night and day, imbues the episode with a sense of mythical atemporality; the Ithaca Falls with their "powdery veils . . . like white curtains blown into a room black with night" (*TE*, 108), prefigure the notion of concealment Sebald allegorizes in his critique of the sanatorium, depicted as a site of enduring misery relating to the torture of the mentally ill. Suspension of time and obfuscation of place suggest the desire to conceal the facts of the evil perpetrated at the ironically named Samaria sanatorium, where the ameliorative role of doctors and the Biblical connotations of "the good Samaritan" are confounded.

Hidden within a rampantly flourishing parkland overgrown by conifers, including mountain hemlocks that suggest the lethal nature of the treatment performed there, the Samaria sanatorium resembles a decaying Tyrolean hunting lodge, a reminder of Sebald's origins in the Allgäu region near the Austrian Tyrol, and the destructive German history that was his legacy. The hunting lodge alludes faintly to Kafka's Gracchus, who dies hunting in the Black Forest, and whose unending exile is allegorical of Sebald's alienation from *Heimat* and national identity. Sebald's critique of psychiatric practice as a coercive regime aimed at social cohesion is implicit in Abramsky's recollection of the mental effects of treatment aimed at "subduing those in its custody, and keeping them in safe detention" (*TE*, 113), including such deleterious results as "the recurrent desolation and apathy of sick patients exposed to continued shock therapy, their growing inability to concentrate, their sluggishness of mind, muted voices, and even . . . cases when patients entirely ceased to speak" (*TE*, 113). The "experimental mania" with which the psychiatrist, Dr Fahnstock, approached the new ECT method, believing it to be "a psychiatric miracle," presents a picture of psychiatrists in thrall to

61    Gilman, *Franz Kafka*, 5–6.

science, and indifferent to the suffering of their patients. The eviscerating effect of treatment on Ambros provides a picture of psychiatric practice as ruthless in its application, resulting in "progressive paralysis of the joints and limbs, probably caused by the shock therapy" (*TE*, 115). Fahnstock is shown to be negligent in the documenting of his experiments, keeping case histories "in a distinctly cursory fashion" (*TE*, 112). Describing Ambros's extreme melancholy, Abramsky notes that "his entire deportment . . . was tantamount to a constant pleading for leave of absence," and "what he ate was no more than the symbolic offerings that were once placed on the graves of the dead" (*TE*, 111), images suggesting the "living-death" that describes the experience of mental illness in Sebald's narrative prose.

In his account of the infliction of extreme pain on another, Sebald drew on Améry's essay on torture as the transformation of the individual into pure flesh and bone through "the radical negation of the other . . . the denial of the social principle as well as the reality principle."[62] Reflecting on his experience of torture, Améry observes: "It would be totally senseless to try to describe here the pain that was inflicted on me . . . The pain was what it was. Beyond that there is nothing to say. Qualities of feeling are as incomparable as they are indescribable. They mark the limit of the capacity of language to communicate. If someone wanted to impart his physical pain, he would be forced to inflict it and thereby become a torturer himself."[63] Sebald's critique of psychiatry is evident in the explicit picture of physical suffering that emerges from Abramsky's description of ECT, and his discovery that it was not the "humane and effective form of treatment" he had imagined, and even in its more evolved form, was the cause of "dislocated shoulders or jaws, broken teeth, or other fractures" (*TE*, 111–12), a faint allusion to Améry's description of the tortures he himself suffered in Breendonk: "And now there was a cracking and a splintering in my shoulders that my body has not forgotten until this hour. The balls sprang from their sockets . . . I fell into a void and now hung from my dislocated arms which had been torn high from behind and were now twisted over my head."[64] A prototype for the suffering of Ambros Adelwarth, the spectral presence of Améry, an authentic survivor of Auschwitz, implies a disturbing equalization of German and Jewish victimhood.

62    Améry, "Torture," 35.
63    Améry, "Torture," 33.
64    Améry, "Torture," 32.

## Max Aurach: The Suffering Artist

Aurach's illness is manifest in the repression of traumatic memory relating to his German past, in agoraphobic resistance to travel, and in his unarticulated but pervasive longing for death, reflected in his perception of Manchester as a metaphorical Auschwitz in which he has found his "place," an implicit acknowledgement of his existence as a "living death." A sickly Jew and a tormented artist figure, he is a trope for a universalized vision of suffering, and for the Romantic notion of pain as enhancing creativity. Aurach's artistic process, and the artworks that emerge from it, arise from his obsession with the Holocaust: his work of continual erasure and destruction is a reminder of the ceaselessly working crematoria of Auschwitz; the charcoal sticks with which he harrows the paper are the residue of burning. With its continuously falling dust, his studio is allegorical of the dissolution of materiality that defines death in the Holocaust. Indeed, Aurach confesses that "he never felt more at home than in places where things remained undisturbed, muted under the grey, velvety sinter left when matter dissolved, little by little, into nothingness" (*TE*, 161), conjuring the event that is at the heart of his repressed trauma. The death aesthetics that inform his art are reflected in his admission that he felt "closer to dust . . . than to light, air, or water" (*TE*, 161).

The inconclusive nature of Aurach's artistic process constitutes him as the paradigmatic Romantic artist, whose work is always "im Werden" (in a process of becoming); never fully realized through his destructive artistic process, his subjects remain "ultimately unknowable" to him (*TE*, 162). Aurach identifies the hardened and encrusted deposit of paint droppings mixed with coal dust on the floor of his studio as "the true product of his continuing endeavours" (*TE*, 161); described as "resembling the flow of lava," his art, and the suffering in which it originates, are seen as deriving from a natural, blameless world of destruction to which illness and pain are endemic.

The Grünewald paintings at Colmar are a screen onto which Aurach projects his own suffering. His identification with the torment of Grünewald's figures is expressed in natural imagery that sees pain "spread to cover the whole of nature, only to flow back from the lifeless landscape to the humans marked by death," and experienced as [rising] and [ebbing] within [him] "like a tide" that subsumes his torment, and the torment of Grünewald's subjects, in a natural history of suffering (*TE*, 170). Grünewald's altarpiece at Colmar stirs in Aurach the epiphanic understanding that "beyond a certain point, pain blots out the one thing that is essential to its being experienced—consciousness—and so perhaps extinguishes itself . . . What is certain though, is that mental suffering is effectively without end . . . One plunges from one abyss into the next" (*TE*, 170), a Benjaminian vision of endless calamity that detaches Aurach's

182 ◆ The Sickly Jew

suffering from the specificity of its causality, and ties it to the destruction that is part of the natural world.

Grünewald's "Entombment of Christ" remains etched in Aurach's memory while he works; with its mourning female figures shrouding the body of Christ, it represents a counter-image to the anonymous Jewish death Aurach attempts to memorialize in his "Zerstörungsstudien" (studies of destruction). The notion of "entombment" is metaphorical of Aurach's repression of memory; indeed, his buried memories of Germany are of a country, "frozen in the past, destroyed, a curiously extraterritorial place, inhabited by people whose faces are both lovely and dreadful" (*TE*, 181). Aurach's fevered hallucination of "entombing" his cat in a shoebox, and burying it under an almond tree, is allegorical of his repression of traumatic memories. The motif of the almond tree under which he "buries" his cat is metonymic of the lingering and malign effect of the traumatic past on his life, linking him to his mother through a shared legacy of loss and suffering. It evokes one of the Grimm brothers' darkest fairy tales, "The Almond Tree," also known as "The Juniper Tree," in which a mother is buried under an almond tree, and in death, becomes a guardian spirit that protects her son from the depredations of infanticide and cannibalism, from which he is resurrected to live "happily ever after."[65] In the context of Aurach's spectral existence in the "mausoleum" of Manchester, the motif of the overshadowing almond tree lacks the resurrective dimension of the fairy tale. Indeed, the past returns to him in visions of a woman in grey, who appears in haste, "like a doctor afraid she may be too late to save a sinking patient" (*TE*, 181), implying Aurach's understanding of himself as ailing. The meaning of the enigmatic "graue Dame" (lady in grey) in Aurach's life is suggested by her allegorical function as an innkeeper in Kafka's writing, the personification of *Lebensmüdigkeit* or world-weariness, and a harbinger of death.[66]

As an elderly man, Aurach returns to Switzerland, to climb Mount Grammont in a reprise of an earlier ascent with his father. The experience catalyzes the return of painful memories that he seeks to repress by locking his hotel door and closing the blinds (*TE*, 173). Attempting again to reach the summit, he is overwhelmed by the self-annihilating desire to plunge down the mountain, but is rescued by the mysterious butterfly hunter, who embodies both the tormenting memory that is the source of the subject's suffering, and the potential for salvation.[67] The memory of his descent down Mount Grammont, and of the butterfly

65   The Brothers Grimm, *Kinder- und Hausmärchen.*

66   This deeply allegorical figure appears in Kafka, *Hochzeitsvorbereitungen*, 90.

67   See Kilbourn, "Kafka, Nabokov . . . Sebald," 54.

hunter, is lost in "a lagoon of oblivion [that] had spread in him . . . and remained a mystery to him however hard he thought about it" (*TE*, 174), an image that abstracts his suffering from the particularity of its origins. Aurach's despair at his inability to capture the elusive image of the salvific figure leads to insomnia, exhaustion, and the use of powerful sedatives that induce in him terrifying hallucinations. His body distorted by pain, Aurach mimics the abject figures depicted in Grünewald's portrayal of the suffering of St Anthony against an infernal background of agony and destruction, an identificatory gesture that subsumes Aurach's suffering in a universalizing history of pain.

The narrator returns to Bad Kissingen on behalf of the dying Aurach, to visit the graves of Aurach's family in the Jewish cemetery of the former spa town. The episode is characterized by absence—of Aurach, who could never bring himself to return to Germany, and of the once-vibrant Jewish guests who enlivened the spa town, now somnolent and deserted, a place of the infirm and the dead. A pervasive sense of finitude is implicit in the daily roll-call of death in the obituary notices; in the newspaper, the "quote of the day" from Goethe reads: "Our world is a cracked bell that no longer sounds" (*TE*, 220), a metaphor for the dissolution of the once-vital Jewish presence, and the efficiency with which the Germans had "cleaned everything up" (*TE*, 225). Imagery of dissolution in nature, "the white down of the poplars was drifting in the air" (*TE*, 220), is mirrored by the memory of historical destruction: the "Orientalized neo-Romanesque style" synagogue of Bad Kissingen, vandalized during *Kristallnacht*, has been erased by a new labor exchange. In the crumbling Jewish cemetery, with its "graves sinking into the ground amid tall grass and flowers" (*TE*, 223), a recent gravestone records the death of Aurach's grandparents at Theresienstadt, and the names of his parents, deported to "a fate unknown" (*TE*, 225). Sebald's indirect approach to Jewish death, his apparent pretense to a lack of understanding — "I stood before [the gravestone] . . . not knowing what I should think" (*TE*, 225)—and his reluctance to confront German agency in the causation of Jewish destruction—result in a consoling and aestheticized picture of natural dissolution that encompasses the absent Jews, the crumbling graves rendered almost anonymous by time and weathering, the stones of remembrance, and the unspoken vision of Jewish erasure implicit in the "unknown fate" of Aurach's parents.

Like most of Sebald's sickly Jewish figures, Aurach longs to end his life, "to put it behind him as soon as possible, one way or another" (*TE*, 231). Dying in a "one-time Victorian workhouse where the homeless and unemployed had been subjected to a strict regime" (*TE*, 231), he is absorbed into the natural world, his labored voice recalling "the rustle of dry leaves in the wind" (*TE*, 231), evoking the voice of Kafka's inscrutable creature Odradek, ambiguous symbol of redundancy and

184 ♦ THE SICKLY JEW

survival. The disintegration of the ailing Jew Aurach connects him with the postwar fading of the town of Kissingen in a natural history of dissolution.

## Austerlitz and the Suffering of the Post-Holocaust Jew

Austerlitz is Sebald's most allegorical character: lacking in self-understanding, he attributes his existential disorientation to incomprehensible, quasi-natural forces, "an agency greater than or superior to my own capacity for thought" (*A*, 60). Paradoxically, he is the character whose mental illness, and its somatic symptoms, are most explicitly manifest, and whose suffering brings him into contact with the world of empirical science through the lengthy periods of hospitalization he endures. Austerlitz's illness relates to the loss of a coherent sense of self—"I have never known who I really am" (*A*, 60), that catalyzes an ultimately futile quest for origins. As depicted by Sebald, psychiatric treatment does not help him, and indeed intensifies his feelings of alienation. In his last work, Sebald presents us with an uncompromisingly bleak view of post-Holocaust Jewish existence that refutes redemption. It is as an alienated, psychologically unstable wanderer that Austerlitz leaves the textual world.

By presenting Austerlitz as a sickly Jewish figure, Sebald pursues a dual aim: the character of Austerlitz is both a trope for incurable Jewish suffering, and a construct through which to critique the theory and practice of psychiatry. Sebald's depiction of Austerlitz's incarceration in various sinister mental institutions reveals a deeply held antipathy towards the field of psychiatry, an antagonism that intensified with the passage of time in response to a shift in the 1980s from the treatment of mental illness as a lived experience towards treating it as a neurochemical imbalance that could be restored by means of drug therapy. Austerlitz's episodes of mental suffering are dramatized within a broader vision of illness that ties it to unjust social conditions, subsumes it as part of a natural world of entropy and dissolution, and constitutes him as a trope for universalized suffering. This encompasses the tormented inmates of Bedlam, the disintegration of his foster-mother, Gwendolyn, the incarceration and death of his foster-father at Denbigh asylum, and the madness of the composer Schumann at Bad Godesberg. Austerlitz's symptoms are not ameliorated by the limited psychiatric treatment he receives, or by recovery of repressed memories of childhood. Sebald's rejection of psychiatry precludes him from investigating psychiatric practice beyond the treatment of patients by medication, invariably shown to be ineffective and harmful. Austerlitz attributes his suffering to mysterious forces, and projects onto the natural world the disorder and dissolution he experiences. As the sickly Jew, Austerlitz is marked by the "imprint" or "negative inscription" of historical violence that suggests, but cannot conclusively confirm, the residual memory of his mother and father. Austerlitz's origins are never validated, and any glimmer of hope is "swallowed up by wavering shadows" (*A*, 190).

To Ilsemann, "*Austerlitz* appears to oscillate between two conceptions of psychological suffering: a man-made history, one that involves the distinction between a victim and a perpetrator and in which the concept of free will and responsibility make sense; and a history that is driven by anonymous, quasi-natural forces and governed by impenetrable laws."[68] An alleged *Kindertransport* child, traumatically ruptured from his mother in his flight from German persecution, Austerlitz's anguished feelings of exile and dispossession can be traced to the impact of historical violence on the individual. By imputing Austerlitz's suffering to inexplicable, natural forces, implicit in his frequent articulation of a sense of incomprehension — "for reasons I could not explain even to myself. . . ." (*A*, 184), Austerlitz becomes an emblem for a universal, morally neutral perspective on suffering that sees it as endemic to the natural world. The ambiguity of Austerlitz's position reflects Adorno's thoughts on "sublat[ing] the usual antithesis between nature and history," articulated in "The Idea of Natural History."[69] Adorno sought to dissolve the dualistic division of nature and history as realms of human experience: "I think that the attempt should be made to behold all nature, and whatever regards itself as nature, as history."[70] Sebald's sublation of history and nature remains unresolved: on the one hand, he acknowledged German responsibility for the Holocaust through Austerlitz's exploration of Adler's comprehensive work on Theresienstadt, and the narrator's investigation of the former Nazi prison of Breendonk. The latter episode establishes the Germans as the perpetrator nation through the vision of SS guards, "former husbands and fathers from Vilsbiburg and Fühlsbüttel, from the Black Forest and the Bavarian Alps" (*TE*, 29), a geographical reference that implicates Sebald himself as a German from the Allgäu region of Bavaria. Nevertheless, Sebald's tendency to depict Austerlitz's illness as contingent on a natural world of suffering and disintegration suggests a reluctance to directly acknowledge German agency in its causation. The implications of Sebald's evasion are noted by Taberner:

> [Sebald] attaches cosmic importance to individual events and posits them as markers in the chronicle of profound suffering that he holds to determine existence . . . Nobody is to blame, no charges may be laid, everything seems inevitable, simply a matter of fate. And if time

68     Ilsemann, "Going Astray," 302.
69     Adorno, "The Idea of Natural History."
70     Adorno, "The Idea of Natural History," 111.

186 ♦ THE SICKLY JEW

is collapsed, there is no opportunity to intervene in the historical process, to demand the redemption of the past in a better future.[71]

Austerlitz embodies many of the ailments historically imputed to the Jew, including mental instability, and a tendency to melancholy and hysteria. I explore Sebald's construction of Austerlitz as the sickly Jewish figure in episodes that contribute to, or reflect his declining mental health.

## The Illness and Death of Gwendolyn

Gwendolyn was a surrogate mother to Austerlitz, and her illness and death are allegorical of Austerlitz's repressed trauma: the loss of his mother that brought him into Gwendolyn's care as a foster-child. Her closed-up sickroom is a metaphor for the buried and traumatic past that torments Austerlitz in moments of resurgent memory, and sees him periodically break down. Everything in the sickroom speaks of dissolution and the obscurity of Austerlitz's unknowable past—the dying Gwendolyn, the unexplained nature of her disease, the "yellowish smoke . . . that never entirely dispersed up the chimney (A, 88), the "obfuscating and repellent" white powder with which she covered herself, and everything else, resembling the ectoplasm of "arsanical horror" ostensibly produced by clairvoyants (A, 87). Laid out in her coffin, Gwendolyn's "white gloves with a great many little mother-of-pearl buttons," are metonymic of Austerlitz's child self, depicted in a photograph as a small page in a costume with six large mother-of-pearl buttons, worn to accompany his mother to the Rose Ball; the gloves arouse in Austerlitz, a faint, unidentifiable memory of Agáta, that fills him with grief—"the first tears I had shed in the manse" (A, 91). Images of gloves and female hands recur in *Austerlitz*, and are metonymic of his lost mother, and other mother-figures: recollecting his austere and loveless Welsh childhood, Austerlitz remembers that, "as [Gwendolyn] went out, she ran her fingers through my hair, the one time, as far as I can remember, she ever did such a thing" (A, 64); as a schoolboy, visiting his friend Gerald, he recalls that Gerald's mother "raised her free hand and put the hair back from my forehead" (A, 157); as an elderly man, recounting his search for traces of his mother in Prague, he has a vision of Agáta, and sees "the scarf slip from her right shoulder as she lays her hand on my forehead" (A, 220).

## The Death of Gerald and Austerlitz's First Breakdown

Sebald traces Austerlitz's breakdowns and their treatment in the psychiatric institutions to which he is committed, reflecting the social critique

71    Taberner, "German Nostalgia?" 188.

THE SICKLY JEW ♦ 187

that underlies the troping of his protagonist. Austerlitz's first described breakdown follows the death of his schoolfriend, Gerald. In Austerlitz's chronicle of illness and despair, Gerald is depicted in imagery of hovering, of drifting smoke, shimmering dust, of intertwined sunlight and shadow, that suggests both transcendence and evanescence: Gerald's home, Andromeda Lodge, has astrophysical associations; his uncanny mother, Adela, is surrounded by "a kind of silvery radiance" (*A*, 157). Gerald's interest in astronomy, and in piloting his small Cessna, constitute him as a metaphor for transcendence and the possibility of hope. This is undermined by the extended metaphor of birds and feathers—the dovecote of Königswart with its dead and dying pigeons, the sinister plucked pigeon feathers lying on the floor of the *Gare d'Austerlitz*—that in *Austerlitz* represent loss of faith in the possibility of hope. This is confirmed by the death of Gerald when his Cessna crashes into the Savoy Alps, an accident Austerlitz perceives as "inevitable," and a catastrophe that precipitates his own mental decline, which he describes as "a withdrawal into myself which became increasingly morbid and intractable with the passage of time" (*A*, 165).

Austerlitz's mental breakdown takes the form of alienation from language, allegorized "as an old city full of streets and squares," and Austerlitz himself as "a man who has been abroad a long time and cannot find his way through this urban sprawl any more" (*A*, 174–75). In his deranged state, Austerlitz perceives language as "a collection of empty shells, wondrous yet lifeless," proleptic of the vitrified specimens in the veterinary museum that, at a later time, will disturb his precarious equilibrium, and plunge him into catastrophic breakdown. Austerlitz experiences his breakdown as a natural phenomenon, a "volcanic" manifestation of "an illness that had been latent in me for a long time [and] were now threatening to erupt" (*A*, 173), an illness that takes the form of "a constant process of obliteration, a turning away from myself and the world" (*A*, 174). He projects onto the natural world the disorientation he feels, lamenting that "the entire structure of language, the syntactical arrangement of parts of speech, punctuation . . . were all enveloped in impenetrable fog" (*A*, 175). Frustrated with his own literary project, Austerlitz expresses his sense of self-dissolution and disgust in images taken from nature: "I could see no connections any more, the sentences resolved themselves into a series of separate words . . . the letters into disjointed signs, and these signs into a blue-grey trail gleaming silver . . . excreted . . . by some crawling creature . . ." (*A*, 175–76). The alienation from language he experiences in his fevered state is reflected in the simile that likens language to "an unhealthy growth . . . something which we use, in the same way as many sea plants and animals use their tentacles to grope blindly through the darkness . . ." (*A*, 175). Overcome by a sense of inauthenticity, by "the awkward falsity of my constructions and the

188 ♦ THE SICKLY JEW

inadequacy of all the words I had employed" (*A*, 172), and by thoughts of suicide, Austerlitz buries his research "under layers of rotted leaves and spadefuls of earth" (*A*, 176), metaphorical of the cycle of growth and decay in nature to which he seeks to return, and a manifestation of Sebald's perception of mental illness as a form of "death."

Austerlitz's suicidal thoughts catalyze his nocturnal wandering on the streets of London, and hallucinations of the undead, in "shapes and colors of diminished corporeality . . . images from a faded world . . . a man in a top hat, a woman wearing the costume of the 1930s" (*A*, 180). In an episode that blurs the boundaries between past and present, the living and the dead, Austerlitz finds himself at the site of Bedlam, "the hospital for the insane and other destitute persons" (*A*, 183), and the paradigm of inhumane psychiatric treatment. Austerlitz's dismayed response to discovering himself at the place where the notorious asylum once stood reflects Sebald's critique of psychiatric practice: imagining "the huge space of the rooms where the asylum inmates were confined," Austerlitz identifies with their residual pain: "I often wondered whether the pain and suffering accumulated on this site had ever really ebbed away or whether they might not still, as I sometimes thought when I felt a cold breath on my forehead, be sensed as we pass through them on our way . . ." (*A*, 183). In a disconsolate vision that dissolves temporal boundaries, he sees the "bleachfields stretching westwards from Bedlam" with shroud-like lengths of linen (*A*, 183), "the diminutive figures of weavers and washerwomen, and on the far side of the bleachfields the places where the dead were buried" (*A*, 184). Anxious and depressed, Austerlitz affiliates with the dead, who he senses "were returning from their exile and filling the twilight around me with their strangely slow but incessant to-ing and fro-ing" (*A*, 188).

### Return to Germany and Mental Collapse

Austerlitz's mental condition is exacerbated following his return to Germany in a reprise of his journey as a *Kindertransport* child. Motivated by the hope of confronting "the original of the images that had haunted [him] for so many years" (*A*, 316), he observes: "I had never before set foot on German soil, I had always avoided learning anything about German topography, German history, or modern German life, and so . . . Germany was more foreign to me than any other country in the world . . ." (*A*, 313). Austerlitz projects onto the world of natural disaster his feelings of panic and anxiety at confronting the repressed origin of his trauma; this is manifest in his perception of having to "struggle against a current growing stronger," and of "standing . . . on the outer edge of this flood of Germans moving endlessly past me" (*A*, 315), a vision that reflects his residual sense of exclusion, as a putative Jew in

Germany. On his train journey through renovated postwar Germany, the landscape evokes the sinister concealment of the past: this is implicit in the natural imagery of "dark forests . . . almost encroaching on the railway embankment. Swathes of mist or low, drifting cloud hung among the dripping pines" (*A*, 312), and the sinister reference to "three gigantic chimneys [that] towered into the sky . . . making the steep slopes of the eastern mountains look like hollow shells, mere camouflage for an underground industrial site covering many square miles" (*A*, 318). A memory of "a nameless land without borders and entirely overgrown by dark forests" (*A*, 316), suggests Austerlitz's deeply repressed recollection of passing through Germany as a traumatized *Kindertransport* child. His buried memories are conveyed in the image of an apparently prehistoric and unexplored realm, obscured by "the trees and bushes on the other bank . . . the fine cross-hatching of the vineyards . . . the slate-grey rocks and ravines leading off sideways . . ." (*A*, 318). Reference to "the great army of mice" (*A*, 319) evokes the medieval legend of the *Pied Piper of Hamelin,* a story that allegorizes the annihilation of an unwanted species, and endows Austerlitz's tragedy with a mythical and universalizing quality that undermines the empathy of Sebald's perspective, and distances Austerlitz's plight from the "actual horror" authored by Germany.

During this period of psychic disturbance, Austerlitz seeks solace in the Tower Hamlets Victorian cemetery, surrounded by a dark brick wall adjoining St Clement's Hospital. His incapacitating anxiety is reflected in imagery relating to the natural world of destruction, in which graves were "tilted or thrown over entirely by the roots of the sycamores which were shooting up everywhere" (*A*, 321), and "the sarcophagi were broken, some of the graves themselves had risen above the ground or sunk into it, so that you might think an earthquake had shaken this abode of the departed" (*A*, 321–22). Fragmented stone body parts—"statues of angels, wingless or otherwise mutilated . . . a stone hand broken off" (*A*, 320–22), prefigure Austerlitz's psychic disintegration, during which he envisages himself as the victim of a natural calamity, "being broken up from within, so that parts of my body were scattered over a dark and distant terrain" (*A*, 323). The broken stone hand is metonymic of what he has lost, his mother's caress, and the loving care of Vera, who peers in astonishment at him from between her "endlessly familiar" hands (*A*, 215). Austerlitz's experience of hysterical blindness, historically attributed to the sickly Jew, is described through the natural image of seeing everything "veiled by a black mist" (*A*, 323). Overcome by anxiety, he seeks comfort by taking home small mementos from the cemetery, and memorizing the names and dates of those buried there. His identification with the dead suggests his perception of his own, deranged life as a form of "death-in-life."

With its "tall brick façade . . . towering behind the wall," St Clement's hospital resembles a fortification that hides, represses, and defends itself

190 ◆ THE SICKLY JEW

against intrusion. It is both a metaphor for Austerlitz's repressed trauma and a symbol of power over the mentally vulnerable. Sebald depicts the lived experience of mental illness as a state of "living death": delivered to St Clement's hospital, "the last in a series of various casualty departments and hospitals" (*A*, 323), Austerlitz is sedated, and spends several weeks in a state of "mental absence" that resembles death. Drug therapy is implied to be detrimental, "paralyzing all thought processes and emotion" (*A*, 323), and recalling the psychiatric treatment of Ambros Adelwarth at the Samaria sanatorium, to which he admits himself in the hope of extinguishing all memory and thought. Austerlitz describes his "curiously remote state of mind induced by the drugs," that cause him to feel both "desolate and weirdly contented" (*A*, 324), reflecting Sebald's negative approach to psychiatric treatment. Austerlitz's sense of mental evacuation is expressed in the metaphor of "feeling nothing inside my head but the four burnt-out walls of my brain" (*A*, 324), a vision that evokes images of buildings with "cracked walls and empty windows through which you saw the empty air" in "Air War and Literature," and conflates Jewish and German suffering in a universalizing vision of annihilation.[72]

Looking out through the hospital window with a telescope that emphasizes his distance from the outside world, Austerlitz sees foxes "running wild in the cemetery in the grey dawn . . . squirrels dodging back and forth . . . the slow wingbeats of an owl in its curving flight over the tombstones at nightfall," a picture of an unfettered natural world that contrasts with his incarcerated existence as an inmate of a mental institution (*A*, 324–25). The transient improvement in Austerlitz's condition is not attributed to psychiatric treatment, but to the remedial activity of gardening, in which Austerlitz finds relief from his symptoms. For Austerlitz, the healing properties of the "constant warm, humid atmosphere, the mossy, forest-ground fragrance filling the air . . ." (*A*, 326), convey a sense of rootedness and well-being that contrasts with the sterile coldness of the psychiatric institutions portrayed by Sebald. While the putatively curative power of gardening is a recurrent notion in Sebald's prose writing, evident in Paul Bereyter's horticultural transformations at Bainlieu, Abramsky's withdrawal from the Samaria sanatorium into nature, and Henry Selwyn's self-exile in his garden hermitage, for these characters, withdrawal from life into nature signals the nearness of death.

**The Salpêtrière: Between Hospital and Penitentiary**

Austerlitz's last reported breakdown follows his visit to the veterinary medicine museum at Maisons-Alfort, repository of grisly exhibits of monstrosity and malformation. Sebald's description of vitrified specimens

72    Sebald, "Air War and Literature," 74.

of deformed nature replaces the objective scientific gaze with one that mythologizes abnormality in nature, evident in the description of "Janus-faced and two-headed calves, Cyclopean beasts with outsized foreheads, a human infant . . . that resembled a mermaid" (*A*, 373), and abstracts disease and suffering to the realm of myth. The process of vitrification is aestheticized as "the desire to secure for the frail body at least some semblance of eternal life by translating its so readily corruptible substance into a miracle of pure glass" (*A*, 374). Here, the morbid beauty of the vitrified objects is undermined by their implicit evocation of Hebel's story of resurrection, and its role in Sebald's narrative prose as an allegory for the hope, but not the reality, of redemption.[73] Distressed by the exhibits, Austerlitz experiences amnesia, crippling physical weakness, and fainting fits he attributes to hysterical epilepsy. Believing himself about to die, "with a phantom pain spreading through my chest" (*A*, 375), Austerlitz recovers consciousness at the Salpêtrière, "to which I had been taken," the passive mode implying his involuntary admission. Sebald's description of the hospital as "a gigantic complex of buildings where the borders between hospital and penitentiary have always been blurred, and which seems to have grown and spread of its own volition . . . until it now forms a universe of its own" (*A*, 376), imputes to it the potential for metasta-cization, that reveals his negative view of the psychiatric institution and the plight of its inmates, whose melancholic mental state is implied in the vision of the "diffuse, dusty grey light which pervades everything in that institution" (*A*, 379). Situated between the Jardin des Plantes and the Gare d'Austerlitz" (*A*, 376), the Salpêtrière hospital is implied as originating in both the natural world, and the man-made, scientifically driven one, echoing Sebald's awareness of the precarious human predicament of "living exactly on the borderline between the natural world . . . and that other one which is generated by our brain cells."[74]

Within the Salpêtrière, Austerlitz experiences hallucinations, imagining himself wandering around a maze of long passages and encountering "armies of unredeemed souls . . . coming towards me . . . their eyes fixed, cold and dead" (*A*, 376), manifesting themselves "in one of the dark catacombs, where, covered in frayed and dusty plumage, they were crouching on the stony floor . . . and made digging motions with their earth-stained hands" (*A*, 376). In this complex and quasi-mythical scene, "catacombs" suggest Austerlitz's unconscious mind, while the digging motions imply the "excavation" of the dead that is Austerlitz's mission. The scene conjures Austerlitz's buried and traumatic memories, rendered ahistorical by the mythological nature of the warriors, whose plumage

---

73   In Hebel's "Unverhofftes Wiedersehen" (Unexpected Reunion), the body of the young miner is vitrified, and perfectly preserved.

74   Wachtel, "Ghost Hunter," 56.

192 ◆ The Sickly Jew

recalls the armour of battle-worn Homeric heroes. The vision of "unredeemed souls . . . their eyes fixed, cold and dead" evokes Wilfred Owen's poem, "Strange Meeting," that imagines the encounter of two enemies, a vision of equivocal reconciliation that posits the faint hope of redemption from the guilt and shame that Sebald found painful to confront.[75]

Sebald reveals psychiatry to be incapable of curing Austerlitz, or helping him beyond palliative sedation. He evinces no interest in the psychiatric dimension to Austerlitz's anxiety, feelings of self-dissolution, or paralysis: beyond depiction of the negative effects of drug therapy, he avoids representation of the diverse aspects of psychiatric therapy, such as history-taking, diagnosis, analysis, or rehabilitation after the head injury Austerlitz sustained before his admission to hospital. He minimizes the role of psychiatric treatment of Austerlitz's condition, condensing a year spent in hospital to just a few lines. Little insight is given into Austerlitz's interaction with psychiatrists or mental health workers, with the exception of a nurse who lends him a telescope through which to watch the natural world outside St Clement's. Sebald attributes Austerlitz's transitory convalescence to the calming effect of gardening, and the salvific role of Marie de Verneuil, valorized, with some irony, as one of the "pious and charitable ladies . . . that had been chosen as instruments of divine mercy" (*A*, 378). Marie de Verneuil's book of ancient remedies, aromatic oils, powders, essences, and infusions (*A*, 379), helps Austerlitz regain "my lost sense of self, and my memory, gradually mastering the crippling physical weakness which had overcome me . . . after my visit to the veterinary museum" (*A*, 379), reflecting Sebald's naive view of mental illness and its treatment.

On a visit to the *Bibliothèque Nationale* during his convalescence, Austerlitz reads Balzac's story of Colonel Chabert, "a gaunt and desiccated old soldier" (*A*, 394), who, after years of wandering across Germany, returns to Paris as a ghostly revenant to claim all he has lost, including "his own name," emblem of Rosenzweigian particularity. The eyes of Chabert are described as "half-blind" (*A*, 394), and his story of loss and quest for restoration is linked to Austerlitz's through the "mother-of-pearl gleam" that veils his eyes, and evokes the photograph that depicts Austerlitz as a page to his mother, the Rose Queen, and the six large mother-of-pearl

---

75    Owen, Wilfred. "Strange Meeting" (1919). It seemed that out of the battle I escaped / Down some profound dull tunnel, long since scooped . . . / Yet also there encumbered sleepers groaned, / Too fast in thought or death to be bestirred. / Then, as I probed them, one sprang up, and stared / With piteous recognition in fixed eyes, / Lifting distressful hands as if to bless. / And by his smile, I knew that sullen hall, / By his dead smile I knew we stood in Hell. . . . / I am the enemy you killed, my friend. / I knew you in this dark; for so you frowned / Yesterday through me as you jabbed and killed. / I parried; but my hands were loath and cold. / Let us sleep now . . .

buttons that are part of his costume. The story of Chabert is an allegory for Austerlitz's own quest to restore to himself his origins, memories, and sense of self. It reinforces for Austerlitz the suspicion that "the border between life and death is less permeable than we commonly think," (*A*, 395), an admission that implies acknowledgment of his own, irreparably deformed, spectral existence. From the *Haut-de-jardin* reading-room, Austerlitz observes the "convoluted traffic routes on which trains and cars crawled back and forth like black beetles and caterpillars," creating the impression that "the body of the city had been infected by an obscure disease spreading underground . . ." (*A*, 399). The vision reminds Austerlitz obscurely of reading the work of a writer "who had previously travelled the deserts of the Orient that are formed, as he said, from the dust of the dead" (*A*, 400). In this complex and diffuse metaphorical writing, Jewish sickness is projected onto the world as a symptom of universal disintegration that erases the boundaries of creature and machine, the living and the dead, the innocent and the guilty.

Sebald's sickly Jewish figures are tropes for Sebald's pessimistic worldview, that sees illness and despair as endemic to a world in a process of dissolution. His sickly Jewish figures are projections of the physical and mental imperfection of his generation, for whom the repressed guilt of the parent generation is manifest in their children as illness. Sebald's suffering Jews reflect a Romantic view of illness as conducive to creativity, and as offering the potential for resistance. In his depiction of suffering Jewish characters, Sebald manifests a reluctance to confront the origin of their suffering, the Holocaust of the Jews and its afterlife. Sebald's troubling tendency to attribute Jewish suffering to obscure natural forces suggests the wish to evade the question of German agency in the conception and implementation of genocide. His reflections on the anarchic process of history, and the trans-European origins of the Holocaust, are further evidence of a universalizing view of Jews and Jewishness, that vitiates Jewish singularity while imputing to his suffering Jews traits of instability, imperfection, and hostility to the world around them.

# Conclusion:
# Sebald and Holocaust Fiction

SEBALD IS WIDELY REGARDED as "the German writer who most deeply took on the burden of German responsibility for the Holocaust," the empathetic "*good German*," who enhanced this concept through an empathy so profound as to conflate his own persona with those of the Jewish victims about whom he wrote.[1] Driven by the desire to restore "real" Jewish lives, and to avoid the stereotyped abstractions of his peers, Sebald proved himself in thrall to the seductions of imaginative writing that constituted his Jewish figures as embodiments of rootlessness, heteronomy, inauthenticity, and incurable disorder. Paradoxically, his empathetic intention to recreate lost Jewish lives was undermined by an elaborately figural mode that contributed to the allegorical and abstract nature of his Jewish characters, who are, in essence, tropes that perpetuate historical perceptions of Jewishness. Sebald's commitment to the allegorical mode—"I believe that the realistic text can support allegorical narrative, indeed, that it should engage with allegory"—resonates with a German substrate of tropes that have traditionally perceived the Jew as rootless, immutably other, inauthentic, and enfeebled.[2] While I do not claim that, in his conception of Jewish figures, Sebald consciously drew on the work of Hegel, Wagner, or Heidegger, I do suggest that Sebald's overwhelmingly figural approach to Jewish lives damaged by the Holocaust abstracts the individuality of the Jewish figures he sought to evoke, and perpetuates discredited historical perceptions of Jewishness. While Sebald acknowledged that the writing process, and in particular, the writing of Jewish lives in the wake of the Holocaust, was "morally dubious," he did not entirely succeed in avoiding the pitfalls involved in fictionalizing the Holocaust and its enduring aftermath.[3]

I have argued that Sebald's empathetic intention of restoring the lives of "real" Jewish individuals is compromised by his privileging of a figural literary mode that subsumes their individuality in a universalizing allegory of exile. His rootless Jews revive the myth of the Wandering Jew and the problematic historical and philosophical foundation to this myth that sees the Jew as innately rootless and alien, implying that there is no place

1    Angier, *Speak, Silence*, 8.
2    Boedecker, "Menschen auf der anderen Seite," 5.
3    Bigsby, "W. G. Sebald in the Potting Shed." 153.

for the Jew in the post-Auschwitz world. In Sebald's narrative prose, the Wandering Jew is depicted as the embodiment of the past that will not die, and a cause of German suffering. He provocatively problematized the Wandering Jew trope by creating ambiguous conflations of Jew and German: Paul Bereyter occupies the unlikely, morally complex position of being both a reviled "Wandering Jew," thrust into exile, and a member of the German *Wehrmacht*, cast in the compromised role of perpetrating atrocities against his own people, a position that serves to equalize Jewish and German guilt. Ambros Adelwarth embodies the Wandering Jew and the suffering German; his "martyrdom" at the hands of Jewish psychiatrists is a disturbing reversal of the roles of victim and perpetrator, and a reminder of Sebald's commitment to the issue of German victimhood, thematized in his essay, "Air War and Literature," a work of deep resentment that reflects the more overtly polemical dimension to his authorial persona. Sebald employed the Wandering Jew trope to articulate the bitterness of the German second generation in relation to a *Heimat* perceived as contaminated, to which they cannot "return." Repudiation of *Heimat* culminates in Aurach's embrace of Manchester as allegorical of Auschwitz, his "predestined place," where he exists as the "living dead," offering a mythologizing and deeply pessimistic view of post-Holocaust Jewish existence.

In his last work of prose fiction, Sebald complicated the Wandering Jew trope by depicting Austerlitz as dispossessed of origins, and consumed by the longing to discover who he really is, and from where he is exiled. Sebald's empathy with Austerlitz's ontological destitution is manifest in his allegorization of Austerlitz's inconclusive journey of self-discovery, in the course of which he traverses false and disorientating worlds, conjured with extraordinary inventive power. At the same time, Sebald's imaginative distortion of the real contributed to a largely abstract and allegorical protagonist who has lost the Rosenzweigian quality of "Eigenheit." Austerlitz's search for origins is detached from historical time and questions of causality, and his resemblance to mythical figures diminishes further his connection to reality. In his construction of Austerlitz as the Wandering Jew who does not know from where he is exiled, Sebald's writing resonates with philosophical perceptions that sought to abstract the Jew to an ontological void, evident in Kant's "euthanasia" of the Jew, Hegel's relegation of the dispossessed Jew to a *Nichts*, and Heidegger's coded allusions to the desert, conceived as a boundless void with no beginning or end, an onto-historical signifier of Jewish deracination and estrangement from the notion of beginning. On his search for identity, Austerlitz responds intuitively to visions of nomadic Jewishness: the motif of the desert, replete with caravan, palm trees, tents, and nomads, recurs in his story, suggesting that his "true" origin or "place" is in the desert of Biblical Jewish wandering, and not in Central Europe, where he engages in a forlorn search for traces of his parents. Sebald's depiction of Austerlitz, a putatively European Jew, as responding instinctively to visions of Oriental nomadism, betrays a problematic view of Jewishness, that sees the Jew as "from elsewhere," unassimilable, and immutably other, and perpetuates the trope that insists that Jews do not belong, and are destined to remain peripheral to society.

Sebald's troping of the Jew as innately heteronomous implies Jewish otherness to be an immutable and ineradicable trait, reviving the perception of the Jew as the most essential outsider of society. His imaginative writing imbues his Jewish figures with the abstract and corrosive features of modernity—the inauthenticity, materialism, and abstract intellectuality that Weininger identified in the figure of the *fin-de-siècle* Jew. Sebald's narrative prose chronicles the conflicts and failure of assimilation; his attribution to assimilated Jews of an intuitive tendency to identify with images of atavistic Jewish nomadism exposes their assimilated lives as fundamentally inauthentic. In the tradition-bound Jewishness that emerges from Luisa Lanzberg's idyllic picture of German-Jewish life, Sebald presents a picture of "authentic" Jewishness that reveals a nostalgic desire for a viable Jewish identity based on an essentialized vision of a destroyed, pre-Holocaust model of Jewish existence.

Sebald's sickly Jewish figures suffer from innate and incurable illness, positing a view of post-Holocaust Jewish life as irretrievably damaged. For the most part, his imaginative figural writing presents the illness and suffering of his sickly Jews as detached from historical contingencies. His enfeebled Jewish figures project onto the world of nature the mental and physical symptoms they experience, and attribute their suffering to the workings of quasi-natural forces that remain incomprehensible to them. While Sebald's reluctance to invade what he may have perceived to be an inalienably Jewish space of mourning suggests a residual form of *Bilderverbot*, it implies a problematic reluctance to confront German responsibility for the deformation of the Jewish lives he sought to restore.

Sebald's portrayal of Jewish figures raises the ethical question of fictionalizing the Holocaust, a question that, with the passage of time, has become increasingly complicated. In criticizing Sebald for "overlooking the ethics of representation, which at the end of the postwar era is still predicated on knowledge and experience, not on imaginative penetration or empathy," Morgan's comments reflect an ethics of Holocaust representation pervasive in the first decade of the twenty-first century:

> The morality of representation will continue to demand informed and enlightened portrayal—and reception—of the truth of Auschwitz in which the roles of victims and perpetrators . . . will be as clearly defined as possible and where the blurring of these roles

in the service of moral ambivalence, political interest, or personal engagement will be open to critical judgement.[4]

In the intervening years, with the demise of all but a handful of survivors, the Holocaust has shifted from living memory to imaginative memory, and the first-hand testimony of the witness generation is yielding to the fictive reality of the secondary witness. This is evident in a tendency to validate fictional efforts to remember the Holocaust, and to replace first-generation Holocaust writing with the work of writers with no personal experience of the Holocaust, a rehabilitation of belatedness that transforms it from a disadvantage into an asset. Fictional representations of the Holocaust increasingly challenge the "sublimity" of the event, exemplified in Fackenheim's totalizing assertion that "all writing about the Holocaust is in the grip of a paradox: the event must be communicated yet it is incommunicable."[5] Reflecting on Holocaust representation in the contemporary world, Robert Gordon observes: "To revisit Auschwitz, literally or symbolically . . . is to walk on a ground that is shifting, something more mobile and displaced than its once solemn status in the postwar cultural field implied, something less conventionally stable as an historical referent, something that has variously been labelled global and cosmopolitan, palimpsestic, transnational, multidirectional, or . . . intersectional, and which, therefore requires new tools or perspectives to decode."[6]

Contemporary approaches to writing the Holocaust reveal a growing tendency to globalized "ownership" of the phenomenon itself, and of Jewish victimhood that derives from it. This is manifest in a culture that routinely and unreflectively employs the Jew as a trope for its own values and anxieties. I have argued that Sebald's troping of Jews and Jewishness is profoundly different from the casual employment of the Jew as a cultural trope in contemporary society: Sebald's Jews are the product of an intensely self-reflective literary process involving self-censure and analysis; they derive from deep research and extraordinary erudition. Their literary existence arises from an avowed sense of guilt and loss, and a desire to restitute "real" Jewish life in the post-Holocaust world. It is troubling therefore, that in doing so, Sebald resorted to time-worn Jewish stereotypes that impute negative qualities to the Jew, disfigure him, and ultimately evacuate the "real" Jew. *Sebald's Jews* is a response to what I perceive as a specific and problematic area of Sebald's writing, namely his literary treatment of Jews and Jewishness. While his legitimacy in writing Jewish lives is not disputed, the mode in which he did so, and its

4    Morgan, "Your Story Is My Story," 200.
5    Fackenheim, *To Mend the World*, 26.
6    Gordon, "Holocaust Intersections," x.

implications, are of significance. Sebald's aporetic depiction of Jews and Jewishness raises literary, ethical, and cultural questions that will, I hope, encourage a more probing approach to a deeply complex writer, at once aware of his own inadequacy, and bafflingly insensitive to the implications of his art. For all the patterning and layering that contribute to the complex weave of Sebald's art, the Jew as individual disappears, to be replaced by the Jew as trope for enduring and invidious perceptions of Jews and Jewishness.

# Bibliography

Abraham, Nicolas, and Maria Torok. *The Shell and the Kernel: Renewals of Psychoanalysis*, vol. 1. Edited and translated by Nicholas T. Rand. Chicago: Chicago University Press, 1994.

Achinger, Christine. "Allegories of Destruction: 'Woman' and 'the Jew' in Otto Weininger's *Sex and Character: Germanic Review* 88 (2013): 121–49.

Aciman, André. "Out of Novemberland." Review of *The Rings of Saturn*, by W. G. Sebald. *New York Review of Books*, December 3, 1998.

Adler, H. G. *Theresienstadt 1941–1945: Das Antlitz einer Zwangsgemeinschaft; Geschichte, Soziologie, Psychologie*. Tübingen: J. C. B. Mohr, 1955.

Adorno, Theodor W. "The Idea of Natural History." Translated by Robert Hullot-Kentor. *Telos: Critical Theory of the Contemporary*, no. 60 (Summer 1984): 111–24.

———. *Minima Moralia: Reflections from a Damaged Life*. Translated by E. F. N. Jephcott. London: *Verso*, 1978.

———. *Negative Dialectics*. London: Routledge, 1973.

Adorno, Theodor W. and Walter Benjamin. *The Complete Correspondence, 1928–1940*. Edited by Henri Loritz, translated by Nicholas Walker. Cambridge, MA: Harvard University Press, 1999.

Adorno, Theodor, and Max Horkheimer. *Dialectic of Enlightenment. Philosophical Fragments*. Edited by Gunzelin Schmid Noerr, translated by Edmund Jephcott. Stanford, California: Stanford University Press, 2002.

Agamben, Giorgio. *Remnants of Auschwitz: The Witness and the Archive*. New York: Zone, 1999.

Aleichem, Sholem. *Tevye the Dairyman and Other Stories*. Translated by Miriam Katz. Moscow: Raduga, 1987.

Aliaga-Buchenau, Ana-Isabel. "'A Time He Could Not Bear to Say Any More About': Presence and Absence of the Narrator in W. G. Sebald's *The Emigrants*." In *W. G. Sebald: History—Memory—Trauma*, edited by Scott Denham and Mark McCulloh, 141–55. Berlin: Walter De Gruyter, 2006.

Allred, Mason. "Foreign Bodies: Border Control, Jewish Identity, and 'Der Student von Prag'" (1913). *Jewish Studies Quarterly* 21, no. 3 (2014): 277–95.

Améry, Jean. *At the Mind's Limits: Contemplations by a Survivor on Auschwitz and Its Realities*. Translated by Sidney and Stella P. Rosenfeld. Bloomington: Indiana University Press, 1980.

———. *Jenseits von Schuld und Sühne: Bewältigungsversuche eines Überwältigten*. Stuttgart: Klett-Cotta, 2002.

———. "On the Necessity and Impossibility of Being a Jew." In *At the Mind's Limits: Contemplations by a Survivor on Auschwitz and Its Realities*. Translated by Sidney and Stella P. Rosenfeld, 82–101. Bloomington: Indiana University Press, 1980.

———. *Örtlichkeiten*. Stuttgart: Klett-Cotta, 1980.

———. "Resentments." In *At the Mind's Limits: Contemplations by a Survivor on Auschwitz and Its Realities*. Translated by Sidney Rosenfeld and Stella P. Rosenfeld, 62–81. Bloomington: Indiana University Press, 1980.

———. "Torture." In *At the Mind's Limits: Contemplations by a Survivor on Auschwitz and Its Realities*. Translated by Sidney Rosenfeld and Stella P. Rosenfeld, 21–40. Bloomington: Indiana University Press, 1980.

Angier, Carole. *Speak, Silence: In Search of W. G. Sebald*. London: Bloomsbury, 2021.

———. "Who Is W. G. Sebald?" In *The Emergence of Memory: Conversations with W. G. Sebald*, edited by Lynne Sharon Schwartz, 63–75. New York: Seven Stories Press, 2007.

Angress, Ruth K. "*A 'Jewish Problem' in German Postwar Fiction?*" *Modern Judaism* 5, no. 3 (Oct. 1985): 215–33.

Arendt, Hannah. *The Origins of Totalitarianism*. New York: Schocken, 2004.

Aristotle. *De Arte Poetica*. Edited by Ingram Bywater. Oxford: Oxford University Press, 1958.

Arnds, Peter. "On the Awful German Fairy Tale: Breaking Taboos in Representations of Nazi Euthenasia and the Holocaust in Günter Grass's 'Die Blechtrommel,' Edgar Hilsenrath's 'Der Nazi und der Friseur,' and Anselm Kiefer's Visual Art." *German Quarterly* 75, no. 4 (Autumn 2002): 422–39.

Arnold de-Simine, Silke. "The Museum, Memory Media and Media Nostalgia in Sebald's *Austerlitz*." Paper at the International and Interdisciplinary Conference on W. G. Sebald at the University of East Anglia, Norwich, September, 2008.

Assmann, Aleida. *Der lange Schatten der Vergangenheit: Erinnerungskultur und Geschichtspolitik*. Munich: C. H. Beck, 2006.

Atze, Marcel, and Franz Loquai, eds. *Sebald Lektüren*. Eggingen: Edition Isele, 2005.

Badiou, Alain. *Ethics: An Essay on the Understanding of Evil*. Translated by Peter Hallward. London: Verso, 2001.

Bartov, Omer. "Germans as Jews: Representations of Absence in Postwar Germany." In *Germany's War and the Holocaust: Disputed Histories*, 216–36. Ithaca: Cornell University Press, 2003.

Bauer, Karin. "The Dystopian Entwinement of Histories and Identities in W. G. Sebald's *Austerlitz*." In *W. G. Sebald: History—Memory—Trauma*, edited by Scott Denham and Mark McCulloh, 233–50. Berlin: Walter De Gruyter, 2006.

Baumann, Zygmunt. *Modernity and the Holocaust*. Cambridge: Polity, 2007.

Beckett, Samuel. *Endgame.* New York: Grove, 1958.

Beissner Friedrich, ed. *Hölderlin, Sämtliche Werke: Große Stuttgarter Ausgabe Erster Band: Gedichte bis 1800.* Stuttgart: W. Kohlhammer, 1951.

Benjamin, Walter. *Berlin Childhood around 1900.* Translated by Howard Eiland. Cambridge, MA: Harvard University Press, 2006.

———. *Briefe II.* Frankfurt am Main: Suhrkamp Verlag, 1966.

———. "Der Erzähler." In *Illuminationen,* edited by Sigrid Unselt, 409–36. Frankfurt am Main: Suhrkamp, 1961.

———. "On the Concept of History." In *Selected Writings* 4: 1938–1940. Translated by Howard Eiland. Edited by Gary Smith, Howard Eiland, Marcus Paul Bullock, and Michael W. Jennings, 389–400. Cambridge, MA: The Belknap Press of Harvard University Press, 1996.

———. *Selected Writings* 2: 1927–1934. Edited by Michael W. Jennings, Howard Eiland, and Gary Smith. Translated by Rodney Livingstone and others. Cambridge, MA: Belknap/Harvard University Press, 1999.

Benz, W. *Das Exil der kleinen Leute: Alltagserfahrung deutscher Juden in der Emigration.* Munich: C. H. Beck, 1991.

Berger, Robert L. "Nazi Science—the Dachau Hyperthermia Experiments." *New England Journal of Medicine* (May 17, 1990): 1435–40.

Bigsby, Christopher. "W. G. Sebald in the Potting Shed." In *Writers in Conversation with Christopher Bigsby* 2, 139–65. Norwich: Arthur Miller Centre for American Studies, 2001.

Bloch, Ernst. *Das Prinzip Hoffnung.* Frankfurt am Main: Suhrkamp, 1954.

Blüher, Hans. *Secessio Judaica: Philosophische Grundlegung der historischen Situation des Judenthums und der antisemitischen Bewegung.* Berlin: Der weisse Ritter, 1922.

Boa, Elizabeth, and Rachel Palfreyman. *Heimat—A German Dream: Regional Loyalties and National Identity in German Culture 1890–1990.* Oxford: Oxford University Press, 2000.

Bodemann, Michal Y. *The New German Jewry and the European Context: The Return of the European Jewish Diaspora.* New York: Palgrave Macmillan, 2008.

Boedecker, Sven. "Menschen auf der anderen Seite. Gespräch mit W. G. Sebald." *Rheinische Post,* October 9, 1993.

Bogdal, Klaus-Michael, Klaus Holz, and Matthias N. Lorenz, eds. *Literarischer Antisemitismus nach Auschwitz.* Stuttgart: J. B. Metzler Verlag, 2007.

Bohrer, Karl Heinz. *Nach der Natur: Über Politik und Ästhetik.* Munich: Hanser, 1988.

———. "Die permanente Theodizee: Über das verfehlte Böse im deutschen Bewußtsein." In *Nach der Natur: Über Politik und Ästhetik,* 133–61. Munich: Hanser, 1988.

Böll, Heinrich. *Der Engel schwieg.* Cologne: Kiepenheuer & Witsch, 1994.

Bosmajian, Hamida. "German Literature about the Holocaust: A Literature of Limitations." *Modern Language Studies* 16, no. 1 (Winter, 1985): 51–61.

## 202 ♦ Bibliography

Bowles, David. "'American Dirt' Is Proof the Publishing Industry Is Broken." Review of *American Dirt*, by Jeanine Cummins. *New York Times*, January 27, 2020.

Boyagoda, Randy. "The *American Dirt* Controversy Is Painfully Intramural." Review of *American Dirt*, by Jeanine Cummins. *Atlantic*, January 30, 2020.

Boyarin, Daniel, and Jonathan Boyarin. "Generation and the Ground of Jewish Identity." *Critical Inquiry* 19, no. 4 (1993): 693–725.

Braidotti, Rosi. *The Posthuman*. Cambridge: Polity, 2013.

Budick, Emily Miller. *The Subject of Holocaust Fiction*. Bloomington: Indiana University Press, 2015.

Büettner, Angi. *Holocaust Images and Picturing Catastrophe: The Culture of Politics and Seeing*. Farnham, UK: Ashgate, 2011.

Buschan, Georg. "Einfluß der Rasse auf die Häufigkeit und die Formen der Geistes-und Nervenkrankheiten." In *Allgemeine Medizinische Central-Zeitung* 9 (1897): 104–5.

Chaouat, Bruno. "Being and Jewishness: Levinas Reader of Sartre." In *Sartre, Jews, and the Other: Rethinking Anti-Semitism, Race, and Gender*, edited by Manuela Consonni and Vivian Liska, 90–106. Berlin: De Gruyter Oldenbourg, 2020.

Charcot, Jean Martin. *Leçons du Mardi médical à la Salpêtrière*. 2 vols. Paris: Progrès Médical, 1889.

Charmé, Stuart. "Varieties of Authenticity in Contemporary Jewish Identity." *Jewish Social Studies* 6, no. 2 (2000): 133–55.

Chiarugi, Vincenzo. *Abhandlung über den Wahnsinn überhaupt und insbesondere nebst einer Centurie von Beobachtungen*. Leipzig: G. D. Meyer, 1795.

Consonni, Manuela, and Vivian Liska, eds. *Sartre, Jews, and the Other: Rethinking Antisemitism, Race, and Gender*. Berlin: De Gruyter Oldenbourg, 2020.

Coplan, Amy, and Goldie, Peter, eds. *Empathy: Philosophical and Psychological Perspectives*. Oxford: Oxford University Press, 2006.

Cosgrove, Mary. "The Anxiety of German Influence: Affiliation, Rejection, and Jewish Identity in W. G. Sebald's Work." In *German Memory Contests: The Quest for Identity in Literature, Film, and Discourse since 1990*, edited by Anne Fuchs, Mary Cosgrove, and George Grote, 229–52. Rochester, NY: Camden House, 2006.

———. "Melancholy Competitions: W. G. Sebald reads Günter Grass and Wolfgang Hildesheimer." *German Life and Letters* 59, no. 2 (2006): 217–32.

———. "Sebald for Our Time: The Politics of Melancholy and the Critique of Capitalism in his Work." In *W. G. Sebald and the Writing of History*, edited by Anne Fuchs and J. J. Long, 91–110. Würzburg: Königshausen & Neumann, 2007.

Cuomo, Joseph. "A Conversation with W. G. Sebald." In *The Emergence of Memory: Conversations with W. G. Sebald*, edited by Lynne Sharon Schwartz, 93–117. New York: Seven Stories Press, 2007.

Curtin, Adrian, and Maxim D. Shrayer. "Netting the Butterfly Man: The Significance of Vladimir Nabokov in W. G. Sebald's *The Emigrants*." *Religion and the Arts* 9, nos. 3–4 (2005): 258–83.

Davies, Mererid Puw. "An Uncanny Journey: W. G. Sebald and the Literature of Protest." *Journal of European Studies Special Issue: W. G. Sebald*, 41, nos. 3–4 (2011): 285–303.

De Gobineau, Comte Arthur. "Essai sur l'inégalité des races humaines." Paris: Editions Belfond, 1967.

Denham, Scott, and Mark McCulloh, eds. *W. G. Sebald: History—Memory—Trauma*. Berlin: Walter de Gruyter, 2006.

———. "W. G. Sebald's Magic Mountains." In *Heights of Reflection: Mountains in the German Imagination from the Middle Ages to the Twenty-First Century*, edited by Sean Ireton and Caroline Schaumann, 320–33. Rochester, New York: Boydell & Brewer, Camden House, 2012.

Derrida, Jacques. *Acts of Literature*. Edited by Derek Attridge. New York: Routledge, 1992.

Di Cesare, Donatella. *Heidegger and the Jews: The Black Notebooks*. Cambridge: Polity, 2018.

Dilger, Martin, and Frank Wössner. "Georg Simmels Exkurs über den Fremden: Eine Textanalyse." Institut für Erziehungswissenschaft, Universität Tübingen, Sommersemester 1997.

Diner, Dan. "Negative Symbiose: Deutsche und Juden nach Auschwitz." *Babylon* 1 (1986): 9–20.

Doerry, Martin, and Volker Hage. "Ich fürchte das Melodramatische." *Der Spiegel* (March 12 2001): 228–34.

Doré, Gustave. *The Wandering Jew*, 12 woodcuts, 1856.

Dühring, Eugen. *Die Judenfrage als Racen-, Sitten- und Culturfrage: Mit einer weltgeschichtlichen Antwort*. Leipzig: H. Reuther, 1881.

Dünkelsbühler, Ulrike. "Zur Irr-Rede gestellt: Was heißt die Frage 'was ist jüdisch?' Kant—Cohen—Derrida." In *Dialog zwischen den Kulturen: erziehungshistorische und religionspädagogische Gesichtspunkte interkultureller Bildung*, edited by Ingrid Lohmann and Wolfram Weisse, 145–54. Münster: Waxmann, 1994.

Dunn, Francis M. *Tragedy's End: Closure and Innovation in Euripidean Drama*. Oxford: Oxford University Press, 1996.

Eckstaedt, Anita. *Nationalsozialismus in der zweiten Generation: Psychoanalyse von Hörigkeitsverhältnissen*. Frankfurt am Main: Suhrkamp, 1992.

Edelman, R. "Ahasuerus, the Wandering Jew: Origin and Background." In *The Wandering Jew: Essays in the Interpretation of a Christian Legend*, edited by Galit Hasan-Rokem and Alan Dundes, 1–10. Bloomington: Indiana University Press, 1986.

204 ♦ BIBLIOGRAPHY

Eder, Richard. "Excavating a Life." Review of *Austerlitz*, by W. G. Sebald. *New York Times*, October 28, 2001.

Etzler, Melissa Starr. "Writing from the Periphery: W. G. Sebald and Outsider Art." PhD diss., University of California, 2014.

Euripides. *Medea and Other Plays: Alcestis/Medea/The Children of Heracles/ Hippolytus*. Translated by John Davie. London: Penguin Classics, 2004.

Fackenheim, Emil. *Encounters between Judaism and Modern Philosophy: A Preface to Future Jewish Thought*. New York: Basic Books, 1973.

———. *To Mend the World. Foundations of Post-Holocaust Jewish Thought*. Bloomington: Indiana University Press, 1994.

Felman, Shoshana, and Dori Laub. *Crises of Witnessing in Literature, Psychoanalysis, and History*. London: Routledge, 1992.

Fermaglich, Kirstin. "Names, Name-Changing, and Family Mobility in New York City, 1917–1942." *Journal of American Ethnic History* 34, no. 3 (2015): 34–57.

Fichte, Johann Gottlieb. *Beitrag zur Berichtiging der Urtheile des Publicums über die französische Revolution*. Edited by Richard Schottky. Hamburg: Felix Meiner, 1973.

Finch, Helen, and Lynn L. Wolff, eds. *Witnessing, Memory, Poetics: H. G. Adler and W. G. Sebald*. Rochester, NY: Camden House, 2014.

Fink, Susanne. "W. G. Sebald—der fünfte Ausgewanderte." In *W. G. Sebald*, edited by Franz Loquai, 214–27. Eggingen: Edition Isele, 1997.

Finkielkraut, Alain. *The Imaginary Jew*. Translated by Kevin O'Neill and David Suchoff. Lincoln: University of Nebraska Press, 1994.

Fischer, Gerhard. "Schreiben ex patria: W. G. Sebald und die Konstruktion einer literarischen Identität." In *W. G. Sebald: Schreiben ex patria/ Expatriate Writing*, edited by Gerhard Fischer, 27–44. Amsterdam: Rodopi, 2009.

———. *W. G. Sebald: Schreiben ex patria/Expatriate Writing*. Amsterdam: Rodopi, 2009.

Fletcher, Angus. *Allegory: The Theory of a Symbolic Mode*. Ithaca, NY: Cornell University Press, 1964.

Franklin, Ruth. "Rings of Smoke." In *The Emergence of Memory: Conversations with W. G. Sebald*, edited by Lynne Sharon Schwartz, 119–43. New York: Seven Stories Press, 2007.

———. *A Thousand Darknesses: Lies and Truth in Holocaust Fiction*. Oxford: Oxford University Press, 2011.

Franzos, Karl Emil. *Die Juden von Barnow*. Leipzig: Duncker & Humblott, 1880.

Fuchs, Anne. "'Ein auffallend geschichtsblindes und traditionsloses Volk': Heimatdiskurs und Ruinenästhetik in *W. G. Sebalds Prosa*." In *Politische Archäologie und melancholische Bastelei*, edited by Michael Niehaus and Claudia Öhlschläger, 89–110. Berlin: Erich Schmidt, 2006.

———. *Die Schmerzensspuren der Geschichte: Zur Poetik der Erinnerung in W. G. Sebalds Prosa*. Cologne: Böhlau, 2004.

Fuchs, Anne, and George Grote, eds. *W. G. Sebald and the Writing of History.* Würzburg: Königshausen & Neumann, 2007.

Fuchs, Anne, Mary Cosgrove, and George Grote, eds. *German Memory Contests. The Quest for Identity in Literature, Film, and Discourse since 1990.* Rochester, NY: Camden House, 2006.

Garloff, Katja. "The Task of the Narrator: Moments of Symbolic Investiture in W. G. Sebald's *Austerlitz.*" In *W. G. Sebald: History—Memory—Trauma,* edited by Scott Denham and Mark McCulloh, 157–69. Berlin: Walter De Gruyter, 2006.

Gasseleder, Klaus. "Erkundungen zum Prätext der Luisa-Lanzberg-Geschichte aus W. G. Sebalds 'Die Ausgewanderten'. Ein Bericht." In *Sebald: Lektüren,* edited by Marcel Atze and Franz Loquai, 157–75. Eggingen: Edition Isele, 2005.

Geller, Jay. "Of Mice and Mensa: Anti-Semitism and the Jewish Genius." *Centennial Review* 38, no. 2 (1994): 361–85.

Gerron, Kurt. Director. *Der Führer schenkt den Juden eine Stadt.* Prague: Aktualita, 1944.

Gilman, Sander. *Franz Kafka, the Jewish Patient.* New York: Routledge, 1995.

———. "Jewish Writers in Contemporary Germany: The Dead Author Speaks." *Studies in 20th Century Literature* 13, no. 2 (1989): 215–43.

Goebbels, Joseph. "Mimikry." In *Die Zeit ohne Beispiel: Reden und Aufsätze aus den Jahren 1939–41.* Münich: Zentralverlag der NSDAP, 1941.

Goethe, Johann Wolfgang. *Faust: Der Tragödie Erster Teil.* Stuttgart: Reklam, 2005.

Goldhagen, Daniel. *Hitler's Willing Executioners: Ordinary Germans and the Holocaust.* New York: Alfred A. Knopf, 1996.

Goldie, Peter. "Dramatic Irony, Narrative, and the External Perspective." *Royal Institute of Philosophy Supplements* 60, no. 1 (August 2007): 69–84.

Goldstein, Jan. "The Wandering Jew and the Problem of Psychiatric Anti-Semitism in *fin-de-siècle* France." *Journal of Contemporary History* 20 (1985): 521–52.

Gordon, Robert S. C., and Emilio Perra. "Holocaust Intersections in 21st Century Europe: An Introduction." Quest. Issues in Contemporary Jewish History. *Journal of Fondazione CDEC* no. 10 (December 2016): 1–27.

Görres, Johann Joseph. *Korruskationen.* In *Gesammelte Schriften,* edited by W. Schellberg. Cologne: Gilde-Verlag, 1926.

Gotterbarm, Mario. *Die Gewalt des Moralisten: Zum Verhältnis von Ethik und Ästhetik bei W. G. Sebald.* Paderborn: Wilhelm Fink, 2016.

Gray, Richard T. "Fabulation and Metahistory: W. G. Sebald and Contemporary German Holocaust Fiction." In *Literarische Experimente: Medien, Kunst, Texte seit 1950,* edited by Christoph Zeller, 271–301. Heidelberg: Universitätsverlag, Winter 2012.

———. *Ghostwriting: W. G. Sebald's Poetics of History.* London: Bloomsbury Publications, 2017.

Grimm, Jacob, and Wilhelm Grimm. *Kinder- und Hausmärchen* (*1812–1815*). Berlin: Edition Holzinger, 2016.

Günter, Joachim. "Der Bombenkrieg findet zur Sprache." *Neue Zürcher Zeitung*, December 7, 2002.

Gunther, Stefan. "The Holocaust as the Still Point of the World in W. G. Sebald's *The Emigrants*." In *W. G. Sebald: History—Memory—Trauma*, edited by Scott Denham and Mark McCulloh, 279–90. Berlin: Walter De Gruyter, 2006.

Gutzkow, Karl. "Plan for an Ahasverus." In *Vermischte Schriften* (1838), 164–66. Translated by Paul Lawrence Rose, and cited in his *German Question/Jewish Question: Revolutionary Antisemitism from Kant to Wagner*. Princeton, NJ: Princeton University Press, 1990.

Gwyer, Kirstin. "An Absence in Context: Holocaust Representation in Testimony, Scholarship, and Literature." In *Encrypting the Past: The German-Jewish Holocaust Novel of the First Generation*, 1–56. Oxford: Oxford University Press, 2014.

———. *Encrypting the Past: The German-Jewish Holocaust Novel of the First Generation*. Oxford: Oxford University Press, 2014.

———. "'Schmerzensspuren der Geschichte(n)': Memory and Intertextuality in H. G. Adler and W. G. Sebald." In *Witnessing, Memory, Poetics: H. G. Adler and W. G. Sebald*, edited by Helen Finch and Lynn L. Wolff, 112–36. Rochester, NY: Camden House, Boydell & Brewer, 2014.

———. "What Comes 'After': The 'Postmemory' Holocaust Novel." In *Encrypting the Past: The German-Jewish Holocaust Novel of the First Generation*, 205–22. Oxford: Oxford University Press, 2014.

Hacking, Ian. *Mad Travelers: On the Reality of Transient Mental Illnesses*. Charlottesville: University of Virginia Press, 1998.

Hage, Volker. "Im Gespräch mit W. G. Sebald." *Akzente*. Special Issue on W. G. Sebald 50 (February 2003): 35–50.

———. *Zeugen der Zerstörung: Die Literaten und der Luftkrieg. Essays und Gespräche*. Frankfurt am Main: S. Fischer, 2003.

Hall, Katharina. "Jewish Memory in Exile: The Relation of W. G. Sebald's *Die Ausgewanderten* to the Tradition of the Yizkor Books." In *Jews in German Literature since 1945: German-Jewish Literature?* edited by Pól O'Dochartaigh, 153–64. Amsterdam: Rodopi, 2000.

Hammerschlag, Sarah. *The Figural Jew: Politics and Identity in Postwar French Thought*. Chicago: University of Chicago Press, 2010.

Hasan-Rokem, Galit. "Jews as Postcards, or Postcards as Jews: Mobility in a Modern Genre." *Jewish Quarterly Review* 99, no. 4 (2009): 505–46.

———. "Joban Transformation of the Wandering Jew in Joseph Roth's *Hiob* and *Der Leviathan*." In *The Book of Job: Aesthetics, Ethics, Hermeneutics*, edited by Leora Batnitzky and Ilana Pardes, 147–71. Perspectives on Jewish Texts and Contexts 1. Berlin: De Gruyter, 2015.

Hasan-Rokem, Galit, and Alan Dundes, eds. *The Wandering Jew: Essays in the Interpretation of a Christian Legend*. Bloomington: Indiana University Press, 1986.

Haury, Thomas. "'Ziehen die Fäden im Hintergrund.' Neo-Globals, Antisemitismus und Antiamerikanismus." In *Gerüchte über die Juden. Antisemitismus, Philosemitismus und Verschwörungstheorien*, edited by H. Loewy, 69–100. Essen: Klartext, 2005.

Hebel, Johann Peter. "Unexpected Reunion." In *The Treasure Chest: Unexpected Reunion and Other Stories*. Edited and translated by John Hibberd. London: Penguin, 1994.

———. "Unverhofftes Wiedersehen und andere Geschichten aus dem Schatzkästlein des Rheinischen Hausfreundes." Zurich: Diogenes, 2009.

Hegel, Friedrich. *Phenomenology of Spirit*. Translated by Arnold V. Miller. Oxford: Oxford University Press, 1977.

———. "Philosophy of Nature." Part 1 of *Phenomenology of Spirit*. Translated by Arnold V. Miller. Oxford: Oxford University Press, 1977.

———. "The Positivity of Christian Religion." In *Early Theological Writings*, edited by H. Nohl, translated by T. M. Knox. Chicago: University of Chicago Press, 1948.

———. "The Spirit of Christianity and its Fate." Translated by T. M. Knox. In *On Christianity: Early Theological Writings* 182–281. Philadelphia: University of Pennsylvania Press, 2011.

Heidegger, Martin. *Anmerkungen I–V (Schwarze Hefte 1942–1948)*. *Gesamtausgabe* 97. Edited by Peter Trawny. Frankfurt: Klostermann, 2015.

———. *The Fundamental Concepts of Metaphysics: World, Finitude, Solitude*. Translated by William McNeill and Nicholas Walker. Bloomington: Indiana University Press, 1995.

———. *The History of Beyng*. Translated by William McNeill and Jeffrey Powell. Bloomington: Indiana University Press, 2015.

———. "The Jewish Contamination of German Spiritual Life." Letter to Victor Schwoerer, 1929. In *Philosophical and Political Writing*, translated and edited by Manfred Stassen. New York: Continuum, 2003.

———. *Ponderings XII–XV: Black Notebooks 1938–1941*. Translated by Richard Rojcewicz. Bloomington: Indiana University Press, 2017.

———. *Überlegungen XII–XV Schwarze Hefte 1939–1941, Gesamtausgabe* 96. Edited by Peter Trawny. Frankfurt am Main: Vittorio Klostermann, 2014.

Hein, Christian. *Traumatologie des Daseins: Zur Panoptischen Darstellung der Desintegration des Lebens im Werk W. G. Sebalds*. Würzburg: Königshausen & Neumann, 2014.

Hell, Julia. "The Angel's Enigmatic Eyes, or The Gothic Beauty of Catastrophic History in W. G. Sebald's 'Air War and Literature.'" *Criticism* 46, no. 3 (Summer 2004): 361–92.

Herder, Johann Gottfried. *Ideen zur Philosophie der Geschichte der Menschheit*, 2 vols. Berlin: Aufbau-Verlag, 1965.

———. *Reflections on the Philosophy of the History of Mankind*. Translated by T. O. Churchill. Chicago: University of Chicago Press, 1968.

## 208 ♦ BIBLIOGRAPHY

Herf, Jeffrey. "'The Jewish War': Goebbels and Antisemitic Campaigns of the Nazi Propaganda Ministry." In *Holocaust and Genocide Studies* 19, no. 1 (Spring 2005): 51–80.

Herzl, Theodor. *Altneuland*. Leipzig: Hermann Seemann Nachfolger, 1902.

Herzog, Werner, director. *Jeder für sich und Gott gegen alle*. Werner Herzog Filmproduktion, 1974.

Hiemer, Ernst. *Der Jude im Sprichwort der Völker*. Nürnberg: Der Stürmer Buchverlag, 1942.

Hirsch, Marianne. "Surviving Images: Holocaust Photographs and the Work of Postmemory." *Yale Journal of Criticism* 14 no.1 (2001): 5–37.

Hitler, Adolf. *Mein Kampf: The Official 1939 Unexpurgated Edition*. Translated by James Murphy. London: Hurst & Blackett, 1943.

Hölderlin, Friedrich. *Hyperion, or the Hermit in Greece*. Translated by Howard Gaskill. Cambridge, UK: Open Book Publishers, 2019.

——. *Sämtliche Werke*, Große Stuttgarter Ausgabe III. Edited by Friedrich Beissner. Stuttgart: W. Kohlhammer Verlag, 1943–1985.

Hollander, Dana. *Exemplarity and Chosenness: Rosenzweig and Derrida on the Nation of Philosophy*. Stanford, CA: Stanford University Press, 2008. Kindle Edition.

Holz, Klaus. "Die Paradoxie der Normalisierung: Drei Gegensatzpaare des Antisemitismus vor und nach Auschwitz." In *Literarischer Antisemitismus nach Auschwitz*, edited by Klaus-Michael Bogdal, Klaus Holz, and Mattias N. Lorenz, 37–57. Stuttgart: J. B. Metzler Verlag, 2007.

Hutchinson, Ben. "The Shadow of Resistance: W. G. Sebald and the Frankfurt School." *Journal of European Studies Special Issue: W. G. Sebald*, 41, 3–4 (2011): 267–84.

Huyssen, Andreas. *Twilight Memories: Marking Time in a Culture of Amnesia*. New York: Routledge, 1995.

Ilsemann, Mark. "Going Astray: Melancholy, Natural History, and the Image of Exile in W. G. Sebald's *Austerlitz*." In *W. G. Sebald: History— Memory—Trauma*, edited by Scott Denham and Mark McCulloh, 301–14. Berlin: Walter de Gruyter, 2006.

Jacobson, Dan. *Heshel's Kingdom*. London: Hamish Hamilton, 1998.

Jay, Martin. "The Jews and the Frankfurt School: Critical Theory's Analysis of Anti-Semitism." *New German Critique* 19, no. 1 (1980): 137–49.

Jeutter, Ralf. "'Am Rand der Finsternis.' The Jewish Experience in the Context of W. G. Sebald's Poetics." In *Jews in German Literature since 1945: German-Jewish Literature?* edited by Pól O'Dochartaigh, 165–79. Amsterdam: Rodopi, 2000.

Johnson, Gary. "The Vitality of Allegory." In *Theory and Interpretation of Narrative*, edited by James Phelan, Peter J. Rabinowitz, and Robyn Warhol, 1–33. Columbus: Ohio State University Press, 2012.

Jünger, Ernst. "Über Nationalismus und Judenfrage." In *Politische Publizistik 1919–1933*, 587–92. Stuttgart: Klett-Cotta, 2001.

Kafatou, Sarah. "An Interview with W. G. Sebald." *Harvard Review* 15 (1998): 31–35.

Kafka, Franz. "The Cares of a Family Man." In *The Complete Stories of Franz Kafka*. Edited by Nahum N. Glatzer and translated by Willa and Edwin Muir. New York: Schocken, 1971.

———. *The Complete Stories of Franz Kafka*. Edited by Nahum N. Glatzer and translated by Willa and Edmund Muir. New York: Schocken, 1971.

———. *The Diaries of Franz Kafka*. Translated by Ross Benjamin. New York: The Schocken Kafka Library, Penguin Random House, 2023.

———. *Hochzeitsvorbereitungen auf dem Lande und andere Prosa aus dem Nachlass*. Frankfurt: Fischer Verlag, 1966.

———. "The Hunter Gracchus." In *The Complete Stories of Franz Kafka*, edited by Nahum Glatzer and translated by Willa and Edwin Muir. New York: Schocken, 1971.

———. "Josephine the Singer, or the Mouse Folk." In *The Complete Stories of Franz Kafka*, edited by Nahum N. Glatzer and translated by Willa and Edwin Muir, 360–76. New York: Schocken, 1971.

———. *Letters to Felice*. New York: Schocken, 1973.

———. *Das Schloß*. Frankfurt am Main: Fischer, 1982.

———. *Tagebücher 1910–1919*. Edited by Max Brod, translated by Walter Sokel. New York: Schocken, 1948.

Kant, Immanuel. *Anthropology from a Pragmatic Point of View*. Translated and edited by Robert Louden. Cambridge: Cambridge University Press, 2006.

———. *The Conflict of the Faculties*. Translated by Mary J. Gregor. Lincoln: University of Nebraska Press, 1979.

———. *Critique of Practical Reason*. Translated and edited by Mary Gregor. Cambridge: Cambridge University Press, 1997.

———. *Kritik der reinen Vernunft*. Edited by W. Weischedel. Wiesbaden: Insel, 1958.

———. *Religion within the Boundaries of Mere Reason and Other Writings*. Edited and translated by Allen Wood. Cambridge: Cambridge University Press, 2018.

———. *Schriften zur Ethik und Religionsphilosophie*. Edited by Wilhelm Weischedel. Frankfurt am Main: Suhrkamp, 1964.

Kermode, Frank. "Secrets and Narrative Sequence." *Critical Inquiry* 7, no.1 (1980): 83–101.

Kertész, Imre. "Who Owns Auschwitz?" *Yale Journal of Criticism* 14, no. 1 (2001): 267–72.

Kilbourn, R. J. A. "Kafka, Nabokov . . . Sebald: Intertextuality and Narratives of Redemption in *Vertigo* and *The Emigrants*." In *W. G. Sebald: History—Memory—Trauma*, edited by Scott Denham and Mark McCulloh, 33–63. Berlin: Walter De Gruyter, 2006.

———. *W. G. Sebald's Postsecular Redemption: Catastrophe with Spectator*. Evanston, Il: Northwestern University Press, 2018. Kindle Edition.

Kim-Cohen, Seth. "What Counts as True? Pictures and Fiction in W. G. Sebald." In *Witness: Memory, Representation and the Media*, edited by

Frederyk Tygstrup and Ulrik Ekman, 191–97. Copenhagen: Museum Tusculanum Press, University of Copenhagen, 2008.

Kittel, Gerhard. *Forschungen zur Judenfrage: Sitzungsberichte der Ersten Arbeitstagung der Forschungsabteilung Judenfrage des Reichsinstituts für Geschichte des neuen Deutschlands vom 19. bis 21. November 1936.* Hamburg: Hanseatische Verlagsanstalt, 1937.

Klebes, Martin. "Sebald's Pathographies." In *W. G. Sebald: History—Memory—Trauma*, edited by Scott Denham and Mark McCulloh, 65–75. Berlin: Walter de Gruyter, 2006.

Kleinschmidt, Erich. "Schreiben an Grenzen. Probleme der Autorschaft in Shoah-Autobiographik." In *Überleben schreiben: Zur Autobiographik der Shoah*, edited by Manuela Günter, 77–95. Würzburg: Königshausen & Neumann, 2002.

Klüger, Ruth. *Von hoher und niedriger Literatur.* Göttingen: Wallstein, 1996.

Köhler, Andrea. "Katastrophe mit Zuschauer: Ein Gespräch mit dem Schriftsteller W. G. Sebald. *Neue Zürcher Zeitung*, November 22–23, 1997.

Köhler, F. "Tuberkulose und Psyche." *Medizinische Klinik* 7 (1911): 1808–13.

Kolenda, Karolina. "The Present Pasts: Image and Text in the Fiction of W. G. Sebald." *Theoria et Historia Scientiarum* 14 (2017): 71–86.

Krauthausen, Ciro. "Sebald: Creci en una familia postfascista Alemana." *El Pais*, July 14, 2001.

Krell, David Farrell. *Contagion: Sexuality, Disease, and Death in German Idealism.* Bloomington: Indiana University Press, 1998.

Kunisch, H-P. "Die Melancholie des Widerstands." *Süddeutsche Zeitung* (Literatur) 80, April 5, 2001.

LaCapra, Dominick. *History and Memory after Auschwitz.* Ithaca, NY: Cornell University Press, 1998.

———. *Writing History, Writing Trauma.* Baltimore: John Hopkins University Press, 2013.

Lang, Berel. *Act and Idea in the Nazi Genocide.* Chicago: University of Chicago Press, 1990.

Lang, Fritz, director. *Die Nibelungen.* Berlin: Decla-Bioscop, 1924.

Langer, Lawrence L. *Admitting the Holocaust: Collected Essays.* New York: Oxford University Press, 1995.

Large, Duncan. "Nietzsche's Orientalism." *Nietzsche-Studien* 40, no. 1 (2013): 420–38.

Leroy-Beaulieu, Anatole. *Israel among the Nations: A Study of the Jews and Antisemitism.* Translated by Frances Helman. New York: G. P. Putnam's Sons, 1895.

Levi, Primo. *The Drowned and the Saved.* Translated by Raymond Rosenthal. New York: Simon & Schuster, 1986.

———. "The Gray Zone." In *The Drowned and the Saved*, translated by Raymond Rosenthal, 25–56. New York: Simon & Schuster, 1986.

———. *If This Is a Man: Survival in Auschwitz: The Nazi Assault on Humanity.* New York: Simon & Schuster, 1986.

Levin, David. *Richard Wagner, Fritz Lang, and the Nibelungen: The Dramaturgy of Disavowal*. Princeton, NJ: Princeton University Press, 1999.

Levinas, Emmanuel. "Heidegger, Gagarin, and Us." In *Difficult Freedom: Essays on Judaism*, translated by Sean Hand, 231–34. Baltimore: John Hopkins University Press, 1990.

Levine, Michael G. "Of Big Ears and Bondage: Benjamin, Kafka, and the Static of the Sirens." *German Quarterly* 87, no. 2 (2014): 196–215.

Levi-Strauss, Claude. *Das wilde Denken*. Frankfurt am Main: Suhrkamp, 2001.

Lipszyc, Adam. *Rewizja procesu Józefiny K.* In "The Present Pasts: Image and Text in the Fiction of W. G. Sebald." Karolina Kolenda. *Theoria et Historia Scientiarum* 14 (2017): 71–86.

Liska, Vivian. "'Le juif, c'est moi': Sartre, Blanchot, Badiou." In *Sartre, Jews, and the Other: Rethinking Antisemitism, Race, and Gender*, edited by Manuela Consonni and Vivian Liska, 243–51. Berlin: De Gruyter Oldenbourg, 2020.

Loewy, Hanno, ed. *Gerüchte über die Juden: Antisemitismus, Philosemitismus und Verschwörungstheorien*. Essen: Klartext, 2005.

Löffler, Sigrid. "'Wildes Denken.' Gespräch mit W. G. Sebald." In *W. G. Sebald*, edited by Franz Loquai, 135–37. Eggingen: Edition Isele, 1997.

Lohmann, Ingrid, and Wolfram Weisse, eds. *Dialog zwischen den Kulturen: Erziehungshistorische und religionspädagogische Gesichtspunkte interkultureller Bildung*. Münster: Waxmann, 1994.

Long, J. J. "History, Narrative, and Photography in W. G. Sebald's *Die Ausgewanderten*." *Modern Language Review* 98, no. 1 (2003): 117–37.

———. *W. G. Sebald: Image, Archive, Modernity*. Edinburgh: Edinburgh University Press, 2007.

Loquai, Franz, ed. *W. G. Sebald*. Eggingen: Edition Isele, 1997.

Löwy, Michael. "'*Theologia negativa*' and '*Utopia negativa*': Franz Kafka." In *Redemption and Utopia: Jewish Libertarian Thought in Central Europe: A Study in Elective Affinity*, translated by Hope Heaney, 71–94. Stanford: Stanford University Press, 1992.

Lubow, Arthur. "Crossing Boundaries." In *The Emergence of Memory: Conversations with W. G. Sebald*, edited by Lynne Sharon Schwartz, 159–73. New York: Seven Stories Press, 2007.

Luther, Martin. *On the Jews and Their Lies*, Parts 11–13, 1543. In *Luther's Works*, translated by Martin H. Bertram. Philadelphia: Fortress, 1971.

———. "That Jesus Christ was born a Jew." In *Luther's Works: The Christian Society* II, XLV, edited by Helmut T. Lehrmann et al., 199–229. Translated by Walther I. Brandt. Philadelphia: Fortress, 1962.

Lyotard, Jean-François. *Heidegger and "the jews."* Translated by Andreas Michel and Mark Roberts. Minneapolis: University of Minnesota Press, 1990.

Mack, Michael. *German Idealism and the Jew: The Inner Anti-Semitism of Philosophy and German Jewish Responses*. Chicago: University of Chicago Press, 2003.

Maddox, John. "A Book for Burning?" *Nature* 29 (1981): 245–46.

Mann, Thomas. "Der Tod in Venedig." In *Gesammelte Werke*, 8. Frankfurt am Main: Fischer, 1960.

Marcus, Kenneth L. *The Definition of Anti-Semitism*. Oxford: Oxford University Press, 2015.

Margalit, Avishai. *The Ethics of Memory*. Cambridge, MA: Harvard University Press, 2000.

Margalit, Avishai, and Gabriel Motzkin. "Der Holocaust: Zur Einzigartigkeit eines historischen Geschehens": *Lettre International* 3, no. 5 (1996): 23–27.

———. "The Uniqueness of the Holocaust," *Philosophy & Public Affairs* 25, no. 1 (Winter 1996): 65–83.

Margry, Karel. "'Theresienstadt' (1944–1945): The Nazi Propaganda Film Depicting the Concentration Camp as Paradise." *Historical Journal of Film, Radio, and Television* 12 (1992): 145–62.

Martin, James R. "On Misunderstanding W. G. Sebald." *Cambridge Literary Review* 4, no. 7 (Michaelmas, 2013): 123–38.

Martin, Laura. "Reading the Individual: The Ethics of Narration in the Works of W. G. Sebald as an Example for Comparative Literature." *Comparative Critical Studies* 11, no.1 (2014): 29–47.

Matteoni, Francesca. "The Jew, the Blood and the Body in Late Medieval and Early Modern Europe." *Folklore* 119, no. 2 (August 2008):182–200.

Mayer, Sven. "Keine Kausallogik: Zum Zusammenhang in W. G. Sebalds Schreiben." In *Über W. G. Sebald: Beiträge zu einem anderen Bild des Autors*, edited by Uwe Schütte, 19–28. Berlin: Walter de Gruyter, 2017.

McCulloh, Mark. "The Stylistics of Stasis: Paradoxical Effects in W. G. Sebald." *Style* 38, no. 1 (2004): 38–48.

———. *Understanding W. G. Sebald*. Columbia: University of South Carolina Press, 2003.

McGlothlin, Erin. *Second-Generation Holocaust Literature: Legacies of Survival and Perpetration*. Rochester, NY: Camden House, 2006.

McGlothlin, Erin, Brad Prager, Markus Zisselsberger, eds. *The Construction of Testimony: Claude Lanzmann's Shoah and Its Outtakes*. Detroit: Wayne University Press, 2020.

Meckel, Christoph. *Suchbild: Über meinen Vater*. Bamberg: C. C. Buchner, 2005.

Meige, Henri. "The Wandering Jew in the Clinic: A Study of Neurotic Pathology." In *The Wandering Jew: Essays in the Interpretation of a Christian Legend*, edited by Galit Hasan-Rokem and Alan Dundes, 190–94. Bloomington: Indiana University Press, 1986.

Merkin, Daphne. "Cordoning off the Past." Review of *On the Natural History of Destruction*, by W. G. Sebald. *New York Times Book Review*, April 6, 2003.

Mitscherlich, Alexander, and Margarete Mitscherlich. *Die Unfähigkeit zu Trauern: Grundlagen kollektiven Verhaltens*. Munich: Piper, 1967.

Modlinger, Martin. "The Kafkaesque in Adler and Sebald's Literary Historiographies." In *Witnessing, Memory, Poetics: H. G. Adler and W. G. Sebald*, edited by Helen Finch and Lynn L. Wolff, 201–31. Rochester, NY: Camden House, 2014.

Moeller, Robert. "The Politics of the Past in the 1950s: Rhetorics of Victimisation in East and West Germany." In *Germans as Victims*, edited by Bill Niven, 26–42. New York: Palgrave Macmillan, 2006.

Monk, Ray. *Ludwig Wittgenstein: The Duty of Genius.* New York: Free Press, 1990.

Morgan, Peter. "The Sign of Saturn: Melancholy, Homelessness and Apocalypse in W. G. Sebald's Prose Narratives." *German Life and Letters* 58, no. 1 (2005): 75–92.

———. "'Your Story Is Now My Story': The Ethics of Narration in Grass and Sebald." *Monatshefte* 101, no. 2 (2009): 186–206.

Morning, Ann. *The Nature of Race: How Societies Think and Teach about Human Difference.* Los Angeles, CA: University of California Press, 2011.

Morris, Leslie. "How Jewish is it? W. G. Sebald and the Question of 'Jewish' Writing in Germany Today." In *The New German Jewry and the European Context: The Return of the European Jewish Diaspora*, edited by Y. Michal Bodemann, 111–28. New York: Palgrave Macmillan, 2008.

Mosbach, Bettina. *Figurationen der Katastrophe: Ästhetische Verfahren in W. G. Sebalds "Die Ringe des Saturn" und "Austerlitz."* Bielefeld: Aisthesis, 2008.

Mosse, George L. *The Image of Man: The Creation of Modern Masculinity.* Oxford: Oxford University Press, 1998.

Müller-Seidel, Walter. *Rechtsdenken im literarischen Text.* Berlin: De Gruyter, 2017.

Nabokov, Vladimir. *Speak, Memory.* New York: Vintage, 1989.

Nadler, Steven. "Why Spinoza Was Excommunicated." *Humanities* 34, no. 5 (2013): 1–8.

Nietzsche, Friedrich. *Beyond Good and Evil: Prelude to a Philosophy of the Future.* Translated by R. J. Hollingdale. London: Penguin, 1990.

Niven, Bill, ed. *Germans as Victims: Remembering the Past in Contemporary Germany.* New York: Palgrave Macmillan, 2006.

Nora, Pierre. "Les Lieux de Mémoire." Paris: Gallimard,1984.

Novalis. *Heinrich von Ofterdingen.* Stuttgart: Reklam, 2008.

———. "Poetik des Übels." In *Schriften* II, edited by Ludwig Tieck and Friedrich von Schlegel, 245–47. Berlin: G. Reimer, 1837.

Nussbaum, Martha. *Poetic Justice: The Literary Imagination and Public Life.* Boston: Beacon, 1996.

O'Dochartaigh, Pól, ed. *Jews in German Literature since 1945: German-Jewish Literature?* Amsterdam: Rodopi, 2000.

Owen, Wilfred. "Strange Meeting." In *Poems of Wilfred Owen*, edited by Edmund Blunden, 116. New York: Viking, 1931.

## BIBLIOGRAPHY

Pelikan-Straus, Nina. "Sebald, Wittgenstein, and the Ethics of Memory." *Comparative Literature* 61, no. 1 (Winter, 2009): 43–53.

Phelan, James, Peter Rabinowitz, and Robyn Warhol, eds. *Theory and Interpretation of Narrative*. Columbus: Ohio State University Press, 2012.

Pöhlmann, Wolfgang. "Ahasver, der wandernde Jude: Eine europäische Legende." In *Glaube-Freiheit-Diktatur in Europa und der USA: Festschrift für Gerhard Besier zum 60. Geburtstag*, edited by Katarzyna Stoklosa and Andrea Strübind, 337–58. Göttingen: Vandenhoeck & Ruprecht, 2007.

Poltronieri, Marco. "Wie kriegen die Deutschen das auf die Reihe? Ein Gespräch mit W. G. Sebald." In *W. G. Sebald*, edited by Franz Loquai, 138–45. Eggingen: Edition Isele, 1997.

Prager, Brad. "The Good German as Narrator: On W. G. Sebald and the Risks of Holocaust Writing." *New German Critique* 96 (2005): 75–102.

———. "Interpreting the Visible Traces of Theresienstadt." *Journal of Modern Jewish Studies* 7, no. 2 (2008): 175–94.

———. "Sebald's Kafka." In *W. G. Sebald: History—Memory—Trauma*, edited by Scott Denham and Mark McCulloh, 105–25. Berlin: Walter de Gruyter, 2006.

Pralle, Uwe. "Mit einem kleinen Strandspaten Abschied von Deutschland nehmen. Interview mit W. G. Sebald." *Süddeutsche Zeitung*, December 22, 2001.

Presner, Todd. *Mobile Modernity: Germans, Jews, Trains*. New York: Columbia University Press, 2007.

Radisch, Iris. "Der Waschbär der falschen Welt: W. G. Sebald sammelt Andenken und rettet die Vergangenheit vorm Vergehen." Review of *Austerlitz*, by W. G. Sebald. *Die Zeit*, April 5, 2001.

Rathenau, Walther. "Höre Israel." *Zukunft* 5 (1897): 454–62.

Reichmann, Eva. "Jüdische Figuren in österreichischer und bundesdeutscher Literatur der 1980er und 1990er Jahre—der schwierige Weg jüdischer und nichtjüdischer Autoren aus dem mentalen Ghetto." In *Jews in German Literature since 1945: German-Jewish Literature?* edited by Pól O'Dochartaigh, 237–50. Amsterdam: Rodopi, 2000.

Rensmann, Lars. *Demokratie und Judenbild: Antisemitismus in der politischen Kultur der Bundesrepublik Deutschland*. Wiesbaden: Verlag für Sozialwissenschaften, 2004.

Reventlow, Ernst. "Was sind für uns die Juden?" In *Der Jud ist schuld . . . ? Diskussionsbuch über die Judenfrage*, edited by Bahr et al., 13–39. Basel: Zinnen-Verlag, 1932.

Ricoeur, Paul. *The Rule of Metaphor*. Translated by Robert Czerny. Toronto: University of Toronto Press, 1977.

Riefenstahl, Leni, director. *Triumph des Willens*. Universum Film AG, 1935.

Rigg, Bryan Mark. *Hitler's Jewish Soldiers: The Untold Story of Nazi Racial Laws and Men of Jewish Descent in the German Military*. Lawrence: University Press of Kansas, 2002.

Robertson, Ritchie. *The "Jewish Question" in German Literature 1749–1939: Emancipation and Its Discontents.* Oxford: Oxford University Press, 1999.

Rose, Paul Lawrence. *German Question/Jewish Question: Revolutionary Anti-Semitism from Kant to Wagner.* Princeton, NJ: Princeton University Press, 1990.

Rosenberg, Alan, and Gerald E. Meyers, eds. *Echoes from the Holocaust: Philosophical Reflections on a Dark Time.* Philadelphia: Temple University Press, 1989.

Rosenzweig, Franz. "'Germ Cell' of The Star of Redemption." Translated by Alan Udoff and Barbara Galli, 45–66. In Udoff and Galli, eds. *Franz Rosenzweig's "The New Thinking."* Syracuse: Syracuse University Press, 1999.

———. *The Star of Redemption.* Translated by William W. Hallo. Notre Dame, IN: University of Notre Dame Press, 1985.

———. *Der Stern der Erlösung.* Frankfurt am Main: J. Kauffmann, 1921.

———. *Understanding the Sick and the Healthy: A View of the World, Man, and God.* Edited and translated by Nahum Glatzer. Cambridge MA: Harvard University Press, 1999.

———. "Urzelle" des Stern der Erlösung." In Rosenzweig, *Gesammelte Schriften* III, *Kleinere Schriften zu Glauben und Denken,* edited by Reinhold Mayer and Annemarie Mayer, 125–38. Dordrecht: Nijhoff, 1984.

Roth, Joseph. *Juden auf Wanderschaft.* In *Werke,* edited by Klaus Westermann, 827–902. Cologne: Kiepenheuer & Witsch, 1990.

Ryan, Judith. "Fulgurations: Sebald and Surrealism." *Germanic Review* 82, no. 3 (Summer 2007): 227–49.

Santner, Eric L. *On Creaturely Life: Rilke, Benjamin, Sebald.* Chicago: University of Chicago Press, 2006.

Sartre, Jean-Paul. *Anti-Semite and Jew: An Exploration of the Etiology of Hate.* Translated by George J. Becker. New York: Schocken, 1976.

———. "Reflections on the Jewish Question: A Lecture." Translated by Rosalind Krauss and Dennis Hollier. *October* 87 (Winter 1999): 32–46.

Saul, Nicholas. "Morbid? Suicide, Freedom, Human Dignity and the German Romantic Yearning for Death." *Historical Reflections* 32, no. 3 (2006): 579–99.

Schlant, Ernestine. *The Language of Silence: West German Literature and the Holocaust.* New York: Routledge, 1999.

Schlegel, Friedrich. *Athenäum Fragment,* 116. In August Wilhelm and Friedrich Schlegel, eds., *Athenäum, 1798–1800,* 204–6. Stuttgart: Facsimile Edition, 1960.

Schley, Fridolin. *Kataloge der Wahrheit: Zur Inszenierung des Autors bei W. G. Sebald.* Göttingen: Wallstein, 2012.

Schmitz, Helmut. *On Their Own Terms: The Legacy of National Socialism in Post-1990 German Fiction.* Birmingham: University of Birmingham Press, 2004.

Schneider, Michael. "Fathers and Sons, Retrospectively: The Damaged Relationship between Two Generations." Translated by Jamie Owen Daniel. *New German Critique*, no. 31, West German Culture and Politics (Winter, 1984): 3–51.

Schneider, Peter. *Vati*. Bamberg: Buchner Schulbibliothek der Moderne, 2001.

Schock, Ralph. "Realismus reicht nicht aus: Gespräch mit Ralph Schock." In *W. G. Sebald. "Auf ungeheuer dünnem Eis": Gespräche 1971 bis 2001*, edited by Torsten Hoffmann, 96–104. Frankfurt am Main: Fischer Taschenbuch, 2015.

Scholem, Gershom. "Against the Myth of the German-Jewish Dialogue," in *Judaica* 2:7–11. Frankfurt am Main: Suhrkamp, 1970.

———. *Jews and Germans: A Commentary Report*. New York: American Jewish Committee, 1966.

———. "Mit einem Exemplar von Kafkas 'Prozeß.'" In *Benjamin über Kafka*, edited by Hermann Schweppenhäuser, 72–74. Frankfurt am Main: Suhrkamp Verlag, 1981.

———. *On Jews and Judaism in Crisis*. New York: Schocken, 1976.

Schopenhauer, Arthur. *Parerga and Paralipomena: Short Philosophical Essays*. Translated by E. F. J. Payne, 2–261. Oxford: Oxford University Press, 1974.

Schowengerdt-Kuzmany, Verena V. "To the Funhouse: W. G. Sebald's Playful Intertextuality." PhD diss., University of Washington, 2014.

Schütte, Uwe. "Ein Porträt des Germanisten als junger Mann: Zu Sebalds dissidenter Haltung gegenüber der Literaturwissenschaft in seinen akademischen Rezensionen." In *Sprachkunst*, Beiträge zur Literaturwissenschaft (2008): 309–32.

———. "Troubling Signs: Sebald, Ambivalence, and the Function of the Critic." *boundary 2*, 47 no. 3 (2020): 21–59.

———. *Über W. G. Sebald: Beiträge zu einem anderen Bild des Autors*. Berlin: Walter de Gruyter, 2017.

———. "Von der Notwendigkeit, ein neues Bild von W. G. Sebald zu zeichnen." In *Über W. G. Sebald: Beiträge zu einem anderen Bild des Autors*, edited by Uwe Schütte, 3–16. Berlin: Walter de Gruyter, 2016.

Schwartz, Lynne Sharon, ed. *The Emergence of Memory: Conversations with W. G. Sebald*. New York: Seven Stories Press, 2007.

Sebald, W. G. "Against the Irreversible: On Jean Améry." In *On the Natural History of Destruction*, translated by Anthea Bell, 147–71. London: Penguin, 2003.

———. "Air War and Literature." In *On the Natural History of Destruction*, translated by Anthea Bell, 1–105. London: Penguin, 2003.

———. "An Attempt at Restitution." In *Campo Santo*, translated by Anthea Bell, edited by Sven Meyer, 206–15. London: Penguin, 2005.

———. *Die Ausgewanderten*. Frankfurt am Main: Fischer Verlag, 2006.

———. *Austerlitz*. Frankfurt am Main: Fischer Taschenbuch, 2003.

———. *Austerlitz*. Translated by Anthea Bell. London: Penguin, 2002.

———. "Between the Devil and the Deep Blue Sea: On Alfred Andersch." In *On the Natural History of Destruction*, translated by Anthea Bell, 107–45. London: Penguin, 2003.

———. *Campo Santo*. Edited by Sven Mayer, translated by Anthea Bell. London: Penguin, 2006.

———. *Carl Sternheim: Kritiker und Opfer der Wilhelminischen Ära*. Stuttgart: W. Kohlhammer, 1969.

———. "Constructs of Mourning: Günter Grass and Wolfgang Hildesheimer." In *Campo Santo*, translated by Anthea Bell, edited by Sven Mayer, 102–29. London: Penguin Books, 2006.

———. "Ein Kaddisch für Österreich—über Joseph Roth." In *Unheimliche Heimat: Essays zur österreichischen Literatur*," 104–17. Frankfurt am Main: Fischer Taschenbuch, 2004.

———. "Eine kleine Traverse: Das poetische Werk Ernst Herbecks." In *Die Beschreibung des Unglücks: Zur österreichischen Literatur von Stifter bis Handke*, 131–48. Frankfurt am Main: Fischer Taschenbuch, 2006.

———. *The Emigrants*. Translated from German by Michael Hulse. London: Vintage, 1996.

———. "Es steht ein Komet am Himmel: Kalenderbeitrag zu Ehren des rheinischen Hausfreunds." In *Logis in einem Landhaus: Über Gottfried Keller, Johann Peter Hebel, Robert Walser und andere*, 11–41. Frankfurt am Main: Fischer Taschenbuch Verlag, 2003.

———. "Das Gesetz der Schande—Macht, Messianismus und Exil in Kafka's *Schloß*." In *Unheimliche Heimat: Essays zur österreichischen Literatur*, 87–103. Frankfurt am Main: Fischer Taschenbuch Verlag, 2004.

———. "Her kommt der Tod die Zeit geht hin: Anmerkungen zu Gottfried Keller." In *Logis in einem Landhaus*, 97–126. Frankfurt am Main: Fischer Taschenbuch, 2003.

———. "Jean Améry und Primo Levi." In *Über Jean Améry*, edited by Irene Heidelberger-Leonard, 115–23. Heidelberg: Carl Winter Universitätsverlag, 1990.

———. "Kafka at the Movies." In *Campo Santo*. Translated by Anthea Bell, edited by Sven Mayer, 156–73. London: Penguin Books, 2006.

———. *Luftkrieg und Literatur*. Frankfurt am Main: Fischer Taschenbuch, 2005.

———. "Der Mann mit dem Mantel: Gerhard Roths *Winterreise*." In *Die Beschreibung des Unglücks: Zur österreichischen Literatur von Stifter bis Handke*, 149–64. Frankfurt am Main: Fischer Taschenbuch, 2006.

———. *Der Mythus der Zerstörung im Werk Döblins*. Stuttgart: Ernst Klett, 1980.

———. *On the Natural History of Destruction*. Translated by Anthea Bell. London: Penguin Books, 2003.

———. "Le promeneur solitaire. Zur Erinnerung an Robert Walser." In *Logis in einem Landhaus: Über Gottfried Keller, Johann Peter Hebel, Robert Walser und andere*, 127–68. Frankfurt am Main: Fischer Taschenbuch, 2003.

218 ◆ BIBLIOGRAPHY

———. "The Remorse of the Heart: On Memory and Cruelty in the Work of Peter Weiss." In *On the Natural History of Destruction*, translated by Anthea Bell, 173–95. London: Penguin, 2003.

———. *Die Ringe des Saturn*. Frankfurt am Main: Fischer Taschenbuch Verlag, 2003.

———. *The Rings of Saturn*. Translated by Michael Hulse. London: Vintage, 2002.

———. "Tiere, Menschen, Maschinen—Zu Kafkas Evolutionsgeschichten." *Literatur und Kritik* 21 (1986): 194–201.

———. *Schwindel. Gefühle*. Frankfurt am Main: Fischer Taschenbuch, 2002.

———. "Das unentdeckte Land—Zur Motivstruktur in Kafkas *Schloß*." In *Die Beschreibung des Unglücks*, 78–92. Frankfurt am Main: Fischer Taschenbuch, 2006.

———. *Unheimliche Heimat: Essays zur österreichischen Literatur*. Frankfurt am Main: Fischer Taschenbuch Verlag, 2004.

———. "Verlorenes Land—Jean Améry und Österreich." In *Unheimliche Heimat: Essays zur österreichischen Literatur*, 131–44.

———. *Vertigo*. Translated by Michael Hulse. London: Vintage, 2002.

———. "Die weisse Adlerfeder am Kopf: Versuch über den Indianer Herbert Achternbusch." In *Manuskripte* 79 (1981): 75–79.

———. "Westwärts–Ostwärts: Aporien deutschsprachiger Ghettogeschichten." In *Unheimliche Heimat: Essays zur österreichischen Literatur*," 40–64.

———. "Die Zweideutigkeit der Toleranz: Anmerkungen zum Interesse der Aufklärung an der Emanzipation der Juden." *Deutschunterricht* 36, no. 4 (1984): 27–47.

Selikowitz, Gillian. "'Connected but not Congruent': W. G. Sebald and the Writing of His Generation." PhD diss., University of Sydney, 2016.

Seuren, Günter. *Abschied von einem Mörder*. Hamburg: Rowohlt, 1980.

Shakespeare. *The Tragedy of King Lear*. Cambridge: Cambridge University Press, 1992.

———. *Hamlet*. Cambridge: Cambridge University Press, 2014.

Shapiro, Susan. "The Uncanny Jew: A Brief History of an Image." In *Textures and Meaning: Thirty Years of Judaic Studies at the University of Massachusetts Amherst*, edited by L. Ehrlich, S. Bolozky, R. Rothstein, M. Schwartz, J. Berkovitz, and J. Young, 157–56. Amherst: University of Massachusetts Press, 2004.

Sheppard, Richard. "Dexter-Sinister: Some Observations on Decrypting the Mors Code in the Work of W. G. Sebald." *Journal of European Studies* 35, no. 4 (Dec. 2005): 419–63.

Shmueli, Efraim. *Seven Jewish Cultures: A Reinterpretation of Jewish History and Thought*. Translated by Gila Shmueli. Cambridge: Cambridge University Press, 1980.

Shulewitz, Judith. "W. G. Sebald Ransacked Jewish Lives for His Fictions." Review of *Speak, Silence*, by Carole Angier. *Atlantic*, November 2021.

Sicher, Efraim. *The Holocaust Novel*. New York: Routledge, 2005.

Sill, Oliver. "'Aus dem Jäger ist ein Schmetterling geworden': Textbeziehungen zwischen Werken von W. G. Sebald und Vladimir Nabokov." *Poetica* (1997): 596–623.

Silverblatt, Michael. "A Poem of an Invisible Subject." In *The Emergence of Memory: Conversations with W. G. Sebald*, edited by Lynne Sharon Schwartz, 77–86. New York: Seven Stories Press, 2007.

Simon, Ulrich. "Der Provokateur als Literaturhistoriker: Anmerkungen zu Literaturbegriff und Argumentationsverfahren in W. G. Sebalds essayistischen Schriften." In *Sebald Lektüren*, edited by Marcel Atze and Franz Loquai, 78–104. Eggingen: Edition Isele, 2005.

Sombart, Werner. *The Jews and Modern Capitalism.* Translated by Mordecai Epstein. Kitchener: Ontario: Batoche, 2001.

Sørensen, Bengt Algot. *Geschichte der deutschen Literatur Band II: Vom 19. Jahrhundert bis zur Gegenwart.* Munich: C. H. Beck, 2016.

Steiner, George. *Language and Silence: Essays on Language, Literature, and the Inhuman.* New York: Atheneum, 1967.

Stoke, Richard. *The Book of Lieder.* London: Faber, 2005.

Strauss, Richard. "Allerseelen." Op. 10, no. 8 (1883). Words by Hermann von Gilm.

Sutcliffe, Andrew. "Reimagining Melancholia: Melancholy and Psychiatry in the Work of W. G. Sebald and David Foster Wallace." PhD diss., King's College London, 2020.

Svenungsson, Jayne. "Enlightened Prejudices: Anti-Jewish Tropes in Modern Philosophy." In *Rethinking Time: Essays on History, Memory and Representation*, edited by H. Ruin and A. Ers, 279–90. Södertörn Philosophical Studies 9. Huddinge: University of Södertörn, 2011.

Szentivanyi, Christina M. E. "W. G. Sebald and Structures of Testimony and Trauma: There are Spots of Mist That No Eye Can Dispel." In *W. G. Sebald: History—Memory—Trauma*, edited by Scott Denham and Mark McCulloh, 351–63. Berlin: Walter De Gruyter, 2006.

Taberner, Stuart. "German Nostalgia? Remembering German-Jewish Life in W. G. Sebald's *Die Ausgewanderten* and *Austerlitz.*" *Germanic Review* 79, no. 3 (Summer 2004): 181–202.

Tagg, John. *The Disciplinary Frame: Photographic Truths and the Capture of Meaning.* Minneapolis: University of Minnesota Press, 2009.

Taubes, Jacob. "Vom Adverb 'Nichts' zum Substantiv 'das Nichts': Überlegungen zu Heideggers Frage nach dem Nichts." In *Positionen der Negativität: Poetik und Hermeneutik* VII, edited by Harold Weinrich, 141–53. Munich: Wilhem Fink, 1975.

*The Holy Scriptures.* Philadelphia: Jewish Publication Society of America, 1955.

Theweleit, Klaus. *Männerphantasien*, 2 vols. Frankfurt am Main: Roter Stern, 1977–78.

Thomas, Alfred. Excerpt from *Prague Palimpsest: Writing, Memory, and the City.* Chicago: University of Chicago Press, 2010.

Trachtenburg, J. *The Devil and the Jews: The Medieval Conception of the Jew and Its Relation to Modern Anti-Semitism.* Philadelphia: The Jewish Publication Society, 1983.

Van der Lugt, Mara. *Dark Matters: Pessimism and the Problem of Suffering.* Princeton, NJ: Princeton University Press, 2021.

Van Rahden, Till. "History in the House of the Hangman: How Postwar Germany Became a Key Site for the Study of Jewish History." In *The German-Jewish Experience Revisited*, edited by Steven E. Aschheim and Vivian Liska, 171–92. Berlin: De Gruyter: 2015.

Vees-Gulani, Susanne. "The Experience of Destruction: W. G. Sebald, the Airwar, and Literature." In *W. G. Sebald: History—Memory—Trauma*, edited by Scott Denham and Mark McCulloh, 335–49. Berlin: Walter De Gruyter, 2006.

Veraguth, Hannes. "W. G. Sebald und die alte Schule: 'Schwindel. Gefühle.,' 'Die Ausgewanderten,' 'Die Ringe des Saturn,' und 'Austerlitz': Literarische Erinnerungskunst in vier Büchern, die so tun, als ob sie wahr seien." *Text +Kritik* 158, W. G. Sebald, edited by Heinz Ludwig Arnold (April 2003): 30–42.

Vesper, Bernward. *Die Reise.* Reinbek bei Hamburg: Rowohlt, 2009.

Von Treitschke, Heinrich. *Unsere Aussichten.* In *Preußische Jahrbücher* 44. Berlin: Reimer, 1879.

Wachtel, Eleanor. "Ghost Hunter." In *The Emergence of Memory: Conversations with W. G. Sebald*, edited by Lynne Sharon Schwartz, 37–61. New York: Seven Stories Press, 2007.

Wagner, Richard. *Judaism in Music and Other Essays.* Translated by William Ashton Ellis. Lincoln: University of Nebraska Press, 1995.

———. *Stories and Essays.* Edited by Charles Osborne and translated by W. Ashton Ellis. London: Peter Owen, 1973.

Ward, Simon. "Ruins and Poetics in the Works of W. G. Sebald." In *W. G. Sebald*, edited by J. J. Long and A. Parry, 58–74. Edinburgh: University of Edinburgh Press, 2004.

Weiner, Marc A. *Richard Wagner and the Anti-Semitic Imagination.* Lincoln: University of Nebraska Press, 1995.

Weininger, Otto. *Geschlecht und Charakter: Eine prinzipielle Untersuchung.* Munich: Matthes & Seitz, 1980.

———. *Sex and Character. An Investigation of Fundamental Principles.* Translated by Ladislaus Löb, edited by Daniel Steuer and Laura Marcus. Bloomington: Indiana University Press, 2005.

Weiss, Peter. "Meine Ortschaft." In Weiss, *Rapporte 2*, 113–24. Frankfurt am Main: Suhrkamp, 1968.

Weissman, Gary. *Fantasies of Witnessing: Postwar Efforts to Experience the Holocaust.* Ithaca, NY: Cornell University Press, 2004.

Weston, Nancy A. "Thinking the Oblivion of Thinking: The Unfolding of *Machenschaft* and *Rechnung* in the Time of the Black Notebooks." In *Reading Heidegger's Black Notebooks 1931–1941*, edited by Ingo Farin and Jeff Malpas. Cambridge, MA: MIT Press, 2016.

White, Hayden. *Figural Realism: Studies in the Mimesis Effect*. Baltimore: John Hopkins University Press, 1999.

Williamson, George S. *The Longing for Myth in Germany: Religion and Aesthetic Culture from Romanticism to Nietzsche*. Chicago: University of Chicago Press, 2004.

Wilms, Wilfried. "Speak no Evil, Write no Evil: In Search of a Usable Language of Destruction." In *W. G. Sebald: History—Memory—Trauma*, edited by Scott Denham and Mark McCulloh, 183–204. Berlin: Walter De Gruyter, 2006.

Wirtz, Thomas. "Schwarze Zuckerwatte: Anmerkungen zu W. G. Sebald." Review of *Austerlitz*, by W. G. Sebald. *Merkur* 55 (2001): 530–34.

Wolff, Lynn L. *W. G. Sebald's Hybrid Poetics: Literature as Historiography*. Berlin: De Gruyter, 2014.

Wolin, Richard. *Heidegger in Ruins: Between Philosophy and Ideology*. New Haven, CT: Yale University Press, 2022.

Wood, James. "An Interview with W. G. Sebald." *Brick. Literary Journal* 59 (1998): 23–29.

Wyschgorod, Edith. *Spirit in Ashes: Hegel, Heidegger and Man-Made Mass Death*. New Haven, CT: Yale University Press, 1985.

Young, James E. *Writing and Rewriting the Holocaust: Narrative and the Consequences of Interpretation*. Bloomington: Indiana University Press, 1988.

Zadoff, Mirjam. *Next Year in Marienbad: The Lost Worlds of Jewish Spa Culture*. Translated by William Templer. Philadelphia: University of Pennsylvania Press, 2012.

Zaenker, Karl A. "The Bedeviled Beckmesser: Another Look at Anti-Semitic Stereotypes in Wagner's *Die Meistersinger von Nürnberg*." *German Studies Review* 22, no. 1 (1999): 1–20.

Zeller, Christoph, ed. *Literarische Experimente: Medien, Kunst, Texte seit 1950*. Heidelberg: Universitätsverlag, 2012.

Zilcosky, John. "Lost and Found: Disorientation, Nostalgia, and Holocaust Melodrama in Sebald's 'Austerlitz.'" *Modern Language Notes* (April 2006): 679–98.

Zukier, Henri. "The Essential 'Other' and the Jew: From Antisemitism to Genocide." *Social Research* 63, no. 4 (1996): 1110–54.

# Index

Abraham (Biblical figure), 74–75, 107–8
Abraham, Nicolas, 46, 139
Achinger, Christine, 127
Aciman, André, 13
Adler, H. G., 92–93
Adorno, Theodor, 11, 24, 30, 96, 135, 185
Agamben, Giorgio, 101
Ahasverus, the wandering Jew, 33, 37–40, 63–65, 67, 69, 72
Aleichem, Sholem, 158
Aliaga-Buchenau, Ana-Isabel, 18
Allred, Mason, 155
Améry, Jean: Améry's *Ressentiment* in Michael Hamburger's dream of return (*RS*), 131–32; as a prototype for Paul Bereyter, 146–47; Sebald's interest in conflicted Austro- and German-Jewish writers, 30; torture of, 180
Améry, Jean, works by: *At the Mind's Limits: Contemplations by a Survivor on Auschwitz and its Realities*, 117; "Jenseits von Schuld und Sühne," 147; "On the Necessity of being a Jew," 37, 121; *Örtlichkeiten*, 122; "Resentments," 131–32; "Torture," 180
Andersch, Alfred, 29, 31
Angier, Carole, works by: *Speak, Silence: In Search of W. G. Sebald*, 19, 157, 194; "Who Is W. G. Sebald?" 12, 24, 58
Angress, Ruth, 125
Antikos Bazar, 89–90
anti-Semitism, 39, 107, 150, 136
Arendt, Hannah, 7
Aristotle, 9
Arnds, Peter, 153

Assmann, Aleida, works by: *Der lange Schatten der Vergangenheit*, 24, 43, 55, 124
ateleological project, 43
Auerbach, Frank, 61
Auschwitz, 6, 7, 61, 72, 94, 96, 101–2, 139, 160, 181, 197

Bacherach, pogrom, 150
Badiou, Alain, 103, 106
Bartov, Omer, 1
Bauer, Karin, 13
Baumann, Zygmunt, 7
Beckett, Samuel, 83
Bedlam, 184, 188
Beissner, Friedrich, 39
Benjamin, Walter: concept of "Jetztzeit," 71–72, 148; death of, 99; evocation of his *Berlin Childhood around 1900* in "Ambros Adelwarth," 58; evocation of his *Berlin Childhood around 1900* in *The Rings of Saturn*, 129; interpretation of Kafka's Odradek, 96; on redemption in Kafka's writing, 86; view of history as calamity, 28, 181
Benjamin, Walter, works by: *Berlin Childhood around 1900*, 58, 86, 129; *Briefe* (Letters) II, 86; "On the Concept of History," 28, 71–72; *Selected Writings* II, 96
Benz, W., 49
Bergen Belsen, 15
Berger, Robert, 95, 123
Bigsby, Christopher, 9, 16, 194
Bitburg, 41
*Blitzkrieg*, 52–53
Bloch, Ernst, 83, 112
Blüher, Hans, 134, 142

Boa, Elizabeth, 36
Boedecker, Sven, 1, 9, 194
Bogdal, Klaus-Michael, 22
Bohrer, Karl Heinz, 28
Böll, Heinrich, 66
Bosmajian, Hamida, 21
Bowles, David, 18
Boyagoda, Randy, 18
Boyarin, Daniel and Jonathan, 106
Braidotti, Rosi, 8
Breendonk, fortress of, 21, 26, 66, 96, 140, 180, 185
Buchenwald, 43
Budick, Emily, 10
Büettner, Angi, 7
butterfly hunter, 44–45, 161, 182
Buschan, Georg, 174, 177

Chaouat, Bruno, 73
Charcot, Jean Martin, 174
Charmé, Stuart, works by: "Varieties in Contemporary Jewish Identity," 137
Chiarugi, Vincenzo, 170
Coplan, Amy, 15
Cosgrove, Mary, works by: "The Anxiety of German Influence," 128; "Melancholy Competitions: W. G. Sebald reads Günter Grass and Wolfgang Hildesheimer," 21; "Sebald for our Time: The Politics of Melancholy and the Critique of Capitalism in his Work," 8
cultural essentialism, 35
Cummins, Joanne, works by: *American Dirt*, 17–18
Cuomo, Joseph, 10, 12, 16, 23, 167
Curtin, Adrian, 161

Davies, Mererid Puw, 25, 168
de Gobineau, Arthur, 175
de Mendelssohn, Peter, 29, 78
Denham, Scott, 116
"Der Dritte" (the "Third"), 126–27
Derrida, Jacques, 8
Di Cesare, Donatella, works by: *Heidegger and the Jews: The Black Notebooks*, 7, 75, 112, 135

Diner, Dan, 24
Döblin, Alfred, 31, 171
Doerry, Martin, 19
*Doppelgänger* (double), 35, 133, 153
Doré, Gustave, 41
Dronske, Ulrich, 31
Dühring, Eugen, 174
Dünkelsbühler, Ulrike, 110
Dunn, Francis M., 45

Eckstaedt, Anita, 167
Edelman, R., 38
Eder, Richard, 1
Etzler, Marissa Starr, 31–32
Euripides, works by: *Hippolytus*, 76
exile, 36–37, 45–49, 67, 69, 70, 77, 98, 101, 179, 190

Fackenheim, Emil, 137, 197
fairy tale, 68, 88, 90, 100, 152–53, 162, 182
Fassbinder, Rainer Maria, 23, 143
Faustian pact, 144–45, 155
Felman, Shoshana, 139
Fermaglich, Kirstin, 115
Fichte, Johann Gottlieb, 39, 105
figural Jew, definition and function of, 7–8
*Figuren* (figures), 101
"Final Solution," 10
Fink, Susanne, 36
Finkielkraut, Alain, 7–8, 138
Fischer, Gerhard, 2
Fletcher, Angus, 3
Frankfurt School, 25, 80, 168
Franklin, Ruth, 14, 33, 166
Franzos, Karl-Emil, 29, 157
Freud, Sigmund, 171
Frohmann of Drohobysz, 67–68

Garloff, Katja, 19
Gasseleder, Klaus, 157
Gebhardt, Thea, 157, 160
Geller, Jay, 126, 141, 152
genocide, 4, 10, 15, 59, 75, 79
German-Jewish symbiosis, 18, 42, 49–50, 56, 62, 68–70, 117–18, 159, 162

INDEX ◆ 225

Gerron, Kurt, 92
Gilman, Sander, works by: *Franz
Kafka, the Jewish Patient*, 108,
144, 178–79; "Jewish Writers in
Contemporary Germany: The Dead
Author Speaks," 143
Goebbels, Joseph, 143
Goethe, Johann Wolfgang von, 144–
45, 183
Goldhagen, Daniel, 52
Goldie, Peter, 15
Gordon, Robert, 197
Görres, Joseph, 169
Gotterbarm, Mario, 19–20, 31
Grass, Günter, 29, 143
Gray, Richard, 13, 18, 115
Grimm Brothers, 162, 182
Grünewald, Matthias, 14, 164,
181–82
Gunzenhausen pogrom, 117
Gutzkow, Karl, 40, 115
Gwyer, Kirstin, 19, 21, 139

Hage, Volker, 19, 88, 166
Hall, Katharina, 18
Hammerschlag, Sarah, 6–8
Handke, Peter, 25, 30, 113, 151
Hasan-Rokem, Galit, works by: "Jews
as Postcards, or Postcards as Jews:
Mobility in a Modern Genre,"
38; "Joban Transformation of
the Wandering Jew," 38; *The
Wandering Jew: Essays in the
Interpretation of a Christian
Legend*, 203
Haury, Thomas, 23
Hebel, Johann Peter, 47, 49, 191
Hegel, Friedrich: on death as the
apotheosis of art, 170; on the Jew
as contagious, 172; on Jewish
dispossession, 11, 74–75, 110; on
Jewish heteronomy, 34, 74–75,
107; on Jewish immutability, 108;
on Jewish rootlessness, 10, 38–39;
relegation of the Jew to *Nichts*
(nothingness), 11
Hegel, Friedrich, works by:
*Phenomenology of Spirit*, 74, 108;

*Philosophy of Nature*, 170; "The
Positivity of Christian Religion,"
172; "The Spirit of Christianity and
its Fate," 11, 39, 74–75, 108
Heidegger, Martin: his association of
the Jew with the desert, 74–75; his
extrusion of the Jew from *Beying*,
76; on the Holocaust as Jewish
self-annihilation, 135; on the Jew
as contaminant, 109; on the Jew
as the embodiment of modernity,
34, 109–10; on the "metaphysical
Jew," 75–76
Heidegger, Martin, works by:
*Anmerkungen* I–V, 135; *The
Black Notebooks*, 109–10;
*The Fundamental Concepts of
Metaphysics*, 75; *The History
of Beyng*, 75; "The Jewish
Contamination of German
Spiritual Life," 109; *Ponderings*
XII–XV, 76, 109
Heiligenstadt, 175
*Heimat*: Améry and loss of, 121–22;
conflicting visions of, 29–30;
connotations of term, 36; and
the dream of return, 67–68;
Germans as grounded in *Heimat*
and *Nation*, 40, 109; Heidegger
and, 110; Jerusalem as the
contaminated *Heimat*, 58; Jewish
cemetery as the *Heimat* of the
Jews, 37, 100; as a lived experience
for Paul Bereyter, 48; as nexus
of home and death, 42–43;
second-generation alienation
from, 24–25, 33, 64; *Unheimliche
Heimat*, 157
Hein, Christian, 31
Heine, Heinrich, 159
Hell, Julia, 103
Herbeck, Ernst, 30, 168
Herder, Johann Gottfried, 10, 137,
174
Herf, Jeffrey, 123–24
Herzl, Theodor, 60
Herzog, Werner, 64, 115
Hippolytus, myth of, 45–46

226 ◆ INDEX

Hirsch, Marianne, 20–21
*Historikerstreit* (historians' dispute),
　23
Hitler, Adolf, 143
Hoffmann, E. T. A., 152
Hölderlin, Friedrich, 39, 169
Holz, Klaus, 8, 104, 122–23, 127
Horkheimer, Max, 30, 135
Hutchinson, Ben, 25, 168
Huyssen, Andreas, 2

Ilsemann, Mark, 165, 185
Israelites, 68, 158
Ithaca, 24, 56, 60

Jacobson, Dan, 79
Jerusalem, 24, 28, 37, 57–61, 112
Jeutter, Ralf, 1, 13
Jewish assimilation, 41, 45, 49,
　105, 118–19, 133–35, 144, 151,
　153–56
Jewish cemetery, 37, 68–69, 99, 100,
　157–58
Johnson, Gary, 3
Jünger, Ernst, 172

Kafatou, Sarah, 147
Kafka, Franz: on Jewish immutability,
　142; on Jewish mimicry, 151;
　negative messianism in, 30, 43–45,
　57, 82, 86, 176; Odradek as
　remnant, 97; Prague social circle
　of, 154; Sebald's essays on, 30; as
　the sickly Jew, 178; *The Student of
　Prague* as relating to, 155
Kafka, Franz, works by: *Complete
　Stories*, 151; *Diaries 1910–1919*,
　154; "The Hunter Gracchus," 13,
　30, 33, 37, 43–45, 57, 66, 79, 84,
　99, 154, 177, 179; "Josephine the
　Singer and the Mouse People,"
　125, 151–52; *Letters to Felice*,
　154, 178; *Das Schloß* (The Castle),
　68–69; "Die Sorge des Hausvaters"
　(The Cares of the Family Man),
　96–97
Kant, Immanuel: "euthanasia" of
　the Jews, 39, 107; on Jewish

heteronomy, 34; on Jewish
　immutability, 107–8; Jews as
　"the Palestinians among us,"
　74–75, 114; repudiation of Jewish
　"bodiliness," 10
Kant, Immanuel, works by:
　*Anthropology from a Pragmatic
　Point of View*, 107; *The Conflict
　of the Faculties*, 39, 107; *Religion
　within the Boundaries of Mere
　Reason*, 107
Kaspar Hauser, 64
Kassack, Hermann, 29, 78
*katabasis*, 65
Kaunas, fortress of, 66
Kermode, Frank, 6
Kertész, Imre, 7
Kilbourn, R. J. A., works by: "Kafka,
　Nabokov . . . Sebald: Intertextuality
　and Narratives of Redemption in
　*Vertigo* and *The Emigrants*," 13,
　45, 182; *W. G. Sebald's Postsecular
　Redemption: Catastrophe with
　Spectator*, 8
Kittel, Gerhard, 174
Klebes, Martin, 171
Kleinschmidt, Erich, 140
Klüger, Ruth, 139
Köhler, Andrea, 53
Köhler, F. 174
Krauthausen, Ciro, 89
*Kristallnacht*, 49, 94, 183
Kunisch, H-P., 25

LaCapra, Dominic, works by: *History
　and Memory after Auschwitz*, 54;
　*Writing History, Writing Trauma*,
　5, 15, 139
Lang, Berel, 6, 10, 107, 132
Lang, Berel, works by: *Act and Idea in
　the Nazi Genocide*, 6, 10, 132
Lang, Fritz, 77, 173
Langer, Lawrence, 3
Laing, R. D., 25
Laub, Dori, 139
Leroy-Beaulieu, Pierre, 142
Levi, Primo, 1, 21–22, 30, 54, 94, 96,
　101, 125

## INDEX ♦ 227

Levi, Primo, works by: *The Drowned and the Saved*, 22, 94, 96, 101, 125
Levin, David, 141, 173
Levinas, Emmanuel, 8
Levine, Michael, 97
Levi-Strauss, Claude, 168
*Liebestod* (love-in-death), 37, 42, 116
Liska, Vivian, 7
literary historiography, 2–4, 9, 14, 25, 90, 165
*Literaturstreit* (literature dispute), 23
Löffler, Sigrid, 28
Long, J. J., 71, 153
"lost brother" trope, 151
Löwy, Michael, 62, 83
Lubow, Arthur, 16
Luther, Martin, 34, 106, 134, 141, 172
Lyotard, Jean-Francois, 8

Mack, Michael, works by: *German Idealism and the Jew: The Inner Anti-Semitism of Philosophy and German-Jewish responses*, 107
Maddox, John, 166
Manchester, 11, 23, 27, 33, 37, 46, 61–69, 105, 133, 181–82, 195
Mann, Thomas, 2, 9, 31
Marcus, Kenneth L., 38, 136
Margalit, Avishai, 21, 94, 167
Margry, Karel, 92
Marienbad, 93–97
Martin, Laura, 13–14
Matteoni, Francesca, 172
*Mauscheln*, 143, 148
McCulloh, Mark, 13, 62
McGlothlin, Erin, works by: *Second-Generation Holocaust Literature: Legacies of Survival and Perpetration*, 26, 42, 86–87
Meckel, Christoph, 26
Meige, Henri, 175
Merkin, Daphne, 13
*Mischling* (a German of partially Jewish ancestry), 49
Modlinger, Martin, 90
Moeller, Robert, 123
Monk, Ray, 122

Morgan Peter, works by: "The Sign of Saturn: Melancholy, Homelessness and Apocalypse in W. G. Sebald's Prose Narratives," 13, 102; "'Your Story Is Now My Story': The Ethics of Narration in Grass and Sebald," 19, 197;
Morning, Ann, 134
Morris, Lesley, 18
Mosbach, Bettina, works by: *Figurationen der Zerstörung: Ästhetische Verfahren in W. G. Sebalds "Die Ringe des Saturn" und "Austerlitz,"* 53
Mosse, George, 155
Motzkin, Gabriel, 94
*Muselmänner, Muselmann*, 34, 101

Nabokov, Vladimir, 13, 44, 182
*Nacht und Nebel* (night and fog), 10
Nadler, Steven, 146
Navratil, Leo, 25, 35, 169
Nazi language, 28, 123–24
negative messianism, 30, 44, 62, 86, 176
*Neuanfang* (new beginning), 54
*Neue Wache* memorial, 23, 41, 55
*Nibelungen, Die*, film, 77–78, 108, 173
Nietzsche, Friedrich, 74
Niven, Bill, works by: *Germans as Victims: Remembering the Past in Contemporary Germany*, 28
Nora, Pierre, 118
Nossack, Hans, 29
Novalis, 114, 149, 162, 169
Nuremberg Laws, 117
Nussbaum, Martha, 22

Odradek, 96, 183
Odysseus, 11, 81, 84
Orpheus, 11, 81
overshadowing tree motif, 42–43, 149, 160, 182
Owen, Wilfred, 192

Palfreyman, Rachel, 36
Pelikan-Straus, Nina, 73

228 ♦ INDEX

*pensée sauvage*, 168
Pied Piper of Hamelin, The, 151, 189
Pöhlmann, Wolfgang, 38
Poltronieri, Marco, 17, 48, 119
post-human, the, 8, 91
postmemory, 20–21`
Prager, Brad, works by: "The Good
    German as Narrator: On W. G.
    Sebald and the Risks of Holocaust
    Writing," 19; "Interpreting the
    Visible Traces of Theresienstadt,"
    93; "Sebald's Kafka," 147
Pralle, Uwe, 129
Presner, Todd, 51

Radisch, Iris, 89
Rathenau, Walter, 142
Reichmann, Eva, 111
Rensmann, Lars, 22
*Ressentiment*, 131–32
Reventlow, Ernst, 108
Ricoeur, Paul, 7
Riefenstahl, Leni, 102
Rigg, Bryan Mark, 52
Romantic wandering, 39
Rose, Paul Lawrence, 38
Rosenzweig, Franz, works by: *The Star
    of Redemption*, 5, 32, 42, 48, 62,
    72, 77, 116; *Understanding the
    Sick and the Healthy: A View of the
    World, Man, and God*, 5, 72, 116;
    "'Urzelle' des Stern der Erlösung"
    ("'Germ Cell' of the Star of
    Redemption"), 5, 72
Roth, Joseph, 29, 68, 157, 160
Ryan, Judith, 48

Sacher-Masoch, Leopold, 29
Salpêtrière, 79, 175, 190–91
Santner, Eric, 102, 165
Sartre, Jean-Paul, 7, 136–37
Saul, Nicholas, 170
Schlant, Ernestine, 1
Schlegel, Friedrich, 39
Schley, Fridolin, 19, 171
Schmitz, Helmut, 1
Schneider, Michael, 25, 37
Schneider, Peter, 27

Schock, Ralph, 9
Scholem, Gershom, works by:
    "Against the Myth of the German-
    Jewish Dialogue," 135, 146; *On
    Jews and Judaism in Crisis*, 31, 86,
    135
Schopenhauer, Friedrich, 39
Schowengerdt-Kuzmany, Verena V.,
    58
*Schuldvorwurf* (accusation of guilt),
    40, 46, 122
Schumann, Robert, 94–95, 184
Schütte, Uwe, 31
Schwartz, Lynne Sharon, works by:
    *W. G. Sebald: The Emergence of
    Memory*, 200
Sebald, W. G.: on allegory, 12–13;
    as a belated Holocaust witness,
    138–41; critical reception of,
    12–14, 18–20; on encountering
    Jews in Manchester, 23; on the
    ethical risks of writing Jewish lives,
    16–17; German context, 22–24;
    on history, 166; on the Holocaust
    as a European phenomenon,
    129; as "Holocaust writer," 1;
    on hope, 82; on mental illness,
    164–65; non-fiction of, 27–32; on
    restitution, 1, 45; on the risks of
    figural writing, 12; and the "Sebald
    Paradox" 5, 14; and the "Sebald
    Phenomenon," 2; and the writing
    of his generation, 15–27
Sebald, W. G., works by:
    "Against the Irreversible: On
    Jean Améry," 30, 49; "Air War
    and Literature," 1, 25–26,
    28–29; "Ambros Adelwarth,"
    55–61, 122–28; "An Attempt at
    Restitution," 206–15; *Austerlitz*,
    71–103; *Die Beschreibung des
    Unglücks*, 164; "Between the Devil
    and the Deep Blue Sea: On Alfred
    Andersch," 29; *Campo Santo*,
    217; *Carl Sternheim: Kritiker
    und Opfer der Wilhelminischen
    Ära*, 31, 171; "Constructs of
    Mourning: Günter Grass and

Wolfgang Hildesheimer," 102–29; "Dr K. takes the Waters at Riva," 175–79; "Eine kleine Traverse: Das poetische Werk von Ernst Herbecks," 168; *The Emigrants*, 42–70; "Es steht ein Komet am Himmel. Kalenderbeitrag zu Ehren des rheinischen Hausfreunds," 49; "Das Gesetz der Schande—Macht, Messianismus und Exil in Kafkas *Schloß*," 33; "Henry Selwyn," 41–48, 114–16, 144–46; "Her kommt der Tod die Zeit geht hin. Anmerkungen zu Gottfried Keller," 49; "Jean Améry und Primo Levi," 30; "Ein Kaddisch für Österreich— Über Joseph Roth," 68; "Kafka at the Movies," 155; *Logis in einem Landhaus: Über Gottfried Keller, Johann Peter Hebel, Robert Walser und andere*," 217; "Der Mann mit dem Mantel: Gerhard Roths Winterreise," 9; "Max Aurach" (Ferber), 61–69, 156–63; *Der Mythus der Zerstörung im Werk Döblins*, 31, 171; *On the Natural History of Destruction*, 26; "Paul Bereyter," 48–55, 116–22, 146–48; "Le promeneur solitaire. Zur Erinnerung an Robert Walser," 172; "The Remorse of the Heart: On Memory and Cruelty in the Work of Peter Weiss," 32; *The Rings of Saturn*, 4, 15, 20, 31, 37, 128–31; "Tiere, Menschen, Maschinen—Zu Kafkas Evolutionsgeschichten," 148; "Das unentdeckte Land. Zur Motivstruktur in Kafkas *Schloß*," 30, 69; *Unheimliche Heimat: Essays zur österreichischen Literatur*, 29; "Verlorenes Land— Jean Améry und Österreich," 30; *Vertigo*: 4, 28, 30, 86, 104, 111, 133, 175–79; "Westwärts—Ostwärts: Aporien deutschsprachiger Ghettogeschichten," 157; Zurich lectures, 25, 27; "Die

Zweideutigkeit der Toleranz: Anmerkungen zum Interesse der Aufklärung an der Emanzipation der Juden," 30
second generation, 25, 34, 49, 52, 58, 69, 86–87, 103, 138, 153, 167
Selikowitz, Gillian, 25
Seuren, Günter, 26
Shakespeare, William, 69, 129
Shapiro, Susan, 40
Sheldrake, Rupert, 166
Shmueli, Efraim, 138
Shrayer, Maxim D., 161
Shulewitz, Judith, 1, 19
Sicher, Efraim, 6
Siegfried, 5, 77, 108, 141, 148, 173
Sill, Oliver, 13
Silverblatt, Michael, 167
Simmel, Georg, 34
Simon, Ulrich, 31
Sombart, Werner, 109, 126, 142
Sørensen, Bengt Algot, 2
Spinoza, Baruch, 106, 146
St Paul, 106
St Sebastian, 155
St Stephen, Feast of, 61
St Teresa of Avila, 84
Steiner, George, 6
Sternheim, Carl, 31, 168, 171
Strauss, Richard, 46
*Student of Prague, The*, (film), 133, 155
student protest movement of 1968, 7
Sutcliffe, Andrew, 32
Svennungsson, Jayne, 106
Szentivanyi, Christina M. E., 219

Taberner, Stuart, works by: "German Nostalgia? Remembering German-Jewish Life in W. G. Sebald's *Die Ausgewanderten* and *Austerlitz*," 14, 65, 100, 185–86
Tabori, George, 143
Tagg, John, 151
Taubes, Jacob, 75–76
Theresienstadt, 77, 79, 85, 88, 90–92
Theresienstadt film ("Der Führer schenkt den Juden eine Stadt"), 92

230 ♦ INDEX

Theweleit, Klaus, 116
"Third Reich," 132
Thomas, Alfred, 170
Torok, Maria, 46
Trachtenburg, J. 172
*Trauerarbeit*, 52
Treichel, Hans-Ulrich, 151
*Trümmerfilme* ("rubble-films"), 67

*Van der Lugt, Mara*, 48
*Väterliteratur* (father literature), 25–26
Vees-Gulani, Susanne, 139
Veraguth, Hannes, 47
*Vergangenheitsbewältigung* (mastering the past), 22, 24
Vesper, Bernward, 26–27
Von Treitschke, 109

Wachtel, Eleanor, 12, 16, 22, 136, 140
Wagner, Richard, 40, 108, 116, 141
Walser, Martin, 23

Walser, Robert, 168
*Wandervögel* youth movement, 36
Ward, Lewis, 165
*Wehrmacht*, 23, 41, 52–53
Weiner, Marc, 173
Weininger, Otto, 127–28, 109
Weiss, Peter, 30, 32, 61–62, 120
Weissman, Gary, 139
Weston, Nancy A., 109
Wilms, Wilfried, 221
Wirtz, Thomas, 19
Wittgenstein, Ludwig, 120–21
White, Hayden, 6
Wolin, Richard, 110
Wood, James, 140

Yizkor books, 18, 158
Young, James, 7

Zadoff, Mirjam, 94
Zaencker, Karl A., 141
Zilkosky, John, 99
Žižek, Slavoj, 106
Zukier, Henri, 34, 105

Printed and bound by CPI Group (UK) Ltd, Croydon, CR0 4YY
17/12/2024

14613665-0001